Real World Scanning & Halftones

THIRD EDITION

INDUSTRIAL STRENGTH PRODUCTION TECHNIQUES

by
David Blatner
Conrad Chavez
Glenn Fleishman
& Steve Roth

 Peachpit Press

Real World Scanning and Halftones, Third Edition
By David Blatner, Conrad Chavez, Glenn Fleishman, and Steve Roth

Peachpit Press
1249 Eighth Street
Berkeley, CA 94710
510/524-2178
800/283-9444
510/524-2221 (fax)
Find us on the World Wide Web at: www.peachpit.com
To report errors, please send a note to errata@peachpit.com
Find the book's Web site at www.rwsh.com

Peachpit Press is a division of Pearson Education

Peachpit editor: Cary Norsworthy
Development editor: Anne Marie Walker
Production editor: Lisa Brazieal
Copyeditor and proofreader: Don Sellers
Compositor: Brigette Schaffarzick
Indexer: Caroline Parks and Jan Wright
Cover design: Aren Howell
Cover illustration: Nathan Clement, StickmanStudio
Interior design: Glenn Fleishman
Part opener designer: Jeff Tolbert

Image Copyright Information

Additional information about the copyright ownership and rights of specific images and illustrators in the book can be found after the index.

ISBN 0-321-24132-0

9 8 7 6 5 4 3 2 1

Printed and bound in the United States of America

Praise from Readers and Reviewers of
Real World Scanning and Halftones, Second Edition

"For years I have referred to *Real World Scanning and Halftones* as the **beat-all, end-all guide for tonal scanning**. Because the information in the book is so invaluable, **scanner manufacturers should include a copy with every scanner they sell.…When it comes to capturing halftones, it's the only book I recommend.**"
– *Neil R. Manausa, Publishing Solutions Specialist,* USA TODAY

"I must tell you that your book is the **easiest to understand on the subject.**"
– *reader Jennifer H.*

"**One of the best technical books I've ever read!**" – *reader Jeffrey R.*

"Wow! A very worthy successor to a great classic. **This book is simply a 'must-have' for anyone doing any kind of commercial reproduction work.**"
– *Wayne Fulton, author of "a few tips on scanning" book and Web site*

"**If you work with scanned images, you should have this book.**"
– *Adobe Systems "Book Picks"*

"…[M]any manuals overlook the finer points of getting a good scan, and making needed corrections. *Real World Scanning and Halftones* takes you through all those important early steps, and onward.… Detailed conceptual explanations provide the foundation on which to expand your personal publishing experience. **Although as glossy and well-designed as a coffee table book,** *Real World Scanning and Halftones* **belongs right next to your scanner.**" – *Dingbat magazine*

"**Here's the book we've all been waiting for!** You read about the original edition of this book…when it brought sage advice on producing top-notch scans and halftones.…They're back! Now the three best-known experts in desktop publishing bring you the latest and greatest in the world of **making your scans kick butt!**"
– *Editor's Pick at The Design and Publishing Center*

"No matter what scanner or graphics program you decide to use, *Real World Scanning and Halftones* **is a book that the beginner should not be without**…Experienced users will also find this book to be indispensable. Advanced topics such as stochastic screening, the fine art of color correction and control, and techniques for producing professional halftones are all covered in depth. In addition, *Real World Scanning and Halftones* takes a **truly cross-platform approach and avoids the trap of defining steps that are specific to one operating system or another**…*Real World Scanning and Halftones* **unravels the mysteries** of producing high-quality computer graphics using a scanner and serves as an **invaluable learning tool for beginning and advanced users alike.**"
– *Borders Books & Music Web site*

"The language, while taking on the most technical subjects, **guides the user through the process clearly.…An excellent guide for beginners and pros alike!**"
– Marketing Higher Education Newsletter

"**You will not find a better source of image information than this.**"
– *Jay Nelson,* Design Tools Monthly

Preface

PRIMAL SCREENS

We've come so far since the desktop-publishing revolution that only the most gray-haired of us remember what the publishing industry was like before 1985.

Before desktop publishing, everyone knew that graphic design was the province of experts. Clerical folks were asked to type, format, photocopy, mimeograph, and staple, while the creative types, often designers and art directors from outside the company, would make design decisions that were implemented by highly specialized production people, some of whom worked for years or decades using X-Acto knives, Rapidograph pens, and hot wax. On the printing side, a swarm of specialized professions dealt with stripping color separations, producing film, running proofs, and making plates.

Desktop publishing has changed all that, allowing CEOs and managers to produce horrific, typo-filled documents that have made their companies look ridiculous. On the other hand, it's also allowed hundreds of thousands—perhaps millions—of people who would formerly have been trapped at IBM Selectric typewriters to learn enough about design and production to have useful, creative jobs inside of otherwise dour companies.

The problem is that too often workers have come in one morning to find a scanner and its manual plunked down on their desk, and a note taped to the monitor: "Please get up to speed this week; you'll be producing our annual report."

This book is, in part, for you folks who found your job description changed, whether you fought for that change or read about it on your new business cards. It's also a primer if you're making the leap to printed media but you've only worked previously with low-resolution visual media such as web design or video production. Finally, we hope to help those who've wrestled with the subject and have nearly pinned it to the ground, but who need some solid, focused techniques for producing consistent results that will take them to the next level in their work.

As Time Goes By

The first edition of *Real World Scanning and Halftones* appeared in 1993. Since then, however, desktop publishing has become professional to the point where a lot of elementary issues are no longer talked about—it's just assumed that everyone knows how to get a good scan and print it well. Paradoxically, it has also become harder to get good information about how to scan images and correct them effectively. Scanners have become better and enormously cheaper, and software has improved, but we still find ourselves answering the same scanning-related questions that we heard 10 years ago. We think that part of the reason for this is that many scanning manuals and books talk about the scanning process itself, but don't relate it well enough to the big picture of a production workflow.

We decided to revise *Real World Scanning and Halftones* because the second edition was six years old, and we wanted to keep you up to speed. Since the second edition, the most dramatic change in the scanning world is that just about everybody now has a scanner, or can easily afford one. When the first edition of this book came out in 1993, a 300 dpi grayscale scanner sold for $1000. By the time of the second edition, scanners had nearly three times the resolution for half the price. Now you can buy a 600-dpi, 48-bit, 1200-by-2400 dpi color flatbed scanner for less than $100. High-resolution film scanners are also more prevalent now because they can be purchased for as little as half of what they cost a few years ago, while their speed, resolution, and quality are close to what you needed a drum scanner for in the early 1990s. Finally, back in 1993 and 1998, our focus was on scanning for printed output, which is why halftones are part of the book's title. Today, scanning images for the World Wide Web is at least as common as scanning for print. We discuss in this book how to design workflows where you can scan once for multiple media without compromising any one medium.

Note that this book is completely bi-platform—Macintosh and Windows. We focus on Mac OS X and Windows XP, but many of the software programs and tricks we mention work in previous versions of Mac OS and Windows as well.

Real World Scanning and Halftones

Ultimately, there's simply no way we can provide you with the exact settings you need for every piece of hardware and software in every situation you'll find yourself in. So we've also done our best to give you the conceptual underpinnings you need in order to address your own publishing environment. While there are many scanning software programs out there, they all control the same conceptual fundamentals—once you understand those fundamentals, you can adjust to different scanning software applications with relative ease. The central concept common to all scanning workflows is this: The choices that you make when scanning are driven by the quality level you want in your final output.

Because we want you to understand not only what button to push, but also why you should push it (or not), you'll find some lengthy conceptual explanations here. Hopefully we've presented them so that you can grasp them easily and without the pain that we've endured figuring this stuff out for ourselves.

Finally, while there are plenty of books out there on imaging theory, hundreds on printing, and thousands on application programs, few are informed by a real-world understanding of the whole production process—from scanning to image-setting to offset printing, not to mention the scan-to-screen workflow for Web and video. What none of these books brings to the party is the understanding of how all these pieces interrelate. And if there's one thing we've learned in the world of scanning and halftones, *everything* relates to everything else.

We didn't want this book to be yet another title that was really about Photoshop. We use Photoshop, as well as other programs, in our examples. In some cases we'll refer you to other fine books that cover subjects outside of the scope of this book. One of those books, *Real World Adobe Photoshop*, was written by David with Bruce Fraser. It focuses on using Photoshop for real-world tasks like scanning, color correction, sharpening, and so on, as well as making selections, using color-management profiles, and creating images for multimedia.

How to Read This Book

So how should you read this book? Since we wrote it, we think you should read it from cover to cover. In a single sitting. Twice.

We realize that's a bit unrealistic. Because all of this stuff is so interrelated, though, it's hard to give any other advice. In some ways, the topics in this book are like Steve's favorite obsession: sailboat racing. You just can't understand sail shape without a good knowledge of hull dynamics, or vice versa. Similarly, you can't understand scanning techniques if you don't know about printing presses and Web graphics, and so on.

There's no single chapter in this book that doesn't rely on information in some other chapter (or several other chapters). Everything depends on everything else. So when you read the book the first time, some things may appear somewhat mysterious. But when you read it again, the patterns and relationships will start to emerge, and techniques that at first appeared odd will begin to make more sense.

First Steps

Nonetheless, if you want to just dip into this book quickly, we suggest you begin with Part 1 and master the concepts in it. That part provides the essential grounding in the essentials of scanning. From there you can wander through each other part of the book, filling in the nooks and crannies of your expertise.

Acknowledgements

Behind every great author stands a myriad of great supporters. We were very lucky to have a number of people who helped in essential ways across all three editions of this book. For this edition, we'd like to thank Bruce Fraser, David's long-time *Real World Photoshop* co-author; Steven Herron, who performed exquisite surgery on our stochastic screening chapter; and Jeff Grandy of West Coast Imaging for his insight into drum scanning.

We had the pleasure of working with several Peachpit Press staffers: our editor Cary Norsworthy who, with the assistance of Anne-Marie Walker, helped us shape this edition into a fresh look at the subject; Lisa Brazieal, our guide into modern print preparation and prepress; and publisher Nancy Ruenzel, whose enthusiasm for a third edition kept us going over the months this book required to revise and produce.

Caroline Parks and Jan Wright did a tag team and outstanding indexing job. And our copy editor and proofreader Don Sellers endured endless page proofs and corrections as we shed detritus of past years and tightened the book up to its current state. Brigette Schaffarzick adeptly handled galley composition and pagination for us in the homestretch. Jeff Tolbert took the whole world in his hands and turned it into a series of distinctive part openers for each section of the title.

From David: "My sincere thanks go to my wife, Debbie, and my sons, Gabriel and Daniel, for their patience and love. Special thanks as well to everyone who has bought this book and my other Peachpit titles over the years, encouraging me to keep trying to explain this stuff better."

From Glenn: "My wife has a certain amount of interest in technical topics, and when I exceed that interest, I write a book. I love her dearly, and appreciate her wit, charm, grace, and support as I wrestle with technical verities. My dad is always a wonderful touchstone on technical writing: a sophisticated user of computers himself, I know that if it doesn't make clear sense to him, I haven't done my job right."

From Conrad: "What carries me through massive projects like this one are the family, friends, and colleagues who continually assure me that it's worth the enormous effort, and then are phenomenally understanding, patient, and supportive during the long journey to press. Thank you all so very much."

From Steve: "Thanks to everyone—especially Glenn—who has contributed to this book over the years, and kept it as a living thing that keeps growing and changing."

Table of Contents

PART 1

Scanning

1

Waltzing Through the Process

AN INTRODUCTION TO SCANNING

There was a time when we got excited about just being able to use type in columns on a computer. Entire layouts that once required typesetting machines, chemical processing, paste-up artists, wax, X-Acto knives, layout boards, Rapidograph pens, and huge vacuum frames suddenly (or so it seemed) only needed a mouse and a keen eye. Oh, but images? Just leave ruled rectangles of the right shape and we'll let the printer drop them in later, manually.

Not so efficient, really, but it took a few years after the advent of typesetting-quality digital output to start incorporating images and type on a single electronic page and have confidence that the results would be predictable and of high quality.

Despite the years that have passed since images and text combined, scanning a conventional photograph, slide, or film negative still seems like a black art to many people in the design community. Those who aren't trained designers, but are required to produce documents with images, may find themselves even farther out to sea, because they have fewer resources and knowledgeable colleagues to turn to.

Most people rely on half-remembered oral lessons to scan images at the correct size or adjust them the right way. We still see people scanning images that take up two or four or even 10 times the storage they need to because someone they can't remember once told them to do it that way. And it pains us when we see anyone using Brightness and Contrast sliders to fix tonal balance.

We're here to tell you that there are simple, consistent, repeatable methods you can use to ensure that you scan, correct, and output your images the right way every time. We'll give you advice on how to approach a new situation and establish your own rules to scan by.

What is Scanning, Anyway?

In essence, scanning is a way to get images—photographs, line art, and drawings—into a computer. This means that the computer must see what we see. We see images because our eyes respond to light, and what we think of as light is actually a specific range of electromagnetic radiation that our eyes can sense. Our brains perceive an image as a continuously varying area of this radiation. Our brains perceive light and dark tones based on the intensities of electromagnetic radiation, and perceive color based on where the radiation falls on the electromagnetic spectrum. Color is measured in various ways: frequency, wavelength, or energy level and intensity (or color temperature).

These measurements are *analog* representations of light because they correspond directly to light's physical properties. But computers can't work with analog data; they don't recognize physical properties. They can only work with numerical values. Exact values. So, if we can describe an image digitally—as raw numbers—we can work with the image in a computer.

Scanners convert analog images into digital images by using a sensor to measure electromagnetic radiation (**Figure 1-1**). They then convert those readings to precise numerical values. Scanners then send those numbers to the computer. An image scanner is sensitive to the visible spectrum, because most people want to scan what their eyes see. Scientists, on the other hand, sometimes need to see things that are invisible to the eye, so they use a sensor that's tuned to sense a range of invisible radiation and map the results to a range of visible light. In this way, they can visualize the invisible. (This is how an infrared night-vision scan of a house's heat output works.)

Like the ancient game of Go, scanning can take less than an hour to learn and a lifetime to master. It's easy to learn, because today's scanners are almost as easy to use as a photocopier. What gets in the way of mastery is that it isn't quite as simple as feeding numbers to your computer. The catch is that those numbers have to be the right numbers. If they're a little bit off, the image might look too dark or too green, for example.

Fortunately, improved scanning and image-editing software have made it easier to generate an accurate scan. However, the real challenge is to produce a scan that has optimal tone and color, and also works perfectly with your output, because output requirements can vary quite a bit.

One of the keys to making a great scan is realizing that it isn't just about the scan or about the output. It's the relationship between the scan and the output. Think

Figure 1-1
Visible light as part of the electromagnetic spectrum

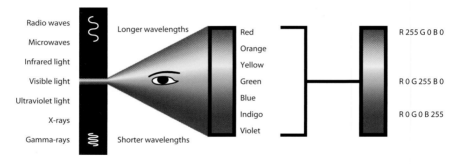

Full spectrum of electromagnetic radiation ▶ Visible colors ▶ Scanner sensor ▶ Digital colors in scanned file

of a scan as a means to an end, not an end in itself. If you keep this in mind, you'll find it easier to make decisions as you scan your images.

Real-World Scanning

The actual act of scanning consists of five basic considerations:

► Type of scanner

► Scanning mode

► Scanning resolution

► Adjusting the scanned image

► Creating final image output

When scanning an image, you need to make decisions in each of these areas. For example, you'll need to decide what kind of scanner you should use, what resolution you should use, and how you are going to output your image. The problem that most people have with scanning is that they don't understand the interconnectedness of each of these decisions.

The scanning resolution depends on your output method; the type of scanner you use depends on the kind of art you have; the types of adjustments you make to the image depend on the manner in which you scan the image; and so on. Chapter 13, *Getting Good Color*, describes just how interrelated each part is. Not only are these decisions interconnected, but they are all ultimately driven by the requirements of your final output.

Let's take a brief look at each of these areas, outlining their key issues. We'll go into more detail in each of these areas in subsequent chapters.

Type of Scanner

The image you want to capture typically determines the type of scanner you should use (as well as your budget, of course). If you have a color transparency, you need to use a device that can scan transparent originals, such as a film scanner, a drum scanner, or a flatbed scanner with a transparency adapter.

For reflective art, you can use a flatbed or drum scanner (of course, you can only use the latter if the reflective art can be taped around a cylinder).

If you need an image of someone's face and you don't already have a photographic print of it, you have to use a device such as a video or digital camera to capture that image. Digital cameras act just like desktop scanners, but you can carry them around more easily.

Another consideration when choosing a scanner is the quality of the scan you're trying to achieve. A scan from a drum scanner often has a much higher quality than a scan from a flatbed device. But a slide or transparency attachment on a flatbed scanner can oftentimes be good enough for your intended output. And almost any current scanner will work well for Web images or other images that will be shown on a video screen.

We look at the various types of scanners as well as their strong and weak points in Chapter 2, *Scanners*. This will help you decide which scanner to use for your purposes.

Scanning Mode

One key to creating a good scan is choosing the correct scanning mode. This means choosing among options such as line-art, dithered, halftoned, grayscale, and color modes. There is usually no reason to scan a black-and-white, line-art image in full-color mode; it's overkill. Similarly, there is usually no reason to scan a beautiful color photograph in high-contrast line-art mode as it won't reproduce at all like the original.

The mode you use depends on what you're scanning, what you plan on doing with the scan on the computer, and what kind of output you're aiming for.

If you're going to retouch an image in Adobe Photoshop, you should avoid the line art, dithered, and halftoned modes. If you're trying to scan type for optical character recognition (OCR), you probably want to use a line art scan. And the printing company that will be producing your output might request halftones, but halftoning usually occurs during output—almost never during scanning. We talk about this aspect of halftones in Chapter 24, *Who Does the Halftone?*

If the words *dithered*, *grayscale*, or *line art* don't mean much to you at this point, Chapter 2, *Scanners* should be enlightening. In addition, a scanning mode generally uses a specific *bit depth*. We cover this topic in Chapter 3, *Getting Your Originals Ready to Scan*, and in Part 2, *Anatomy of a Scanned Image*.

Scanning Resolution

To choose the correct scanning resolution, you need to think about file size, output resolution (whether for press or screen output), screen frequency (if it's a grayscale or color scan), and the size of the image—both the original image and the final image that you print or display on screen. All of these items interrelate. Fortunately, today's software goes a long way toward helping you calculate the right resolution for your scan.

We discuss these topics and the difference between dots per inch (dpi) and samples per inch (spi) and tell you how to use all of this information in Chapter 11, *Image Resolution*.

Adjusting the Scanned Image

Once your artwork is scanned in, using a particular scanner in a particular mode and resolution, you have to save it as a file on a disk. And once your image is on disk, you can change its tonal levels (highlights, midtones, and shadow detail) or color balance (hue and saturation), manipulate the picture (move a tree in the background, delete a person from the scene, and so on), and make it crisper or sharper. We talk about these issues in Chapter 12, *Tonal Correction*, Chapter 13, *Getting Good Color,* Chapter 15, *A Sharper Image*, and Chapter 16, *File Formats*.

Most scanners let you perform these adjustments as you scan. You can also perform these functions—plus create lots of other effects—in programs like Adobe Photoshop or Jasc Paint Shop Pro. Of course, there are many other less expensive (and less powerful) programs on the market that you can use to adjust images, such as Adobe Photoshop Elements, Microsoft PictureIt!, and Ulead Photo Express. However, you should only consider the less expensive programs if your output is not going to be printed on a printing press. The low-cost programs won't give you the degree of control as would a professional-level editor such as Photoshop, but they're fine for creating Web images or images you will only print on a desktop color printer.

Creating Final Image Output

You also need to think about how to get your image from the computer and into another form—from the digital world back to the analog, real world. This includes printing as halftones to black-and-white imagesetters (Chapter 24, *Who Does the Halftone?*), printing to a color device like a six-color inkjet printer or a film recorder (Chapter 8, *Scanning for Color Photo Printers*), or formatting an image for the World Wide Web (Chapter 7, *Scanning for the Web and Video*).

But the issue is larger than just deciding on the final output medium; it also includes several factors, like screen frequency of halftones, file size, and file format. To guide you through the maze of decisions you need to make, we've included chapters that are specific to particular media: Chapter 6, *Scanning for Prepress*; Chapter 7, *Scanning for the Web and Video*; Chapter 8, *Scanning for Color Photo Printers*; and Chapter 9, *Scanning for the Office*.

With all these topics to consider for what seems like a simple scan, it's amazing that anyone ever gets them right! We're confident that after you read Part 1, *Scanning*, you'll have most of the information you need to create great scans. And once you've done it a few times, choosing the correct options will become second nature.

Should You Do It Yourself or Send It Out?

At this point, you're either excited about scanning or totally overwhelmed. Now you need to decide whether to make the scan yourself or send it out to a service. Even if you own a great scanner and have become a scanning expert, there may be times when it might be better to have somebody else scan your images for you. Consider the following, which is summarized in **Table 1-1**:

Quality requirements. Although the performance of inexpensive and moderately priced scanners has increased markedly in recent years, they still can't match the capabilities of top-end equipment such as a drum scanner, which can cost tens of thousands of dollars. If you take on a project such as a coffee-table book, where the size and quality of the scans you need is beyond the capabilities of your own equipment, an outside imaging service might be the only way to go.

Table 1-1
Comparing outsourcing methods and scanning images yourself

Method	Advantages	Disadvantages
Scanning images yourself	Limited only by your equipment's capabilities, your ability, and your time.	Limited by your equipment's capabilities, your ability, and your time.
Kodak Picture CD	Uses standard JPEG RGB files. Widely available service.	Not directly usable for prepress due to lack of resolution and CMYK color.
Kodak Photo CD	Color quality and highest resolution are usually suitable for prepress use.	Uses proprietary file format that may require special software; must be converted for on-screen or printed output.
Kodak Pro-Photo CD	Higher maximum resolution and dynamic range than Photo CD.	More expensive and harder to find than the Photo CD service.
Standard file formats, CD/DVD delivery	Scans can be made to your exact specifications and saved in standard file formats such as TIFF.	Ideal results depend on precise communication with your imaging service and the quality of their expertise and equipment.
Standard file formats, Web delivery	Potentially the fastest delivery method. Scans can be saved in standard file formats.	Large files may take a very long time to download.

Your ability. You might find scanning to be an activity you love to do, and you know you'll master. Someday. But you might be working on a project that requires a particular level of quality and consistency, and you realize you're not going to reach that skill level by the time the scans need to be done. A good scanning service can fill the gap here.

Your level of interest. Do you really want to "do it all?" You might have the motivation to become proficient at creating a good scan when you have to, but you might not be interested in scanning every image that crosses your desk.

Large volume of images. Many scanners come equipped with document feeders that can automatically scan stacks of pages or slides, or all of the frames in a filmstrip. Some flatbed scanners are smart enough to let you place multiple photos on the scanner and make a separate file for each photo. But the time it takes for the actual scan doesn't include the time to load and unload your originals, test and perfect your batch settings, adjust settings for non-typical images, and organize the scanned files into disc archives.

Say you're thinking about scanning a high-quality archive of 1000 historical photos; this can represent as few as 27 rolls of film. Scanning each photo might take a couple of minutes, and checking and fine-tuning each scan (fixing dust, scratches, tone, and color) might take another 5 to 10 minutes—if you're lucky. In total, this project could take 167 hours, or an entire month of 8-hour days, with no breaks!

So if scanning isn't the number one item in your job description, taking the time to scan numerous images might not be the best use of your time. If it's not possible to hire a skilled worker to run your scanner, you have a good reason to outsource your project to an imaging service.

Delivery Media and Methods

It used to be that getting an outside scan done meant sending in your original images and getting the scans back on floppy disks or CDs. However, you can now choose from several CD formats, or just pick them up on the Web. But be sure to choose your format carefully because each option has its advantages and disadvantages. Some formats are targeted for the modest needs of consumers, whereas others are intended for professional publishing. A list of the formats follow, but we talk more specifically about comparing, opening, and editing each of them in Chapter 16, *File Formats*. **Table 1-1** summarizes the major pros and cons.

Kodak Picture CD. You might recognize the words Kodak Picture CD as a checkbox on film envelopes at your local drugstore photo lab. The quality of this format is more than good enough for the Web, and images are saved as standard JPEG files. However, for print media, Picture CD is only good for jobs with moderate quality requirements, like a real estate catalog or community newspaper. The images only have enough resolution to be printed at rather small sizes.

Kodak Photo CD. For graphic arts uses, Photo CD is more useful than Picture CD. But be sure not to confuse the two. Each image is stored at five resolutions in a Kodak format called Image Pac. The scan quality of images can be excellent (depending on the competence of the person scanning them), and the highest-resolution scans can be adjusted for prepress output and other forms of high-resolution printing. In some cases, you might need a Photo CD plug-in to open the images, because the Image Pac file format is proprietary.

Kodak ProPhoto CD. This format is the same as Photo CD, but adds a sixth resolution, 4096 by 6144 (that's 87 Mb of data). This resolution allows for better enlargements (you could fill a full tabloid-size page with good results) and accommodates scanning 4-by-5 film frames (Photo CD is limited to 35mm and APS film formats). ProPhoto CD scanners are also capable of producing a subtle range of tones than Photo CD.

Regular CD or DVD. Any imaging/scanning service can scan your film or prints using its scanner, and burn the resulting image files onto a Macintosh or Windows CD or DVD using standard file formats. There really isn't an official name for just creating a CD or DVD with images; it's the same as if you scanned your images and saved them on a CD or DVD yourself. Because there is no standard for the format or image specifications that end up on the disc, to get the kind of images you want you have to communicate very clearly with the imaging service. Talk with the service in terms of the attributes of scanned images we discuss in Chapter 10, *What is a Bitmap?*, such as size, resolution, color model, and bit depth, with all specs derived from the type of output in which the images will be used.

Web pick-up. Although most services return your finished scans on a disc such as a CD or DVD, some services might allow you to download them, which can be handy if you're working with a service that's in a different city. This works well for images scanned at low resolutions for Web use or home printing. But if you're having the service create a large number of prepress-quality scans, the files can be so large that the total downloading times may become

 In all cases, it's always best to comparison-shop and request test scans to make sure your imaging service's scans will work properly within your output workflow.

impractical. Also, few services provide a secure or private FTP site, so it may be easy for one client to see or download another client's files (like yours). This can be an issue if you're working with confidential images or material not yet released to the public. As with files received on a regular CD, you have to be very clear about the specifications of the images you want to receive from the service.

Why You Need This Book

Remember that scanning is just a means to an end. After you get your scans back from the imaging service, you still need to adjust your scan to your output. We cover the variety of ways you can adjust your scanned images throughout Parts 2, 3, 4, and 5.

Even when you don't perform the actual scan, this book helps you get the most out of your outsourced scans by providing you with information on what to ask for and how to recognize whether or not your imaging service gave you what you asked for. By specifying scans correctly relative to the type of output you need, you'll vastly increase your chances of getting your project done on time, on budget, and at the level of quality you need. And if you exhibit a familiarity with scanning concepts and terms, you'll earn the respect of your imaging service and build a more satisfying working relationship with the service.

2

Scanners

WHAT YOU NEED AND WHAT YOU GET

Choice is good. We like having as many options as possible. But too much choice makes your head spin on its axis. Every day, it seems, a new scanner model or three appear—faster, more powerful, and less expensive than the ones preceding it.

Every scanner does basically the same thing: it takes a picture of a physical image, like a photograph, and turns it into something your computer can use. All scanners carry out this task in pretty much the same way. But we're going to tell you how each part works so you can understand what's really going on at each step of the way.

In this chapter, we explain what different kinds of scanners can do—and what they can't do—as well as what makes a good scanner. You can use these guidelines when searching for a unit yourself or reading product comparisons or marketing literature. We'll also talk a bit about digital cameras, which have a surprising number of similarities to scanners but have a different purpose and different options.

Scanning Factors

Before buying a scanner, it's useful to consider what factors play into how well a scanner will work with your hardware and software, and fit into your workgroup, if you're part of one. Here's a quick overview, followed by an in-depth look at each.

Resolution. How many samples per inch (spi) can the scanner capture? This seems simple, but isn't always. There's *optical resolution* and *interpolated resolution*, and more isn't always better. Resolution needs vary depending on the size and kind of material you're scanning. (Resolution is explored in Chapter 11, *Image Resolution*.)

Dynamic range and bit depth. How many bits per sample does the scanner capture and how well? Again, a simple number doesn't tell the whole story. All 48-bit scanners are not created equal—if they were, one wouldn't cost $150 and another $1,500. The real question is how wide a range of colors the scanner can capture and how well it can differentiate tones across that range and at the difficult extremes—whether grayscale or color.

How your scanner sees. The ability of a scanner to capture your original depends largely on how well its sensor and hardware are matched to your original. The density of your original may come into play if it's outside the range your scanner can handle. Some sensor types are better than others, and the level of quality can vary even within the same type of sensor. The best sensors capture a wide range while representing each recordable tone accurately and without introducing noise.

Light source. How does the scanner illuminate the image? Do you need to worry about replacing the light source as it ages?

Software. What capabilities are built into the scanning software? Does it just capture an image and drop it on disk, or can it apply tonal correction and sharpening as it scans? Does it let you make precise corrections to the actual scanner data, before saving the final scanned image? Does the scanner only work with a standalone application, or can you access it via plug-in modules from within other programs? Does it work with the industry-standard TWAIN format? (See Chapter 5, *How to Read Your Scanning Software*, for more on this subject and a definition of TWAIN.)

Scanner types. Is the scanner a flatbed, film scanner, or drum scanner? Does it use CCD, CMOS, or PMT to capture samples? Or is it a more specialized unit, like a video-capture system or sheetfed scanner? The type of scanner you use determines the types of images you can capture, and different types have different strengths and weaknesses in the four previous areas.

Color management. Can the scanner use device profiles to represent color more accurately? Is the scanner ready to be integrated into a color-managed workflow? Can color management be customized or turned off?

Hardware interface. How do you connect the scanner to your computer? Which interfaces are faster and easier to use?

Networking. Can you operate the scanner from any machine on the network? Is this an option you should consider?

Resolution

It seems like it should be easy to compare different scanners' maximum resolutions. One scans at 1200 spi (samples per inch)—manufacturers like to say "dots per inch," but as you'll see in later chapters, that's not really accurate—and another scans at 2400 spi. So the 2400-spi scanner is better, right?

Not necessarily. Manufacturers often list their scanners' *optical resolution* and *interpolated resolution* in their marketing materials. Optical resolution is the maximum number of samples the scanner takes per inch, but it's not always easy to find or clearly labeled. You can read Chapter 11, *Image Resolution*, to find out what interpolated resolution means, but we can tell you right here that the scanner simply can't capture more usable information than the optical resolution. You can ignore interpolated resolution as a factor when you compare scanners—just compare the optical resolutions. Higher is almost always better.

But there is one catch: higher resolution doesn't necessarily give you a sharper image. Even though two scanners have the same optical resolution, it's possible for one scanner to be sharper than the other if one scanner has better lenses. Hardware quality issues like this help to explain why two scanners can have similar specs but very different prices—in general, you do get what you pay for.

Some scanners list two values for optical resolution, such as 1200 by 2400 spi. This is because the resolution along the short side of a scanner is determined by the scanner's sensor, while the resolution along the long side is determined by the drivetrain of the stepper motor that moves the sensor across the original (or the original past the sensor, depending on the model). The resulting scanned samples are square, so when evaluating scanners with two optical resolution values, err on the conservative side and use the smaller of the two values for comparisons to other scanners.

Keep in mind that you need a much higher resolution—more samples per inch—for slides and film than you do for reflective art because you're usually enlarging a 35mm slide an order of magnitude more than a 4-by-6–inch print. We'll explain more about resolution in Chapter 11, *Image Resolution*.

Dynamic Range and Bit Depth

In terms of tone and color, to get a good scan of an original your scanner must have these characteristics:

A See the full range of tones in the original, without clipping off the lightest or darkest tones that have detail. For color scans, a scanner needs to detect an original's full tonal range in each color channel it senses (the red, green, and blue channels).

B Distinguish as many steps as possible between the lightest and darkest tones it records.

C Represent tones accurately between the lightest and darkest tones it records. For example, 25%, 48%, and 76% black sample points in the original are recorded precisely at those values in the scan.

D Record all of the above in the final file it saves.

Scanner spec sheets provide a limited amount of insight into how well a scanner can achieve these goals. To understand how scanners and their advertising address the goals of scanning, it's necessary to understand some basic, and sometimes challenging, terminology.

Dynamic range. Dynamic range addresses goal A in our list above. Dynamic range expresses how broad a range of tonal values a scanner can capture; this is similar to the photographic measure of *density* (discussed in detail in "Density of the Original," later). A scanner's dynamic range is set by the lightest and darkest levels that the scanner's sensor can recognize. But scanner spec sheets don't represent dynamic range consistently.

Dynamic range should represent the entire system from the sensor through the scanning software—and like any system, it's only as strong as its weakest link. Some scanners have hardware that's capable of a nice wide range but aren't fitted with a sensor that can fill that range. The scanner's spec sheet advertises the wider, unrealistic range. This is like advertising 2-liter bottles of soda that are filled by a machine that can only dispense 1.5 liters per bottle.

Bit depth. Bit depth addresses goal B in our list above, by describing how many different tones can be recorded within a given range of tones. Bit depth is measured, naturally, in bits: single binary digits that represent either zero or one. An antiquated 1-bit-per-sample (or bilevel) scanner could only capture two colors: black and white. An 8-bit grayscale scanner grabs 256 levels (2^8); and a 24-bit scanner can measure any of more than 16 million different colors (2^{24}). Most scanners today work at even higher bit-depths. Scanning at bit depths higher than 8 bits per channel can provide extra flexibility for images that need rather extensive tonal or color adjustments. We talk about bit depth in more detail in Chapter 10, *What is a Bitmap?*

Our friend Bruce Fraser likes to compare dynamic range and bit depth to a staircase: the dynamic range describes the height of the staircase and the bit depth describes the number of steps from the bottom to the top. A scanner with an enormous dynamic range (able to capture information from the very light to the very dark) but with only 256 steps doesn't offer much of an advantage; neither does a scanner with lots and lots of tiny steps (like a 36-bit scanner) that spans only a tiny dynamic range.

Tonal sensitivity. Now we address goal C in the list above. Neither density nor bit depth tells you how sensitive the scanner is to tonal changes, or the ability of a scanner to accurately represent similar, adjacent tonal values as distinct from each other. Some scanners are great in the lighter and darker areas of a scan, but muddy in the midtones, where most of the Caucasian flesh tones are found. Unfortunately, there isn't a number that can represent tonal sensitivity on a scanner spec sheet.

It should be clear by now that reading manufacturers' figures on dynamic range, bit depth, and tonal sensitivity doesn't help you compare scanners as much as you'd like. When scanners were less capable, those numbers were more useful. Generally, but not always, higher numbers are better, and

the more expensive the scanner, the better it performs in all of these areas. Beyond that, you should read as many published scanner reviews as you can before buying.

What about goal D above, recording all of this information into a file? That depends on the quality of the scanner's internal processing hardware and the capabilities of the scanning software you use to drive the scanner. If a scanner has 16-bit capability and you drive it with software that can edit and save a 16-bit file, they're well-matched.

You can see a visual map of the whole process in **Figure 5-9** in Chapter 5, *How to Read Your Scanning Software*. In the rest of this chapter, we talk about concepts and factors that affect how well a scanner handles dynamic range and bit depth.

How Your Scanner Sees

The most important stage of scanning is when the scanner and the original meet face-to-face. It's kind of like two people on a first date: The scanning hardware encounters the original image, and if they're well-matched, both are happy. If not, someone's going to be disappointed. This section describes factors that contribute to love at first sight or a first date being the last date.

Density of the Original

If you combine dynamic range and bit depth into a measure of the range and extent of tones that can be captured, you're pretty close to the photographic term *density*. The amount of light that film records is measured as density, using the symbol "D." Density is actually a measure of how opaque the film is, or how much light can shine through it (or reflect off it, in the case of prints). The more opaque or dense the film is, the more chemical that's been deposited on the film stock, and the greater tonal range the photographic emulsion can capture.

Figure 2-1 Film density versus scanner exposure

The lightest and darkest tones a particular film can capture—the minimum and maximum tonal values—are called the "DMIN" and the "DMAX". A film's entire tonal range is measured by subtracting the minimum from the maximum, like a DMAX of 3.3 minus a DMIN of 0.3 means an overall density of 3.0D. Negative film is rated around 3.0D, while prints are usually less than 2.0D, and transparencies or slides are as high as 4.0D.

The densest areas of film and prints are hardest for scanners to capture. This is because scanners measure light in a straight line, while film records—and the human eye perceives—light as a sharply increasing logarithmic curve (**Figure 2-1**).

The curve is steepest in the densest areas, which are also the darkest in film transparencies and reflective art; this is called the *shadow detail*. In film negatives, the densest areas represent the lightest tones or *highlight detail*, because the film is reversed out.

It can be a challenge for a scanner to record tonal details smoothly across the entire density curve because digital steps progress evenly from dark to light, while the density curve does not. Along the steep parts of the curve, the tonal differences between each digitally recorded value are larger than they are along the shallower parts. Scanning at a higher bit depth

addresses this by providing more digital steps, as long as the scanner's sensor is good enough to distinguish those tonal differences in the first place (**Figure 2-2**).

Most professional scanners have density ratings these days, which makes it easier to decide whether a given scanner can adequately capture the detail in the work you need to scan. If you're scanning mostly reflective art, a scanner with 2.8D is fine. If you're digitizing transparencies day in and day out, you'd better get a scanner with at least 3.3D. You don't necessarily need a higher density rating than your originals' density.

Unless you always use large-format transparencies and drum scanners, or subjects lit perfectly in a studio, you'll always be making some compromises in density, sacrificing some tones at the upper or lower end of the scale. This might come when actually shooting the film—exposure time, aperture, and lighting affect density at that stage; or, it might happen when making the scan, where you use scanning software to capture more highlight or shadow detail, and give up some tones on the opposite end of the scale.

Sensor Types

A scanner's dynamic range, bit depth, and tonal sensitivity all depend on the hardware—specifically, two different pieces of hardware that act together: sensors that respond to the intensity of light hitting them, and the analog-to-digital converter that takes measurements from the sensors and turns them into numbers that the computer can understand.

Every scanner has sensors that measure the light *reflecting* off art or *transmitting* through film negatives and transparencies. There are three main kinds of sensors: CCD, CMOS, and PMT. CCD (charged-coupled devices) and CMOS (complementary metal-oxide semiconductor) sensors are found

Figure 2-2 Different bit depths and their exponential number of tonal and color levels

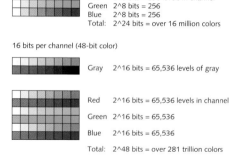

8 bits per channel (24-bit color)

Gray	2^8 bits = 256 levels of gray
Red	2^8 bits = 256 levels in channel
Green	2^8 bits = 256
Blue	2^8 bits = 256
Total:	2^24 bits = over 16 million colors

16 bits per channel (48-bit color)

Gray	2^16 bits = 65,536 levels of gray
Red	2^16 bits = 65,536 levels in channel
Green	2^16 bits = 65,536
Blue	2^16 bits = 65,536
Total:	2^48 bits = over 281 trillion colors

in flatbed scanners, digital cameras, and desktop film scanners, while PMTs (photomultiplier tubes) are exclusively the province of rotating drum scanners.

CCD and CMOS

These sensors work just like the light meter in a camera: light coming in is measured and then plotted on a scale. The more light that comes in, the higher the mark on the scale. (The scale itself has an arbitrary top mark based on the density of the scanner; see "Density of the Original," above.)

The difference between a camera's light meter and a scanner is that a scanner has several thousand sensors in a row (or *linear array*). Each sensor takes in a single sample point of data (if there are 400 CCDs per inch on the linear array, you can say the scanner has a resolution of 400 samples per inch, or 400 spi). CCDs have been around for decades, and have improved in quality to the point where high-end CCD scanners rival drum scanners.

CMOS sensors first appeared in digital cameras in 1996, and started showing up in inexpensive flatbed and sheetfed scanners in late 1997 in the form of CISs (Contact Image Sensors). They're similar to CCDs, but have the advantage of being made using the same techniques that chipmakers use to create memory chips and processors; they benefit more quickly from improvements in that field. CCDs also have separate sensors, analog-to-digital converters (see "Quality of Measurement," below), and other electronics, while these are in a single package for CMOS sensors.

Sensors are bulk manufactured and aren't perfect; virtually any scanner that you buy has a very small number of damaged units. Manufacturers pack in enough sensors so that if an occasional one doesn't work or is out of whack, its neighbors pick up the slack. This happens in hardware or as the data is read.

PMTs

Drum scanners use PMTs, which are one of the last incarnations of good old vacuum tubes. A PMT amplifies incoming light into a signal strong enough to be measured easily, so exposure time can be very short; CCD and CMOS sensors require a longer exposure time because they need to have more photons hit them before they can make an accurate reading.

All PMTs used to have a much greater overall dynamic range than CCDs. It's now hard to find a new drum scanner; their days are numbered.

Quality of Measurement

Getting from a sensor's reading to a color or tone requires a bit of conversion. The scanner has to take the signal the sensor creates and turn it into a number. To do this, it uses an analog-to-digital (A/D) converter. The quality of your scanner is dependent on the A/D converter's ability to sample voltage output by a sensor and suppress or correct for noise. (*Noise* is the introduction of random fluctuation into information.)

An A/D converter works the same for CCD, CMOS, and PMT sensors. These sensors react to light by producing an *analog* electric signal; there are no bits or bytes or anything digital about it at all. The A/D converter fits in the scanning process as the mediator between the sensor and the scanner's primitive onboard computer. The converter has a bit depth that represents its precision: the number of digits to which it can accurately measure the analog signal coming from the sensor.

During a scan, sensors measure light and produce a voltage. The voltage varies directly in response to the intensity of the light being focused on the sensor; the light's intensity varies as a function of the spot on the image being scanned.

The sensors pass on this voltage to the A/D converter, which samples the values and produces a discrete number—a digital value representing the tone. Some scanners actually send the voltage through two or more different converters and average the results to try to correct for noise.

In the case of sensors and converters, noise shows up as values that are too high or low compared with the original image data that was sampled. Noise is an artifact of analog sensors. Noise can be attributable to ambient temperature, a subtle flaw in the sensor, a tiny change in the scanner's AC power, or almost anything that would alter sensor performance. The good news is that after the analog signal is translated to a digital value, no more noise is introduced during digital editing and output. But there's no meaningful way to determine a scanner's noise level by looking at a scanner's spec sheet.

Because noise can be induced by inconsistencies in electrical power, you can try to minimize this type of noise by plugging the scanner into a *line conditioner*. This type of gadget filters electrical power so that the scanner is shielded from the voltage spikes, drops, and power line noise that are happening all the time. This kind of filtering goes well beyond what a cheap surge protector can do. If you already use an uninterruptible power supply (UPS) to prevent data loss during power outages, check the manual—there's a fair chance that it also has power filtering features built into it.

Discerning Tonal Detail

All scanner elements have a linear response to light; that is, there's a one-to-one ratio between the brightness of the light and the intensity of the outgoing signal. However, photographic film and the human eye both record light in a logarithmic fashion—we are actually more sensitive to detail in the deep shadows of an image (**Figure 2-1**, earlier in the chapter).

The result is that two points that appear clearly different to us may appear the same (or only a tiny bit different) to a scanner. Detail in images is entirely a factor of samples being different from each other; the more they differ, the more obvious the detail. The deeper the bit depth in a scanner, the better it can record detail.

The problem is that the tiny differences in pixel values that the scanner picks up are often completely overwhelmed by noise that naturally occurs when the scanner's A/D converter tries to interpret the very low electric signals that the sensors generate.

In Chapter 12, *Tonal Correction*, we discuss how you can emphasize the details in shadow areas with tonal correction—accentuating the differences between adjacent samples—and how you lose detail in the highlights in the process: either they wash out to white or they all become too similar to display much detail.

There are also a few methods you can use to combat noisy shadows in scanner hardware and software. Each of these should be evaluated before you buy or use a scanner.

Capture extra bits. While some very low-end scanners only capture 8 bits of data per channel (a single channel is either black, red, green, or blue), decent scanners on the market today capture at least 12 bits of data—or 36 bits overall. Some scanners can record as many as 48 bits per color sample.

When we wrote the first edition of this book in 1993, it was too expensive for anybody but a service bureau or dedicated department in a larger company to buy a 30-bit color scanner; at this writing, there are 36-bit flatbeds available for under $100. Of course, you still have to pay at least $300 for a flatbed unit that's more suitable for professional work, and some are in the $1,200 to $1,500 range for the right combination of hardware and software to do a wide range of scanning in a managed and consistent environment. Film scanners tend to cost a few hundred dollars more, and drum scanners can range into the tens of thousands of dollars.

Most scanners that capture more than 24 bits for each color sample automatically reduce the image data down to just 24 bits per sample when saving out the final scan file—the scanning program or plug-in removes extra data by averaging samples. Files that contain more than 24 bits per sample are called *high-bit* files. High-bit files take up more disk space and are slower to process. But if you want to make major tonal or color corrections using more powerful image-editing features than your scanning utility provides, see if your scanning utility can save a high-bit file that you can then work on in an image editor that supports high-bit files.

Photoshop can open and edit files with up to 48 bits of color data per sample (16 bits of data per RGB channel). A 16-bits-per-channel file is also useful for creating high-quality images that you can use as masters for multiple media uses, which we discuss in Chapter 18, *Creating Master Images*.

We'll talk more about bit depth in Chapter 10, *What is a Bitmap?*; more about scanning software support in Chapter 5, *How to Read Your Scanning Software*; and more about deep tonal adjustment in Chapter 12, *Tonal Correction*, and Chapter 13, *Getting Good Color*.

Adjusting exposure time. Many scanners can adjust the amount of time that each scanning element is exposed to light. Most figure the exposure automatically, by doing a prescan and then adjusting exposure based on the density of the image. By increasing the exposure time, you can push data lower on the density scale by letting more light pass through or reflect off your source image. This can blow out detail at the less dense end of the scale, but it is a way to spread detail in the densest area over a greater range. By doing this at scanning time, you capture better information, which you can balance in your image-editing software.

Adaptive analog-to-digital converters. Some scanners use adaptive analog-to-digital converters. If the image you're scanning concentrates most of its tonal values in a narrow band, adaptive A/D converters can use the CCD's full ability to discern tonal differences but apply it to a narrower range of values, resulting in better dynamic range. The hardware, in cooperation with the scanning software, handles this automatically; many scanners also allow you to do this manually using their software, as well. This automatic adaptation is less important with scanners that have very high bit depths but is a great trick for a 24- or 30-bit scanner.

Multi-sampling. Some scanners let you take multiple samples of the same point on the image. This reduces noise by averaging the samples to arrive at a less distorted tonal value, making your scanner more effective in shadow areas. We cover this technique in more detail in Chapter 5, *How to Read Your Scanning Software*.

Light Source

For the scanner sensor to read the original image, the original must be illuminated by a balanced, consistent source of light. A few years ago, most of the scanners on the market used fluorescent lamps to illuminate the original, but many recent scanners use light-emitting diodes. The light source you choose depends on the types of originals you scan, and how much you use your scanner.

Fluorescent Lamp

Many scanners use a fluorescent lamp that works like the ones that hang from ceilings in shops and offices. Gasses inside the lamp fluoresce, or give off light, when an electrical current passes through them. The particular type of lamp used in many scanners is called a *cold-cathode* lamp.

As a fluorescent lamp ages, it becomes dimmer and its *color balance* can change, possibly causing the scanner's representation of colors to change. Many scanners use a self-calibration routine that can compensate somewhat for this effect, but eventually a fluorescent lamp will dim or shift so much that it needs to be replaced. Estimated lamp life is often noted in the scanner's technical specifications, and can run anywhere from 1000 hours to 10,000 hours and up. If you aren't scanning every day, you'll probably replace the scanner with a newer model before the lamp wears out. But if you plan to do a lot of scanning, you might want to consider the rated lifetime of the lamps for different models, and how easy they are to replace.

To prolong the life of the lamp, the software that comes with many scanners includes an option to automatically turn off the scanner lamp when it isn't used for a certain amount of time. If you're scanning occasionally it may be best to let the lamp turn itself off. Because the lamp should be warmed up for best results, you should disable this option if you're scanning continuously or quite frequently.

LED (Light-Emitting Diode)

Some scanners use an array of red, green, and blue LEDs to illuminate the original. LEDs have several advantages compared to fluorescent lamps. They last longer, and they are ready to use practically instantly—no need for the half-hour warm-up time normally associated with fluorescent lamps. LEDs also take up less space than a lamp. For all of these reasons, LEDs have turned up in everything from high-end film scanners to low-end and super-thin flatbed scanners.

All of these reasons would seem to make LEDs the winner in the light source wars, but there is one situation where some prefer to use fluorescent-lamp scanners: scanning grainy film or dirty, scratched originals. The issue is one familiar to veterans of traditional "wet" darkrooms. In a traditional darkroom's black-and-white film enlarger, you can use a *collimated* (focused, or point) light source, or a *diffuse* (soft) light source. In a film enlarger, a collimated light source is generally thought to produce sharper images, but can also over-emphasize silver film grain and other unwanted details like dust and scratches.

This also seems to be the case when scanning: some photographers feel that, due to their collimated nature, LED scanners over-emphasize grain, dust, and scratches. You might take that opinion with a grain of salt, because LED scanners such as the Nikon line are widely used by professionals. The issue may not actually be such a big deal unless you scan a lot of black-and-white silver negatives. In that case, you should test typical examples of your originals on both fluorescent and LED scanners before buying one.

Also, unwanted artifacts resulting from LED scanning can be somewhat mitigated by hardware-based defect removal features such as Digital ICE (used in the Nikon line of LED film scanners)—which is probably a large reason why hardware-based defect removal appeared first in the Nikon film scanners. We talk more about hardware-based defect removal in Chapter 5, *How to Read Your Scanning Software*.

Software

Scanning software has improved to the point where you might carry out a variety of corrections using the software before transferring the scan into an image-editing program. We used to sniff at the very thought. But whether you buy the scanning software separately—like LaserSoft's Silver-Fast—or use what's bundled with the scanner, you should focus on tonal correction, sharpening, and plug-in modules.

We talk in more depth about working with scanning software in Chapter 5, *How to Read Your Scanning Software*.

Tonal Correction

If your scanning software allows you to apply tonal correction while you scan, you can save a lot of time when producing multiple scans. Without this capability, you need to scan, save, open the picture in an image-editing program, correct it, then save again.

The tonal correction that is offered, of course, has to be *good* tonal correction. As we point out later in Chapter 12, *Tonal Correction*, linear correction (usually consisting of contrast and brightness adjustments) is essentially worthless. You need good tools for nonlinear correction, and (perhaps) for ICC color management or closed-loop calibration. We talk about ICC color management in Chapter 13, *Getting Good Color*; some kind of monitor calibration is necessary so that you can accurately preview your corrections on screen.

A major influence on the tonal and color quality you get from your scanning software is whether or not the software's corrections are performed at the scanner's maximum bit depth, which depends on how the scanning hardware and software work together. Let's say you have a 16-bit-per-channel color scanner, and your final output requires an 8-bit-per-channel RGB color scan. If the scanning software applies your corrections on the original 16-bit scan data before it converts to 8 bits, you obtain the best quality. But if the scanning software converts the original 16-bit data to 8 bits before applying your corrections,

removing subtlety in the details, the quality of the correction could be much poorer. We discuss how and when certain adjustments happen during the scanning process in Chapter 5, *How to Read Your Scanning Software*.

Sharpening

Sharpening is always needed before final output. Sharpening usually isn't handled by the scanning hardware, but by software—either the scanning software, or your image-editing program, the latter being the best place to sharpen. But if you're scanning for simple output like home, office, or the Web, sharpening in the scanning software can be convenient. We cover this in detail in Chapter 15, *A Sharper Image*.

If you want to keep it simple and sharpen images only once, sharpen after you're finished applying tonal correction and performing other image-editing tasks. Usually, you won't be concerned about the quality of the sharpening options in your scanning software, because you'll sharpen images later using your image-editing software.

Access from Other Programs

Almost every scanner comes with a standalone application for controlling the scanner and capturing scans, but it's also convenient if you can scan images from within an image-editing application. If your scanning application doesn't offer (good) tonal correction and sharpening, scanning directly into Photoshop or the like can partially short-circuit the multiple-save routine.

Most scanners come with either a Photoshop plug-in or a TWAIN module that lets you control the scanner and acquire a scan into a new, untitled window without leaving your image-editing program. Photoshop plug-ins work not only with Photoshop, but also with some other Adobe software, like Adobe Photoshop Elements, and with some competitors' software, like

DeBabelizer. TWAIN modules can be used with virtually every image-editing program for the Mac and Windows.

Scanner Types

As we mentioned in Chapter 1, *Waltzing Through the Process*, the sort of scanner you need at any given time depends mostly on the sort of image you're trying to get into your computer. Different scanner types also perform differently in the areas discussed above, such as resolution, dynamic range and bit depth, and software. Let's take a quick overview of the various types of scanners, considering them for types of artwork that they support. We'll also take a dip into digital cameras, which work just like scanners, but require different considerations. **Table 2-1** offers suggestions for the type of scanner you should consider for different kinds of output and resolution.

Flatbed Scanners

Flatbeds are cheap, good, and ubiquitous. They usually look like some weird cross between a photocopier and a packing carton for an alien computer. The idea behind flatbed scanners is that you can place flat artwork down on a sheet of glass, and a scanning mechanism moves under it, bouncing light off the material so the reflected light lands on the image sensors. Flatbed scanners are generally set up for *reflective* art (like photographic prints, printed pages, and so on), but they can often be fitted with *transparency* attachments that enable them to scan film (slides, negatives, or other transparent art). Many flatbeds are sold with the attachment as a bundle.

In the reflective mode, a light source is typically mounted below the glass on a motor-driven arm that sweeps by the material being scanned. The scanner has a series of mirrors that focus the reflection of the art onto the sensors. When scanning transparencies, the light source usually looks more like a light box, which is sometimes built into the scanner cover, and it's above the art in question. The light shines through onto mirrors that redirect the light onto the sensors.

Flatbed scanners can be incredibly cheap: at the time of this writing, you can buy a 1200-by-2400 spi, 36-bit scanner for $75. But as with all computer equipment, you do get what you pay for, and a $750 Hewlett-Packard or $1,500 Microtek scanner will have some advantages in sensor quality, software controls, and durability over a lower-cost unit. Problems crop up in less expensive scanners with blurry or jittery scans when the scanning mechanism itself doesn't move smoothly or is on a shaky surface. And light sources wear out or their color and brightness may shift as the light source ages. Cheaper models may not hold up well in an office where people scan all day long.

Higher vertical resolution. Some scanners have different horizontal and vertical optical resolutions, which they achieve by having a better "stepper" motor that moves the image sensors along the length of the bed of the scanner. We describe this in more detail in "Resolution," earlier in this chapter.

Multiple optical resolutions. If you need a transparency attachment for a flatbed scanner, it's important to check before buying on what the highest optical resolution is for the scanner. The more expensive scanners have two sets of resolutions, and often two sets of optics (lenses). When scanning reflective art, the flatbed might scan at 600 or 1200 spi over an 8.5-by-14–inch area. When you switch to transmissive film scanning, the scanner can swap in a different lens for 2400 spi or higher scanning by focusing a smaller area (usually 4 by 6 inches or smaller) onto the same sensors.

If you need to scan ▸ / when your final output is ▾	Reflective art or photos	Photographic film	In color	...for printing at a max. line screen (lpi) of ...	...minimum scanner specs should be...
Just text; photos are stripped in by the printing service	FPO[1]	No	Yes	n/a	Flatbed, 300 dpi, 24-bit color
	FPO	FPO	Yes	n/a	Flatbed, 300 dpi, 24-bit color with transparency attachment
	No	FPO	Yes	n/a	Film scanner, 2000 dpi, 24-bit color
Newsprint, one-color	Yes	Yes	No	85	Flatbed, 300 dpi, 24-bit color with transparency attachment
Uncoated, one-color	Yes	No	No	133	Flatbed, 600 dpi, 30-bit color (10 bits for grayscale)
Quick print color offset	Yes	No	Yes	133	Flatbed, 600 dpi, 30-bit color
High-quality color offset	Yes	No	Yes	200	Flatbed, 1200 to 4800 dpi, 36-bit color
	Yes	Yes	Yes	200	Flatbed, 1200 to 4800 dpi, 36-bit color for reflective; low-end drum, 4,000 dpi, 36- to 48-bit color for film ...or... Flatbed with transparency attachment, 4000 dpi for film, 600 to 1200 dpi for reflective, 36- to 48-bit color
	No	Yes	Yes	200	Film or drum scanner, 4000 dpi, 36- to 48-bit color

[1]FPO = For Position Only for dummying images.

Table 2-1 Choosing the right scanner for the right output

Density. Reflective art, such as a photographic print, has a maximum possible density (Dmax) of about 2.0D, while film captures a range as high as 4.0D—that's 100 times as many tones. Most flatbed scanners are geared toward reflective art; just putting a transparency unit on it won't improve the tonal differentiation. So when choosing a flatbed, check that its density is in the right range if you're planning to use a transparency attachment.

Film Scanners

Film scanners are designed to scan photographic film. Flatbed scanners equipped with a transparency unit aren't always as good as film scanners because they interpose a sheet of glass between the sensors and the film, and the light is not usually as intense as in a dedicated film scanner. Furthermore, because of the very short depth of field in flatbeds, you sometimes need to unmount transparencies from slide mounts to get the image in focus. A matter of tenths of millimeters can affect the sharpness of the scan.

A flatbed may be okay for occasional film scans, especially on a budget, but a film scanner is the way to go when you're scanning to produce large prints or prepress above newsprint quality, or if you'll need to scan a large volume of film frames.

A film scanner's closest relative is a drum scanner. Film scanners are typically CMOS or CCD based, and they pass the film by the sensors rather than rotating the film around at high speeds as on a drum scanner. While film scanners are generally lower quality than drum scanners because of the lower intensity of light and less precise tonal differentiation—although sometimes, hardly so—they're catching up. An interesting offering, for instance, is the Imacon Flextight 343, a $5,000 desktop CCD scanner that has near-drum-scanner performance characteristics and can scan both film and reflective art. The Flextight is still not quite as good as a PMT drum scanner, but it is far closer to that level of quality. It's like a drum scanner at a film scanner price.

Focus. Film scanners use an auto-focus mechanism, but many provide manual focus control when needed. Unlike a flatbed, in which you contact an image flat against the scanner glass, film in a film scanner is usually held only by its edges in a carrier or frame. This means that there's a chance that the film might be slightly warped, especially if the film curls up when it's not in the scanner. If a film scanner has a relatively short depth of field (range of focus), film that isn't totally flat in the scanner can result in out-of-focus areas in the scan. Some scanners come with alternate film holders that can hold the film flatter than the automatic feeding system, and some scanning software lets you position the point of focus within the scanning area.

Format. Typically, film scanners are geared toward the 35mm format, since it's the most popular. If you need to scan the Advanced Photo System (APS) format (slightly smaller than 35mm), you might want to get a scanner that supports this format out of the box—with some scanners, you have to buy an adapter at additional cost. The former large price gap between flatbed and film scanners has narrowed considerably; at the time of this writing, Prime Film and Umax have bargain-basement 35mm/APS film scanner models available for $200 and below. For more discerning uses, higher-quality 35mm/APS film scanners tend to cost between $500–$1,000. For those above $1,000, you're usually paying for higher resolution (for bigger enlargements) or a wider dynamic range (for better shadow and highlight detail).

If you want to scan larger film formats, such as 120 or 4x5 film, the cost of entry goes up to $1,800 for the Microtek ArtixScan 120tf, with most other models above $2,000. If you run a shop that provides high-quality scanning services all day long for customers, you might purchase a high-volume scanner from a company like Kodak or Durst. These heavy-duty film scanners can cost more than $5,000.

Batch processing. The more expensive film scanners have some way to perform multiple scans unattended. Most will scan all the frames in a six-frame filmstrip in one pass, while a few will even scan an entire roll. Some scanners can be fitted with a bulk slide loader, such as the one for the Nikon line that can feed up to 50 slides through the scanners while you take a long lunch break.

Resolution, bit depth, and density. Scanners dedicated to film start at around 1800 spi, but 4800 spi or higher may be necessary for reproducing 35mm film to magazine-size resolutions. Don't accept less than 3.4D for a device you can't use for anything but film. Typically, the CCDs or other sensors are of a higher overall tolerance than you find in a flatbed scanner. It's rare to find a 24-bit film scanner—these days, they're usually 36 bits or more per RGB sample.

Drum Scanners

Drum scanners rotate a cylinder at extremely high speeds while a sensor moves along the length of the drum. A high-intensity point-source light shines from inside the transparent drum, through film that's taped on the drum, onto the optics that carry the light to the sensors. The sensors take rapid-fire measurements, sampling the image at high speed as it rotates by, then stepping the optics in tiny increments down the drum. Drum scanners can often perform reflective scans as well by using an opaque drum and using a different light source to illuminate the art.

The optics consist of a series of mirrors that reflect and then refract the light to three separate PMT sensors that record the red, green, and blue components of each sample.

Drum scanners traditionally offered the very highest-quality scans. The key advantages of drum scanning—besides quality—are high resolution, wide density, low noise, large film format, and batch processing. Drum scanners can be tightly integrated with a complete imaging and color separation system, but that's not always the case with a lower-priced unit.

High resolution and density. Drum scanners are still the best way to make extremely high-resolution scans (exceeding 9600 spi) with a wide density—as high as 4.2D, or 10 to 15 times the number of tones of a good flatbed with an attachment. It's also one of the best ways to scan large-format film at high resolution, such as 8-by-10–inch artwork at 4000 spi.

Batch processing. Batch processing is a wonderful tool for efficiency. Glenn worked with an Optronics ColorGetter on which he could load 50 35mm images, select each one individually, apply unique cropping and resolution settings to each image, and then walk away for a few hours

while each was acquired. Batch processing is just about essential if you're doing a huge job, like scanning years of archives, or if you're providing scanning services to outside clients. Today, many film and flatbed scanners also offer batch processing.

Integration. Drum scanners are often incorporated into complete image-scanning and processing systems (though some can just plug directly into your computer). This makes it possible to get a great scan that can be corrected and output in a tightly calibrated environment. You might never touch the scan at all in those circumstances, but instead have the service bureau handle the correction, and just give you a *for-position-only* (FPO) link to place on a page.

The availability of drum scanners is rapidly dwindling as CCD-based scanners provide close to drum-scanner quality at a much lower price. The price of a PMT scanner can climb into the tens of thousands of dollars, but the best of the CCD scanners tend to cost between $3,000 and $15,000. Because the best CCD scanners are still not as good as the best drum scanners, those who want the absolute best quality—typically fine art photographers and high-end publishers—still choose to seek out and pay for drum scans.

Specialized Scanners

For certain kinds of scanning, you might need to get something other than the standard flatbed or film scanner. For instance, using a sheetfed scanner is appropriate for massive text processing, whereas video-capture software is necessary when trying to "scan" something from a videotape.

Sheetfed scanners. Sheetfed scanners are meant mostly for performing optical character recognition or OCR (see Chapter 9, *Scanning for the Office*). These scanners take a few sheets or a few thousand and process them automatically. They generally pull or push an image past a stationary scanning mechanism. Their biggest problem is that they can only scan artwork flexible enough to be pulled through the pasta-making innards. Mounted pictures and books are out. And, often, smaller images have to be mounted on a larger piece of paper before they can successfully navigate through the scanner. It's also extremely difficult to feed the art accurately so that horizontal and vertical lines end up horizontal and vertical. Some of these scanners are meant for use with a desktop computer, such as the 4-by-6 photo feeder on the HP ScanJet 5500c; others are $100,000 devices used by legal firms to turn acres of typewriting into computer text.

Video. Acquiring images from video sources, like cameras and videotapes, isn't the easiest way to capture images—or, more precisely, it's not easy to get good quality images. However, it is possible; you just have to work hard to do it. We talk more about acquiring video scans in Chapter 7, *Scanning for the Web and Video*.

Multifunction Units

You might be tempted to save space by purchasing a single machine that combines scanning, printing, and faxing. Thanks to the falling costs of good-quality scanning components, these units can be quite acceptable for low-volume scanning for images used on Web pages or in low-end desktop publishing. As you might guess, combining functions results in compromises in performance and quality. If you're serious about getting good scans, a dedicated scanner is a better bet. Of course, there's also the dark side of multifunction units: if your all-in-one machine breaks, you can't scan, print, or fax until it's fixed.

Digital Cameras

Back in the 20th century, if you wanted a digital image of something that didn't fit on a scanner—like an office building—you had to take a picture of it with a film camera, develop the film, and then scan the resulting film. Or you could make a print from the film, and scan that. But today, you can use a digital camera to bring that office building to your computer screen.

Digital cameras have had several generations to mature, and they now come in all ranges of quality and cost. While there have long been expensive digital cameras capable of producing photos good enough to print in a magazine, the requisite level of quality can now be yours in pocket-size models available for under $1,000. The more you spend on a camera, the closer the results match photographic film—or even exceed its possibilities.

In many ways, a digital camera is a handheld version of a desktop scanner. They both use a CCD or CMOS sensor to digitize the light from an image plane, but with a digital camera, the image sits behind the camera lens, exactly where a film frame would in a film camera. Where a scanner is always tethered to a computer via an interface, most digital cameras are designed to grab-and-go, connecting to a computer only to transfer images.

Digital cameras typically use memory cards to store images. These cards come in an unfortunately large variety of incompatible formats, which include Compact Flash, Secure Digital, and Sony Memory Stick, plus a few other also-rans. Some formats can even contain miniature multi-gigabyte hard drives such as the Hitachi MicroDrive.

To transfer images to your computer, you connect the camera to your computer via a USB (Universal Serial Bus) or FireWire/i.Link/IEEE 1394 cable, or you can remove the card from the camera and insert it into a card reader directly connected to your computer. Some larger and more expensive studio cameras require a tripod and are intended to be connected to the computer at all times because they operate at extremely long shutter speeds or use a linear array that scans across the camera's focal point; they also generate files far too large to be stored in quantity on a memory card of any kind. Studio cameras can capture very high resolutions and are used in place of film cameras in still shots or in capturing objects like paintings that can't be handled on a flatbed scanner.

Color Management

If you use color management, you need to make sure your scanner software can produce images that work properly with color management. Most current scanners have at least some support for color management. If you aren't using color management, make sure you know how to turn off color management in your scanning software.

Digital Cameras vs. Film Scanners

If you have years of experience with film cameras and thick binders of filmstrips to show for it, you may wonder what kind of digital camera compares favorably to your trusty old equipment, if such a camera is available or affordable, and how it might compare to scanning frames you shoot with your film camera. A comparison between digital cameras and film scanners isn't always straightforward.

Resolution. At the time we're writing this, a film camera/film scanner combination can produce more megapixels than a digital camera of the same price. For example, for $1,000 you can produce 22 megapixels from a 35mm film frame using a 4000 spi film scanner and a 35mm SLR. However, the raw numbers are misleading. Many photographers claim that because a digital camera image has no film grain, it needs far fewer pixels to reach the same image quality as a film scan.

Speed and convenience. While a film camera/film scanner team can potentially produce more megapixels, this advantage is often outweighed by the speed and convenience of digital photography. Shooting digitally, you avoid time spent scanning, possible image degradation from moving the image through a second set of optics (in the scanner), and having to master the art of scanning each film type in just the right way. But digital photographers still have to spend time adjusting photos for their final medium.

Storage. When you shoot physical film, frame storage is a matter of how many film rolls you bring. For a digital camera, storage of new frames entirely depends on the capacity of the memory cards you have with you and the file sizes of the frames you shoot. After you get back to your home or office, original film is easy to store; you can keep many rolls of film in a binder by storing the filmstrips in plastic pages. You must store and organize digital camera photos on digital media like hard drives, CDs, or DVDs. The twist is that when you scan film, you then have to manage the storage of both the film and the resulting digital files.

Color. For film, good color depends on your film choice combined with how well your scanner digitizes your film type. For digital cameras, good color depends largely on how well you set the camera's white balance. Both film and digital photos can be integrated into a color-managed workflow.

While digital is not always superior to film, trends indicate that digital is closing the gap on all fronts. It's simply a matter of time before shooting on film becomes as rare as making halftones in a process camera. (If you're asking, "What's a process camera?" you know what we mean!) As digital cameras become suitable for more jobs that currently require film, film scanners will be used less for scanning freshly developed film and more for migrating existing film archives into the digital domain.

Digital Camera Array Types

Digital cameras come in two main flavors: *area array* (or instant capture), and *linear array* (also called a "scanning back").

Area array. The vast majority of digital cameras being sold today are area array cameras. They use a two-dimensional matrix of image sensors—all of which are exposed simultaneously to light. In this way, an area array works like a film frame. Some cameras have a single array with different elements painted red, green, and blue to filter light. Others—though this is rare—have three separate arrays, each exposed at the same time through red, green, and blue filters. The newer Foveon image sensor stacks the RGB arrays and relies on each wavelength to work its way down to its sensor array. Most conventional designs stagger the RGB arrays, leaving gaps between, for example, each red pixel. The stacked Foveon design is supposed to allow more pixels to be crammed into the same space, though Foveon-based cameras are quite rare at the time of this writing.

Linear array. A linear-array scanning-back camera is a lot like a flatbed scanner placed behind a lens: a single row of image sensors comprises the scanning element. To fill a frame with an image, the sensor row scans each line of the image plane. The exposures can take minutes, because the device is usually doing long exposures. Obviously, you don't want the subject to move while the sensor is moving, or the image will be distorted. This kind of camera is primarily used to shoot still art in studio settings for jobs like catalog work where the highest quality is required, and lighting and vibration can be tightly controlled. The image elements in scanning backs are usually the most expensive made; even tiny defects in a few of the thousands of sensors are enough to reject it for use. Some backs can be attached to existing high-quality medium- and large-format cameras. Other backs are purchased as part of a custom-designed unit. They're always directly tethered to a computer so that the image is acquired directly into the computer, just as with a flatbed scanner. Because these cameras and backs are made entirely for studio purposes, they're all very high resolution, up to 10,000 samples in the linear array. (For reference, an image at 10,000 by 10,000 samples could reproduce at 33 by 33 inches at 300 lines per inch.) They range from just below $10,000 to more than $50,000.

ICC/ICM Profile Support

Color management only works if you have accurate descriptions of how your devices represent color. ICC (Image Color Management) and ICM (International Color Consortium) profiles are identical, interchangeable formats that store color descriptions of scanners, printers, presses, monitors, and even theoretical color spaces. There are three different ways that scanning software can use ICC profiles.

Tagging an image with the scanner profile. At the most basic level, a scanner can support color management simply by tagging the files it saves with an ICC profile that describes how the scanner sees color, so that when you open the image in a color-managed image editor, it can represent the image's colors accurately. The software bundled with many scanners includes such a profile; in other cases you can download a profile from the manufacturer's Web site.

Converting an image to a specific color space. Some scanning utilities can convert images to another color space before saving them. For example, you might want a series of images to be saved out of the scanning utility as a standard press-style CMYK file. Some scanners may allow conversion to a preset list of color spaces, but better scanners will let you choose any ICC profile on your machine to use as the color space to convert to.

Using the monitor profile to display the file accurately on screen. It's very helpful if your scanning software can apply a monitor profile to the software's preview of the scan. This corrects the image for the idiosyncrasies of your monitor so that the on-screen preview is more accurate, making it much easier to perform color corrections in the scanning utility instead of in another image editor. Without monitor profile compensation, you can't tell how far off the color is, so you don't know how much correction is really needed.

Raw Output Support

In some workflows, it's helpful to save the raw, uncorrected scanner image data so you can open it in your image editor. This is usually the preference of those who feel that the scanning software doesn't properly support color management, doesn't provide enough control over color or accurate feedback on the monitor, or can't be trusted to do a color conversion without losing image quality. David likes to bypass the scanning software's controls and just grab the raw data because he prefers to use Photoshop's controls to edit images.

Raw support lets you set the scanning software to output a raw file (no tonal or color correction, no reduction from the scanner's native bit depth), so that you can use a professional image-editing application like Photoshop to perform precise color correction. In some cases, this can be as simple as using the image editor to apply the scanner's ICC profile. Also, raw output capability is necessary if you're profiling the scanner, because a scanner profile has to be created from uncorrected scan data.

Hardware Interface

It's been said that the great thing about standards is that there are so many to choose from, and this certainly applies to the methods used to connect a scanner to a computer. We have so many scanner interface options at this writing because we're still in the transition from the SCSI (Small Computer System Interface) and parallel interfaces of the 1990s to the USB and FireWire connections of the 2000s. If you're shopping for a new scanner to connect to a new computer, you really only need to look at scanners with USB or FireWire interfaces.

In the past, obtaining, installing, and using the right scanner driver software was a regular source of consternation. Today, the plug-and-play technologies in Mac OS X and Windows XP have almost entirely eliminated driver hassles. The one exception is when you have a scanner that's no longer sold, but for which the manufacturer has released updates for newer versions of the operating system; this was a common issue with Mac OS X and early USB scanners.

USB

USB (Universal Serial Bus) was created by several computer makers. They designed USB to replace traditional serial and parallel interfaces, which used big, bulky connectors, finicky cabling, and were just not very user-friendly. USB was first introduced on a large scale by Apple, when they built USB ports into the original iMac in 1997. USB is currently the most popular interface for connecting computers to scanners, digital cameras, and many other types of peripherals. Unlike the older interfaces (**Figure 2-3**), USB devices can be connected and disconnected without turning them off (they're *hot-pluggable*). USB can also supply power to peripherals, but not very much—about enough for low-power devices like keyboards and mice. Still, there are some USB scanners that draw power directly from the USB interface. But glitches can result when bus-powered devices don't get enough power from a particular USB hub or port.

When USB and FireWire were new, the main difference between them was speed. USB 1.1 was limited to a top speed of either 1.5 or 12 megabits per second (Mbps), depending on the kind of device, or about $\frac{1}{25}$ of the original FireWire. For a more realistic alternative to FireWire, a consortium developed USB 2.0, which has become the de facto USB standard found in Macs and PCs, and an increasing num-

Figure 2-3 USB and FireWire ports
Left: USB port
Center: FireWire 400
Right: FireWire 800

ber of peripherals that need to move a lot of data. USB 2.0 has a raw top speed of 480 Mbps, although the original 400 Mbps FireWire has better throughput and consistent speed in real-world use.

To get the most out of USB, buying a scanner with the newer, faster standard will optimize your whole workflow. Computers that only have the older USB 1.1 interface can often be retrofitted with a $50 to $100 PCI card that brings it up to speed, often with three to five dedicated high-speed ports. It may not be possible to upgrade a computer that doesn't have PCI slots or a PC card slot. If you must use a USB 2.0 scanner with a 1.1 port, don't share the port with a keyboard or mouse as that will make your other activities jerky.

FireWire

FireWire is the marketing name for the IEEE 1394a standard, which is a high-speed serial interface pioneered by Apple Computer and adopted by Sony as i.Link. Apple created FireWire for reasons similar to those that motivated the creation of USB: to provide a simpler, more user-friendly way to connect peripherals. But Apple wanted high performance for its SCSI replacement. FireWire originally ran at 400 Mbps, but a newer FireWire 800 (IEEE 1394b) flavor operates at 800 Mbps (**Figure 2-3**). Apple now calls the original version "FireWire 400."

Like USB, FireWire is hot-pluggable, and can supply power to a device. However, FireWire can provide a lot more juice than USB, so a FireWire device is less likely to need a separate cord cluttering up your power strip. (Sony's i.Link flavor can't power a device, unfortunately.)

What really solidified FireWire's place in the computer industry was its ability to transfer data in the raw Digital Video (DV) format. Most DV cameras use FireWire ports because it's the easiest way to move massive video files quickly, which is also useful for moving huge scanned images from the scanner to your computer. If you work with high-resolution scans, such as those used in full-page magazine-quality ads, pick a FireWire scanner.

If you have a computer that doesn't have FireWire ports, you can add them using an inexpensive PCI card or PC card often for as little as $50. If you're going to get a card, consider buying one that has both FireWire and USB 2.0 ports on it. Then you'll be ready for any new scanner.

FireWire has a minor advantage over USB in that each FireWire device has a dedicated chipset that handles its communication and data processing. It's possible for FireWire devices to talk to each other without a computer at all. In comparison, all USB processing must take a trip through the computer's CPU, which means the CPU can become a USB bottleneck. This is more of an issue on older, slower computers; current computers have sufficiently speedy CPUs that you shouldn't notice much of a slowdown unless you perform other CPU-intensive actions while scanning, such as editing other images.

SCSI

SCSI (pronounced "scuzzy") was developed in the early 1980s but was upgraded several times with progressively faster top speeds (**Figure 2-4**). SCSI was the de facto standard for the Mac since its earliest days and was a popular add-on to PCs until IDE interfaces became common and faster. Most systems have migrated to USB and/or FireWire, but SCSI has its legacy and its adherents.

Figure 2-4 SCSI
port with SCSI ID
and terminator
switches visible
above port

The earliest SCSI standard, SCSI-1, ran at 5 megabytes per second, while later and more expensive flavors run from 10 to 320 megabytes per second. SCSI speeds are usually measured in bytes, not bits, so the fastest SCSI is about three times faster than FireWire 800.

The downside of SCSI, and what doomed it to the scrapheap of technology piles for the average user, is that it was always relatively expensive to implement and tricky to configure—so much so that the term "SCSI voodoo" emerged to describe the often frustrating process of troubleshooting a misbehaving SCSI bus. SCSI devices can't be hotplugged (so you have to power down your computer before adding or removing a SCSI device), and a SCSI bus could only support a limited number of devices. And what about those "standard" connectors? Glenn has a box full of SCSI-1, -2, -3, -4, mini-SCSI, and other adapters all intended for a very small number of devices and interface cards.

SCSI is increasingly found only in high-performance environments where the customer is willing to pay a premium for the very fastest data transfers.

The number of new SCSI scanners has dwindled in recent years. But because of the popularity of SCSI scanners a decade ago, you can still find quite a few on eBay or in design offices that have kept them around, usually connected to older computers. Having an older computer is probably the main reason why anyone would look for a SCSI scanner today.

Parallel

Before USB was widely accepted, most scanners were connected to IBM PC-compatible computers via a parallel port (**Figure 2-5**). The parallel port was the connector used for most PC peripherals, such as printers and CD burners. The Enhanced Parallel Port specification allows data rates of up to 2 megabytes per second (about 16 Mbps), which is no match for the speeds found with USB 2.0 or FireWire. While you can still find parallel ports on some new PCs, they are generally supplemented by USB and FireWire ports. Like SCSI, as time goes on, you'll see fewer parallel scanners sold new in stores, and you will be more likely to encounter them connected only to older PCs.

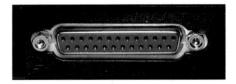

Figure 2-5 Parallel port

Networking

Even as the cost of a good flatbed scanner has plunged below the $100 mark, you may find yourself in a workgroup that can only afford one scanner. (Don't laugh! This is not uncommon in the nonprofit world.) Some scanners can be networked, which means you can run them from any machine on the network. To find out if your scanner supports networking, check the scanner's user guide or support Web page. Networking a scanner usually requires that the scanner's software be installed on all workstations that will be used to run the scanner.

Networking is an ingenious idea, but it's not without some potential bottlenecks:

Performance of the scanning computer. Even though the computer connected to the scanner isn't supposed to be involved in the scanning process, that machine still gets the job of receiving the incoming scan and sending it to your machine. This processing happens in the background. If the scanning workstation isn't a fast computer, it can get bogged down as it scans and sends in the background—which can really annoy the person who's trying to get their own work done on that workstation.

A related performance issue varies based on the interface for transferring data. USB 1.1 is both slow and CPU-dependent, so it's more likely to bog down the connected computer, especially on an older, slower CPU. FireWire and SCSI are faster and don't rely on the CPU, because their own chipsets process the transfer.

Network speed. Slower networks will need more time to get the scan from the scanning computer to your computer. This can slow down both the scanning computer and your computer. This is more of an issue in workgroups with older networking equipment, such as 10 Mbps Ethernet, and less of an issue if you're running 100 Mbps or Gigabit Ethernet.

Sneakernet. You still have to walk to the machine to which the scanner is connected to place the original on the scanner.

Putting Bits in a Bucket

In scanning, as in most of life, you get what you pay for. Scanner specifications tend to be about as optimistic and theoretical as the advertised gas mileage of cars

or the battery life of laptops. For example, it's possible to find two scanners that both list 2400 spi resolution and 48-bit color (16 bits per channel), yet one of these scanners might cost half as much as the other. The less expensive one must be quite a deal, right? In reality, these numbers by themselves can't describe the actual image quality a scanner can produce.

While both scanners can produce a file that has 48 bits of data in each sample, an image from the more expensive scanner is likely to have a sensor that produces less noise and more accurate color, better software with more control, and might also have better production features like batch scanning.

It's a good idea to check the Web for reviews of scanners you're considering. For consumer scanners, you can check `epinions.com` and Amazon.com. For higher-end scanners, you can try sources like `photo.net` or the Usenet newsgroup `comp.periphs.scanners`. (Use `groups.google.com` if you don't have Usenet access via your Internet service provider.)

Choosing a suitable scanner can often be the most important part of setting up your workflow. Getting the right bit depth, the right resolution, the right set of features—whether they're on a cheap flatbed or a $100,000 drum scanner—saves time and effort throughout the whole process. The more you can do at the time of the scan, the less you have to do later. We continue this theme in the next chapter, *Getting Your Originals Ready to Scan,* because it takes a lot less time to get a good scan from a good original than from a flawed original.

3

Getting Your Originals Ready to Scan

QUALITY IN, QUALITY OUT

"Garbage in, garbage out," is the familiar geek aphorism that means the results you get out of the computer are automatically limited by what you put into it in the first place. With scanning, the results you obtain are based on the quality of your original and your work process. The time you spend obtaining the best possible original can save you the time it would take to fix up a bad original after the scan.

What's going to take you less time: wiping the scanner glass before you scan a photo or going on a search-and-destroy mission to remove dust and hair in Photoshop? Correcting and cleaning up images is one of the most onerous and time-consuming chores of scanning, so it's well worth your while to avoid it through good planning and by using the highest-quality originals you can find.

Size Matters

For reproducing reflective art in print, it's best to use an original that's at least as big as its final reproduction size. If your original is smaller than the size you need, you can provide enough data for its final, larger reproduction size if you compensate by increasing the scan resolution. We explain the relationship between scaling and resolution (a concept called *effective resolution*) in Chapter 11, *Image Resolution*, and we show an example in **Figure 5-6** in Chapter 5, *How to Read Your Scanning Software*.

The downside to having an original that's smaller than you need is that any defects in the original will be magnified when you enlarge it—cleaning up those imperfections will add to any post-processing chores you perform on that scan.

An original that's larger than the size you need it isn't a bad thing at all, because size reduction doesn't reduce quality. Again, you can adjust the scan resolution proportionally so that you end up with the right resolution for the final output size. For example, if you have a 4-by-6–inch snapshot to reproduce at 2 by 3 inches in a magazine at 300 dpi, scan it at 150 spi at 100% scaling. We explain these calculations in Chapter 11, *Image Resolution.*

But large originals can be an issue when they're too big to fit on a flatbed scanner. You can try to fit your original into your scanner's limits by photographing the original. Hang the original on a wall or lay it on a floor, and then shoot it with a digital camera on a tripod using high-quality settings. Make sure the original is as flat as possible and evenly lit with no hot spots or glare; and if you're shooting for color reproduction, use color-balanced lighting. If this seems too complicated or you don't have a digital camera that can produce enough effective resolution for your final output size, you can send the original to an imaging service that digitizes oversized originals.

In Range and On Target

When Aunt Millie hands you an old photograph to scan for the family web site, take a good look at it first. The ideal original has a full range of tones from black to white, isn't too dark or light overall, and is color-balanced. If Aunt Millie's original has faded and yellowed from 30 years of display in a bright room, ask her if there's another copy in a photo album somewhere. A photo hidden away in the dark is less likely to have suffered the ravages of atmospheric contaminants and daylight.

If you're using a film scanner that produces good-quality scans, see if Aunt Millie has the original slide or negative that the photo was printed from. If the film hasn't deteriorated too much, it will contain a wider range of tones and colors than the print, giving you the possibility of making a print that's sharper, deeper, and more vivid than the treasured old print.

Film scanners vary in how well they interpret color negatives. Adding to the challenge, color negatives use an *orange mask*—that characteristic amber tint you see on all color negative film. Color negatives need the orange mask to help compensate for imperfections in color dyes. For best results, scanning software must have a way to account for the orange mask when color-balancing color negatives. Some scanning utilities include correction presets for specific film types, which can result in a good scan without much work. Others use balancing algorithms that try to detect and remove the orange mask and then calculate the right color balance.

Old film may have also faded or lost its original color balance, making the scanning job even tougher. When the scanning software's calculations are wrong, you get to fix those settings. (Some scanning software includes a fade-compensation feature for old film; see Chapter 5, *How to Read Your Scanning Software.)*

If you find yourself spending too much time trying to correct a negative scan to make it into a good image, it might be easier to first have a photo lab make a high-quality print from the original negative, then scan that print on your flatbed. This can sometimes result in a better scan, because color labs print color negatives on photographic papers that are carefully engineered to match specific films.

Gotta Look Sharp

If you want a sharp scan, you have to start with a sharp original. While today's image editors contain powerful tools for enhancing image sharpness, they work by accentuating edge contrast so that your eye thinks there's more sharpness than there actually is, and there isn't much leeway before the image starts to appear obviously *over-sharpened*. If you're scanning in order to reproduce an original at a smaller size, you're in luck. Reducing an image increases its apparent sharpness by packing the image's existing detail into a smaller space.

When you have no choice but to work with a scanned image file that's out of focus, blurry, or contains too little data, you might want to apply an artistic filter to the image, such as noise or brush strokes, using an image editor (**Figure 3-1**). This technique can be effective when you resample an image to its final output size and resolution before applying the filter. Applying a filter creates new details at the current resolution, which can distract the eye from the fact that the image content's inherent resolution wasn't very detailed.

Figure 3-1
Applying a filter to hide low resolution *Top:* original low-resolution file (72 dpi); *middle:* upsampled to 300 dpi; *bottom:* Rough Pastels filter applied to low-res file

Dot's Not What You Want

One of the most annoying scanning tasks is working with originals that are already halftoned or screened, such as a photo from a magazine or newspaper. Unlike true photos, which appear to have continuous tones when you look at them under a magnifying loupe, halftones represent tonal changes using a grid of tiny dots of varying sizes that your eyes optically merge into apparent tones and colors when you view them from a normal distance. We talk about halftones in more detail in Part 5, *Halftones*.

The problem with scanning halftone images is that halftones are optimized for reproduction at a certain size, resolution, and set of press conditions. When you scan an image that's already halftoned, the halftone grid can clash with the scanning sensor grid, resulting in a *moiré* pattern. This pattern can persist or become worse when the image is then fed through the final output device's dot grid (**Figure 3-2**).

If you have the choice between a halftone image and the original photographic print of the same image, choose the photograph. If you have no choice but to scan a halftone image, see if your scanner has a *descreening* feature. A descreening feature attempts to cancel out the halftone screen by converting the halftones back to continuous tones and colors. Be aware that descreening features don't always work very well, and usually blur the original.

There are also manual image-editing techniques you can use to minimize the effects of a halftone screen, but these techniques are all very tedious and not always successful. We describe some of these techniques in Chapter 28, *When Grids Collide*.

Neatness Counts

So far in this chapter, we've talked about how to select an original image that will give you the best possible scan. Now we talk about the two surfaces of an image: The paper (or other material) it's printed on, and the scanner's glass if the scanner is a flatbed. You can save yourself a lot of

Figure 3-2
Descreening
option in Canon's
ScanGear software

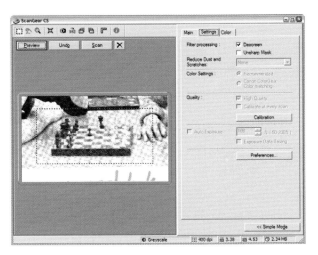

Original

Descreened

retouching time if you check both surfaces before you scan. Here are some tips on how to keep those surfaces clean.

Shmutz and fingerprints. As our grandmothers would say, shmutz is bad. Keep dirt and dust off scanners, film, and prints. Keep a can of compressed air (the kind that won't destroy the Earth's ozone layer) or a small compressor on hand to gently eliminate dust. For stubborn stains or fingerprints, you might need to use a solution like PEC-12 by Photographic Solutions (www.photosol.com)—but if you do, follow the directions precisely.

Don't use facial tissues, for heaven's sake. Facial tissues are made from wood pulp and can microscopically—but within a scanner's resolution—scratch the glass on a flatbed and leave marks on film and prints. Gently remove dust from photographic materials and scanner glass using a photographic blower brush or a clean, soft, lint-free cotton cloth. You can also purchase special, one-time-use cotton wipes.

Clean your flatbed's glass frequently. Be sure to purchase a cleaner that doesn't streak; window cleaners should not be used on scanner glass.

Fingerprints on film can be unremovable. The skin's oils can chemically change film emulsion. A cleaner like PEC-12 can help remove fingerprints; never use water. Photographic stores also sell pairs of cotton gloves you can use for handling originals.

Newton rings. If you're scanning at very high resolutions, you can see a phenomenon called *Newton rings*, which are interference patterns resulting from the contact of film stock and glass. These are most commonly seen on drum scanners, where the film is taped up against a cylinder, but high-resolution flatbeds can demonstrate the same problem. The solution is to use a special mounting oil between the film and the glass that floats the film and removes the appearance of rings. You can get this oil from photographic stores, although they might not recognize the term Newton rings; they are familiar with the problem, however.

Legalize It

As our society becomes ever more litigious, with lawsuits flying at every perceived offense, it's worth making sure you have the rights you need to scan and reproduce an original. You might think it isn't a big deal for a family's private project, like a slide show

Newspapers or other thin, semitransparent papers can be tricky to scan. You can sometimes end up with an unwanted ghost image of the text or graphics on the other side of the sheet. To prevent this from happening on your flatbed scanner, place the original on the scanner as you normally would, then lay a sheet of black paper over the back side. This will stop light from bouncing back through the paper so that the printing on the other side won't be revealed.

for a wedding or birthday party, but using copyrighted materials in a more public setting—even on a personal, noncommercial Web site—can still expose you to corporate lawyers whose job is to find unauthorized uses of their clients' intellectual property. For example, fans of television shows such as Star Trek have found that media companies do not always appreciate having photos and logos used without permission, and may request their removal. Copyright law is very clear: The owner of a set of rights controls their use unilaterally and the owner can pursue those rights through the courts.

The issue is a bit more immediate when you reproduce an image for commercial sale. In recent years, designers and photographers have been the subject of legal action by various property owners who believe that they reserve all rights to graphical depictions of their buildings, particularly if the buildings are quite distinctive. For example, the designers of the nighttime lighting of Paris's Eiffel Tower claim that the lighting display is a design that's protected by copyright law, and they require the payment of a fee if you want to sell or publish a photo of the Eiffel Tower lit up at night. They don't restrict daytime photos, because their lighting design isn't visible then. You can examine their wording at `http://www.tour-eiffel.fr/teiffel/uk/pratique/faq/index.html`

You should also use caution when someone else's artwork appears in your scan. A lawsuit filed by the United Farm Workers claimed that their copyright to their San Francisco street murals were being violated by Corbis because photographs of the murals were being sold as stock photography. In Seattle, a sculptor sued a local designer who, without permission, sold postcards featuring the sculptor's popular, and copyrighted, statue of a troll under a bridge. In other words, just because it's out on the street doesn't mean it's royalty-free—or at least, doesn't mean someone won't make a legal case of it.

While we can't provide specific legal advice on this issue, we thought we should at least make sure you were aware of these issues. There are still many gray areas being worked out by the legal system—court decisions so far haven't always been consistent. But no one needs a lawsuit, so the safe way to proceed is to check with a copyright lawyer before reproducing scenes where recognizable people, property, artwork, or trademarks are involved. Based on what you find out, you can plan accordingly by avoiding questionable subjects, or obtaining signed releases from models, portrait subjects, artists, and property owners as necessary. And although samples of release forms are all over the Web, it's best to have a lawyer help you modify them for your particular needs.

Off to a Good Start

Great scanning starts with flawless originals. Once you are in possession of a stack of clean, sharp, balanced, and rights-cleared images, you need to make sure your computer is set up to handle all of the scanning you're about to do. To set up your computer, let's move on to the next chapter: *Getting Your Computer Ready for Scans.*

4

Getting Your Computer Ready for Scans

SET UP, TUNE UP, BACK UP

If you create a lot of scans, you inevitably end up with lots of big files on your hard drive. Let's say, for instance, that you get an assignment to digitize decades' worth of your company's slides and negatives. The first couple of days, everything goes well. You and your scanner are happily filling up a folder of scans on your hard drive. A week later, the company wants to use some of the images on a Web site. Two weeks later, the marketing department wants to use a few images for the annual report. By the time you're a month into your scanning project, you find yourself both running out of space and losing track of which image is which. Things can get out of hand pretty quickly unless you do a little advance planning. In this chapter, we try to help you anticipate what your long-term needs might be for storing and managing scans.

Location, Location, Location

When scanning software completes a scan, it can either leave the image file open onscreen and unsaved, or it can automatically save the image to disk, closing the image file. (Some scanning software lets you choose between these two options.) If your software leaves images open, you can just save them wherever you want. But if your scanning software immediately saves the document to disk, you want to think about where all those scans will go.

Most programs default to storing any new file in your documents folder: Documents in Mac OS X or My Documents under Windows. Smarter scanning utilities save scans in your computer's image folder: Pictures in Mac OS X or My Pictures under Windows.

After using your computer for more than a few weeks, you realize that if you don't change the default folder location, your documents or pictures folder will become cluttered with unorganized files. You could spend several minutes every time you try to find an image scrounging among the grab bag of other files.

Fortunately, many scanning utilities let you change the default folder for newly scanned images. Instead of making a new folder simply called "Scans," we recommend naming the folder something like "Raw Scans" or "New Scans" so that you can distinguish the scans you have and haven't reviewed. Similarly, you might want to create other folders for the different versions you create, such as folders called "In Progress," "Print," "Web," "Rescan," or "Ready" (**Figure 4-1**).

Figure 4-1
One possible way to base folder organization on workflow

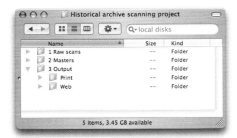

Mac OS X and Windows XP can automatically create and display large preview icons for image files directly in folders on the Desktop or in Windows Explorer (**Figure 4-2**). Your system's Pictures or My Pictures folder might already be set up this way, but you can set any folder to show these previews. Here's how to do this on both platforms.

If the icons don't fill the entire Mac OS X Finder window, choose the Arrange Icons By from the View menu and choose any option. This command fits all rows within the width of the window.

Mac OS X. In the Finder, open a folder that contains images. Choose the As Icons item from the View menu, and then the Show View Options item. In the View Options palette, make sure This Window Only is selected; otherwise, you're changing the default options for all windows that haven't been customized as Check Show Icon Preview. If you think the previews are too small, drag the Icon Size slider to the right until they're the size you want, up to 128 pixels square.

Windows XP. Browse your hard drive using My Computer or Windows Explorer, and open a folder that contains images. Click the Views button and choose either Filmstrip or Thumbnails. The Filmstrip view lets you click through the images in the folder in order, displaying a large preview of the currently selected image. The Thumbnails view shows small previews of all images in the folder.

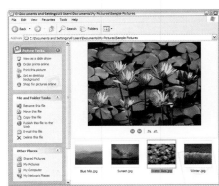

Figure 4-2 Photo-oriented folder views in Mac OS X and Windows XP

What's in a Name

It might seem obvious at first how you name your scans: a short, descriptive name is enough, right? If you scanned a photo of Dad, you would probably call it Dad. But what happens when you're scanning a lifetime's worth of photos of Dad? Here's Dad in 1975 next to the family Vista Cruiser. Here are five photos of Dad fishing in the Yakima River in 1965, three of Dad at Christmas 2002, ten from his 48th birthday, six from last year's family picnic. How do you name all of these and still be able to tell them apart? And how do you know which film negatives they came from if you want to scan them again?

You face a similar problem if you have photo shoots in which entire rolls are of the same subject. You're pretty much forced to use filenames like "Sally 021" and "Sally 022," so that they match the original film frames. But let's say you shoot the same person four months later, and you want to distinguish that shoot from an earlier one. You might try keeping them in separate folders, but unless you make each set's filename slightly different, you might end up with duplicate filenames if you ever need to mix photos from each set—which might accidentally wipe out one of the files if they were to end up in the same folder. That might prompt you to add the date to the filenames.

A related problem is tracking multiple revisions to a single source image; this task is collectively called *version control*. You may need to distinguish earlier versions with later or finished versions. You could use numbers, but then what would "Sally 005" mean? Is it the fifth frame in the roll or the fifth version of a particular frame?

What we've tried to prove with these scenarios is that all of the commonsense approaches you might take to organize your files by name and folder will ultimately fail once you have a sufficiently large collection—which could be as soon as a few days of scanning images or a single download from a digital camera.

The One and Only

Many professional photographers have found that the only practical way out of the filenaming maze is to develop a system that produces a completely unique name for each image. They do this not just to be unique for its own sake, but also for consistency and structure, so that they can tell a lot of production details about an image just by looking at its name. There are many ways to do this; here's one example:

20010503-0418-01PRT-Dave.tif

In this example, the first eight characters describe the date the photo was taken: May 3, 2001. The next five characters, -0418, indicate that this image was scanned from the 18th frame of the 4th roll shot that day. (The original film would be labeled the same way, so that you can always locate the original frame.) The -01 is set aside for version control: this is the first version of the file. The next three characters, PRT, indicate that it's a print-resolution version of the file. "Dave" is included just as a human-readable clue, and because there are a few characters left to use. And of course the .tif is the filename extension.

Here's another file in that folder:

20010503-0418-FLWEB-Dave.jpg

This looks a lot like the first example, but it has a couple of differences. Instead of 0418-01, it reads 0418-FL. In this particular case, this is a code for Final, but it could also stand for Flattened (an optional but irrevocable final step after working with layers in a image editor like Photoshop). Instead of PRT, it reads WEB, so it's the low-resolution Web version of the same image. And it's clearly a JPEG file instead of a TIFF. So it's the same frame and roll as the other image, but it's been finalized for the Web at a much lower level of quality than the TIFF version.

There's no single naming system in use; the one we just described is hypothetical but based on the naming schemes that photographers and agencies have used successfully. You can see what other people use by entering terms like "photo filename naming system" into a Web search engine. You can also examine the ways digital cameras name the files they generate: Digital cameras will typically generate unique filenames endlessly, until the counter for that function is manually reset.

When you devise your file-naming system, try to think of every possible way you might confuse two similar files, and design your filename system to distinguish them. Also, make the filenames portable across platforms and environments, avoiding reserved characters like slashes and colons (which are used by different operating systems to signify paths). Although it may be painful, limit the filename's length to 31 characters for multiple platform compatibility. The 31 characters must include the file extension which can have more than three characters on modern operating systems. Also notice that the roll numbering in our example is 0418, not 418; by keep-

ing each code length constant, you know for sure that this is roll 4, frame 18, and not roll 41, frame 8.

Pay attention to how you sequence the filename codes from the beginning to the end of the filename. A hierarchical approach often works best: Start with broader, non-unique information at the beginning of the name and work toward more precise and unique details as you move to the right. How you order your filenames determines how they'll sort in a folder listing—the naming system used in our example will list files by date, then roll, then frame, then version. This is also why many people choose to write the date as year, month, then day, so the files sort in that order. If the dates of the sample names were written using the American month-day-year sequence, or 05032002, all of the images from May 3, 2002 would list before those from May 4, 2001.

Once you develop your filenaming system, be sure to document it. Write down exactly how your naming system is set up (**Figure 4-3**).

By now, you might realize that this method of naming is a lot like those mysterious serial numbers you find on your software CDs: They look like gibberish, but every character actually has a specific meaning. It's a valuable system for soft-

Figure 4-3

Example of a "filename decoder" reference sheet for a filenaming system

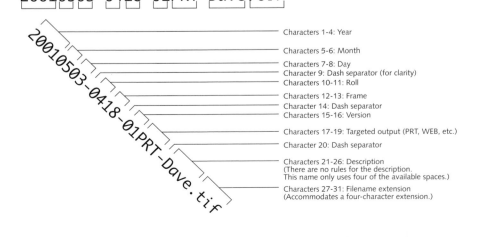

20010503-0418-01PRT-Dave.tif

Characters 1-4: Year

Characters 5-6: Month

Characters 7-8: Day
Character 9: Dash separator (for clarity)
Characters 10-11: Roll

Characters 12-13: Frame
Character 14: Dash separator
Characters 15-16: Version

Characters 17-19: Targeted output (PRT, WEB, etc.)

Character 20: Dash separator

Characters 21-26: Description
(There are no rules for the description.
This name only uses four of the available spaces.)

Characters 27-31: Filename extension
(Accommodates a four-character extension.)

ware companies, and it can be for you too. However, you also might be saying, "That's going to keep everything organized, but it doesn't exactly help me tell the images apart." True. Now that you've designed a way to avoid filenaming conflicts, you have to find a different way to identify subject matter. That's actually a topic we cover later in this chapter, in the section "Using Image-Management Software."

The Rename Game

The first step in implementing an image-naming system is to start with your scanning software: It might be able to automatically name files sequentially. If you master your scanning program's naming system, you can end up with a folder of perfectly named images right off the bat. But what if your scanning software can only do part of the job, and what about those hundreds of images you already have? You might find that renaming hundreds of files is more than a little tedious. Fortunately, there's help. There are many free or inexpensive ways to rename entire batches of files.

Many scanning utilities automatically increment filenames as you scan additional images, so the first image you scan would be named Image01, the second is automatically named Image02, and so on. Better utilities, like NikonScan, let you specify exactly what the name is, so if you name the first scan 20030918-01, the next scan will have the default name 20030918-02 (**Figure 4-4**).

The VueScan utility has an interesting feature where the plus (+) and equals (=) symbols create different types of automatic numbering if you use either symbol in a filename. The plus sign means, "always number sequentially starting with this number." The equals sign means, "number sequentially based on the order of the frames relative to the starting frame." For instance, if you are scanning a strip of four film frames and you have set the first frame number to 5, you can enter the filename Park-05=.tif. If you scan the third and second images in the strip (in that order), VueScan will name them Park-07.tif and Park-06.tif, respectively, because it follows the frame numbers. If you enter the filename Park-05+.tif and scan the third and then the second images in the strip, VueScan will name them Park-06.tif and Park-07.tif (the reverse of the previous example) because it numbers them in the order you scanned them.

If you need to rename files you've already scanned, you can use a batch renaming utility. Batch renaming is a feature of some image editors and photo organizers. Some renaming utilities support more features than others. These features include:

▶ **Find and replace.** If you started out naming your files with a hyphen between the year, month, and date, and you then realize that uses up too many characters, you can find instances of "2002-" and change them to "2002."

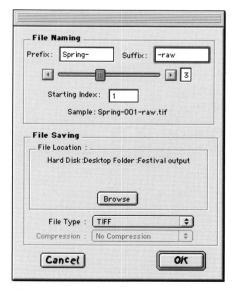

Figure 4-4 Batch renaming in NikonScan

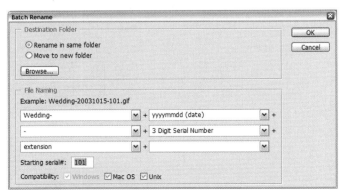

In Photoshop, batch renaming is part of the File Browser. See the section "Adobe Photoshop CS File Browser" later in this chapter.

▶ **Add or remove characters at the beginning or end of a filename.** If you forgot to add the date to all of the images in a folder, you can add it to the beginning of all of their filenames. Or if a number of GIF images were sent to you without the proper filename extension, you can add .GIF to all of them at once.

▶ **Number images sequentially.** If you want a set of images to be numbered, you can add those numbers with this feature.

Many image organizers, such as iView Media Pro and Ulead Photo Explorer, include batch-renaming features (**Figure 4-5**). If you don't have any of these programs, go to **www.versiontracker.com**, select your OS, and search for "rename." You'll find a number of shareware and freeware batch-renaming utilities covering a whole range of capabilities.

Using Image-Management Software

So far in this chapter, we've explained how to set up a sensible set of folders for your scans, and how to make sure each version of each image can be uniquely identified. But we still haven't told you how to figure out what's *in* each image, or how to find an image quickly. As we mentioned earlier, many filenames turn out to be inadequate for labeling files. Even though newer operating systems let you type novel-length 256-character filenames, trying to read those in a folder listing is totally impractical.

You can approach organizing and locating images more sensibly with image-management software that lets you assign and find images by keywords. You can categorize photos using keywords that are independent of the image's filename. You can use keywords to represent names, places, or any other concept that would apply to an image. The only downside to using keywords is the fact that at some point you have to sit down and actually *assign* all the keywords.

Image Organizing Programs

As scanners and digital cameras drop in price and rise in popularity, a variety of image organizers has emerged at all price points and levels of capability. At the low end, image organizers provide a more direct and convenient way to work with folders of images. More sophisticated organizers give you more options for tasks like exporting to HTML for Web photo galleries, printing contact sheets, or burning image collections to CD or DVD.

Adding scans to an image organizer is usually as simple as dragging image files (or folders containing images) to the image organizer. With many image organizers, you can import images directly from a scanner (usually by using TWAIN) or a digital camera.

Simple and Free or Cheap

On Mac OS X, iPhoto 4 (**www.apple.com**) is a logical program to start with, because it has more features than most free programs and is easy to use.

Figure 4-5
Batch renaming in Photoshop

iPhoto 4 comes free with any Macintosh purchased starting in January 2004. Otherwise, it's part of the $49 (single user) or $79 (five home user) iLife '04 software bundle from Apple that also includes iTunes, iMovie, iDVD, and Garage-Band.

On Windows, you might try XnView (**perso.wanadoo.fr/pierre.g/xnview/enhome. html**) or Vallen Jpegger (**www.vallen.de/ freeware/index.html**). Adobe (**www.adobe. com**) produces Adobe Photoshop Album, a slick standalone image organizer. The Photoshop Album Starter Edition is a free download, but the Starter Edition's feature set is quite limited compared to the paid version.

Inexpensive Yet Capable

As we mentioned earlier, the folder views in Mac OS X and Windows XP now offer many options for viewing and handling images. As a result, free image organizers don't add as much value as they did for older versions of Mac OS and Windows. You can enjoy a big jump in power and flexibility just by moving up to one of the many program options available in the $30-$50 range.

In this price range, you can find useful options such as automatic generation of contact sheets and Web image galleries, advanced keyword and metadata support, and batch processing of images. Some organizers in this price range make it easier to manage large numbers of images across multiple disks and disks that are not connected, such as archived CDs. A few programs provide simple image-editing capabilities.

Some popular organizers in this price range are iView Media (**www. iview-multimedia.com**, Mac and Windows), ACDSee (**www.acdsystems.com**, Mac and Windows), ThumbsPlus (**www.cerious.com**,

Windows only), Graphic Converter (**www. lemkesoft.de**, Mac only), Ulead Photo Explorer (**www.ulead.com**, Windows only), and the paid version of Adobe Photoshop Album (**www.adobe.com/products/ photoshopalbum/main.html**, Windows only).

Seriously Professional

Professional-grade image organizers go beyond being just an electronic photo album. The programs we list below save independent database files that you can use to track and sort images from any folder, instead of being limited to the folder organization on your hard disk. They can also catalog file types other than images, so you can track other project files like fonts, movies, and sounds. Of the programs listed below, all except iView Media Pro are network-aware, so that a workgroup can share the organization's image databases over a network. Of course, power comes at a price, and that price is generally $90 and up.

Popular professional image organizers include Canto Cumulus (**www.canto.com**, Mac, Windows, and UNIX), Extensis Portfolio (**www.extensis.com**, Mac and Windows), iView Media Pro (Mac only), and ThumbsPlus Pro (Windows only). If you're a professional photojournalist, PhotoMechanic (**www.camerabits.com**, Mac and Windows) is worth a look; it's optimized for selecting newsworthy images under deadline conditions through quick image comparisons, captioning, and metadata entry.

Adobe Photoshop CS File Browser

We mention this program feature separately because so many people who scan also own the full version of Photoshop CS. The File Browser built into Photoshop offers the features of a mid-level image browser without the ability to save standalone catalogs (**Figure 4-6**). You bring up the

Figure 4-6
File Browser
in Adobe
Photoshop CS

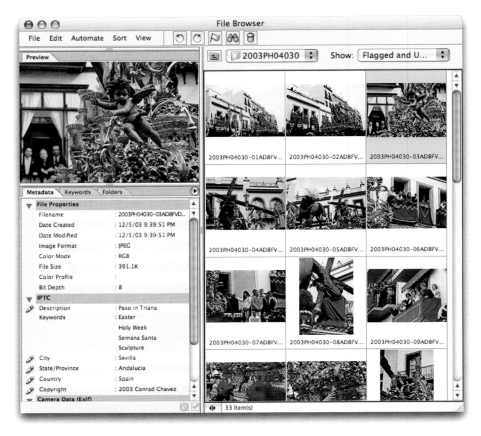

File Browser by choosing the Browse item from the File menu. The browser generates thumbnail previews of all of the images in a folder and can sort images in various ways such as by size or date.

One of the most valuable File Browser features is batch processing—the ability to select any set of images in the File Browser window and then run a Photoshop Action on the selected images. You can also simplify your naming scheme by choosing images and then selecting Batch Rename from the Automate menu that's part of the File Browser. The popup menus in the Batch Rename dialog box provide preset formats for bulk naming.

The File Browser doesn't create a standalone image database—you can only browse images folder by folder.

How Keywords Work

Depending on the image organizer you use, you usually start by viewing lots of images in the window of your image organizer. Then you select certain images and apply a keyword to them. For example, when viewing 24 images containing different dominant colors, you can manually select the photos that are predominantly red, and assign the keyword Red to them as a group (**Figure 4-7**). Later, when you need to find red photos, you enter the keyword into the search feature of the image organizer and all of the red photos will appear.

Setting up keywords can be a hassle, but most likely you would have put in the same amount of effort trying to invent descriptive yet unique filenames for each image without gaining the flexibility that keywords offer.

Figure 4-7
Using simple
keywords in iPhoto

As with filenaming, it's best to develop a keyword system that fits your needs. Apply keywords consistently so that you don't end up duplicating terms by using different spellings or forms of the term. Otherwise, this will throw off your searches. For example, if you search on "gray" but a co-worker has tagged a bunch of images as "grey," you'll miss a lot of images.

Also, find out what information your image organizer automatically reads for each image, so you don't needlessly use keywords for that data. For example, if your image organizer lets you find images by using the file-creation date or last-modified date, which are attributes of the image file, you don't need to make and assign keywords for 2002 or March. Generally, you don't need to use keywords for metadata that already exists in the file, either, as we discuss next.

Beyond Keywords: Metadata

Keywords are actually a form of *metadata*, a term that means "data about the data." Metadata came into being because people started realizing that there needed to be a place to store information about an image in the image itself. But older image file formats only provide two places to store data: the image's bits themselves (all graphical information) and the filename. Neither location can handle extended data, such as copyright information, subject, or category.

While there have been places to enter this kind of data in operating systems (such as the Comments field in the Mac OS Get Info dialog box), they were neither standardized nor cross-platform. As digital photography advanced, demand grew for a way to include extended information about an image, and metadata standards emerged.

Metadata is now supported by many types of hardware and software, such as digital cameras and image organizers. When you take a photograph with a digital camera, it encodes information such as the aperture, shutter speed, date, and time into each image. The metadata generated by digital cameras conforms to the Exchangeable Image File Format (EXIF) standard (**Figure 4-8**). (Yes, we know the name doesn't match the acronym, but that's what their official Web site says. You can study EXIF specifications at **www.exif.org**.)

If you expect to work with major media organizations, you should become familiar

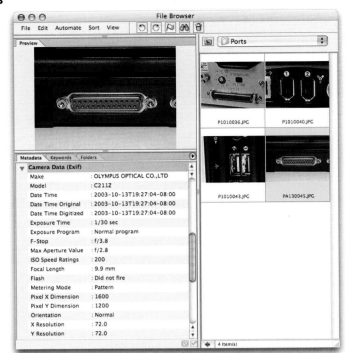

Figure 4-8
EXIF metadata in
the Photoshop CS
File Browser

work best and fastest when there's a lot of free hard disk space to use for virtual memory and other housekeeping tasks. In some cases you can start to see performance degradation and instability if you have less than a gigabyte of space free on your hard disk. A rough rule of thumb is that you need at least twice as much free space on your drive as memory installed in your computer.

But even before you have the necessity of archiving your files, you should be creating regular—and we mean regular!—backups of all images on your hard drive. Everyone procrastinates about backups, but it's not a question of if but when a hard drive will fail.

Have you spent days, months, or weeks of your life scanning? Will you be able to find the time to scan from scratch all over again, along with whatever retouching you've already done? Do you still have access to every one of the originals in case you need to scan them again? Probably not. If you've been using a digital camera, the files on your hard disk are the originals—in the event of a hard disk failure, they'll be gone forever.

Our other rule of thumb: always back up critical data to at least two different kinds of media. If you back up to DVD, also make a copy on a removable hard

with the standard categories and practices they use. One place to study metadata is the International Press Telecommunications Council (**www.iptc.org**); its Web site contains descriptions of the IPTC Subject Reference System used by journalists to categorize their images. In Adobe Photoshop, you can add metadata in standard IPTC categories by choosing the File Info item from the File menu when an image is open.

Archiving and Backing Up Your Scans

Image file sizes being what they are, you will fill up your hard disk eventually, particularly if scanning is a regular part of your job or your life. If you're editing video and music files, free storage space will disappear even faster.

Actually, you need to get stuff off of your hard disk long before it actually fills up, because operating systems generally

 Glenn has a high-tech consulting cousin who has had the impossible happen: five hard drive mechanical failures in three years, even though both the drives and the computers they were installed in were made by top manufacturers in their respective fields. Another colleague of ours can make machines die by hitting a few keys. It can happen to you.

drive. If you use tape, write discs, too. If you choose one method that's erasable (like tape or a hard drive), use another that's physical, like CD-R or DVD-R, which actually burns pits in the medium.

Backups and Archives

What's the difference between a backup and an archive? We loosely use the terms interchangeably, but they're actually two separate concepts.

▶ A backup is a copy of the current state of a drive, a folder, or a set of files. It's a complete or selective snapshot of the current contents of those files or locations. A backup is often overwritten with new data as it comes available.

▶ An archive is a discrete point in time for a given set of files, folders, or drives. An archive is typically maintained over time. Each newer copy of a file is added to an archive, while all or a selected number of older copies are retained in the archived set.

Depending on the kind of media you use and the way you need to store your data, you might choose to backup or archive. We generally backup our hard drives so they can be easily restored to a certain point. And we archive files when we need multiple versions of files we might either want to retrieve later or have deleted altogether from our hard drive.

Backup and Archival Media

Let's take a look at some of the media options you have to make copies of your files.

 CDs and DVDs may not be stable over long periods of time; bacteria discovered in Belize can eat discs (the plastic and metals) in the right sultry conditions.

Compact Discs

Burning CDs of images is tried and true, and a very popular method. A CD can store up to 700 Mb. CD-R (recordable) is used as an archiving method since the discs can't be rewritten. CD-RW (rewritable), which is slower and the media for which costs more, is both a backup and an archival method.

The number of images you can store on a CD has been declining because newer scanners and digital cameras are creating larger files. Also, the increasingly sophisticated feature sets of image editors tend to encourage more complex and heavily layered files. A full-page, press-resolution Photoshop composition made up of many layered scanned images can run into the hundreds of megabytes; you can only fit a few of them on a CD.

We're also hearing more and more reports that recordable and rewritable CDs can fail within a few years, even in the best storage conditions. So not only should you be making backups of the same data to multiple CDs, but you should refresh your CDs by duplicating them every few years.

DVDs

When CDs aren't big enough, DVDs can come to the rescue. A recordable or rewritable DVD data disc can store 5 or 10 Gb of data, depending on the format. Newer formats will squeeze in even more. Like CDs, DVDs can be written or rewritten and can be used as backup or archive.

You need a DVD drive that can write DVDs, but prices of these drives have fallen to where CD writers were a few years ago, and most computers designed for graphics professionals have a DVD-R/RW or SuperDrive (Apple's name for a DVD-R/RW and CD-R/RW drive).

Hard Drives

Two problems with CDs and DVDs are that they are markedly slower than your hard drive, and you have to manage a growing library of discs. As hard drive prices have dropped and the storage on a single drive has climbed dramatically, they have become a more viable way to archive and backup data.

But as we said earlier, hard drives fail more frequently than we'd like. If you decide to store your scan backup on a big hard drive, it's best to buy at least one additional hard drive and maintain a second backup. NASA calls this redundancy, and it's what NASA does to safeguard its missions when the consequences of equipment failure would be very high. See the next section for more information about redundant storage.

Tape Drives

Writing to tape is a time-honored way to back up data, going back to the days when tape was the cheapest way to archive endless gigabytes of data. Tapes remain useful even as hard drive prices have fallen, because the small tapes are reliable and don't take up much space—they fit eas-

 Glenn just bought a 320 Gb drive to back up his entire office network of machines— and the only reason he bought that small a drive was because the 500 Gb drive was backordered.

ily inside secure offsite locations like safe-deposit boxes. Most tape backup technologies expand their backup capacities further by using data compression.

Tapes are primarily used for archiving because a tape drive writes sequentially to its medium; rewriting is a very slow option and not often available. You generally write to each tape in a set until it's reached the end and then pop in the next tape. Often, you can keep several different sets of multiple tapes each of them representing a discrete period of time.

It takes much more time to read and write files on a tape compared to disk media, and it's especially time-consum-

Figure 4-9
Rotating three offsite backup sets (A, B, and C) with your onsite location

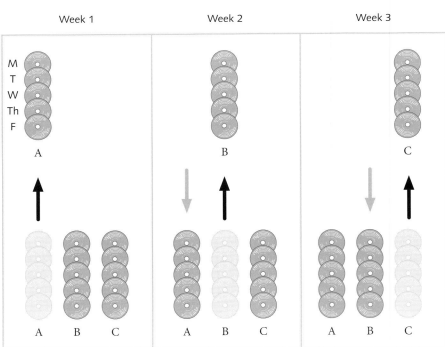

ing to retrieve files from backups that are spread over several tapes. Also, the price of tape drives and media hasn't fallen as quickly as the price of CD and DVD drives, because the market for tape drives is so much smaller and manufacturing costs haven't dropped as far.

Tape formats are a sea of acronyms—ADR, AIT, DDS, DLT/SDLT, LTO, SLR, and VXA. Smaller studios are more likely to use DDS drives, which use DAT (digital audio tape) format tapes, or VXA drives. The higher-capacity tapes can store 20 to 50 Gb per tape. Higher-end drives cost more than $1,000 and tapes for those drives cost $35 to $50 or even more. Some studios use tape cartridges that allow 5 or 10 or more tapes to be loaded or unloaded automatically, providing terabytes of backup storage "online" with no human intervention.

Rotating Archives

When making a backup, you may want to retain that snapshot indefinitely or refresh it constantly with new data. But for an archive, you probably want to retain files for quite a while—weeks or months. We recommend building a media rotation schedule so that you always have a full set of all your data up to a given date. If you don't rotate sets of media, then you're overwriting part of your full backup whenever you restart from the beginning. With at least two sets in rotation, you have a worst-case scenario plan (**Figure 4-9**).

To set up a rotation, you might start with three sets of drives, discs, or tapes named Set A, B, and C (one set per week). During week 1, you back up to Set A, during week 2 back up to Set B, and so on, alternating the set you back up to each week. This provides a full snapshot and archive of all of your systems, which can prevent total catastrophe if even one full set is damaged or unreadable.

Another approach is to rotate sets on days of the week: have five sets for Mon-

day through Friday/weekend. With this approach, you have a complete backup of all your files that's only a single day old, and multiple sets in case a corruption occurs during the week. If you have many tapes and are less concerned, you can rotate just by filling up a set number of tapes, drives, or discs and rotating to the next set when that number of media items is filled.

Finally, you should rotate your image backups offsite—to a place that won't be affected if something truly horrible happens to your home or office, like a fire or flood. You can keep your offsite backup at a friend's house or in a safe-deposit box at the bank. Some photographers are sufficiently paranoid that they attempt to protect their image backups from Biblical-scale worst-case scenarios by storing their offsite backups well away from the flood plain or fault line they live on.

When deciding what you need to do, simply ask yourself how much of a financial, emotional, or functional loss you or your business would suffer if all the scans you ever made suddenly disappeared. If your business can't withstand the loss of even one day's work, you'll want to back up to an offsite location (say, over a network) every day.

Mass Migration

You may not need to think about this just yet, but as time goes by, newer storage media are always larger and cheaper per megabyte than the media they replace, rendering older media obsolete. Eventually, it may become impossible to acquire service, support, and supplies for the drive you are using, which would be a major issue if your archiving hardware ever developed a problem or failed outright.

One of the most significant examples of this is the vast archives of scientific data accumulated by NASA in the 1960s. Recorded on large reels of magnetic tape, the data is unreadable because there aren't any functioning machines that can play the tapes, and the data was never copied to a newer medium.

Also keep in mind that even if the hardware functions, your data can be stranded simply because there isn't a software driver compatible with that shiny new operating system you upgraded to.

Before it's no longer economical or practical to continue archiving your scans on the media you've been using for the last few years, be ready to migrate your data to current media. Yes, it's a hassle, but you can minimize the hassle if you anticipate and plan for it, which is why we're bringing it up now. And it's usually worth it, because newer media is typically capable of storing so much more data that it becomes a lot easier to manage the media and retrieve images. We can now store 15 of the once popular 45 Mb SyQuest disks on a single CD-ROM that costs, even in constant dollars, about $\frac{1}{100}$th of what that SyQuest set did.

If all of this seems like a chore, keep in mind that it's not just your dilemma—every organization that creates digital archives has to have a way of continually migrating their archives from obsolete, unsupportable media to current media. Instead of thinking of your image archives as a stationary house of data, think of your archives as a nomadic tribe, whose survival depends on recognizing the right time to move on to greener pastures.

Now Scan in Peace

Once that scanner gets going, it's easy to fill up your hard disk with images without realizing that that virtual pile of data is becoming unmanageable. But if you've developed a solid scanning plan and have a system to organize, locate, and safeguard all of your scans, you can scan away with a lot more peace of mind.

5

How to Read Your Scanning Software

A ROSETTA STONE FOR SCANNING SOFTWARE

We've probably used a thousand software applications, but the ones we find most baffling are the programs that ship with scanners. This is not to say they're not powerful and sophisticated and cool. But they are too often slightly batty: their interface design is non-intuitive or too clever, program functions are given non-standard names, and important features are nested three dialog boxes deep. (To get out of that nesting you have to do what our colleague Steve Broback calls the Joe Pesci method: "ok, ok, ok, ok.") Too often, we're not given an option other than entering numbers we have to figure out in our heads—and that's what a computer is supposed to help us with.

Throughout the rest of the book, we discuss how to use tonal correction, unsharp masking, and other techniques to get the best possible scan. But it may not be clear how to implement our suggestions

when you're actually sitting in front of the scanner. We hope that this chapter helps bridge the gap between theory and practice, especially in cases where the scanner's own manual doesn't adequately relate the features of the scanner to the process of scanning. While your scanning software might look a little bit different than the tools we cover, the basic process is likely to be the same because there are certain adjustments that need to be made no matter what kind of scanner you use. And if you understand the process of scanning, you can transfer that skill to any scanning utility you come across.

Most of the software programs we refer to in this chapter have been around for a few years without much improvement. (We still hope for scanning packages that are as easy and straightforward to use as Photoshop.) We also discuss a couple of

Hewlett Packard seems to have cornered the market on multi-year confusion. We found their Desk-Jet software terrible back in 1990. Now, over a decade later, it's still terrible, but in an entirely different, bewildering fashion.

general software features to think about, notably the TWAIN standard and third-party packages that you might prefer to use to drive your scanner.

Here's the short version of the general scanning process. You may not need to take all these steps every time. We'll cover each of these steps in more detail in this chapter.

1 Insert the original.

2 Preview.

3 Crop, rotate, and flip.

4 Set output resolution and dimensions.

5 Set tonal range and bit depth.

6 Adjust color space and adjust color balance.

If you don't spot most of the options in your scanning software that we talk about here, check to see if your scanning utility is set for an Easy, Simple, or QuickScan mode. These "training wheels" modes are great for quick-and-dirty scans, but you can't really see or control what the scanner does. You may need to turn one of those modes off or choose Advanced, Expert, Full Menus, or a similar option.

Before you begin, make sure the scanning software is installed, of course. Follow the instructions for your scanner's software to complete the install. You should be aware of whether you're running the software as a plug-in or as a standalone application; see "Plug-in or Standalone?" later in this chapter.

7 Apply digital restoration and enhancements.

8 Make the final scan.

Let's begin, shall we?

Loading the Original

It's easy to place an original into a flatbed scanner. Like a photocopier, you open the lid, position the original on the glass (make sure it's straight!) and close the lid. Close the lid slowly; sometimes, the simple act of closing the lid creates enough of a breeze that it shifts your carefully positioned original out of square. (For a clever way to make sure your original remains aligned after the lid is closed, see "Rotation," later in this chapter.)

With a film scanner you may find various methods to load your original media. With some film scanners, you place your filmstrip into a film holder and then insert the film holder into the scanner. With others, you gently push the end of the filmstrip into the machine and a little motor pulls it inside, like putting your bank card into an ATM. Certain scanners allow both approaches. For APS film, you typically use an adapter that lets you insert the entire APS cartridge, then the scanner retrieves the frame.

Whichever method you use, keep your original media and your scanner clean. With flatbed scanners, keep the glass clean; with some film scanners, you might need to blow dust out regularly using compressed air. (Use the non-ozone-layer-destroying variety of canned air or consider investing in a tiny electric compressor.) We talk a little more about using quality originals in Chapter 3, *Getting Your Originals Ready to Scan.*

Some scanners have a sweet spot, which is an area of the scanner bed where the scanner produces the highest quality results. You can try to find this

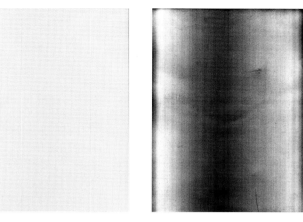

Figure 5-1 Scan of empty scanning bed before (left) and after (right) applying Equalize command

Figure 5-2 SilverFast's Prescan button (labeled Preview in most other utilities)

sweet spot by creating a scan of the entire imaging area using a white original (a low-resolution scan is all you need), then applying the Equalize command in Photoshop or another image editor—or just increasing the contrast to a high setting (**Figure 5-1**). Look for areas that are excessively noisy or dark: some cheaper scanners have definite darkening around the edges or dark streaks. Once you locate these areas, you can position originals to avoid areas that are less than optimal.

Sometimes you need to tell the scanner what type of media your original is. Depending on the scanning utility you use, this option might be labeled something like Media Type, Original, or Input.

If you're using a film scanner or transparency adapter, the media type might have some additional variations that you should pay attention to, such as Color Neg-

 If you're using a flatbed scanner without a transparency attachment or tray, there might not be a media type setting because you're always using reflective media.

ative, Black and White Negative, or Slide. You may also need to select the film format (35mm, APS, 4x5). There might even be a film type option that adjusts the scanner to the specific film stock you're scanning, such as Fuji Velvia slide or Kodak Portra 160NC negative.

Preview

A scanner can take a few minutes to make a high-resolution, high-quality scan, but you don't want to wait that long just to see if your settings are right. That's why most scanning utilities have a preview function.

 If the scanner's performance is so inconsistent that the optimal areas aren't large enough to be useful, you might think about getting a better scanner.

A preview is a low-resolution scan—typically just at screen resolution at 100 percent of the area shown on screen—that provides you with enough detail so you can make any necessary setting tweaks before you complete your final scan. Most scanning utilities have Preview and Scan buttons next to each other in the main window (**Figure 5-2**).

Some scanning utilities let you adjust the resolution of the preview as well. But if you're interested in speed, set the scanning resolution as low as you can stand, making sure that you can still see enough detail to make good decisions about your settings. To maximize preview performance, your scanning utility might suppress features that won't affect the most important adjustments like cropping, tone, and color. For example, it might not apply multi-sampling or dust-and-scratch removal to previews. Your scanning documentation can tell you about any limitations of your scanner's preview mode.

You can also often select just part of the scanning area to preview. This is usually very fast and can be seen through a marquee that lets you select and zoom in to receive a detailed close-up of the area.

If you're interested in quality, see if your scanning utility lets you increase the resolution of the preview scan. With more samples, the automatic settings for tone and color should be improved. Previews will take longer, however.

Figure 5-3
Histogram affected by crop area

Crop and Set Orientation

This step is pretty straightforward. You can crop the overall scanning area to just the part of the flatbed glass or film frame that you need, usually by using a crop or marquee tool to draw a rectangle around that area. You can also use rotate or flip features to correct the orientation of an image in case you put the original in the wrong way.

Cropping

You might think that cropping is a simple cosmetic operation that can be postponed until you open the scan in an image editor. However, in a lot of cases it's critical to crop correctly during the preview stage. This is because scanning software generally measures tone and color levels based on the image inside the scanning area. Areas within the cropping rectangle that aren't part of your final selection may distort the automatic image analysis (**Figure 5-3**). Even if you're making adjustments manually, empty areas may foul the information you get about the tonal range or color balance of the image. These concerns may be less of an issue if your scanning utility has an auto-crop feature that automatically tries to crop out empty areas.

Another reason to crop is when your original is much smaller than the total scanning area. If your scan includes large empty areas, the scan will take longer than it needs to, and the resulting file will be much larger than necessary.

The precision of the crop depends mostly on the precision of the scanner preview. Scanner previews can be imprecise enough that you need to crop again in your image editor. After scanning a few images, you'll acquire a sense of how accurate your scanner preview is.

Aspect ratio locked   Unlocked

Figure 5-4
Cropping with the
aspect ratio locked
and unlocked

Aspect Ratio

Aspect ratio is the proportion of width to height in the crop box. You can usually choose an option to maintain the aspect ratio so that the proportions of your crop are preserved when or if you resize it. Most scanning utilities use a lock or chain icon to do this (**Figure 5-4**).

Rotation

For flatbed scanners and individual slides, rotation is mostly a matter of convenience, since you can simply rotate the original by hand on the scanner bed. Rotation is more useful with filmstrips, because you can't put a filmstrip in sideways, and it saves you a step in processing an image.

Most scanning utilities don't let you rotate in less than 90-degree increments. If the original isn't straight when you put it in, you have to rotate the resulting scan a few degrees in your image editor. One of our helpful readers sent in a great way to line up a crooked original so that it scans perfectly straight: Find a sticky note that's big enough to extend past the edge of the

 If you've put a film negative or transparency in the scanner upside down, with the emulsion facing the wrong way, reload it—don't use the flip or mirror option to correct it.

scanner. Now attach the sticky note to the original, and line up any of its edges with the horizontal or vertical axis of the original image, ignoring the edge of the paper. After you close the lid, move the part of the sticky note that extends past the lid until it's lined up with the edge of the scanner.

Flipping

Flipping usually rotates a frame 180 degrees. This is useful for film, because it's easy to insert film upside down. (But don't flip film back to front; see note at lower left.)

Set Output Resolution and Dimensions

Setting the resolution and dimensions of a scan confuses most people new to scanning because there are many variables that interact with each other; changing one option makes other numbers change, too, which makes it hard determine the direct cause-and-effect relationship.

The resolution and dimensions section of your scanning software usually includes options like size (physical dimensions, represented by width and height), file size, resolution, scaling, and halftone screen (**Figure 5-5**).

Each of these options has its counterpart in both input (which describes your original) and output (which describes your final output). For example, the input reso-

Figure 5-5
Original and output dimensions in SilverFast

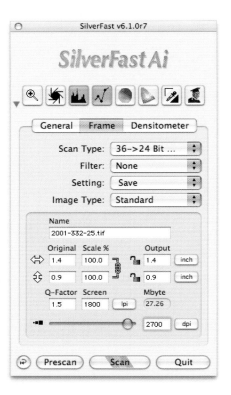

Printing at the same dimensions as the original. If you're scanning for printed output and the size of your original matches the size at which you want to print it, then no scaling is necessary. Once you've confirmed the output dimensions and entered the output resolution, you can move on to the tonal correction stage.

Printing at different dimensions than the original, or scanning for the Web or video. Enter the dimensions for the final image in the appropriate unit of measure for the output medium (**Figure 5-6**). For print, use inches or metric units; for Web or video, use pixels. (Using inches or metric units for screen output isn't practical, as we explain in Chapter 11, *Image Resolution*.)

Good scanning software should automatically calculate and enter the values for the scaling and scanning resolutions by looking at the cropping rectangle you drew and the final dimensions you entered.

Options for Resolution and Dimensions

You might notice that we haven't talked about changing scan resolution, scaling, file size, or halftone screen options. The reason is that these aren't the values you should consider at this point. As we discuss in the previous section, if you can draw a cropping rectangle, specify output resolution, and specify output dimensions, the rest of the numbers are derived directly from those values. However, if your scanning software doesn't seem to do the calculations properly or at all, you might need to understand these options after all. So let's talk about them now.

Scan Resolution

Scan resolution is rarely a value that you can enter by hand because it's usually calculated by the software utility, which uses the original dimensions and the output dimensions you enter. Here's the formula:

lution will be used by your scanner, and the output resolution will be used by your printer. In many scanning utilities, the user interface doesn't make the distinction between these input and output settings clear.

Your first step should be to enter and lock the output resolution. In a lot of scanning software, the output resolution is automatically locked: it doesn't change as you change other settings. That's the way it should be. If you don't know what the output resolution should be, see Chapters 6 through 9, where we discuss settings for specific types of output. Note that you rarely need to scan photographs at an output resolution above 300 samples per inch (spi) at the final output size, even if your printer has a much higher resolution.

When you set output dimensions, it comes down to two scenarios: Either the original and the printed final image are the same dimensions, or they aren't.

Figure 5-6
Relationship of
dimensions to
resolution when
resizing

Offset and other printing

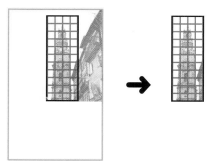

If the original is already at the same dimensions as your output size you scan at the same settings as your output specs.

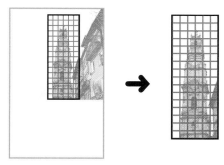

If the original and the output are different sizes, you set the output dimensions and resolution to match the final output specs.
Original size: 3 x 8 inches
Output specs: 4.25 x 11.5 inches at 300 dpi
Resulting scanner resolution: 425 dpi

On-screen graphics

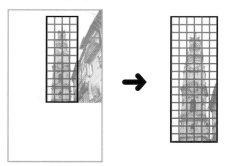

For the Web or video, you need to generate just enough pixels to match the required on-screen width or height.
Original size: 3 x 8 inches
Output specs: 600 pixels tall
Resulting scanner resolution: 75 dpi

```
Scan resolution = (print resolution
÷ original width or height) × (print
width or height)
```

For example, if you have an original that's 5 inches wide and you want to print it 4 inches wide at 300 dpi, then scan it at (300 ÷ 5) x 4 or 240 spi.

Scaling

Like scan resolution, the scaling percentage is calculated using the original dimensions and the output dimensions, but this time the result is a ratio. The formula for this one is as follows:

```
Scaling percentage = Output height or
width ÷ Original height or width
```

For example, if you have an 8-by-10–inch photo and you want to shrink it to 3 inches wide while scanning, the scaling percentage you want to use is 8 divided by 3 or 37.5 percent. There may be times when you find it convenient to change the output dimensions by entering a scaling percentage—for example, when you know you need an image blown up 200 percent. But we think it's more likely that you're targeting specific dimensions on a layout, and thus would enter the precise output measurements instead of a percentage.

> ⊕ *You can use either height or width for both sides of the division. As long as the image is scaled proportionately, the results are the same.*

The horizontal and vertical scaling percentages should normally be locked, preserving the aspect ratio. Unlocking them lets you "stretch" the scan by entering different horizontal and vertical percentages. Stretching an image can be useful as a special effect or to adjust for output that uses non-square pixels, such as video.

File Size

You may often see the size of a scanned image referred to in terms of the amount of space it takes up on disk. For example, an art director may tell you that he needs a 20 Mb TIFF file, and a lot of publications ask for images in terms of maximum size, not resolution and dimensions. They're used to their own production methods, and all of the files they make are about that size. Also, sometimes asking for sizes with a few parameters produces a more consistent submission for their purposes without confusing less experienced clients or colleagues.

The problem is that file size alone doesn't tell you very much about the image, because changing image attributes can cause significant changes to the file size. A 20 Mb TIFF file can be an 8-by-10–inch RGB TIFF image—if it's uncompressed 8-bit color, with no extra channels or layers, at 300 dpi. A 20 Mb TIFF file could just as easily be a 6-by-7–inch RGB TIFF image that happens to have 16 bits of color.

If your scanning software has a File Size option, you can refer to it as a reality check for your other settings (**Figure 5-7**), but you should concentrate on making sure your output dimensions and resolution (and other settings coming up in this chapter) meet the requirements of your project.

Figure 5-7 File size readout in NikonScan

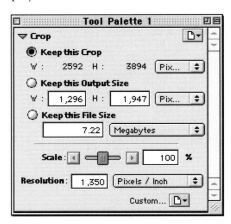

Halftone Screen

Some scanners let you specify a halftone screen value in lines per inch (lpi). This option isn't designed to provide a halftoned image (usually), but rather to help you target your scan for the final halftone output. When you enter a screen frequency value, the scanning software calculates the resolution required to achieve that halftone screen.

The math for this isn't hard; many printers recommend that the output resolution should be between one and a half times to double the desired line screen. If you're scanning an image for a magazine that's printed at a halftone screen of 150 lpi, you'd scan at two times 150, or 300 spi. Similarly, if you enter 150 lpi into a scanning utility's Halftone Screen option, the software will probably set the output resolution to 300 spi. Some scanner software utilities let you set this multiplication factor.

Interpolation

When the scanning resolution is beyond the optical resolution of the scanner, the scanning software may offer interpolation to create more pixels by analyzing the existing pixels and adding similar pixels around them. Your image editor probably can do just as well, if not better, so there's no reason to have your scanning software do it.

We talk about interpolation in Chapter 11, *Image Resolution*, and include reasons why you probably should not use your scanner software for interpolation. In general, we recommend turning it off. If there's no "off" option, look for a "bicubic" or "anti-aliased" setting and disable it.

Set Tonal Range and Bit Depth

To get a good-looking, high-quality image, you want your scanner to make the best use of the image's tonal range available in the final output file. Today's scanners do a rather decent job of this, on average images at least. But to get the best results or to work successfully with more challenging images, you need to know how to read a histogram—the distribution of tonal values in an image—and how to adjust tonal controls in the scanning software. (We tell you all about histograms in Chapter 12, *Tonal Correction*.)

Unfortunately, if you want to understand how the scanner and the software process image data, you often can't easily tell by looking at your software's features. Scanning utilities tend to group controls by function instead of by their role or step in the image-processing sequence. The tonal range of a scanned image is the result of two distinct stages: the scanning hardware preparation before the scan and the scanning software's processing after the scan.

What happens before the scan (in hardware). When you preview an image, the sensor data is analyzed by the scanner to determine the auto-exposure setting by measuring the densities of the red, green, and blue channels. When you carry out the final scan, the sensor captures the image using the exposure setting, and sends the entire, unmodified (raw) contents of the sensors to the scanning software.

Most people have never seen a raw scanner image, because scanner data isn't useful in its raw state—it looks like a scan gone wrong (**Figure 5-8**). (We tell you why in Part 2, *Anatomy of a Scanned Image*.) The scanning software's preview is the image data after it's been processed by the options selected at the software stage. The only way you can affect the raw scanner image is to change the exposure setting. (See the Exposure description later in this section.)

What happens after the scan (in software). Just about all the tonal controls available to you in the scanning software are applied

to the raw scanner data after it's come in from the scanner. This includes the options you normally see in the tonal section of scanning software: black and white points, gamma, levels, curves, brightness, and contrast (**Figure 5-9**).

The way the interface for most scanning software presents its options it would appear that all the settings control the scanner directly. They don't. If you find your images have blown-out highlights or filled-in shadows and you've already set the black and white points to their limits, that's an indication that the tones you want weren't part of the raw scan, which is usually because the auto-exposure value was a little off.

 To fix an auto-exposure problem, preview the original again, shift the exposure or lamp brightness option to include the tonal range that was clipped, carefully check the histogram and preview to make sure you got the missing tones, and then rescan the image.

Let's go over the options you'll find in the tonal controls of typical scanning software.

Automatic Tone Controls

Because automatic controls work well a lot of the time there's nothing wrong with trying them first.

Auto Exposure

As we discuss earlier, the auto-exposure control sets the sensor so that it acquires the best range of tones from the original, based on the original's density (**Figure 5-10**). You can override auto exposure by using exposure or lamp brightness manual controls.

Figure 5-8
Raw scans and other views

Upper left: Raw scan of color negative

Upper right: Inverted figure is too blue

Lower left: Color neg scanned using specific film type setting

Lower right: Image is easier to correct from scan at lower left.

Auto Contrast

The auto-contrast control attempts to optimize contrast by stretching the tonal range of the raw data (**Figure 5-11**). Some scanning software automatically applies contrast adjustment, while other packages let you decide to apply it or not. If you're not happy with the results, turn off auto contrast and adjust the contrast yourself using levels/histogram or curves.

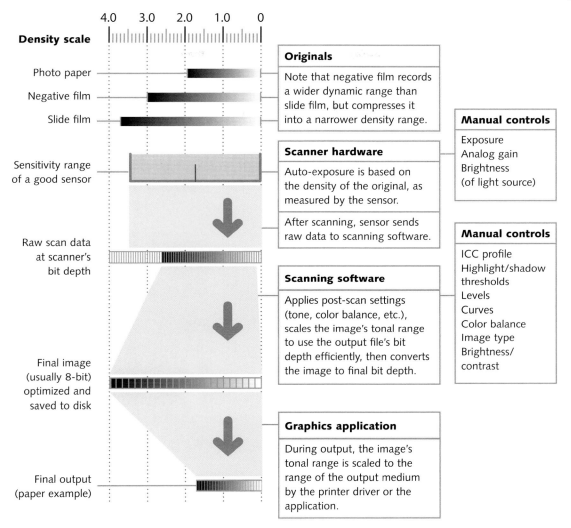

Density scale

4.0 3.0 2.0 1.0 0

Photo paper
Negative film
Slide film

Originals

Note that negative film records a wider dynamic range than slide film, but compresses it into a narrower density range.

Manual controls

Exposure
Analog gain
Brightness
(of light source)

Sensitivity range of a good sensor

Scanner hardware

Auto-exposure is based on the density of the original, as measured by the sensor.

After scanning, sensor sends raw data to scanning software.

Manual controls

ICC profile
Highlight/shadow thresholds
Levels
Curves
Color balance
Image type
Brightness/contrast

Raw scan data at scanner's bit depth

Scanning software

Applies post-scan settings (tone, color balance, etc.), scales the image's tonal range to use the output file's bit depth efficiently, then converts the image to final bit depth.

Final image (usually 8-bit) optimized and saved to disk

Graphics application

During output, the image's tonal range is scaled to the range of the output medium by the printer driver or the application.

Final output (paper example)

Figure 5-9 Sequence of tonal processing

If you're never happy with the results, try to find an auto-contrast preference (**Figure 5-12**). This setting might let you adjust what the auto-contrast algorithm aims for in terms of white, black, and gray, and clipping or tonal removal from both ends of the range. This last preference is often called something like black-and-white thresholds.

The auto contrast feature may also be called auto levels, auto adjust, or similar names, depending on which software utility you are using.

Because post-scan adjustments drop image data, we suggest that you rarely use an auto-contrast option unless you've confirmed that its settings aren't dropping data you want to keep. Auto contrast is often most useful as an experimental starting point for your own adjustments; that is if you try auto contrast without permanently applying it.

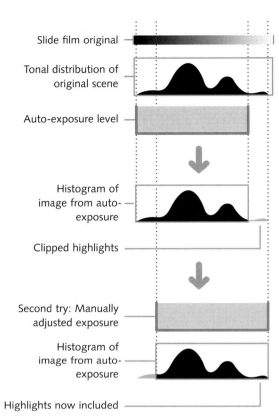

Slide film original

Tonal distribution of original scene

Auto-exposure level

Histogram of image from auto-exposure

Clipped highlights

Second try: Manually adjusted exposure

Histogram of image from auto-exposure

Highlights now included

Figure 5-10 How auto exposure works

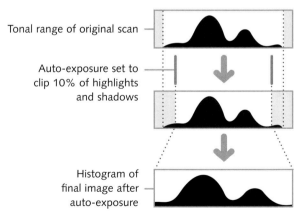

Tonal range of original scan

Auto-exposure set to clip 10% of highlights and shadows

Histogram of final image after auto-exposure

Figure 5-11 How auto contrast works

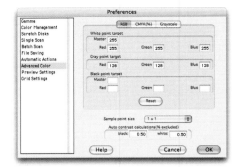

Figure 5-12
Auto-contrast preferences in NikonScan

Figure 5-13
Image types in SilverFast

scenes that are naturally brighter, darker, or less neutral than average, such as snow scenes, night scenes, sunsets, or metallic subjects. These subjects may be misinterpreted by automatic tonal correction.

Manual Tone Controls

When automatic controls don't quite do the job, you can override them using other controls, but many of these controls

Image Type

Some scanning utilities provide an Image Type or Scene Type option (**Figure 5-13**). This feature tries to compensate for

Figure 5-14
Analog Gain in
NikonScan

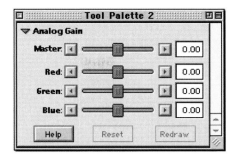

are redundant. There's usually no reason to apply adjustments using both the curves and levels controls, because they accomplish the same task using different approaches. The more controls you touch the easier it is to lose track of what changes you've made and why. If you've been taking good notes as you read this chapter, you know that it's okay to change both the exposure and curves options: exposure happens during the scan, and curves are applied after the scan.

Exposure

Exposure changes the period of time while the sensor reads the original. Consequently, it affects the original's tonal range in the raw scan file: a longer exposure can result in either blown-out highlights or more detail; a shorter exposure provides less highlight and more shadow detail, or it can fill in the darkest areas.

The auto-exposure analysis in today's scanners is usually quite good, but if the preview or the histogram reveals problems,

you can manually override the exposure if your scanning software has that option. You won't have to fiddle with exposure at all for reflective originals because they always fit within the dynamic range of the sensor; exposure adjustments are more likely needed for wide density range transparent originals like slide film.

When working with typical originals, the need for manual exposure adjustment should be pretty rare. Depending on the scanner software you use, this option might appear under another name; for example, Nikon calls it Analog Gain (**Figure 5-14**).

Brightness

In a few rare cases, you might come across an option labeled brightness or lamp brightness that is somewhat buried in the software's user interface. This control alters the intensity of the light source as opposed to the sensor's exposure time. It's unfortunate that this feature is labeled brightness because you might ignore it in favor of a more common and less useful brightness control at the top level of the scanning software's user interface that doesn't relate to the lamp; see "Linear Correction or How to Ruin an Image" in Chapter 12, *Tonal Correction*.

Histogram

The manual way to optimize contrast is to use a histogram control to set the lightest (highlight), darkest (shadow), and in-between tones (midtones). Some scanning utilities label histogram as levels, because this feature is essentially the same as the Levels feature in Photoshop. A histogram is a graph representing the density of tones at each tonal point, and you use the controls to specify the range of tones you want to expand to fill the contrast range of the image. In many scanning utilities, levels sliders are found at the bottom of the curve controls (**Figure 5-17**, below). We cover histograms, levels, and curves in more depth in Chapter 12, *Tonal Correction*.

Testing Brightness

If you're not sure how your scanning software's brightness control works, you can test it. Scan an image using automatic settings, and save the file. Change the brightness value and save a second version of the file. Open both files and compare their histograms. If your scanner is adjusting light source brightness during the scan, the histogram will look more like the first histogram in **Figure 5-15**. But if the second file's histogram looks more like the second one in **Figure 5-15**, then the option is a typical post-scan brightness adjustment—the kind we tell you not to use.

Figure 5-15
Comparing levels and brightness adjustments

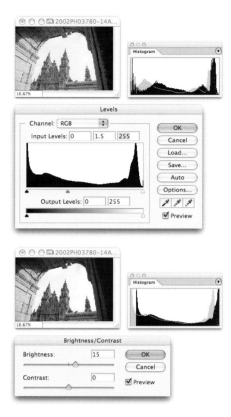

The Levels adjustment preserves the original tones (top), while Brightness/Contrast removes shadow detail and loses highlights (bottom).

Curves

As in Photoshop, the curves feature lets you adjust contrast arbitrarily throughout the tonal range of the image (**Figure 5-16**). While curves appears intimidating, the feature is just an expanded version of the histogram control. The two endpoints on a curves graph set the levels to use as the darkest and lightest tones, just like the end sliders in the histogram. The difference is that the histogram provides one additional control to set the midtone, while curves lets you add many more control points that aren't necessarily on a linear or perfectly curved scale between the darkest and lightest levels. This gives you more control.

Eyedroppers

If, while viewing the preview, you can see specific areas containing the tones that you want to use as the lightest, middle, and darkest tones in the image, you might prefer to set your black and white points by eye rather than using the more abstract histogram or curves controls. Using the highlight, midtone, or shadow eyedropper (**Figure 5-16**, far right), click the location on the image that you want to use for a highlight, midtone, or shadow level, respectively.

Bit Depth

Most newer scanners can capture 12 to 16 bits of color or gray data per channel. Older scanners are typically limited to 8 to 12 bits per channel. But the vast majority of output types, including print and Web, don't benefit from more than 8 bits of data in the final output file.

The main reason to scan at greater than 8 bits is to preserve tonal and color quality through large adjustments, such as when color-correcting raw negative scans into usable images. You can scan at less than 8 bits for non-photographic originals like black-and-white line art (for example, a pen-and-ink drawing) or when scanning text for OCR.

Working with higher bit depths is slower and requires much more disk space and RAM, so you need to choose when to trade time and space for efficiency. If you can produce an acceptable image directly from the scanner, so that it needs little to no adjustment in an image editor, then scanning at 8 bits per channel is sufficient. (We cover these issues in more depth in Part 2, *Anatomy of a Scanned Image*.)

Set Color Space and Adjust Color Balance

Color correction during the scanning process works a lot like tonal correction. Some adjustments are applied before the scan, and some are applied only to the raw data that's already scanned. During the initial exposure analysis we talk about in the last section, the sensor measures the density

Figure 5-16
Curves feature in different scanning utilities

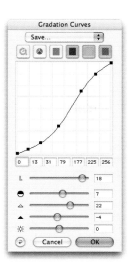
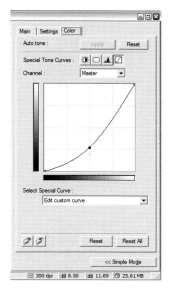
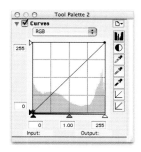

of each of the red, green, and blue color channels in order to work out the optimal exposure for each channel.

Optimizing exposure for each channel can also help result in the proper color balance, although the bulk of that analysis happens after the raw scan data comes in. If a scan looks off and the histogram indicates that tones were clipped at the ends of one or more channels, you can try manually adjusting the exposure or lamp brightness of the channels that were off.

You can make better color judgments on screen if you calibrate your monitor and your scanning software lets you use your monitor profile. See Chapter 13, *Getting Good Color.*

Color Space

The color space is the range of colors you make available for image storage and editing. You might not see this option on less expensive scanners, but it's present on professional devices. We provide output-specific color space recommendations in the next four chapters, but here are the basic guidelines.

▶ Adobe RGB (1998) is a safe choice for materials headed for high-quality output, like offset printing or a photo-quality inkjet printer.

▶ sRGB is more appropriate for images that will end up on a video screen (like the Web or television), or for home and office printing where color requirements aren't critical.

While there are many other color spaces available, they're meant for more specialized uses and often require special handling. For example, some are not good editing spaces unless you scanned a 12- or 16-bit image. (There's a more detailed discussion of color spaces in Chapter 13: *Getting Good Color.*)

Automatic Color Controls

Color correction is tricky enough if you're human with fallible and non-color-corrected eyesight, and even more challenging for a computer that doesn't have human eyes. (Glenn discovered a distinct five percent red cast in his left eye during his color-correction days.) Fortunately, humans program computers, which means that today's color-correction algorithms are surprisingly good most of the time.

However, when an original contains large areas of a dominant color (like a sunset) or lacks neutral whites, grays, or blacks, automatic color correction can get it wrong. Before running for the manual controls, look a little deeper to see if your software has the following color-balancing options that might be more appropriate for the image you're trying to scan.

White balance. Scanning software automatically attempts to remove color casts from a scan by analyzing the balance of red, green, and blue across the available tonal range. In some scanning software, there is a white balance menu with choices for situations where the color balance is naturally different, such as fluorescent or incandescent lighting. When none of the automatic options seem to help, see if there's a neutral or off option so that no automatic color correction is applied, and then move on to the manual controls.

Another time to consider turning off white balance is if it overcorrects. For example, using white balance on a sunset can drain much of the dramatic color out of the scene, because white balance tries to neutralize color casts. Sometimes, setting the image type option (next) can help in these situations.

Image type. If the scanning software has an image type or scene type menu like the one we mention earlier (in "Set Tonal Range and Bit Depth"), you might also find modes for special color situations like sunsets, flesh tones, or landscapes with large areas of green grass and blue skies. If your initial scan strays too far from the actual colors that you know should be in a scene, these modes may take you more quickly to your goal of correction for the image.

Manual Color Controls

As you've probably figured out by now, manual controls are for those times when the automatic controls fail you or when you just want more control.

Color balance. Manual color balance controls may be available as a color wheel, or in the form of RGB sliders as in the Color Balance dialog box in Photoshop. The color wheel is a little easier to use because it's a visual representation of how colors are opposed.

Eyedroppers. For color images, the eyedroppers have a bit more functionality than for tones. Instead of simply setting the gray level for the highlight, midtone, and shadow at the location you click, the control attempts to neutralize the red, green, and blue channel values where you click. If you click the shadow eyedropper at a location that has an RGB value of 4, 10, and 7, the scanning software will reset all three to the same value. You can usually set this value in the scanning utility's preferences, because the right answer depends on your output device. For example, images for a press normally target a narrower tonal range than images being prepared for fine-art output on an inkjet printer, because a press can't reproduce as many colors and tones.

You can also set the target value for the midtone eyedropper. While you might want to leave it at a perfect 50 percent (or 127, 127, 127 in RGB notation), you can adjust the preference when you want images to be a little warmer or cooler than neutral.

Or, Why Not Procrastinate?

If you aren't completely happy with the tone and color controls in your scanning software, or if you don't think the preview's good enough for you to make accurate decisions, don't bother making your corrections in that software. Conrad prefers to make color corrections using Photoshop's color tools, like many users. After all, if you're going to wind up in Photoshop anyway, why waste time in the scanning software? The goal before and during the scan then becomes getting the basic adjustments right (like the initial tonal range of all channels); postpone all of the fine-tuning until the image is opened in your favorite image editor.

Apply Digital Restoration and Enhancements

For years, scanner manufacturers concentrated on a rather literal transfer of an image from analog reality to digital virtuality. Scanning software was designed to reproduce the original as faithfully as possible. "But isn't that the entire point?" we can hear you say. Generally, yes, but scans can also be too faithful, reproducing every film scratch, every speck of dust you didn't quite wipe off the scanner, and the unfortunate fading and color shifts of a slide stored for decades in less-than-ideal conditions. Let's look at each of these new features in turn that can correct for problems in the media and scanner.

Defect Removal

As scanning hardware became a commodity and scanning software became more refined and mature, manufacturers started looking for new ways to stand out in the market. One result was the development of *defect removal* as a way for scanners to be "new and improved."

Many users were naturally suspicious of defect removal claims, because older dust-and-scratches filters were rather crude, destroying image detail or tonal data along with the defects and often not worth the trouble. But many current implementations of scanner-based defect removal actually detect and eliminate dust, scratches, and fading while preserving image quality. It's an amazing feature, which makes it possible to use images that might not have been worth the time to salvage in the past. Along the same lines, scanning manufacturers have added convenience features like sharpening.

Ideally, your scanning software should let you control the intensity of the digital restoration and enhancement features, instead of simply turning them on or off. To determine the correct setting, start with a low value and increase the value until the image loses too much real detail, then back off. For a feature like defect removal, you may not be able to wipe out all defects without softening the image too much. To preserve image quality, try using a setting that removes the majority of problems, and then take care of the few remaining defects using manual tools like the Healing Brush in Photoshop.

Recall when we explained how exposure is performed by the sensor in hardware and auto contrast is done in software? Well, defect removal falls into either category, too, depending on whether it's applied during or after the scan.

Hardware-based. The best defect removal features analyze the physical characteristics of the original. For example, the physical characteristics of a scratch are completely different than the physical characteristics of

Defect removal is one of those features that each company names differently to make it sound like they're the only ones who have this option. Nikon and Minolta use a technology called Digital ICE, LaserSoft's software approach is GANE (Grain and Noise Elimination), Canon calls theirs FARE, and so on. The acronym you encounter isn't as important as whether the scanner uses hardware-based defect removal, which is the feature you want..

undamaged film emulsion. To a hardware-based system, a scratch appears as a 3-D canyon in what would normally be a relatively flat surface. If a scanner can detect the difference, the scratch can be subtracted from the image with little danger that it was mistaken for an actual part of the image (**Figure 5-17**). This is best done in hardware, because that's when the original can be analyzed in three dimensions.

When you scan an image as an RGB file, all you have is a flat set of color values, making it much harder for software to tell the difference between a dust speck and an actual specular highlight that should not be removed.

Hardware-based defect removal lengthens scanning time. If you know there are just one or two little specks in the image, it might be faster to remove them yourself in your image editor.

Software-based. Some types of defect removal work in software on a file that's already scanned. They use clever algorithms to attempt to recognize the characteristics of the image content so that they can get rid of anything in the image that doesn't match. For example, most of a scanned film image will have a grain pattern, but a scratch won't, so the software recognizes the scratch isn't part of the image. As we've explained, hardware-based defect removal is much better at recognizing what's really a defect, but recent versions of software have improved a bit.

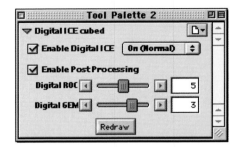

Figure 5-17 Before and after applying Digital ICE

Software-based approaches still tend to soften images too much, removing detail along with defects, grain, and noise.

Dust and scratch removal. Hardware-based dust and scratch removal attempts to identify artifacts that aren't part of the image by analyzing the physical characteristics of the original being scanned. Some scanners (such as the Nikon film scanners) remove defects by scanning an infrared channel in addition to the red, green, and blue channels. This infrared channel contains the additional information necessary for the scanning software to distinguish actual film content from things on the film (like dust) or damage to the film (like scratches).

You receive superior results from hardware-based dust and scratch removal, but there are specific cases where infrared dust-and-scratch removal isn't effective. Infrared analysis doesn't work well with silver-based black-and-white film, because infrared defect removal looks for physical deviations from a smooth film emulsion. With silver-based films, the actual silver

Your scanning software may be able to save the infrared defect data in an extra channel included with the uncorrected original scan. Because excessive defect removal can soften the image, this technique lets you experiment with defect removal settings without tedious re-scanning. VueScan can both save an infrared channel with a scan and read that channel for later defect removal. See "Plug-in or Standalone?" later in this chapter.

grains appear as large boulders compared to the rather flat dyes used in color films. The scans end up looking too poor to use unless you turn off the feature.

Some types of infrared defect removal are also less effective with Kodachrome film, because the layers of Kodachrome dye are relatively thick compared to other film types, so as the sensor does its infrared scan across different colors and tones, it sees cliffs and valleys. If you want to shoot film that works with infrared defect removal, you should probably test it first. For black and white, consider shooting chromogenic (non-silver) black-and-white film such as Kodak T400CN, or shooting using non-Kodachrome color film and converting to black and white.

When some defects require a level of defect removal that would soften or damage the rest of the image more than you'd like, you can use techniques that let you apply different amounts of defect removal to various areas in the same image (see "Handling Specific Areas" in Chapter 14, *Freshening Up).*

Plug-ins. When hardware-based defect removal isn't an option, you might try a plug-in such as Polaroid's Dust and Scratch Removal software. The Polaroid plug-in is free, and you can install it as both a standalone application and a Photoshop-compatible plug-in. You do have to watch your settings carefully; because it's a software-based solution, it can unintentionally remove real detail and specular highlights. You can download the Polaroid software from **www.polaroid.com/service/software/poladsr/poladsr.html**.

 Polaroid has discontinued its own line of scanners, so it's unclear how long the company will provide this software.

Tone and Color Restoration

Clever engineers have come up with two broadly defined methods to manipulate the scanning process to help solve problems with old or difficult originals: restoring color from faded dyes and capturing a broader tonal range.

Fade and color restoration. Film dyes can fade in just a few years, depending on the quality of processing and film storage, and each dye color fades at a different rate. When images are balanced by analyzing the film base or by using data about a film type you selected, faded colors might not be corrected if the condition of the color dyes isn't taken into account. Color restoration attempts to rebalance image color. Some methods adjust color levels based on the typical fade rates of each dye color. When performed in software, this involves resetting the highlight, shadow, and midtone values. But as with dust and scratch removal, color restoration works much better when performed in hardware because the actual exposure of each color channel can be adjusted to compensate for fading, providing the best channel data to work with in the software.

Wide tonal range processing. An original with a very wide tonal range can be difficult to scan. For example, your original might be of a person wearing dark clothing in the shadowed doorway of a building with white stucco walls, and you want to keep a range of detail all the way from light to dark. On lesser scanners, the tonal range of the original might be wider than the sensor can capture, so a single scan would clip highlights, shadows, or both. Even on better scanners, the sensor might not be able to maintain the same level of image quality from the highlights to the deep shadows.

Some scanning utilities have an option to scan the same image at two different exposures: One optimized to make sure highlights are included, and the other optimized to include all shadow detail. The utility then merges the two scans, combining both scans' highlight and shadow information into a single image. This is a tricky operation that your scanning software may or may not handle well. If you don't like the results, you can do it manually in an image editor by making the same scan at two different manual exposures, layering the two images, and then using masking or erasing techniques to combine them. In VueScan, this option is called Long Exposure Pass.

Noise Reduction

Grain and digital noise are not helpful when you're making a super-sized enlargement or when you're aiming for the best possible image quality. Fortunately, scanner companies have been working on this problem as well, adding the following features that help take care of these issues.

Multi-sampling (noise reduction). Noise creeps into just about all analog-to-digital converters, like the sensor in your scanner. Noise is most visible in shadow areas. Generally, the more you pay for the scanner, the less noise you have to put up with. Different methods exist to try and reduce noise, but one particularly effective technique is called *multi-sampling*: The sensor measures each part of the image multiple times, and then averages the values to minimize any randomness introduced by noise. Scanners typically support up to 16x multisampling, but scanning every part of your original 16 times is very slow—especially at the scanner's maximum resolution. Settings between 4x and 8x seem to provide the best return relative to the extra time it takes; try higher values only if there's still too much noise.

Multiple pass scanning. This technique is similar to multi-sampling—the difference is subtle but easy to understand. In multiple-pass scanning, the sensor scans the entire crop area once before making a second pass. With multi-sampling, the sensor scans the same spot multiple times before moving on. Multi-sampling is generally better, because of possible issues with scanner alignment. If the sensor doesn't move while it takes multiple samples, you know the three samples are really from the same spot. But if the sensor travels all the way across the crop area before returning, as in multiple pass scanning, there's a chance that the motor didn't position the sensor in exactly the same place. Use multiple-pass scanning only when the scanner doesn't support multi-sampling.

Grain removal. Because grain is actually part of an image and not a defect (depending on your personal aesthetic), grain removal is more of a digital enhancement than a restoration. If removal is adjustable, it usually works best at low, subtle settings. Higher settings can soften the image too much, resulting in the feature taking out actual image texture along with the grain.

Sharpening

We talk about sharpening in Chapter 15, *A Sharper Image*, but here are some basic guidelines for sharpening at the scanning stage. In general, you don't need to sharpen at this point, and if you convince yourself you do, don't sharpen very much at all. Sharpening is one of the final steps before output, so you don't want to sharpen before you have done any necessary editing or correction (if any).

There is, however, one reason to sharpen the scan within the scanning software. Digitizing an image can make it softer than the original, because on many scanners, the red, green, and blue sensor arrays are offset. That means two green sensors aren't right next to each other, but instead are interspersed with the red and blue sensors. It's that gap that can cause softening. For this reason, some people like to apply a very tiny smidgen of sharpening as they scan, *only* for the purpose of restoring the original's sharpness. Even if you decide to make this particular correction, postpone full, output-based sharpening until later in the process.

Make the Final Scan

When you think you're ready to press the Scan button, it's a good idea to double-check your settings. It's a waste of time to wait for a high-quality scan to finish, only to discover that one of your settings was wrong. If your scanning software lets you save settings to a file, consider that option so you don't have to remember exactly how you set up a particular scan.

 Some scanning software may prompt you to name the final scan so it can save it; for some naming advice, see Chapter 4, Getting Your Computer Ready for Scans.

If you're about to scan a large image or a batch of images, you may want to make sure you have enough free disk space to store the new scans.

When everything checks out, go for it. Small, individual scans can be made quickly, but if you started a high-bit, high-resolution, multipass scan or a batch of film scans, many minutes may pass—take a break while the scanner does its thing.

Other Production Options

Even though you might think we've comprehensively covered all of the features in

scanning software and hardware controls, there are a few more in each category that you should be aware of.

Additional Software Options

Although the features in the following list aren't essential to basic image quality, some of them can be useful for production.

Batch scanning. If you're scanning multiple images, batch features can save a lot of time and labor in loading. Some scanners can automatically feed and scan all of the frames in a filmstrip, or a stack of slides. Some flatbeds let you arrange a number of small originals (like snapshots) as a grid on the scanning glass and can automatically save each original to a separate file. And of course, some flatbed scanners have automatic document feeders that work like the ones on photocopiers, so that you can load a stack of paper or 4-by-6–inch prints, walk away, and come back to a computer full of scans, automatically numbered and saved.

Automatic naming and numbering. If you're scanning multiple images, it's handy to have those scans named consistently or numbered sequentially' use automatic naming or numbering to handle that task. Many scanning utilities increment file names by default (Image_01, Image_02, and so on) so that you don't accidentally overwrite your previous scan. (We also discuss using automatic filenaming features as part of an overall file-naming strategy in Chapter 4, *Getting Your Computer Ready for Scans.*)

Output folder. Instead of letting the scanner save files into its own default folder and then having to move the files to their final destination, you might want to have them saved to a folder you already use for image production.

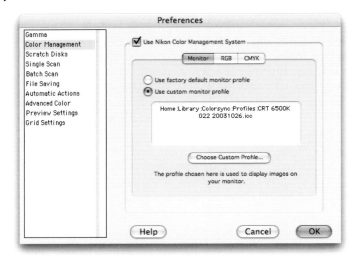

Figure 5-18
ICC profile support
in NikonScan

ICC scanner and monitor profiles. If you're comfortable using ICC-based color management and you have a color profile that accurately describes the scanner's color space, see if your scanning software supports color management (**Figure 5-18**). If you don't have a good scanner profile, don't use this option at all; it can do more harm than good. You can make a profile for a scanner if you have a profiling target. For more information about color management and profiling, see Chapter 13, *Getting Good Color*.

Raw file support. Serious digital-camera users are already hip to the advantages of a raw-file workflow, where the raw sensor output is saved directly to disk without being processed by the camera or its software. Some scanners and scanning utilities also support this workflow, letting you save the sensor's raw scan data without applying the tone and color controls in the scanning software. This is only for experts who know what they might need to adjust in a raw file.

If you're happy with the tone and color correction tools in your scanning software, you probably don't need to concern yourself with raw-file workflows. But if you feel that your scanning software's own image processing removes too much quality from your scan, you might want to study your scanner's raw-file capabilities.

Saved settings/presets. The more options your scanner has, the harder it is to keep them straight. Maybe you scanned half a roll of film three weeks ago, and you want to finish scanning that roll now. If you don't have a record of the settings that worked, you might have to spend time testing and working them out all over again, hoping to match the previous results. If your scanning software lets you save the current settings, you can easily reproduce old scanning jobs.

Every time Conrad scans a roll of film, he does a quick draft-quality scan of some frames on the roll, and then saves a settings file named after that roll. Later, if there's a frame he wants to enlarge, he just has to load up the settings saved for that roll. All that's left to do is adjust the settings to increase the quality (for example, by increasing resolution and multi-sampling values) and hit the Scan button again.

Other Scanner Hardware Options

We've already discussed options that actually alter the behavior of the scanner software, such as exposure and infrared defect removal. There are a couple more options that you don't normally have to deal with, but you should know that they're there.

Hardware calibration. Many scanners periodically calibrate their light source to compensate for the slight shifts in color temperature that can happen as a light source ages. You may not notice automatic calibration when it happens, because it may be a regular part of a scanner's startup routine. By the time you have your original positioned and are back in front of the computer, the scanner has usually taken care of any startup tasks it needs to do.

Many scanner utilities provide a calibration command so that you can manually run the calibration procedure. You can try this if you notice a fundamental degradation in the scanner's reproduction of tones and colors.

 Hardware calibration is not the same as profiling the scanner, which we talk about in Chapter 13, Getting Good Color.

Focus. Just about all scanners have autofocusing, which they perform automatically by comparing the contrast of adjacent pixels in certain areas or lines and increasing and decreasing the focus setting until contrast is at maximum. However, you might sometimes see a scan that's still out of focus. Your scanner utility may have a command that lets you run the autofocus procedure at any time.

Some of the higher-end scanning utilities also provide manual focus control, which usually involves a slider or value that you enter. Some utilities, like VueScan, let you specify the location within the frame where the scanner should be in focus. This can help with curled film originals that go out of focus towards their edges or when scanning three-dimensional objects on a flatbed.

Plug-in or Standalone?

Depending on the scanning software that comes with your scanner, you may have two options for scanning images into your computer: using a Photoshop plug-in or a standalone scanning utility.

If your workflow requires one method or the other, see what your scanning software supports. While some software can run as either a plug-in or a standalone utility, others function only as one or the other.

TWAIN and Photoshop Plug-ins

Scanning software can be provided as a Photoshop-compatible plug-in—a software module that adds a new scanning menu command to Photoshop or any program that can use Photoshop plug-ins (many image editors can). When you scan with a Photoshop plug-in, the completed scan opens as a new image in Photoshop. This is obviously very convenient if you spend your whole day in Photoshop anyway.

 Photoshop requires a lot of RAM to start with, and when you use plug-ins, they increase the amount of RAM Photoshop needs. Also, you usually can't use Photoshop to edit other images while the plug-in is open.

A more commonly found plug-in supports TWAIN, which is a widely supported consistent standard that allows any software program that uses the TWAIN interface to access scanners. TWAIN plug-ins can be used in Photoshop via its TWAIN module. The TWAIN approach lets a scanner software developer write a single acquire module that works with any TWAIN-enabled program, from image editors to word processors.

Under Windows, you are more likely to find a plain TWAIN module because

 In our minds—and in our books—TWAIN has always stood for its original expansion as Technology Without An Important Name, but the TWAIN group claims TWAIN don't stand for nothin'. Either way, it's a great concept, and one carried out with some degree of success.

of the large variety of desktop-publishing applications that support it as opposed to Adobe's dominance on the Mac.

Under Mac OS X, TWAIN support has been built into the operating system since version 10.2, and the Image Capture utility takes advantage of scanners that come with TWAIN data sources.

Standalone Software

With a standalone utility, you use the scanning software as a separate program that you start up to begin scanning. Completed scans can either be opened immediately in your image editor or automatically saved to a folder on your disk. A standalone utility can be operated separately from your image editor. This is great if you want to edit images in Photoshop while the scanning utility scans away in the background, or if you don't want huge tracts of RAM to be occupied by Photoshop just so you can use the scanner.

When scanning in bulk, the ability to automatically name, save, and close each scan as it's completed is a great plus. If you're scanning with a plug-in that can only leave completed scans open in Photoshop, and you've loaded a bulk slide loader with 50 slides to scan, it may result in 50 open image windows in Photoshop. This can take up an awful lot of RAM, potentially slow down the whole machine, and leave a lot of unsaved data vulnerable in the event that there's a crash before you get around to saving all the images.

Alternative Standalone Software

If you don't like the software that comes with your scanner, you may not have to use it. The included software might be too hard to use, might lack certain professional-level controls, or might not even be available for the operating system you're using. Alternative scanning utilities can fill these gaps and many aren't tied to any scanner manufacturer.

In addition, some people like to use alternative software because they own multiple scanners and want to use a single user interface to run them all, instead of having to remember the subtle differences between each scanner's own software.

Here are some independent scanning utilities you might want to check out.

LaserSoft SilverFast (`silverfast.com`). Many professionals like SilverFast's deep feature set, which has enough control and precision to make production-ready scans straight from the software. SilverFast comes in different flavors that are optimized for specific scanners, so you need to buy the version of SilverFast that's specifically engineered for your scanner. SilverFast also has special versions for high-bit scanning, digital cameras, and other specialized workflows. Because it's geared to professionals, SilverFast is generally developed for higher-end film and flatbed scanners, and not for inexpensive consumer scanners.

VueScan (`hamrick.com`). Available in Standard and Professional editions, this software doesn't really look like any other scanning utility on the market. It's not "pretty" like many of the easy-but-limited utilities that come with consumer scanners, so it can be hard to learn. But people who like to use VueScan tend to be quite loyal, due to the rather impressive breadth and depth of VueScan's capabilities.

VueScan can run almost any scanner; it has a long list of devices it supports, including orphaned products no longer currently supported. VueScan runs under recent versions of Mac OS, Windows, and Linux, and provides access to almost all of a scanner's features, sometimes giving access to features not supported by the scanner's own software. The developer constantly updates the software for new scanners and features, too.

Operating System Support

Mac OS X and Windows XP come with utilities that represent yet another way to scan images out of your scanner if it's supported via TWAIN or other drivers. Mac OS X includes the Image Capture application, and Windows XP provides the Scanner and Camera Wizard.

These system utilities are aimed at home and consumer users: they are very basic, and they don't provide the amount of control that we believe you are trying to achieve by reading this book. You're better off using the software that comes with the scanner or the more professional packages mentioned earlier.

You Want That Pre-Cooked or Raw?

The fundamental trade-off in this chapter is whether to use Adobe Photoshop or a similar program to handle all of your adjustments, or to rely in part or whole on your scanning software. Let's review your options:

Make the scanning software do everything. If your scanning software's controls are good enough to produce final output without further work in an image editor, you might be able to do all of your adjustments without an image editor. This workflow works best when your scanning software is superb; that is, capable of accurate, high-quality previews and supporting color management so that you can take advantage of scanner, monitor, and printer ICC profiles.

You'll also need to configure the scanning software so that it produces final files exactly the way you need them. For example, if your job is to scan photographs for reproduction on a printing press, make sure the software is capable of exactly the CMYK conversion your printer dictates, which may require that the software supports conversion using a CMYK profile of the press or proofing standard. If you can successfully go this route, you should be able to use the time-honored settings for scanning: 8 bits of raw RGB scan data, processed and converted in the scanning software, with the image for final output converted to press CMYK and saved.

Send a raw file to the image editor. Your project might have output standards that outstrip the capabilities of your scanning software, or you might have a strong familiarity and preference for your image editor's capabilities and editing interface. If you want your scanning software to have a minimal role, you can set up a raw-file workflow: In your scanning software, make sure the exposure is correct, convert a negative scan to positive (if necessary), and apply restoration or defect removal options—but don't bother adjusting tone or color settings.

In many cases, this workflow works better if you set the scanning and output bit depth to more than 8 bits (typically 16 bits), because you're probably going to make some major adjustments in your image editor. When the scan is done, open it in your image editor and make your tone and color corrections there, using the steps in Part 3 of this book, *Image Correction*. After you've completed all major corrections, convert the file to 8 bits per channel before preparing the image for final output.

Split the difference. It's not always easy to make scanning software do everything well, from scanning through editing and final output. On the other hand, image editors like Photoshop are extremely capable, but it can be a real challenge to manually interpret uncorrected data that's fresh out of a scanner. You'll probably find that the best solution involves letting the scanning software do what it does best (maybe it's very good at converting color negative scans, for instance), and then using your image editor to take the image the rest of the way.

When splitting the workflow, remember to preserve image quality. The fewer corrections you plan to make in the scanning software, the more you should consider scanning and sending a 16-bit file to the image editor. If you're leaving major changes to the image-editing stage, tonal and color quality is more likely to survive if you scan a 16-bit image. On the other hand, the closer you can get to the final image in the scanning software, the more you can save disk space by sending it to the image editor as an 8-bit file, because you'll only need to apply minor changes in the image editor.

One common hybrid workflow is to send a quick low-resolution scan to Photoshop, use Photoshop's more powerful tools to work out the corrections, and then send the correction data back to the scanning software to make a properly adjusted final scan. This is possible because some scanning utilities can read and write Photoshop curve files. You'll find Save and Load options in dialog boxes such as Levels and Curves in Photoshop, and in corresponding dialog boxes in some scanning utilities. Use a Photoshop dialog box's Save button to create a file containing the adjustment, then use a Load option in a scanning utility's dialog box to open and apply the adjustment from Photoshop.

6

Scanning for Prepress

MAKING A GOOD IMPRESSION

Even with advances in high-volume digital printers, the printing press remains the best way to output thousands or millions of printed pieces because offset printing provides excellent tonal and color reproduction with a correspondingly high level of consistency. To take best advantage of offset printing, all of the elements that go into your printed piece—fonts, imported graphics, and images—need to start out at a high quality, and then be adjusted further for the idiosyncrasies of a printing press.

While the recommendations we provide are typical, the exact information you need varies for different combinations of prepress software, imagesetters, presses, papers, and inks. Always discuss your job and workflow with your prepress service provider—they know how to make files work best with their equipment and workflow. They can point out opportunities for saving you time and money, and for improving the quality of your job. Similarly, they can steer you away from creating poorly prepared files that can cost you in terms of time, money, and quality.

Guidelines for the Initial Scan

Images you scan for prepress need to have enough resolution to support the screen frequency of the final output, and contain a color range that can accommodate and make best use of the press's color space.

Prepress *is the term for the preparatory stage prior to printing, when your service bureau receives and prepares your layout, image, and font files so that they'll run perfectly on press.*

> *Adobe InDesign, QuarkXPress, and Adobe Page-Maker have a Print dialog box option that automatically downsamples image resolution to two times the screen frequency at print time. This option can be useful when proofing document text on laser printers: the job prints faster when less data goes down the cable. In general, however, it's better to use your image-editing program to resample images to the appropriate size and resolution before importing them into your layout program.*

Because prepress output requires high quality, you need to ensure that the best possible image data makes it out of the scanner via its scanning software and into your image editor (**Figure 6-1**).

We look at, in turn, resolution, bit depth, and color model and color space, as well as the best file format to save in.

Resolution

Your service bureau should be able to provide you with their recommended output resolution for your scans based on the final screen frequency that your printer uses to reproduce halftoned color and grayscale images. (You can get an idea of the typical ranges of screen frequencies for common reproduction methods in *Chapter 21, Frequency vs. Gray Levels.*)

Most service bureaus recommend scanning images at a resolution value that's 1.5 to 2 times the screen frequency value; ask your printer for their preferred formula. If your job will be printed at a screen frequency of 150 lines per inch, you probably need to scan for an output resolution of no more than 300 samples per inch at the image's final output size.

Ultimately, only images that have very fine detail—like line art, rigging on a sail-boat, or a baby's hair—need resolution higher than 1.5 times lpi. In these cases, you can lose image detail at lower resolutions, and run into two other quality problems: aliasing and mottling. You can also use a workaround to avoid a problem with line art at any ratio.

Aliasing. Hard diagonal edges in lower-resolution images often display aliasing, or jaggies. A sailing ship's rigging in front of a bright sky, for instance, can often look quite "stair-steppy" at lower resolutions. This effect is accentuated by sharpening. If hard diagonal edges or fine lines, like those found in a baby's hair, make up important elements in the image, you should consider using a higher resolution.

Mottling. Lower-resolution scans can sometimes display mottling in areas of smooth gradation. In people's faces, it looks like a poor complexion. This is mainly a problem with scans from lower-quality scanners that have a lot of noise—usually, samples in uniform gray areas that don't match their surroundings. Since sharpening works by accentuating the differences between adjacent light and dark pixels, it increases the mottled effect. The solution is a higher-resolution scan.

Line art. If you're scanning line art—art without gray shades or colors—scan the art at the resolution of the final output device, up to around 1200 spi. Above that resolution, the slowdown in processing that many pixels starts to outweigh any perceptible increase in sharpness. To increase performance on imagesetters, you can try scanning line art at one half, one quarter, or one eighth of the final output resolu-

Figure 6-1 From scanner to image editor

Scanner hardware — Scanner software — Image editing software — Press

tion. If you're creating output at 2400 dpi, you can try 600 or 1200 dpi as your final size. (For more tips, see "Line Art," later in this chapter.)

Bit Depth

For images that don't need much correction, scan at a bit depth of 8 bits per channel. If an image requires extreme adjustments, consider scanning it at 16 bits per channel. If you go the 16-bit route, you'll probably need to convert the image down to 8 bits per channel before you create final output or import it into other applications because not all programs can support 16-bit channels. While it may make sense to scan line art in bitmap or line art mode, you can sometimes achieve better results by scanning line art in 8-bit grayscale; we explain why in "Line Art," later in this chapter.

Color Model and Color Space

When you scan color images, you can decide at the outset whether to scan directly into CMYK mode for the printing press or to scan into a more generic RGB that lets you create both press and on-screen images from a single source file. Let's compare the two models.

CMYK. If you decide to scan into CMYK, make sure you scan into the right kind of CMYK—inks and press conditions vary. Get the proper CMYK specifications from your service bureau. If your scanning software lets you specify an ICC profile as the output color space, and if your service bureau can provide an accurate CMYK profile for their press, you might be able to scan images directly into the press color space. This method works best when the image will only be reproduced on that particular press, and not used for other purposes (Web, video, framed inkjet prints, and so on).

Scanning into CMYK forever constrains the colors of the image to the restricted CMYK gamut. This is not a good idea if you also need to use the image in RGB color spaces that can reproduce more colors.

For example, CMYK doesn't produce a wide range of blues, so if the image has brilliant blue skies and you want to use it in an RGB-based medium like the Web or a computer slide show, the blue skies in a CMYK source image are unlikely to be anywhere near as intense as the original.

RGB. By scanning into RGB, you can create both press and Web versions of the image without excessively compromising color fidelity in either medium. If you plan to edit the image further, many image editor features that work in RGB don't work in CMYK mode. Finally, RGB images may take up less disk space than CMYK images, because RGB images have three color channels (one per color) instead of CMYK's four.

For a chart listing your color model options, take a look at workflows A, B, and D in **Figure 13-1** in Chapter 13, *Getting Good Color*. Workflow A is also a traditional workflow from a drum scanner where the scanner operator scans into CMYK.

File Format

Save your scans in TIFF or Photoshop (PSD) format. Both are tried-and-true formats for prepress. They preserve the level of quality that's required for a printing press, and they support the CMYK color model. Although Photoshop can open both TIFF and PSD files, you should scan into the PSD format if you plan to save the image with Photoshop-specific features.

Because it's widely supported, TIFF is a safer choice if you'll be using the image in many other print design applications. You can also reduce storage space or transmis-

Drum Scanners and CMYK

You might hear older drum-scanner operators insist on scanning as CMYK. This was the preferred workflow in the past, when the majority of images were headed for a specific press in a specific shop. But more flexible workflows (like workflow D in **Figure 13-4**) are now popular for scanned images that also need to be output on devices with a wider color space than the press. In these newer workflows, you scan once into a working RGB space that's large enough to accommodate your anticipated output color spaces, edit the image, and then convert copies of the image into each output path's color space.

You might also run into someone who insists that drum scanners are CMYK scanners. This may appear to be true at first glance, because prepress scanners typically output CMYK data. In traditional prepress scanners, the RGB-to-CMYK conversion may be done in hardware, which can lead to the illusion that it actually scans in CMYK. But all scanners use RGB sensors, regardless of the output they create—there's no such thing as a CMYK sensor.

This may seem like incidental trivia, but it's actually an important point: Because the color characteristics of the scanning hardware are always different than the color characteristics of the output device, there is always a conversion from the scanner's own RGB color space to the output color space, even if you can't see or control the conversion directly.

sion time by using TIFF's built-in lossless compression; some service bureaus ask you to turn compression off.

Use other file formats only if your service bureau recommends them.

Preparing the Final, Corrected Image

After an image is initially scanned and edited, you need to adjust it for the following conditions of the CMYK press where it will be printed (**Figure 6-2**).

▶ Spot gain and loss

▶ Upper and lower tint limits

▶ Black replacement

There are two ways to adjust for those three sets of conditions. If your service bureau supports a color-managed workflow, you may be able to adjust your image simply by converting it using the offset press's CMYK profile. If your printer hasn't built color management profiles, your service bureau should be able to give you instructions about making these adjustments manually in your scanning software or image editor, using features like the Levels or Curves dialog boxes. Chapter 12, *Tonal Correction*, describes these adjustments in more detail.

There are also two places in the workflow where you can make these adjustments. If you're using powerful, precise scanning software like SilverFast, you may be able to produce a prepress-ready image within your scanning software. Otherwise, plan to open your scans in your image editor and do your final preparations there.

Color Conversions

If you have images with highly saturated colors, you may find—as we noted earlier—that some colors don't translate well to CMYK, such as deep blue. It's possible to let your scanning software or image editor simply apply its default conversion to CMYK, but this can cause deeply out-of-gamut colors to be either clipped or compressed depending on how you do the conversion. If these results aren't satisfactory, you may need to reduce the saturation of these colors using a feature like Photoshop's Hue/Saturation command.

Figure 6-2 From editing to press

Scanner hardware   Scanner software   Image editing software   Press

Because these issues are related to using halftones to render tones and colors, we describe these factors in more detail in Chapter 22, Reproducing Halftones.

If your image editor has a soft-proofing feature, you can use it to preview the effect that converting to CMYK will have on the colors in the image. In Photoshop, the Proof Colors command can do this well if you have accurate profiles of your monitor and your output conditions (such as an output profile representing SWOP CMYK inks on your press on the exact paper stock you'll use).

Sharpening

Prepress images are probably the highest-resolution images you create on a routine basis, but the halftoning or dithering process tends to soften images. For these two reasons—the large amount of data in your original image and the softening process—you can generally use more aggressive final sharpening settings than you would with screen-resolution images. An image that's properly sharpened for a press usually looks a little too sharp on screen, which can make it hard to judge when you've got it right. Chapter 15, *A Sharper Image*, provides sharpening examples that we created at prepress resolutions.

The more important the print job is, the more helpful it is to have your service bureau run a test print of a sheet containing the same image at various sharpening settings. That way you can see which settings work best under your press conditions. We've averted disasters and improved our results by requesting a press test.

Line Art

In Chapter 5, *How to Read Your Scanning Software,* we talk about line-art images. These are always black and white; each sample point in the image is described with one bit of information. Bilevel scans are great for reproducing straightforward line drawings, and even images as complex as the finely etched pictures in those old-fashioned Dover clip-art books.

To achieve line-art quality approaching that of photographic reproduction, and to avoid the jaggy look (**Figure 6-3**), you need very high resolution and sharpening. We

Figure 6-3 Jaggy edges in line art reduced as resolution increases

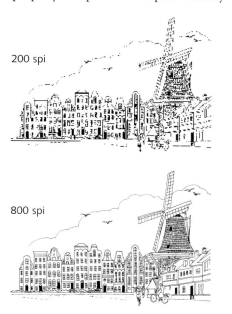

200 spi

800 spi

400 spi

1200 spi

We talk about soft-proofing and profile-based color conversions in Chapter 13, Getting Good Color, or you can find a much more thorough explanation in Real World Color Management.

discuss sharpening in Chapter 15, *A Sharper Image* (but we will say here that sharpening improves line-art scans *dramatically*). We'll cover the details of line-art resolution here. To preserve or enhance the quality of line art, use either or both of the following techniques.

Large originals. A simple solution for quality line art is to use large original art. Scan at your scanner's maximum resolution, and then scale the image down in your page-layout software, increasing the resolution (or, if your scanning software lets you, scale the image down and raise the resolution in one fell swoop at scan time). If your original art isn't big enough, you can enlarge it photographically (even using a high-quality photocopier) with minimal loss of quality. (Photocopiers generally use lenses to enlarge art, which avoids jaggies you'd get digitally.)

Cool grayscale-to-line-art workaround. You'd never think this technique would work, but it does. This method uses the extra information captured in a grayscale scan, and converts that information into higher-resolution line art. You can actually increase your line-art resolution by a factor of two over your scanner's true optical resolution by using this technique.

Figure 6-4 Cool grayscale-to-line-art workaround

1

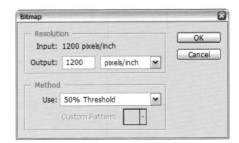

2

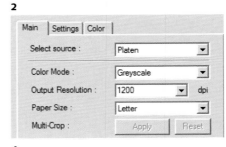

3

4

Because today's scanners can usually match the output resolution of an image-setter, this technique is now used primarily to control the overall line weight and edge smoothness of line art. Our thanks to Rob Cook for explaining this technique. See **Figure 6-4** for the settings and controls to use in Photoshop. Here's the step-by-step procedure.

1 Scan the image in grayscale mode at the resolution of your output device; we assume 1200 spi for this example.

2 Sharpen the image using your image program's unsharp mask filter, setting Amount to 500 percent, Radius to 1 for Photoshop and 2 for most other programs, and Threshold to 5. (See Chapter 15, *A Sharper Image,* if you haven't used unsharp mask before.) You may need to increase the Radius or Amount at higher resolutions.

3 Use the threshold control to adjust the level where gray pixels jump to white or black. This control will make the lines thinner and thicker in the process. Aim for a value that's above the point where lines break up and below the point where spaces between lines block up.

4 Convert the image to black and white with the 50-percent threshold option selected if your image-editing program offers it. You've already turned everything into 0 or 100 percent with the threshold feature; converting to black and white simply freezes that change into the file.

5 Finally, convert to a black-and-white bitmap. If your image editor won't let you convert the art to a bitmap, try converting it using a flattened grayscale copy of the file.

You can also use this technique to increase your line-art resolution by up to a factor of two over your scanner's true optical resolution by resampling the image to the higher resolution before you perform the sharpening step. Note that some scanning software packages provide a feature called *interpolation* that performs this process automatically. While we don't encourage the use of interpolation for grayscale and color images, interpolation can benefit 1-bit line art.

Keeping Tints and Lines Printable

If you're preparing images for a press, you may need to adjust the images' output levels so that the resulting image doesn't include highlight or shadow dots that can't be reproduced on press (see Chapter 22, *Reproducing Halftones*).

Similarly, you may need to make sure line widths are above the minimum width below which point they would disappear on certain paper stocks. **Table 6-1** shows typical ranges for three classes of printing paper. The second column performs the arithmetic for you, noting which output levels you should specify in the Levels dialog box in Photoshop (**Figure 12-9** in Chapter 12). The principle applies to any scanning or image-editing software with a similar function.

Table 6-1 Output level settings for press

Printing Stock	Percent Range	Output Levels	Minimum line width
Newsprint	12–88	30–225	0.75 pt
Uncoated stock	10–90	25–230	0.5 pt
Coated stock	5–95	12–243	0.3 pt

These values are guidelines; talk to your printer to determine the best settings for their equipment and paper.

If your service bureau or printer uses color management and ICC profiles, you may not need to limit your images' output levels. If in doubt, consult with them.

Hitting the Sweet Spot

Aiming for the press involves well-known, easily quantifiable and profile-able properties, which have been perfected over time. In the next chapter, *Scanning for the Web and Video*, we look at fuzzier final results that make scanning more challenging.

Scanning for the Web and Video

FOR A GLOWING REVIEW

If you're used to scanning for print, scanning for on-screen media like Web pages and digital video requires a mind-set that may seem upside down and backwards. As an output medium, video involves transmissive light that reaches the retina directly instead of the reflected and absorptive light of print. The color models follow accordingly: RGB instead of CMYK.

Your scan may be viewed on a wide range of monitors—most of which are probably not adjusted correctly—rather than a fixed and calibrated output medium like paper printed on a profiled offset press. There are no halftones, color separations, or spot gain—but these issues are replaced by another set of considerations. Even the term *screen* has a different meaning than in print.

In this chapter, we introduce you to the new terminology and concerns that will allow you to start out with your best foot forward and avoid washed out, overcorrected, undersaturated images that don't take advantage of these transmissive media.

From Toner to Liquid Crystal

When desktop scanning started to gain momentum in the 1980s, it was driven by desktop publishing—the newfangled ability to create entire pages that combined graphics and good-looking, professional fonts on a desktop computer. And then be able to print them out at 300 dpi on a black-and-white laser printer that only cost…$7,000.

The promise of precise creative control at such a low, low price attracted people like Glenn, David, Steve, and Conrad to desktop publishing. (In fact, most of us based our careers on performing DTP and writing about it.) The desktop scanners of the 1980s could create images that were good enough for printed output for the ultimate target of desktop publishing: quick-print newsletters, offset but low-frequency halftones in newspapers, and coupons and flyers.

In the 1990s, media emerged that didn't have printed output: what you saw on the screen was what you got. We were early adopters of the Web, with Glenn founding a Web design and development company back in 1994. We quickly realized that the World Wide Web would change the scanning equation. With offset or other printing, you can control what the final output looks like, whether it's a print or a run of a million books. With the Web, the screen is the final output—any screen, not just the one on which we were previewing and adjusting the scan.

As we passed the turn of the century, the rapid spread of digital video production and DVD authoring gave us more reasons to scan images with on-screen output in mind. More and more of our art was being viewed without a drop of ink in sight.

We divide on-screen graphics into two categories: Web graphics—and everything else. While these two categories have a lot in common, compression separates them. Web graphics need high levels of compression because they're often sent over the Internet, where bandwidth is an issue even with high-speed connections.

In contrast, most on-screen graphics that aren't headed for the Web are retrieved internally over your computer's high-speed data bus; are converted to analog signals, like traditional TV; or are compressed later in digital video authoring software. None of these paths requires initial compression.

But no matter where your screen graphic is headed, you should go about your initial scanning and image manipulation the same way.

Guidelines for the Initial Scan

The same basic scanning guidelines we use for other initial scans also apply for Web and video scans: start with the output requirements, and then determine the input requirements from there. This makes scanning for the screen a lot easier than scanning for print. The low pixel count of on-screen images results in faster scans that take up less disk space.

To save bandwidth, Web-bound graphics are usually delivered in compressed formats, which are not good formats for editing. To preserve image quality as you bring the scan into your image editor (**Figure 7-1**), scan on-screen graphics using higher quality settings than those needed to create the final output. Screen-bound graphics will retain the higher quality of the scan.

Resolution

To set resolution for images that display on screen, follow the guidelines we provide in step 4 of Chapter 5, *How to Read your Scanning Software*. But use pixel dimensions to specify the output *size*, and ignore the output *resolution* (the dpi

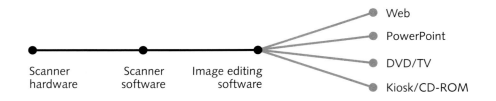

Figure 7-1 From scanner to image editor

Scanner hardware — Scanner software — Image editing software — Web / PowerPoint / DVD/TV / Kiosk/CD-ROM

A beneficial side effect of scanning slightly more pixels than you need for output is that you can use the same source image to generate graphics for just about any screen-based display device, whether it's a television, a monitor showing Web pages, a mobile phone, or a handheld device.

value). Then let the scanning software calculate the scanning resolution needed for the original.

The reason you want to go by pixel dimensions instead of resolution is that resolution has a different meaning for on-screen images than it does for printed images. As we discuss in Chapter 11, *Image Resolution*, measuring on screen in inches or dots per inch isn't reliable because dpi can vary with differences in each monitor's settings. Instead of trying to use resolution in the print sense (dots per inch), use the screen definition of resolution (width by height in pixels). For example, instead of entering output settings like "3-by-2 inches at 96 dpi" into your scanning software, enter dimensions in pixels, such as "300 by 200." The image size will still vary on different monitors, but you can count on the pixel dimensions as a consistent measurement (**Figure 5-6** in Chapter 5).

Similarly, the relationship between dpi and output size is different for print and on-screen display. In print, scanning an original at a higher dpi setting retains more detail in the same physical dimensions, while for on-screen images, scanning an original at a higher dpi setting increases its dimensions. The GIF graphics format used so widely on the Web doesn't even have a place to store a dpi value. Therefore, it sometimes doesn't matter what you enter for dpi, because for on-screen images, one image pixel always corresponds to one screen pixel.

If you haven't quite decided how to crop or size your image, feel free to increase the output pixel dimensions somewhat so that you have some room to work out your final composition. The goal is to avoid ending up with too few pixels.

Bit Depth

In general, you can leave your scanner set to scan at 8 bits per channel. As we describe in Chapter 13, *Getting Good Color*, television sets and most of the monitors used around the world for viewing Web pages are uncalibrated, so if you were to scan at more than 8 bits per channel, few people would notice the difference. If you come across a couple of images that need major tonal or color correction, you can scan those exceptions at more than 8 bits per channel.

If you're scanning images for motion-picture film, DVD, or high-definition television, the tonal and color quality of the final output media actually has a chance of being consistently accurate. For these media, you may be able to benefit from scanning and editing at 10 to 16 bits per channel, because the quality you preserve might actually be noticeable in the final product.

Even though some formats, like GIF, can be saved with fewer than 8 bits per pixel to save bandwidth, you should still leave the scanner set to 8 bits per channel to preserve quality for when you edit

You might be wondering why people say that the Mac OS screen resolution is 72 dpi and the Windows resolution is 96 dpi, and whether your cross-platform images have to account for two different resolutions. Here's the short answer: Don't worry about it. For the reasons we mention in this section, the dpi setting doesn't really apply to images you display on screen. However, these dpi values do play an important role in how each operating system calculates the size of on-screen text. The TidBITS online publication has one of the best explanations of this subject at `http://db.tidbits.com/getbits.acgi?tbart=05284.`

If you're working with black-and-white line art, you may want to try the techniques in the Line Art topic in Chapter 6, Scanning for Prepress, instead of scanning line art at 1 bit per pixel from the start.

the image. Reducing the bit depth should be the last step, which we discuss at great length in the next section, "From Scan to Screen."

Color Model, Color Space, and Color Management

Choosing color settings for Web and television graphics is pretty straightforward: You should scan, edit, and output images using the RGB color model with the sRGB color space. sRGB was designed to describe a typical computer monitor or television set. In addition, sRGB is the color space for high-definition television. We talk about color spaces in Chapter 13, *Getting Good Color*.

The only reason we can think of for scanning into a color space other than sRGB is if you plan to use the same scan as a source file for media with a different color gamut. For example, if you want to scan just once for on-screen and print media, you might scan into the prepress-friendly Adobe RGB color space since it also encompasses most of sRGB.

File Format

On-screen graphics are frequently saved as JPEG or GIF files, particularly for Web pages (**Figure 7-2**). However, when scanning your source files, it's better to scan into a format like TIFF. As we mention in Chapter 16, *File Formats*, JPEG and GIF are lossy, which means they degrade every

time you edit and save them. Lossy formats are best used for final output, not editing. For a clean start and high-quality editing, save your original scans in TIFF or Adobe Photoshop (PSD) format, edit them as needed, and then as needed, save a copy into a lossy format after you've completed editing.

From Scan to Screen

No matter what method your image is output to screen—in a Web browser, a CD-ROM or DVD-ROM multimedia program or game, or a television—the trick is to pick the right optimizations to take the initial scan to its final stages. And that's what we're going to dive into right now.

Resolution

If the image isn't already set to the final on-screen pixel dimensions, change the dimensions just before you save the copy. In your image editor's resizing feature, make sure that the resampling option is turned on so that the pixel dimensions can change. The Save for Web feature found in many of Adobe's Creative Suite applications lets you resample the image directly in the Save for Web dialog box (**Figure 7-3**).

Bit Depth

The issue of bit depth for on-screen images is no longer as critical as it was in the 1990s. Back then, there were far fewer computers that could display 24-bit color (8 bits for each RGB channel). Now, most desktops and laptops, and even some newer handhelds, display 24-bit color out of the box. If you know your audience has reasonably current equipment, this greatly simplifies

Figure 7-2 From image editor to screen output

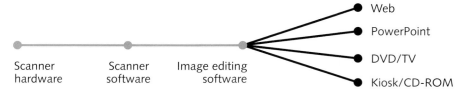

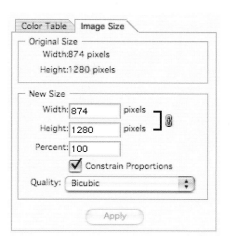

Figure 7-3 Image size in Save for Web

color issues. You can simply use the colors you want to use.

However, your images may still be subjected to bit-depth constraints. For instance, many users with older computers might surf your Web site. (Java, JavaScript, DHTML, and other features might already make it impossible for an older computer to access the site reliably.)

Computers that can't display 24-bit color are almost always capable of 8-bit color—just 256 colors. While that's enough to create a grayscale image with an adequate range of tones, it's really not enough colors for a high-quality full-color image.

Another bit depth constraint may be the file format you use; the GIF format can only handle a maximum of 256 colors. If you need to optimize color for a GIF image or you know your audience includes many older computers that don't have 24-bit color, you may need to make some compromises to preserve the colors you want to display. These compromises are available in the form of specialized color palettes and the technique called *dithering*, which we discuss later in this section.

Web-safe palette. For the Web, GIF files often use what's called the "Web-safe palette," which is a set of 216 colors that both

the Mac OS and Windows operating systems can display without using a patchwork of other colors to simulate ones it can't display. (This patchwork is called dithering.)

The safe palette limits itself to 216 colors, leaving 40 colors free on an 8-bit video display for the Macintosh or Windows (or even Unix) operating system to use for its own purposes. A safe palette can produce distorted color because of the large number of tradeoffs made to map a wide range of colors to the safe palette's limits.

Master palettes. The Web-safe palette is just one of a large possible set of 216 colors that can safely be used across images on the same page without dithering. These sets of 216-color palettes are called master palettes, and it's easy to create one from a set of images to maximize photographic quality.

In Adobe ImageReady, you can create a master palette by selecting the Image menu and then using the Master Palette submenu commands. Open an image, choose Add to Master Palette from the Master Palette submenu, and repeat for each image containing colors you want to add. Then select the Master Palette submenu and choose the Build Master Palette command to combine the colors you added. (Creating a single palette across multiple images is also a specialty of Equilibrium DeBabelizer, which calls them Super Palettes.)

You can also obtain software packages and Photoshop plug-ins that do a nice job presenting dithers made up of color palettes you select—like the Web-safe palette—to better control your final images.

When working within an 8-bit, 256-color palette, we still recommend using only 216 colors; otherwise, the image will have dithering. The main reason to use a master palette is to represent natural images in a manner that's not as distorted as you'd get from the Web-safe palette.

Dithering. Some image-editing software can substitute a patchwork of dot patterns to simulate the colors it can't produce. This doesn't help when editing images or checking details, for sure, because as you zoom in, you see those patterns—not areas of different tonal values. But it's better than pure posterization, where abrupt transitions appear instead of a gradual tonal variation. Dithering is usually visible to the naked eye as a kind of speckling; it's terrible to view in flat colors because it completely stands out. It's better hidden and put to better use when it appears in photographs, giving the impression of a real tonal range (**Figure 7-4**). Most Web graphics tools provide a fair amount of control over how colors are dithered.

What about television? Bits are a digital measurement, but traditional TV is an analog medium where bit depth doesn't apply directly. For practical purposes, think of an analog TV as a 24-bit display device, although its color rendering is somewhere between 8 and 24 bits. Digital television and HDTV provide 24-bit digital color or better.

Color Model, Color Space, and Color Management

If you're editing an image in the sRGB color space, your image's colors should appear on your audience's screens somewhat close to the way you see them. However, if you've been working with your image in a color space other than sRGB, remember to convert the image to sRGB before you save the final version. If you don't convert to sRGB, chances are that your image's colors will not appear the way you expect.

Converting to sRGB is necessary because most other applications (like

Figure 7-4
Dithering

24 bits

Full photographic color

Detail view of continuous tones

Flat colors

64 colors

Photograph using palette generated from photo

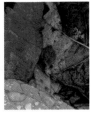

Detail view of dithering

Flat color using its own adaptive palette

Flat color using photo's palette

Conrad likes to take care of these color issues by running Web-bound images through a Photoshop action that was recorded with all necessary steps like color space conversion and sharpening. The only thing he has to remember is to run the images through the action.

PowerPoint and just about all Web browsers) don't use color management, so they can't use profiles to interpret color. They assume all colors exist in sRGB or a similar generic color space, so colors stored in another color space won't look right. (The Mac OS version of Microsoft Internet Explorer can use color profiles through a preference setting, but almost nobody turns it on and Microsoft has canceled that browser's development.)

It's easy to forget to convert the color space for every image that might need it. To make matters worse, many Web export commands (such as Adobe Save for Web) do not provide for color space conversion during Web export.

If you're only going to use an image on screen in non-color-managed applications, you don't need to embed a profile into the image: it's ignored and takes up space. On the Web, embedding profiles that won't be used can actually be a measurable waste of bandwidth on slow Internet connections like dial-up or through cell phones. As long as the image is in a color space like sRGB, you are doing the best you can for the many uncalibrated monitors in existence.

If you're using an image that was originally targeted for press output, it might already be stored as a CMYK image. So, you might consider bumping up the saturation of CMYK images to better fill the RGB gamut; otherwise, they may appear relatively flat when displayed on screen next to full-range RGB images.

Gamma

Gamma measures how tonal values are distributed in an image or a video display. It's usually displayed as a curve on a graph, showing where values are compressed, expanded, or shifted. Macintoshes typically have a much lower gamma (1.8) than Windows video (2.2), which means that an image that looks perfect on a Macintosh can be far too dark on a Windows machine (or television, which also uses gamma 2.2). Therefore, you may need to adjust image gamma before sending images to the Web or other on-screen media, especially if you aren't using color management to convert images to sRGB.

On the Web, setting image gamma to look identical on both Mac and Windows has been a significant problem, as there's no happy medium in between the two platforms' gammas. How do you know whether an image's gamma will look right? The obvious way is to set up standard Mac and Windows systems with video cards capable of 16-bit color or better, and then connect them over a network so you can view the same file on both machines. However, there are much easier ways to preview gamma. Some image editors let you directly preview cross-platform gamma settings within the program. For example, in Adobe ImageReady CS you can choose from three commands on the View menu's Preview item: Uncompensated Color, Standard Macintosh Color, and Standard Windows Color.

If you're familiar with the Curves command in Photoshop, Gamma is like dragging the curve midpoint back and forth, which makes an image appear lighter or darker without clipping highlights or shadows.

If you find that the image will appear too light or too dark on one platform or another, here are a few ways you might approach the problem:

▶ Aim for a 2.0 gamma, between the typical 1.8 level found on a Mac and 2.2 or higher found in Windows. This is what we typically try for, but you may or may not be happy with the compromise.

▶ Save the image using the gamma of the majority of your audience. This might make sense if you think it's better for most viewers to see the image correctly rather than for no viewers to see it correctly. Sites designed for Mac users or sites for companies that sell Windows-only software might want to have their images snap on those platforms.

▶ Convert images to sRGB, which will encode them using gamma 2.2. The image will look about right on Windows, but a little too light on the Mac. In Photoshop, you achieve this by choosing the Image menu, Mode submenu, Convert to Profile option, and specifying sRGB.

The gamma of an image is entirely separate from the gamma values for your monitor profile, your Photoshop working space, and your printer. Problems occur when gammas don't match and you aren't using color management to automatically compensate for different gammas.

The PNG file format can store a gamma curve representing the display of the machine that created it, so that a PNG image theoretically could automatically display correctly on any computer. However, the various Web browsers support PNG gamma inconsistently, so this is not a complete solution… yet. Once again, the life of a color-sensitive online publisher would be easier if Web browsers would simply provide full support for industry standards.

File Formats

Everything you need to know about how a graphic file format works can be found in Chapter 16, *File Formats*. But here we want to explain which files work on the Web and how browsers can handle them. **Table 7-1** compares the Web file formats. (Issues about formats' color spaces are found in Chapter 13, *Getting Good Color*, and formats' compressions in Chapter 17, *Compression*.)

Standards. The current standard file formats for the Web are GIF and JPEG; these are well supported by all major browsers. Use JPEG for photographic or continuous-tone images, and GIF for images that use solid, flat colors, transparent areas, or animation. PNG is a more recent standard that promises to provide the best of GIF and JPEG without their drawbacks. The catch is that while current Web browsers display PNG images, some browsers don't support all of the features of PNG.

There aren't any hard-and-fast standards for video editing, DVD, and PowerPoint presentations, but TIFF and JPEG are good choices depending on what your authoring software supports. If you save a JPEG using high-quality settings, it should look just as good as a TIFF but take up a lot less disk space. In Windows, WMF and BMP graphics are also popular (but we hate them; see Chapter 16).

Compression and file size. Although we devote Chapter 17 to compression, you should also be thinking here about the final file size of images you put on the Web. JPEG is often preferred to GIF because of its massive compression ratios: for example, a full-screen image might compress into a several-hundred-kilobyte GIF but only a 50 K JPEG. And though GIF can display the same way on many different machines, it's not the best way to represent

For-mat	Displays in browser	Inter-lacing	Transparency	Browser color modles	Device-indepen-dent color support
TIFF	No				Yes
EPS	No				
GIF	Yes	Yes	One color	8-bit indexed	No
JPEG	Yes	Yes[1]	No	Grayscale or 24-bit RGB/CMYK	No
PNG	Yes[2]	Yes	One color or alpha channel	Indexed, gray-scale, or 24-bit	Yes

[1]Multiple settings for interlacing.
[2]While many browsers display PNG, not all browsers support all PNG features.

Table 7-1 Major bitmap formats as they work on the Web

photographic images. Flat colors compress well and look good as GIFs; photographic images are better suited for JPEG even if there's some variation between how the image looks on different computers.

Sharpening

If you're used to sharpening images for print, get ready to adjust your sharpening habits. On-screen images are displayed at far lower resolutions than printed images. Because the effects of sharpening are resolution-dependent, on-screen graphics need a lot less sharpening than print images. If you apply print-resolution sharpening settings to an on-screen graphic, chances are the graphic will be way oversharpened. When applying Photoshop's Unsharp Mask command to on-screen graphics, try using these settings as a starting point: Amount of 100 percent, Radius of 1 pixel, and a Threshold of 0 levels. See Chapter 15, *A Sharper Image* for more in-depth explanations of these settings.

Although you generally want to avoid oversharpening, it's especially important with JPEG images. With JPEG compression, sharp images result in larger files than blurry images because sharpness creates more details to store. That's why you might find a Blur option in JPEG export features

like Adobe Save for Web. If the exported file size is larger than you want it to be, you can try increasing the Blur value slightly to try and lower the file size without losing too much sharpness.

Web Specials

There are a few things you can do on the Web that you can't do in the prepress world. It's a cross between true multimedia—which encompasses animation, transparency, and fading effects—and flat media, like print, which can use transparency and translucency to some great effect. Any technique can be overused, but transparency, interlacing, and animation can make Web pages seem a bit more interesting if done well.

Transparency

An image that has transparency—whether a single color or an entire channel—allows other images or text behind it to show through wherever that color or tone appears. It is used to knock out shapes in prepress, and to better blend images and type on the Web.

The difference between creating composites in Photoshop that are intended for print and using an alpha channel in a Web-bound image is that you can combine and recombine different Web images on the fly with different backgrounds, or several times on the same page for varying effects.

GIF and PNG both allow transparency information to be encoded, but have a giant difference in their sophistication.

GIF

GIF transparency is limited to knockout colors, not partially transparent mixes. Most programs that allow you to set transparency in a GIF let you select either a single or multiple colors. However, the colors you select don't mix with the underlying colors; a transparent GIF color sample just shows through whatever color underlies it in the browser window. It's either on or off, not a blend. If you want a graphic to have semitransparent areas, try the PNG format instead.

In Photoshop, any transparency that's already in the file is preserved when you choose Save for Web from the File menu (**Figure 7-5**). The Save for Web window shows your indexed color palette or color map, and you can select any image colors you want to add to the transparent area.

Figure 7-5
Save for Web
in Photoshop

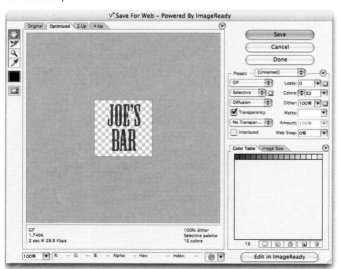

This can take a bit of back and forth to perfect, because typically you have a color or a background image showing through the transparent images, not just a dark gray. Sometimes it's better to create "fake" transparency, using the Save for Web dialog box's Matte option to match the background color of the Web page that will contain the graphic.

PNG

In Photoshop, the Save for Web dialog box lets you export PNG-8 (8-bit) and PNG-24 (24-bit) images. For PNG-8, you can control transparency using methods similar to those you use for GIF. For PNG-24, Save for Web creates an alpha channel to preserve the original file's transparency.

Interlacing

Interlaced images display gradually on a Web page by storing the image data out of sequence. The image data is stored in an alternating form in the file to achieve this effect so that the image gradually loads in lines or a blur as the file is retrieved. This effect seemed like the greatest thing since sliced bread when it was first introduced, but the advent of better compression and optimization, 56K modems, and broadband Internet has made interlacing's trick a necessity of the past—unless your entire audience is using 10-year-old technology, which is true in some areas of the world.

Here's how to set interlacing in GIF, JPEG, and PNG files.

GIF and JPEG. GIF and JPEG use line-at-a-time interlacing, and these are both easily set. Many Adobe applications let you set interlacing in the Save for Web dialog box. When you select a format that supports interlacing, the Interlacing option appears (**Figure 7-5**). If you need more options for JPEG, use the Save As command and choose JPEG, where progressive display can be set to 3, 4, or 5 lines of alternation for each pass.

PNG. PNG interlacing is two-dimensional—a bit harder to picture. Single pixels are extracted both down and across the original image in a regular, progressive pattern. The PNG specs point out that the first pass of a PNG image can display in one-eighth the time of the first pass of a GIF image. There's less detail in each pass, but the effects are quite nice and it does appear to appear faster.

As you would expect, Adobe's PNG options appear in the Save for Web dialog box after you select PNG as the file format. Progressive rendering is done through the Adam7 algorithm; it's not descriptive, just a funny name.

TV Specials

You may not think of yourself as a television engineer, but if you make DVDs or connect your laptop to a projector to give a PowerPoint presentation, you may need to work around the technical limitations of traditional television formats. Many of the limitations exist because analog television is built on top of the technology of the 1930s, involving many techniques and workarounds that are no longer necessary with 21st century technology but still get in the way.

Pixel Aspect Ratio for Video

When scanning images for video editing, DVD production, or anything else that might be translated through a television format, you may encounter the concept of *pixel aspect ratio*. We talk about aspect ratio in Chapter 5, but that discussion refers to the proportions of an entire image. Pixel aspect ratio describes the proportions of the little pixels that make up an image. That's right—in video, pixels can be rectangular, not square. If you draw a square on a rectangular-pixel system like a television graphics workstation, then move that file to a square-pixel system like a Mac OS or Windows computer, the square will look unnaturally thin because the square computer pixels aren't the same proportions as the rectangular TV pixels.

For example, the aspect ratio of a digital video (DV) pixel used in digital camcorders is .9:1, which means its width is .9 times its height. Photoshop uses the Pixel Aspect Ratio submenu on the Image menu to indicate the pixel aspect ratio (**Figure 7-6**), and the aspect ratio's scaling factor is at the end of each menu item. The only video formats that use square pixels are certain digital high-definition standards, because they have more in common with computer formats than traditional video formats.

Figure 7-6 Pixel aspect ratios in Photoshop

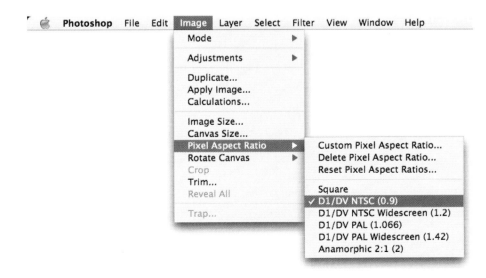

Seeing straight. You can test how your video application handles your scanned images by importing an image. Use a scan that contains something that's obviously supposed to be a perfect square or circle, so you can easily see whether scans are going to be distorted. There's actually a fair chance that everything will be fine, because many video editing applications try to auto-detect the correct pixel aspect ratio for imported files. If your scan imports an undistorted image, your video editor has guessed correctly, and you won't have to worry about it.

Squaring off. If you do see distortion, see if your video editing application has a setting that lets you indicate the imported image's pixel aspect ratio. For example, you can indicate an imported image's Pixel Aspect Ratio using the Item Properties window in Apple Final Cut Pro (Mac OS X) or the Interpret Footage dialog box in Adobe Premiere Pro (Windows). Choose Square Pixels (1.0 aspect ratio) for any image you acquired using a scanner.

If the image still looks distorted in the video editor, try using an image editor to resample the image first. For every video format that uses non-square pixels, there are recommended square-pixel frame dimensions that correspond to the frame's non-square pixel dimensions. **Figure 7-7** shows a list of popular frame sizes that Photoshop provides for new images; in this list the equivalent of a 640 by 480 square pixel image is 720 by 480 rectangular pixels. In Photoshop, choose Image Size from the Image menu, uncheck Constrain Proportions, and enter 720 by 480 or another appropriate set of dimensions from **Figure** 7-7.

When you resample for rectangular pixels, the image may appear distorted on a square-pixel computer monitor, but should look fine on a rectangular-pixel television monitor. You can use Adobe Photoshop CS to preview such an image correctly on a square-pixel computer monitor. Select the View menu to choose the Pixel Aspect Ratio Correction preview command. To embed pixel aspect ratio information into an image so that it's interpreted correctly when opened, use Photoshop's Pixel Aspect Ratio submenu on the Image menu.

Avoiding Flicker and Moiré

If you're scanning images to be shown on a television, watch out for very fine lines and patterns that might flicker or produce a shimmering moiré. Flicker and moiré are caused by *interlacing*, a display technique used by televisions. Instead of drawing each video frame from the top down, interlaced displays draw each frame in two passes, similar to an interlaced GIF. One pass contains the odd-numbered lines, and the other pass contains the even-numbered lines. This technique was developed so that motion would be smoother on early televisions that could not produce the frame rates of today's monitors. Interlacing lets a device achieve the same frame rate using half the bandwidth that a non-interlaced (progressive scan) frame would need.

A side effect of interlacing is that adjacent horizontal lines exist on different fields. So if a scanned (or drawn) image contains a horizontal line that's less than two video lines tall, alternating parts of it will repeatedly disappear and reappear as the fields it sits on redraw, and the line appears to flicker. If you want to avoid this, try to make sure the horizontal lines on your television graphics are several pixels

For the most accurate test, display the video-editing application's preview window on an actual rectangular-pixel video monitor instead of on a computer monitor.

Figure 7-7
Non-square video
resolutions built
into the New
document dialog
box in Photoshop

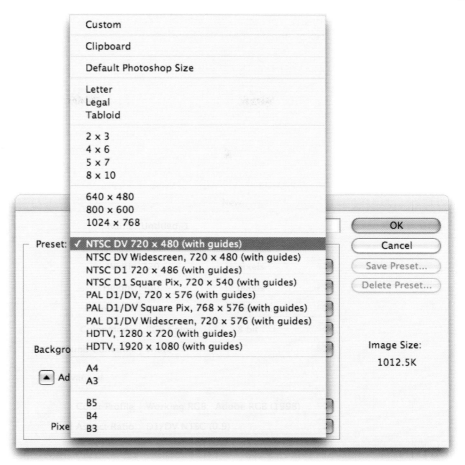

tall. That includes watching out for skinny typeface features like strokes and serifs. If you're working with a scanned image that has fine lines in it and if thickening the lines is too labor-intensive, try using your image editor to blur the lines slightly.

A related television problem is moiré. This isn't the same as the moiré patterns you might see on printed material, but the cause is similar. If a pattern in your scanned image (like a woven pattern on clothing) interferes with the television display grid, you see new, distracting moiré patterns. Another way you might encounter a moiré is by scanning a printed image that contains a halftone dot pattern, like a magazine photo, forgetting to descreen

it, and then zooming in on it in your video. To avoid video moiré, try not to use scanned images with fine patterns in a television presentation. Blurring patterned areas slightly may help here too.

Capture Strategies

Scanning images for video is one thing; acquiring images from video is another thing. Digital video capture is fairly straightforward if you use digital camcorders which produce a DV stream. With a Mac, plug a DV camera into your Mac's FireWire port and use the free iMovie software to import a short segment of video. To turn a frame into an image file, select the frame you want to export and choose Cre-

We didn't think that video scanning was a reasonable way to capture images (everything we'd seen looked terrible) until a friend of ours showed us the poster he produced that included 50 video captures. Now we know it's possible to get good images from a videotape or video camera; you just have to work hard to do it, and not print them very large. A good starting point for color-correcting a captured video frame is to use an image editor to tag it with a likely ICC color profile, such as the NTSC (1953) profile that's installed with Adobe Photoshop.

ate Still Frame from the Edit menu (**Figure 7-8**). Importing DV is almost as easy in Windows because many PCs now come with FireWire ports. For software, Windows comes with Windows MovieMaker, which has a convenient Take Picture button to capture still frames. If your computer lacks a FireWire port, inexpensive add-in cards are available for desktop and laptop computers. Some FireWire cards come with a CD of other video-capture software you can try.

Figure 7-8
Creating a still image from video in iMovie

Analog video capture setups are trickier because you typically need a board or add-on that you plug into your computer, which is necessary to convert the analog video to digital video. Once you get the hardware working, the video comes in through a cable, and you control the capture of a particular frame of the video through software.

Video resolution is typically low by print standards; it's measured in horizontal lines that sort of match up with vertical monitor-pixel depth. VHS has about 400 lines of resolution, while Hi-8, DV, and professional Beta have 500 or more. This is below the level of a small computer monitor. The most obvious side effect of such low resolution is that video images print best at very small sizes. The pixel count of a frame captured at the highest-quality "high-definition" video standard, 1920 by 1080 pixels, allows a maximum size of 6.4 inches by 3.6 inches if printed at 300 dpi. Not exactly magazine-cover material.

The interlacing behavior we talked about earlier also affects video capture. Televisions update their pictures 60 times a second. However, they only show half a frame at a time, alternating lines—or interlacing—each time. Video boards can typically grab two successive *fields* to make a full image capture, but this synchronization adds to the blurriness and jitter of videotape. Some video cameras can shoot in progressive scan mode, which captures whole frames without interlacing. If you're shooting video with the intention of grabbing still images from them and your camera can record in progressive-scan mode, you may want to see if progressive-scan mode gives you better images.

If you're going to capture video images from tape, do it from DV footage with a FireWire connection whenever possible—it's the best, cheapest solution.

Video Out

The Web and television are remarkable media capable of reaching both far and wide in an instant, but trying to appeal to the least common denominator can be an ongoing and tiring effort. Choose your battles well, though: There's nothing like completing a project only to find that you have to redo every image on a site because of browser limitations—or the CEO's old low-bit-depth video display. Our final piece of advice: Save your originals (in RGB mode, if possible); most likely you'll be revisiting them to create new versions of the same images in the future.

8

Scanning for Color Photo Printers

GOING OFF THE DEEP END

If you're making thousands or millions of copies of an image as part of a catalog, magazine, or newspaper, then creating CMYK color separations—discussed in Chapter 6—is the way to go. However, if you're printing just a few copies (as few as one) on your inkjet photo printer, or at the imaging service provider down the street, or at an online service across the country, the requirements are a bit different. This chapter focuses on copies of very high-quality color images on devices like inkjet or dye-sublimation photo printers, film recorders, and digital photo printers that use a laser to expose photographic paper.

Scanning for a photo printer is different than scanning for a press. Some of the differences are subtle, but significant. Images that will be printed on a press are scanned and edited for factors that include coping with CMYK color and the press color gam-

ut, screen frequencies, spot gain, and black and white points. When you scan an image for a color photo printer, you need to be concerned with RGB color, and you often have a larger tone and color gamut available than on a press.

Although various photo printing technologies have different characteristics for factors like spot gain and tonal response, color management profiles provide a one-step way to compensate for such differences if a profile is available for your output device.

Nice and Nicer Printers

Color photo printers range from desktop inkjets to room-sized printers, which create poster- or gallery-sized output. On any of these devices, you can aim for adequate quality or all-out maximum quality. While the factors that go into both levels of quality are the same, the amount of effort you put into producing either level is different. Throughout this chapter we refer to these levels as *consumer* or *professional* printing.

Consumer printing. You want snapshots and moderate enlargements to look nice, but you don't need them to be meticulously crafted works of art. You plan to print the photos on your own desktop printer or send them to an outside service like Ofoto, Shutterfly, or the digital minilab down at the Wal-Mart.

Professional printing. You want big, beautiful prints. You're on a mission to preserve the most quality you possibly can from your original and your scanner, and when you print your images, you want to push your output device to its limits. To get the level of quality you want, you're printing to a high-quality inkjet like the Canon i9000, a large-format inkjet flagship like the Epson Stylus Pro 9600, or you're sending your images out to a calibrated Lambda or Lightjet photo printer using museum-quality Fuji Crystal Archive paper.

Guidelines for the Initial Scan

Color photo printers are very different animals from printing presses, which affects how you scan images for them. Print-ing presses are constrained to the gamut of industry-standard CMYK inks, while each color photo printer might use its own set of dyes or pigments with a correspondingly unique color gamut and tonal response. The trick is to make sure your file is well-matched to the output device you send it to.

The good news is that scanning for color printers is really not that different from scanning for the press; they have similar requirements in terms of resolution and bit depth. The main difference is in how you plan your color workflow (**Figure 8-1**).

Resolution

Because the useful resolution of a scan is determined by the final output device, the logical next step is to understand what kind of resolution a particular color photo printer needs.

In Chapter 6, we say that the typical output resolution for a press-targeted image is typically two times the halftone screen, which usually results in a resolution of 150 to 300 samples per inch (spi). However, the resolution you need for a photo printer depends on the specific technology that the printer uses. When you use a printer that dithers or halftones, you don't need to provide an image at the printer's output resolution, because the printer must use its smallest dot size to build its spots and specks. In other words, never send a 2880-dpi image to a 2880-dpi inkjet printer—your image probably doesn't need to be higher than 360 dpi. On the other

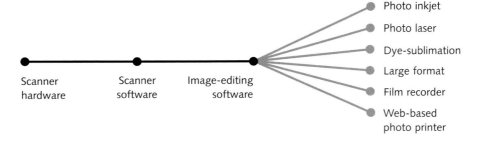

Figure 8-1 From scanner to image editor

Scanner hardware

Scanner software

Image-editing software

Photo inkjet

Photo laser

Dye-sublimation

Large format

Film recorder

Web-based photo printer

hand, continuous-tone printers often used for photographic prints generally need an image that's about the same as the printer's output resolution because they can change the tone of each dot they produce.

The resolution numbers given for each printer we discuss in the following list are provided as general guidelines. Because printer models and their drivers are updated and replaced frequently, you should check your printer's or imaging service's user guide or technical support to verify the optimum resolution for your job. Unless we've noted otherwise, the dpi values mentioned in the following list are relative to the final output dimensions. Also, remember to bump up the resolution a little if you'll need to crop the image (so that after cropping, you don't end up with fewer pixels than you need).

Inkjet printers. In general, you get the best results when you start at an output resolution of about 240 dpi; you are unlikely to see any improvement beyond 360 dpi. As mentioned earlier, due to the nature of inkjet reproduction you should not work with an image at an inkjet printer's maximum hardware resolution, which at this writing is surpassing 5760 dpi in some inexpensive inkjets.

 There's nothing wrong with setting the printer driver to its maximum output resolution. In this section, we're referring to the resolution of the image that you send to the printer.

Photographic laser printers. Printers like the Durst Lambda and Gretag Cymbolic Systems Lightjet use red, green, and blue lasers to expose photographic paper that's developed in traditional photochemicals unlike toner-based laser printers. They produce continuous-tone output, which under a loupe appears much more like a traditional chemical photo print than dith-

ered output. These huge, expensive printers can cost as much as a single-family home, so they're found only at high-end imaging service providers.

These printers produce top-quality prints when you provide images with output resolutions of 200–400 dpi. Models such as the Lightjet 403 can take advantage of the detail in a 400-dpi image, but other models are limited to around 200 dpi. Check with your imaging service provider for the specifications of its equipment.

Companies like Noritsu and Fuji make *minilab* versions of photographic laser printers, which look and work a lot like the older, film-based minilabs made by the same companies but with one exception: they accept memory cards and CDs of images instead of rolls of film. These digital minilabs are increasingly common at drugstores and shopping malls. Digital minilabs are appealing because they make prints that look a lot like traditional drugstore snapshots and enlargements, yet have a superior image quality because of the digital imaging processing. They're also very affordable at a per-print price.

The resolution guidelines for minilabs are usually similar to those for Web-based photo printing services (see below), but your best bet is to call ahead and ask your minilab what resolution works best on its machine. Since the folks who operate them require less training than an imaging service bureau operator, they may not have detailed advice for you. You should also plan on testing some sample images before committing to a lot of prints.

Dye-sublimation printers. These output devices print on special paper that contains dye layers. The printing process releases the dyes. Unlike photographic laser printers, dye-sub desktop printers are affordable. Depending on the printer you use, an output resolution of 150–200 dpi is appropriate.

Large-format printers. Inkjet, photographic laser, and electrostatic (liquid toner) output devices all come in large-format models. You can follow the guidelines for resolution up to this point for prints up to about 30 inches on a side. However, as prints approach and exceed that size, imaging service providers recommend lowering the resolution to maintain a manageable file size. Don't be alarmed: Large prints generally don't need as much resolution, because resolution requirements drop as the viewing distance increases. For very large posters or banners that will be seen from a distance, you may be able to drop an image's output resolution to as low as 50 dpi. If this seems too low to you, go outside, find a billboard, banner, or wall-sized poster containing a photo, and get as close to it as you can. You'll probably see huge dots that you never noticed from your car.

When scanning for large format prints, find out what your service provider's recommended resolution is for the final physical dimensions you want, then enter that resolution (in dpi) and the physical dimensions into the output options of your scanning software or image-editing program.

Film recorders. You can output to a film recorder when you want to transfer your scan to film, such as a slide. Less expensive film recorders (also called slide recorders and film writers) create an image on very high-resolution, compact CRTs (cathode-ray tubes). In other words, they make a picture on a tiny TV. But where a normal television can only display a few hundred pixels vertically and a low-res computer monitor can display 1600 pixels from top to bottom, film recorders use CRTs that can display up to 16,000 lines of pixels or more.

A CRT film recorder has a set of three colored filters, and it carries out one pass each for red, green, and blue exposures. The CRT displays just grayscale, and the

 In the movie industry, special film recorders write digitally mastered movies back to motion picture film, one frame at a time.

filters rotate into place for each different color exposure. Some newer film recorders expose the film with lasers instead of a CRT: the Kodak LVT film recorder is capable of printing at up to 3048 dpi.

We've mentioned how resolution is sometimes expressed as pixel dimensions instead of dots/samples/pixels per inch. Unlike photo printers, which describe resolution in dots per inch, some film recorder services refer to pixel dimensions, and many others specify resolution in *lines* from 2K to 16K (K stands for a thousand lines of horizontal resolution). You need to convert from one set of units to another.

Let's say you're going to send an image to a 35mm film recorder with 4K resolution. The actual dimensions of a 35mm 4K image are 4096 pixels wide by 2731 pixels tall. If you want to know what that is in dots per inch, divide the pixel dimensions by the physical dimensions of a 35mm photographic film frame (1.42–by-0.945 inches); the result is approximately 1409 dpi. If you send 4K output to a larger frame size like 4-by-5–inch film, the dpi will drop proportionally.

LVT film recorders use a "Res" measurement. A typical LVT film recorder might support Res20 through Res120. The Res number is actually the number of pixels per millimeter, so you have to convert it to inches to compare it to dots per inch. There are 25.4 mm in an inch, so Res40 (a common default) works out to 1016 dpi.

So how does all of this tell you how to set the output resolution in your scanning software? In many cases, it's probably easiest to learn the pixel dimensions of the film recorder, and enter them as the output pixel dimensions of the scan. For example, if you are scanning a 6-by-4–inch (4 by 6 wide) print for output to a 2K film recorder, and your scanning software lets you specify pixel dimensions for output, enter 2048 by 1365. That will cause the scanner to scan at an input resolution of about 341 spi.

 An film recorder resolution of 3048 dpi may seem extraordinarily high, but the film that's produced is typically not the final output medium—it's simply an intermediate medium on the way to a projection screen or print enlargement that's much larger than the output film frame. The high resolution of a film recorder helps to ensure that the details in the film image can survive significant enlargement. We talk about how scaling affects resolution in Chapter 11, Image Resolution.

Web-based photo printing services. You can order good-quality, glossy snapshots or enlargements of digital photos by sending files to a Web-based consumer printing service such as Ofoto or Shutterfly. Before uploading your image files, check their Web sites for resolution recommendations. For an 8-by-10 print, for example, they'll probably tell you that your image should be about 1600 by 1200 pixels, which works out to roughly 150 dpi. Guidelines found at professional service like Pictopia.com or West Coast Imaging (**www.west coastimaging.com**) will typically recommend a higher pixel count—at least 200 dpi at its final output dimensions, but probably 300 dpi. It all depends on the photo printing technology they use, and better service providers have a number of output technologies you can choose from. They may use the digital minilabs mentioned above. As always when working with an outside service your best bet is to talk to them about the requirements of their specific output device before you send anything.

Often, an imaging service's Web site will tell you what you need to know.

If you're not sure what the final output device is, it's usually safe to aim for 240 and 360 dpi at the final output dimensions. We talk more about this in the topic "Set Output Dimensions and Resolution" in Chapter 5, *How to Read Your Scanning Software.*

Bit Depth

If you're scanning well-exposed originals that don't need much correction, you can scan your images at 8 bits per channel. If an image requires extreme adjustments that cause posterization problems at 8 bits per channel, you might scan that particular image at 16 bits per channel. While some professional programs, printer drivers, and imaging services may be able to print directly from a 16-bit image file, consumer-oriented printer drivers and photo services are likely to support 8-bit files only. So if you scan and edit an image at 16 bits, you may have to convert it to 8 bits for final output.

Some fine-art digital printmakers scan 16-bit files all the time, but for reasons that are specifically relevant to a fine-art workflow. A gallery show might involve only 10 or 20 images, so disk space is less of an issue. On the other hand, a magazine or catalog might need hundreds of images, so 16-bit scans would eat up many more megabytes of disk space for only occasional benefit. Many of the ink and paper combinations used by fine-art printmakers can reproduce more tones and colors than the inks and papers used on a printing press, so an artist may decide to edit in 16-bit mode to take full advantage of the printer's tonal range and color gamut.

As we mention in the next section, fine-art printmakers may find advantages in using larger color spaces like EktaSpace; 16-bit editing is often the only way to successfully edit in a larger color space.

If you're working with black-and-white line art, you may want to try the techniques in the Line Art topic in Chapter 6, Scanning for Prepress instead of scanning line art at 1 bit per pixel.

 It does no good to scan at 8 bits and convert to 16 bits for editing. If you want to edit at 16 bits, scan at 16 bits.

Color Model, Color Space, and Color Management

Your scanner saves scans in some kind of color space, so if your scanner gives you a choice, it's good to know which one might be best for the photo printer output you're targeting. Again, your choice depends on whether you want consumer or professional prints and what output device your image is headed for. Here are the choices:

sRGB. For consumer output like snapshot prints, you can simply scan and edit using the sRGB color space. If you don't know what color space you're using and the service doesn't reveal this information, your image will probably end up in sRGB or something a lot like it because most consumer scanners, printers, and image-editing applications are preset or optimized for sRGB, as are consumer imaging services like Ofoto and Shutterfly.

Pros turn up their noses at sRGB, but in reality, sRGB doesn't look all that awful to most people. sRGB might not let you see all of the colors that are in your original image, and it might not use all of the colors that an output device can produce. But if you're just printing pictures of houses for sale or snapshots of a family picnic, sRGB is usually more than adequate.

Adobe RGB (1998). If you want to at least match what a printing press would give you, and you're working with an output device or imaging service that supports color management, consider scanning and editing in the Adobe RGB color space.

CMYK. There's really no reason to scan an image as a CMYK file when your output device is a photo printer. "But wait," you say, "don't inkjets use CMYK inks?" That's misleading. The reality is more complex than that. Because most people (outside the prepress industry) work with RGB files, the vast majority of the printer drivers for CMYK inkjets are written to receive RGB data. This is because most programs cannot send CMYK data (think Microsoft Word or Excel, digital camera software, photo organizers, and so on). This concept applies to any output device that uses RGB-based output hardware, such as a film recorder.

But even if the driver could accept CMYK data, CMYK output would not be so straightforward because an inkjet's CMYK inks are chemically different than the CMYK inks formulated for a printing press, so some kind of conversion would still be necessary. We talk more about the output side of this issue in the next section, "Preparing the Final, Corrected Image"; all you need to know here is to avoid scanning into CMYK for images that will only be sent to a photo printer.

Wide-gamut color spaces. Some high-end scanners can scan images into wide-gamut spaces like EktaSpace or ProPhoto RGB. Most people do not need to mess with these color spaces, which can be challenging to use, but some pros make very good use of them. Wide-gamut spaces can be useful for making extreme corrections, archiving all of the colors in transparency film, or editing scans of color negatives. If you've mastered how to convert from the image color space to the output device color space, a wide-gamut color space may let you take full advantage of an output device's complete color range. Wide-gamut color spaces work best with images scanned and edited at 16 bits per channel. And it really helps to have a working knowledge of color management, 16-bit editing techniques, and soft-proofing (see the Proof Setup submenu in Photoshop).

 Bruce Fraser and David cover wide-gamut color spaces in their book Real World Adobe Photoshop *and include a technique for quickly interpreting color negatives while preserving and optimizing their entire dynamic range.*

The scanner's own color space. Should you just leave the scan in the color space of your scanner when you save and edit it? There's not much point in doing so. The recommended workflow is to convert an image from the scanner's color space into a working space (a good color space for editing) like sRGB or Adobe RGB, which is why scanner software does this by default. A scanner's color space usually doesn't have the right attributes to be a good editing space, because it's a record of the individual quirks of a particular scanner's hardware.

File Format

For consumer printing where you aren't making major changes, you might get away with scanning to a high-quality JPEG file. If you have more than a passing interest in preserving image quality, scan into TIFF or Photoshop (PSD) format.

If you're scanning for professional photo output, TIFF and PSD are the logical choices for the format of your original scan. They're capable of preserving the image's details, tonal range, color range, and any bit depth or color space you're likely to use during editing and output.

Preparing the Final, Corrected Image

For consumer photo printing, a typical workflow consists of scanning images as 8-bit TIFF files in the sRGB color space, aiming for an output resolution of 200 to 300 dpi at the final output size of your print (**Figure 8-2**). After editing, you either send the image directly to your own photo printer, or, you can make JPEG-compressed copies of your images and send the copies out to a service.

For professional photo printing, scan images as 8-bit (or if needed, 16-bit) TIFF or Photoshop files in the Adobe RGB (1998) color space and aim for an output resolution of 300 dpi at the final output size of your print. After editing, either send the images directly to your own photo printer, or, if you're sending them out to a service, adjust copies of the images to meet the specifications provided by the imaging service. You may need to adjust the resolution, bit depth, color space, and file format, and in many cases you might be asked for an 8-bit RGB TIFF file.

Figure 8-2
Output workflows

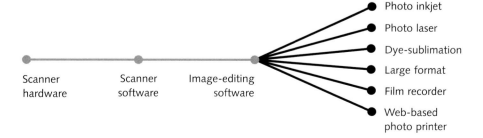

Resolution and Dimensions

If you followed the resolution guidelines we listed in the previous section, your file should already contain enough pixels for quality output. Before you send the image out for final output, make sure that your file's physical dimensions also match up with what the output device is expecting. For example, if you want to output an 8-by-10–inch print of a 3827-by-2551 35mm film scan, make sure it actually says 8 by 10 inches in your image-editing application. Otherwise, you might end up with a very high resolution image that's no bigger than the original tiny film frame.

If you can't provide the resolution that your imaging service needs, ask if they have any high-quality digital scaling options; some image services can do a better job of scaling images up than you can with your own image editor. They may provide this service through specialized scaling software that uses advanced algorithms or through a similarly advanced scaling feature built into the high-end output device they use.

If you're preparing output for a film recorder, you may want to make sure that the aspect ratio of your image matches the film you're printing to. For example, an 8-by-12 image equals the aspect ratio of a 35mm film frame, while an 8-by-10 image does not. Printing an 8-by-10 image on a 35mm film frame without cropping will leave unused space on two sides, so you may want to crop the image to properly fill the intended frame proportions. If you're using Photoshop, you can easily constrain its cropping tool to a specific aspect ratio by first selecting the cropping tool and then entering your required dimensions into the options bar at the top of the screen.

Some online services have cropping tools that are preset to the output dimensions they provide. You use their Web site to crop your image. It's a good way to help prevent costly output mistakes.

Bit Depth

Eight bits is the standard or default bit depth used by just about every scanner and image editor you're likely to use at home or in most offices, so it's pretty much a given that an output device will take an 8-bit-per-channel file. Many consumer output devices and imaging services only take 8-bit files. If you've been working in 16-bit mode, you may need to create an 8-bit version before printing it. Even if your output device or imaging service has no problem accepting 16-bit files, keep in mind that the software driver for the output device will typically convert the image to 8 bits per channel before it actually sends it to the device.

Color Model, Color Space, and Color Management

The easiest part of an image to ruin is its color as you move from the image file on the computer to an output device. You can avoid pitfalls by understanding how your output device produces color, and how its software driver interprets files coming in. Fortunately, most of the possibilities fall into two categories: non-color-managed devices for consumers, and professional, color-managed devices.

If you're creating output from CMYK images, you may face bigger challenges with a photo printer than when you start with RGB images. In some cases, you need to convert an image's color space to get the very best output.

Consumer or non-color-managed devices. Regardless of the color space your image

 If the color concepts in this topic make your head spin, particularly those involving color management or color conversion, you might want to jump ahead to Chapter 13, Getting Good Color.

started in, the best results come from converting your image to the sRGB color space before sending it to a consumer output

Using Profiles for Better Consumer Output

Even if you output to a consumer device that doesn't have direct support for color management, it's possible to get better-than-average color. Make or obtain an accurate ICC profile for the printer or service. Use software that can either convert the image using the profile or send output in the profile's color space.

If you use a device in your own home or office, you can profile it if you use profiling hardware and software, which we talk about in Chapter 13, *Getting Good Color*. When you send images to an outside consumer service like a drugstore, it's unlikely that the staff will be able to provide any help for color management issues. However, there is a way around this: Surprisingly, you can download profiles from the Dry Creek Photo Web site (www.drycreekphoto.com) for the digital minilabs located in many neighborhoods around the world. If you're in a large city, Dry Creek may already have an accurate profile of a digital minilab just a few minutes away from you.

"Now wait a minute," you say, "if the people down at the Costco photo counter know nothing about color management, who made a profile for that particular machine?" The answer is clever and appealingly subversive. You start by downloading Dry Creek's standard profiling target file. Then you send the target file through the minilab as part of one of your regular orders, and the machine prints out the image of the target file. (You do have to tell the staff to turn off all automatic image processing for your job.) You send the resulting print to Dry Creek, where they figure out the difference between the target's ideal state and the print you received from the minilab, which represents the typical state of the minilab.

Later, you download Dry Creek's updated profile of your local minilab, and you convert a copy of your image to that profile without embedding the profile. You then send the image to the minilab, again requesting that automatic processing be turned off. You should get a print that hopefully has better color than you were getting before. See the Dry Creek site for more detailed explanations and additional tips on working with a minilab. This method works well as long as the staff regularly runs the minilab's built-in calibration, which the staff should be doing daily.

device or service. If you've been using consumer applications all along, your photo is probably already in sRGB or something like it. If an output device or imaging service is set to expect sRGB and you send it a file that uses a different color space (like Adobe RGB), the colors won't look right. If a file's color space is larger than sRGB, the output will probably look flat and unsaturated.

If you're using an inexpensive image editor that doesn't seem to have an option for changing the color space, it's probably set permanently to sRGB.

Professional or color-managed devices. If you're aiming for optimum quality on a high-end photo output device, your best bet is to find out what color spaces its driver expects by default and whether it supports color management and ICC profiles. You can then use color management to give the device what it expects. For instance, Conrad needed 35mm slides of some Photoshop images he wanted to enter in a competition. He went to the tech support section of his imaging service's Web site and found that it recommends Adobe RGB (1998) as the color space for files sent to its film recorder. Before sending copies of his files to the service, he made sure that each image was in Adobe RGB (1998), converting them if necessary. (He also used the service's sizing guide to make sure the images were properly composed within the aspect ratio of a 35mm frame.)

While some professional imaging services may recommend a common color space like Adobe RGB (1998), others may tell you to convert your image to their output device's specific color space. This can mean that the imaging service is interested not only in making your color predictable, but also in making the best use of the device's available color gamut. They can probably provide a device profile that you can download and use to convert the images you want to send in. Actually, you need to make sure you convert copies of your images, because the conversion to a device-specific color space may limit some or all of the original image's colors.

Printing from a CMYK image. The main reason to send a CMYK file to a photo printer is because it's the only version of the file you have, since an RGB image would (in theory) make better use of the wide gamut of most photo output devices. However, you might have a really good reason for sending CMYK images to a photo printer. For instance, you might be working with images that were scanned by a prepress service provider and immediately converted to the CMYK specifications of the press used for a specific job. This is a

common and traditional scenario for projects where print is the only targeted medium, particularly for the millions of images that were scanned only in CMYK in the years before it became important to also have good RGB versions for the Web.

There is, however, an unfortunate double whammy when printing CMYK images to a photo printer. As we mention earlier in this chapter, most photo printers expect RGB data, so an application may need to convert a CMYK image to RGB just so it will be accepted by the device's driver. Then there's the usual conversion from RGB to the actual CMYK data relevant to the specific inks or dyes used by the device. These two conversions may change the image's color unless you can anticipate and control them. If you frequently need to output CMYK images accurately (say, for press proofing), consider using an output device that's designed to receive CMYK data, such as a press proofer, or replace the output device's driver with a RIP (raster image processor) software driver that can process CMYK directly.

Another consideration is that because the original CMYK image was probably optimized for the limited color gamut of a CMYK printing press, it's unlikely to take full advantage of a photo printer's color range, which is typically larger. This is not a big deal if you're proofing, because your only concern is that the device be constrained to match the gamut of the press.

Manual Override

If you don't have a CMYK-based driver for a photo printer and you don't trust how the image will be converted to RGB for the driver, there is one possible escape route if you are comfortable with color management. If you know the RGB color space that works well with the printer driver, convert the image to that RGB color space manually, so that you can evaluate and correct its color before sending it off to print.

With a professional image editor like Photoshop, you can preview and control the conversion precisely, and maybe even bump up the saturation and contrast a bit to try and use more of the device's color gamut and dynamic range.

In Photoshop select the Image menu, choose the Mode submenu, choose Convert to Profile, and then choose the RGB color space the driver might expect from most programs. (If you don't know what that might be, try sRGB or Adobe RGB.) The Preview button in the Convert to Profile dialog box shows you the conversion, allowing you to adjust it for better anticipated results.

After the conversion you can adjust the image to make it look better. Then, if you know your way around Photoshop's View menu's Proof Setup option, you can then preview how the image will look when printed. (We talk a little more about Proof Setup in Chapter 13, *Getting Good Color*.)

File Format

For output you send to one of your own photo printers, your image just needs to be in a file format you can print from. If you're sending the file out to an imaging service, find out what file formats they support.

Consumer imaging services, particularly minilabs or Web-based printing services, often require that files be sent in JPEG format (set JPEG compression to medium or high quality for decent results). If you scanned and edited your image in TIFF or Photoshop format, you'll need to save it in the version your imaging service requires. Double-check the format requirements before you send anything.

Professional imaging services will probably ask for a TIFF or Photoshop file, which you may already be working with. However, you still need to read their requirements carefully, because they may not want to take just any TIFF or Photoshop file. For example, many services don't want you to send in complex files with numerous layers, channels, and live objects like type and effects; or files in weird color modes like LAB. For the sake of clarity and efficiency, some imaging service providers accept only a flattened TIFF RGB file (at their resolution, bit depth, and color space specifications).

A Photo Finish

It's obvious that the sheer number of photo printer technologies and services means that there isn't a single best way to send a file to all photo printers. Become familiar with the specifications for your own typical photo printing jobs, and your prints should meet or exceed your expectations.

Scanning for the Office
IMAGES AT WORK

We think of office scanning as digitizing images that you want to use in general office communications using applications in Microsoft Office. You then print the document containing the image on a laser printer or run it down to a copy shop or quick printer. The types of jobs we have in mind are newsletters, memos, brochures, and reports. These jobs don't need to strive for the high aspirations of large-format Photoshop artists or the technical exactitude of brand-name product catalogs or magazines. However, they are jobs that simply need to be done, at a level of quality that's compelling and attractive.

Fortunately, the quality requirements of office scanning aren't burdensome when compared to other types of output, and the defaults for many of the less expensive scanners are already set up for office documents. But since you bought this book to

do better than the defaults, let's dig a little bit deeper into the available options.

As it is with scanning for other output types, the file format we recommend you scan into may be different than the file format you save after editing, especially if the final format uses a compression method that would degrade the image during editing. For example, although a JPEG might be the best format for a scan you want to send through e-mail, you'd want to save the original scan in the lossless TIFF format for later higher-quality reproduction and maximum flexibility. We cover aspects of file formats in Chapter 16, *File Formats*.

For most image scans, you can leave the color mode set to 8-bit RGB or grayscale, or black-and-white (1 bit) because that preserves enough detail without wasting time, effort, and storage (**Table 9-1**). In a general office environment, you almost never need to use other modes like CMYK.

Table 9-1
Scanning guidelines for office documents

Output	Output resolution	Format of final file
E-mail	200 by 300 pixels (vertical or portrait) at 72 dpi	8-bit RGB JPEG; choose GIF for solid-color graphics
Faxing	100–200 dpi	1-bit TIFF; use up to 8 bits if the fax software converts well
Photocopying	100–200 dpi	8-bit TIFF or JPEG
Laser printing	100–200 dpi; may use 300 dpi for line art	8-bit TIFF or high-quality JPEG
Inkjet printing	150–300 dpi; may use 300 dpi for line art	8-bit TIFF or high-quality JPEG
Out-of-house quick printing	150–300 dpi; may use 300 dpi for line art	8-bit TIFF or high-quality JPEG
Adobe PDF	72–96 dpi for on-screen viewing only; 100–300 dpi if you want readers to print or zoom in	8-bit TIFF; Acrobat can compress further
OCR	At least 200 dpi, usually at 100 percent of original; preferably at 300 dpi	1-bit file in any format supported by the OCR software

Editing Scans in Office Applications

You might find yourself tempted by the image-editing features in many office applications. For example, you can make adjustments to brightness, contrast, and color in Microsoft Word by choosing Picture from the Format menu. However, we recommend that you avoid editing scans in your word processor. Image controls in office applications are generally rather imprecise, and office applications normally don't support color management. Also, the adjustments you make typically apply only to the instance of the image in the document that contains them, so if you use the same image somewhere else you have to correct it all over again (**Figure 9-1**).

We think you're better off getting the original scans right, either in the scanning software or in a good, inexpensive image editor like Adobe Photoshop Elements. This way, your scans output correctly from whatever application you put them in.

E-mail

When you scan something that you want to send out in e-mail, keep its file size as small as possible. For people using slow Internet connections like a dial-up modem, oversized attachments are time wasters and line cloggers. If you've enjoyed a privileged life and have never had to use a slow connection, imagine what it would be like to wait five minutes for a single e-mail to arrive because somebody attached three 500K images that didn't need to be that big.

Figure 9-1
Output workflows

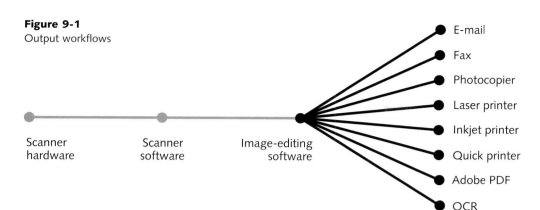

- E-mail
- Fax
- Photocopier
- Laser printer
- Inkjet printer
- Quick printer
- Adobe PDF
- OCR

Scanner
hardware

Scanner
software

Image-editing
software

Even if you are sending images across a fast corporate internal network, it's easier and faster to display, store, and back up small, efficient attachments.

Fortunately, the guidelines for making e-mail-friendly scans are essentially the same as the guidelines for making Web-friendly scans. In general, use the Web guidelines we lay out in Chapter 7, *Scanning for Web and Video*. For resolution, scan to the pixel dimensions you want the image to have in the e-mail. This usually means you want the image to fit inside a typical e-mail window.

There's no real standard for the size of an e-mail window or what form it will take. Some e-mail programs open messages in a pane inside a larger window, whereas others open them in an entirely new window. What we do know is that an e-mail window is usually a fraction of the size of the entire screen. Try starting with pixel dimensions like 200 by 300, making it larger if necessary.

For photos, you should end up with an 8-bit JPEG file compressed as much as the image can stand without becoming unrecognizable or completely jaggy. Graphics with just a few colors may be smaller if sent as GIFs, but avoid GIF if you want the recipient to be able to print the image well.

One exception to the usual guidelines is when you want your e-mail recipient to be able to print the image at a decent size without it looking blocky or pixelated. Because an image needs more pixels to print than to display on screen, you'd need to increase the pixel count of the scan you send. Let's say you want to send your recipient an image that will print 3 by 5 inches on an inkjet printer. For a level of quality that's good, but doesn't need to be great, you might want your recipient to be able to print the image at 150 dpi at that 3-by-5–inch size. Three inches times 150 dots is 450 pixels wide, and 5 inches times 150 dots is 750 pixels tall. So you should aim for 450 by 750 pixels when scanning the image.

 Many companies, online mail services, and individuals reject all attachments these days even from trusted or known senders because of the variety of viruses that disguise themselves in attachments as images or other files. You might not be able to send images in e-mail readily for that reason.

If you and your correspondent both have computers with Adobe Acrobat on them, e-mailing PDF documents is a higher-quality, lower-cost alternative to faxing, particularly when color and detail are involved.

Fax

Sometimes you need to send a scan straight from your computer through a fax modem, or print out a scan that will be recognizable after being sent through a fax machine. Even a high-resolution fax prints at a lowly 200 dpi. Like e-mail, the importance of compression over quality is mostly due to the desire to move those faxes through the machine as quickly as possible, particularly on expensive long-distance telephone lines.

While modern fax machines and fax modems can handle 200 dpi ("fine"), they default to a lower and faster resolution setting of 100 dpi ("standard"), and people generally don't change it. In addition, fax images are generally 1-bit, so the reproduction of grays is usually rather crude. And color? Even if you do have a color fax machine, there's no point in sending a color fax unless the person at the other end also has a color fax machine, and that's quite rare.

Resolution

For any image type, the useful range of resolution for faxing is between 100–200 dpi. You'll probably find that 100–150 dpi is all you need if you aren't regularly using your scanner's highest quality setting.

Text Originals

Text-only documents are the bread-and-butter of fax machines. With no color and no shades of gray, you can often just scan these documents using your scanner's 1-bit mode, which is often called line art, text, or black-and-white mode.

Color and Grayscale Originals

With color or grayscale documents, things are a little trickier. The scan's continuous tones and hues must survive as best they can when translated into the coarse black-and-white dither of a fax machine's transformation. You might want to control the quality of the conversion by doing it yourself.

Start by scanning the original as grayscale (even if the original's in color). Adjust it so that it has enough contrast to be recognizable after being faxed. For help with tonal adjustment, use the guidelines we discuss in Chapter 12, *Tonal Correction*.

Next, use your image editor to convert it into a 1-bit image. In Photoshop or Photoshop Elements, choose Bitmap from the Image menu's Mode submenu; for a color original, you'll have to choose Grayscale from the Mode submenu first.

These options will convert the image's gray tones to fax-friendly 1-bit tones in a way that you can control. If your image editor presents you with options for conversion, choose a dither or halftone screen option. Don't choose a "threshold" option, which removes all tonal gradations, resulting in a solid silhouette.

The 1-bit image that you get from the conversion should be adequate for faxing. If it isn't, try the conversion again with slightly different settings.

Graphics Modes

If your fax machine or fax modem has special modes for graphics or photos, test those modes. If they adapt color and grayscale images well for fax transmission, you may not need to make any image changes on your end. In particular, you may not need to convert it to a 1-bit image.

Manually converting your scans to 1-bit images might still provide more consistent results because you can't always be sure what your recipient will receive (**Figure 9-2**).

Figure 9-2
Converting a grayscale image to 1-bit using a diffusion dither

Scanning a Fax

If you need to scan a fax, set your scanner to 1 bit and 150 spi or lower. If it's a high-resolution fax, there may be some benefit in scanning it at 200 spi, but that's a rather rare scenario. Save the scan as a TIFF with compression turned on, and the file should be nice and compact.

Photocopiers

There may be times when you want to scan for a photocopier as the last output device in the chain from creation to distribution—think flyers, presentations, posters, and other ephemera. For example, you might want to create 500 handouts for a conference by printing one and then making 499 photocopies of it. Or you might want to distribute a document to a series of offices, instructing the staff to photocopy it as needed.

Photocopying is like faxing in that the process tends to increase contrast and reduce the number of tones and colors. However, photocopying preserves a lot more detail than faxing does. The general increase in contrast can also result in higher color saturation (sometimes too much) and clipped highlights and shadows. You can easily see these effects by photocopying a good photograph and comparing the original to the copy, although newer color copiers are much better at maintaining color than older models.

Because photocopying adds contrast, the logical countermeasure is to reduce the original image's contrast slightly. For color copies of color scans, you might also want to reduce the original's saturation. Of course, if you're the one running the copier, you could make these adjustments at the copier instead of making new versions of your originals. Check to see if the copier has a "photo" mode. If you're using a color scan in a document that's intended to be photocopied on black-and-white copiers, you might want to test it to make sure it looks good in grayscale, or simply convert it to grayscale and remove all doubt.

Resolution

Setting resolution is simple for photocopiers, a nice change from more complicated output devices with tonal options.

Text and Line-Art Originals

Text and line-art documents are already at 100 percent contrast, so don't bother to optimize them. However, copying reduces resolution, so keep text and line-art originals as crisp as possible by scanning them at an output resolution of 200 dpi or higher. There isn't much benefit beyond 300 dpi.

Color and Grayscale Originals

For color or grayscale originals, a setting of 100–200 dpi should be enough. Additional resolution is likely to be obscured by the halftoning, dithering, or other image processing that the copier may apply to reproduce the original's continuous tones.

Printing to a Copier

Your office might have a photocopier that's also a networked printer. If you send output directly to it from your computer, you're using it as a printer, so the guidelines we just talked about don't apply. Instead, treat it as a printer and use the guidelines we provide for you in the "Laser Printers" section just below.

Scanning a Photocopy

For good-quality photocopies where tones or colors are visible, set your scanner to 8 bits per channel RGB or grayscale, and to 200 spi. You can decrease or increase the resolution depending on the quality of the photocopy. If the photocopy is just text or line art, set your scanner to 1-bit mode instead (which might actually be called text or line art).

Office Printers

Office printers used for color printing of charts, graphs, or proofs tend to come in just two types: laser printers and inkjet printers.

Laser Printers

When you print a scan on a laser printer, its tones are halftoned or dithered into patterns that can be represented by tiny black or colored dots at 600–2400 dpi. You can't use those numbers as a guide for scanning output resolution, because the printer builds halftone patterns out of those dots, If you want to know more about how that works, see Chapter 21, *Frequency vs. Gray Levels*.

Older laser printers rendered tones using the press-style halftone dots we talk about in Part 5, *Halftones*. Using traditional halftone dots at the 300-dpi resolution of these old printers limited them to about 25 shades of gray (**Figure 9-3**). Current laser printers can print many more levels of gray and many more colors because they use alternative halftoning methods such as stochastic screening or plain old dithering, and because they can print smaller dots. A pretty average laser printer should have 600 dpi as a default option with 1200 dpi as its enhanced mode.

For good results on a desktop laser printer, scan your color and grayscale originals at 8 bits per channel for an out-

Figure 9-3 Low-frequency halftone from a laser printer

put resolution of between 150–300 dpi. For line art, you can go up to 1200 dpi or the maximum resolution of the printer, whichever is lower. Going above that resolution on a laser printer doesn't provide visibly better quality, even though the file takes up more disk space and opens, responds to changes, and prints more slowly.

If you're printing something that's intended to be photocopied, you should also adjust the scan according to the guidelines in the "Photocopiers" section earlier in the chapter.

The guidelines for scanning a photocopy in that section also apply to laser prints. You should use higher-quality settings more often with laser prints than with photocopies.

Inkjet Printing

Inkjet printers create output using methods similar to those of recent laser printers. They tend to use dithers—scattered dots that simulate smooth tonal values—to render tones and colors. For general office printing, you can follow the guidelines for consumer output in Chapter 8, *Scanning for Color Photo Printers*. Typically, scan 8-bit files at 150 dpi and higher.

The guidelines for scanning a photocopy, described earlier, also apply to inkjet prints. You'll probably use higher-quality settings more often with inkjet prints than with photocopies.

Out-of-House Quick-Print Shop

The "right" scanning specs for an outside quick-printing service like Kinko's are whatever works well on the specific equipment the service uses for your job. Some quick-printing jobs are output on high-speed laser printer/copiers, which means you'd set up your images for a laser printer as described earlier.

Part 1: Scanning

You might be surprised: Even small job printers might be using high-quality short-run multi-color presses (two to six colors per pass) with computer-to-plate output. It's so efficient that it can rival quick printing.

Other jobs might be sent to an offset printing press which eschews the metal plates from a platemaking machine or plate-setting output device. These jobs would be completed using inexpensive paper or plastic printing plates intended for lower-quality (but cheaper) offset reproduction. In this case, you would treat your project as more of a prepress job with higher quality specifications like the ones we talk about in Chapter 6, *Scanning for Prepress*.

Before you send your files out to a quick printer like Kinko's, tell the service what types of originals you have and ask for its scanning guidelines.

Adobe Acrobat PDF

Figure 9-4
Acrobat scanning dialog box

Today, many office documents are being converted into the Adobe Acrobat PDF format. Adobe is quite interested in accel-

erating this trend, so it's been closing the workflow gap between scanning images and making PDF files. If you have Acrobat Standard or Acrobat Professional (not just the Adobe Reader), you can scan images directly into PDF, which makes it easy to send the scan to people who might not be familiar with how to open bitmap formats like TIFF. Recipients can open the scan with the free Adobe Reader program.

We explain PDF at length in Chapter 16, *File Formats*. But you can generally consider PDF as a container format that stores many other kinds of files as well. When you scan into PDF, you're really scanning into an image format that's stored inside PDF like a photo in a shoebox. PDF stores scans using TIFF and JPEG, and offers many options for the storage resolution and compression method. However, Acrobat's scanning feature doesn't provide many options, and only two of them affect how the scan is saved.

To scan using Acrobat, click the Create Adobe PDF button on the toolbar and choose From Scanner (**Figure 9-4**). Or choose From Scanner from the Create PDF submenu in the File menu. After choosing a device, set the following two options. Each option affects scan quality.

Adapt Compression to Page Content. In general, turn on this option because it causes Acrobat to try to detect the types of images on the page and compress the overall scan using an appropriate method. You should turn off adaptive compression if you plan to apply optical character recognition (OCR) to the scan.

Higher Compression/Higher Quality slider. If it's more important for the file to be small, drag this slider to the left. If it's more important for the image to be scanned at high quality, drag it to the right.

If you want to work with a PDF scan as an image (adjusting tones and colors, crop-

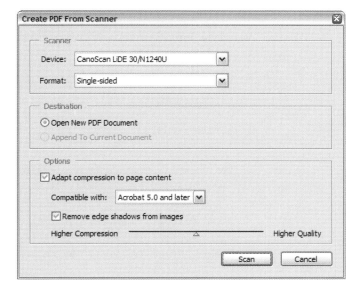

ping it, or painting on it), the best way is to open it in Photoshop or Photoshop Elements. Either program can open a PDF image just like any other bitmap or scan. You can then save it in any of the formats it supports. If you just want to convert the PDF scan to a format like TIFF, use Acrobat's Save As command, which gives you a choice of file formats.

OCR

As scanners became less expensive and easier to use, people started asking the question: "How much space could we save in our file cabinets if we just scan all that paper onto the server?" This sounds like a good idea, until you run into the next question: "How the heck would I find anything if it's all just images of pieces of paper?"

OCR uses a combination of built-in pattern recognition and heuristics (adaptive and trained learning) to identify characters and words in a scanned image, and converts them to true editable text. As real text, it's searchable, and that's appealing to companies with huge paper archives that are not really searchable as long as they remain on paper. And because it's real text, it can take a fraction of the space to store as the original scanned image at a legible resolution.

OCR is the rubric for a variety of software techniques that analyze a scan of printed text and turn it into letters, words, and sentences. A computer has to perform hard work when it analyzes a scan for text, and it's only in the last decade—as PCs have become really powerful—that OCR has become less hype and more truth as a real desktop solution.

Many applications can perform OCR, and there's a fair chance one of them came with your scanner, possibly in an older or "light" version with limited features. If you have Adobe Acrobat Standard or Profes-

sional, it too can perform OCR. Select the Document menu and then the Paper Capture submenu's Start Capture item. Adobe Acrobat's OCR engine works best on images that have a resolution of at least 200 dpi, and this is a good guideline to follow with any OCR software in general—though you should still check your OCR's manual to make sure.

You might need to increase the resolution to 300 dpi for small text or text with little details, like serifs, which might not be properly imaged at a lower resolution. However, if you're getting good results at 200 dpi, don't make larger files.

Because text is naturally high-contrast content, there's no need to scan in grayscale or color, so it's usually appropriate to set your scanner to 1-bit (line art) mode. Again, check the manual accompanying your OCR software, because some OCR software can take advantage of the extra information in a grayscale scan.

Once the page is scanned and analyzed, you should check the resulting words for suspected errors, or *suspects*. Each application has its own way of doing this, but you can usually check the OCR program's interpretation against how the word appears in the original scan. You may not want to do any bulk OCR until you're confident that the settings aren't creating too many suspects.

Getting Down to Business

The office is increasingly a place filled with images—and with the expectation that everyone in an office can handle scanning, producing, and outputting images for a variety of sometimes difficult-to-use devices. With the tips and guidelines in this chapter, you should be well on your way to becoming the office wiz.

PART 2

Anatomy of a Scanned Image

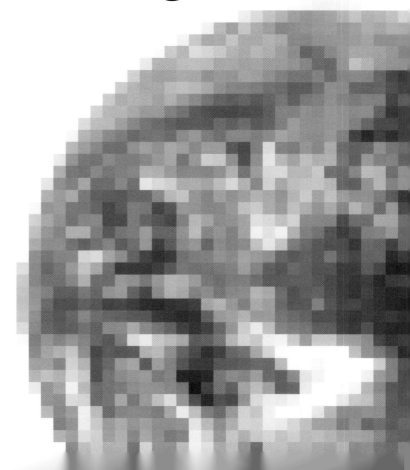

10

What Is a Bitmap?

BIT BY BIT

There's an amazing phenomenon that happens whenever someone talks about desktop publishing: every time the word *bitmap* is mentioned, people's eyes glaze over. Really; try it sometime. You can say, "Scan that photograph, drop it in the page-layout program, and print the halftone on the imagesetter," and everyone will nod their head and smile. Then say, "The resolution of the bitmapped graphic doubles when you reduce the image's size by 50 percent," and your audience will be asleep before you finish the sentence.

Bitmapped images do not make for exciting conversations. But it is a topic that is incredibly important to know about when working with scans. All scans are represented as bitmaps, and in the next few chapters we cover everything you need to know about how bitmapped images work and how to handle them. We promise it

isn't as confusing—or as boring—as it sometimes seems.

The word *bitmap* is confusing only because its two constituents, "bit" and "map," both sound so technical. A bit is just the tiniest unit of computer storage, representing either a one or a zero. A map is jargon for a table, like a spreadsheet—the information is organized two-dimensionally, into rows and columns. A bitmap is a table that describes where bits are located—as in an image.

In this chapter we describe the characteristics of bitmapped graphics—the attributes that define them—and how those characteristics relate to file size.

Meet the Bitmaps

A bitmap describes all the points in a rectangular grid of dots. In plain English, a bitmapped file might read, "The point at coordinate 1,1 is black; the point at coordinate 1,2 is white; the point at coordinate 1,3 is black," and so on.

Sample Points

When we talk about points in a bitmapped graphic, we call them *samples* or *sample points*. We use this term because a scanner *samples* an image—checking what color or gray value it finds—every $\frac{1}{300}$ inch, every $\frac{1}{100}$ inch, or whatever. So we talk about the resolution of bitmaps in *samples per inch*, or spi.

Samples are not the same as *dots* (the small round marks that laser printers and imagesetters make) or *spots* (the elements of a halftone) or *pixels* (the "picture elements" on a computer screen), so we prefer to use a distinct term for them.

Characteristics of Bitmapped Graphics

Every bitmapped graphic has four basic characteristics: dimension, resolution, bit depth, and color model. People use these terms all the time without really knowing what they mean, and then make poor decisions based on a faulty understanding. So let's look at what these words refer to, and why they're important.

Dimension

Bitmapped images are actually big rectangular grids. Like checkerboards or parquet floors in your kitchen, these big grids are made up of little squares. And grids always have dimensions—specifically, two dimensions (**Figure 10-1**). A chessboard is always eight squares by eight squares. The grid of pixels that makes up your computer screen might be 1024 by 768.

The dimensions of a grid—the number of squares tall and wide it is—are independent of the actual *size* of a grid. A chessboard can be a 6-inch square (the traveling set) or the size of an outdoor college campus quadrangle (the Renaissance Fair set). The chessboard is still just eight squares by eight squares; it's independent of *resolution*.

However, increasing the dimensions of a bitmapped image increases file size geometrically. So if you double an image's dimensions, you increase file size by a factor of four. Increase the image to three times dimensions, and file size increases by a factor of nine.

Resolution

The word *resolution* is so misunderstood and overused that we've devoted an entire chapter to it: Chapter 11, *Image Resolution*. The resolution of a bitmapped image is the number of samples (or squares in the grid) in each unit of measurement. If we're talking in inches, we talk about spi.

If your bitmapped image has 72 samples per inch, and it's 72 samples long on each side, you know that it's an inch long on each side. We can take the same bitmapped image and change it to 36 spi (change its resolution without affecting the underlying grid dimensions), and suddenly the image is two inches on each side—same *number* of samples, but each one is twice as big (**Figure 10-2**). Changing resolution of an existing scan doesn't change the file's size.

You can also look at bitmap resolution in another way: If you know the pixel dimensions of an image and its resolution,

Figure 10-1
Dimensions of a bitmapped image

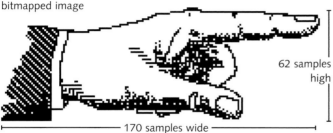

62 samples high

170 samples wide

Figure 10-2
Changing bitmap
resolution

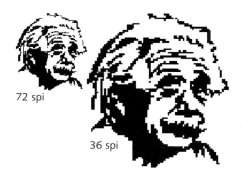

72 spi

36 spi

you can figure out its physical dimensions. When you scan a picture that is three inches on each side at 100 spi, you know that the bitmapped image has 300 samples on each side (100 per inch). If you scan it at 300 spi, the dimensions shoot up to 900 dots on each side. Because each sample takes up room on the disk, the more samples, the larger the disk file.

Bit Depth

In Chapter 2, *Scanners,* we explained what bit depth meant when scanning samples. Each sample in a bitmapped image can be black, white, gray, or a color; the key is the number of bits used to describe it. A sample that is defined using one bit of information can only be black or white—zero or one. If you have two bits of information describing a sample, there are four possible combinations (00, 01, 10, and 11), hence four possible colors or gray levels (**Figure 10**-3). Eight bits of information gives you 256 levels of gray; 24 bits of information results in over 16 million possible colors (with 24-bit images, each sample actually has three 8-bit values—one each for red, green, and blue).

The number of bits is called the image's *bit depth*. We call a 1-bit image a *flat* bitmap; it's also called a bilevel image. A *deep*

You'll rarely hear the term deep bitmap *any more; it's more historical in nature, dating from a time when it was less common.*

bitmap is any image that has more than one bit describing each sample (**Figure 10-4**).

Bit depth also affects the image's file size. An 8-bit image is eight times the size of a similar 1-bit image: it uses eight bits to describe each dot instead of one. A 24-bit image is 24 times as big, and so on. Increasing bit depth increases file size arithmetically. Here are strategies for deciding your bit depth.

How many bits do you need? For editing photographic-quality images, you should use at least 8 bits per channel (24-bit RGB color). Most equipment and software support 8 bits per channel by default, so you usually don't have to do anything special to achieve this result.

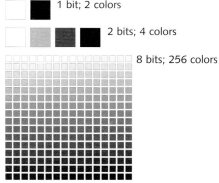

1 bit; 2 colors

2 bits; 4 colors

8 bits; 256 colors

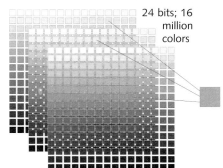

24 bits; 16 million colors

Three 8-bit values (red, green, and blue) combine to make 16 million colors

Figure 10-3 Bits per sample

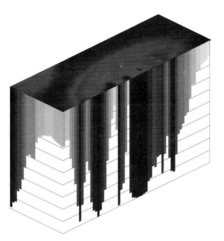

Figure 10-4 A deep bitmap

While you can use techniques like dithering and indexed color to create great-looking images at minimal bit depth, these techniques cut so many corners in simulating a full range of colors that you can't easily edit those images without ruining them—the color fidelity is too poor. Bit depths below 8 bits per channel are appropriate only for versions of the image that will be viewed using a narrow-bandwidth medium like dial-up Internet connections.

Will more bits get you better color? One of the most acrimonious holy wars raging in digital imaging circles is whether bit depths above 8 bits per channel are worth using when the human eye can't even distinguish among the majority of tones in the more 16-million-plus colors present in a 24-bit RGB image. The simple answer is that 8 bits per channel may be enough for your scans if they don't need much adjustment to make them suitable for your final medium.

Some applications define bitmap more narrowly than others. For example, although many people think of a bitmap as a map of bits of any bit depth, Photoshop uses the term only to describe 1-bit images.

Images acquired at 16 bits per channel from a scanner or digital camera provide a lot more flexibility when you edit them: their tones and colors won't posterize, or stair-step, as quickly as an 8-bit image. However, you perceive this difference only when you make major or repeated changes, or work in a color space with a very large gamut. If your images don't need such a dramatic level of editing, the extra bits may not be worth what they will cost you in terms of the additional RAM, storage space, and processing power required to store and edit them.

A bit misleading. Bit depth doesn't directly correspond to image quality. You gain nothing by converting 8-bit images to 16 bits, and a well-done 8-bit scan may be preferable to a poorly done 16-bit scan. It's like buying a bag of 16 apples on sale at the store—if you get home and find that 12 of the apples in the bag are bruised or rotten, you would have gotten a better deal picking out eight perfect apples by hand. To take full advantage of 16-bit images, remember that what you really want are 16 *good* bits. The guidelines in Chapter 5, *How to Read Your Scanning Software*, can help you scan good image data at the bit depth you choose.

Color Model

The final attribute of a bitmapped image is the color model, which really only applies to color images. The most common color model is RGB (red, green, and blue), in which each color is represented by an 8-bit value for a total of 24 bits.

Some bitmaps are described using the CMYK color model, defining values for each of the four process printing colors: cyan, magenta, yellow, and black (represented by K). While this results in 32 bits per sample, it doesn't add more colors; it's just a different method of describing the colors—a method that's required for most offset printing and many color printers. For more on CMYK bitmaps, see the discussions of the TIFF and EPS formats in Chapter 16, *File Formats*.

We use RGB because monitors display color by striking red, green, and blue phosphors with an electronic beam; monitors use RGB because those three emitted colors can be mixed to create most of the visible spectrum. CMY without K (black) is the reflective equivalent of RGB; when white light strikes cyan, the ink absorbs all the other colors, and so on. To make red on a monitor, you excite just red phosphors; to do this on paper, you print magenta and yellow ink, which together absorb everything but red light. CMY add up to black, but impurities in the ink and limitations on how much ink paper can hold require the use of black.

Device-independent (CIE) color. This class of color model emerged to work with the color-management systems that improve color correspondence between your screen, color printouts, and final printed output. These *device-independent* or *perceptually based* models don't describe a color by the components that make it up (RGB or CMYK, for instance). They describe *what a color looks like*. All of them are based, more or less, on the standards defined by the Commission Internationale de l'Eclairage (CIE) in 1931.

The problem with RGB and CMYK color models is that a given RGB (or CMYK) specification doesn't really describe a color. A color specified using RGB may look totally different on your monitor than it

does on color-printer output. Perceptually based color definitions describe what a color looks like; it's up to your color-management software to decide what RGB or CMYK values are needed to create that color on a given device.

Indexed color. Indexed color is a method for producing a file that uses a specific color table. Indexed-color bitmaps can use a table containing up to 256 colors chosen from the full 24-bit RGB palette. A given sample's color is defined by reference (an *index*) to the abbreviated table: "this sample is color number 123, this sample is color number 81," and so on.

While indexed color can save disk space by using 8 bits per sample point at most, rather than the full 24, you only have 256 colors available. The colors can be optimized for that image, however. You might want to convert indexed-color bitmaps to true RGB for editing, though the image isn't improved any in the process—you still have access to just 256 colors.

 Color-management systems and their associated color models are discussed in Chapter 13, Getting Good Color.

On the other hand, you can't use indexed color for files with a bit depth higher than 8 bits, because the color table becomes too large to be practical and no longer saves any significant disk space. While an 8-bit color table can easily be shown as a 16-by-16 grid of 256 colors, a 24-bit color table would comprise over 16 million squares—not very easy to edit!

Indexed color is used primarily in GIF files, which is the standard—though imperfect—image format used on the World Wide Web. (See Chapter 7, *Scanning for the Web and Video*.)

 Professional image-editing software and high-end scanners support the LAB color model, which is based on CIE color.

Unlike resolution and bit depth, the color model of a bitmapped image doesn't necessarily have a direct bearing on file size. However, if you change the color model, the computer might need to change the image's bit depth, which will change file size. For example, if you convert a CMYK image to a grayscale image, the computer changes the bit depth from 32 bits (8 bits for each of the four channels) to 8 bits. This reduces the file size by 75 percent. Similarly, if you change a flat, bilevel bitmap into an RGB bitmap, the computer has to add 23 bits to each pixel, making the file size 24 times as large.

Bitmaps and File Size

You've no doubt noticed that throughout this chapter we've commented on how different bitmap attributes affect file size. We've done so because it's a really important topic. Big files are hard to work with, hard to print, and hard to transfer. So it's well worth reducing file size when you can.

To encapsulate what we discussed earlier in the chapter, here's a rundown of the characteristics of bitmapped images that affect file size.

Dimensions and resolution. Increasing the number of samples in a bitmap by increasing the dimensions raises file size geometrically: 200-spi bitmaps are four times as big as 100-spi bitmaps, and 300-spi images are nine times larger. Resolution is independent of dimensions; it's the measurement of samples against a scale, like 300 spi.

Bit depth. Increasing bit depth increases file size arithmetically. A 24-bit image is three times as large as an 8-bit image. A 16-bit-per channel color file (48 bits) requires twice as much storage as a 24-bit color file.

Color model. Color model doesn't necessarily increase file size, but going from RGB to CMYK color models does because CMYK requires an additional color channel.

Figuring File Size

Now that you know the factors that affect the size of bitmaps, it's a simple matter to calculate file size using the following formula.

$$\text{Resolution} \times \text{Width} \times \text{Height} \times \text{Bits per sample} \div 8{,}192 = \text{File size (in kilobytes)}$$

This formula works because 8192 is the number of bits in a kilobyte. For example, if you have a 4-by-5–inch 1-bit image at 300 spi, you know that the file size is 220 K. You multiply 300 squared (or 90,000) by 4 by 5 by 1; divide by 8192 and you get right about 220. A 24-bit image of the same size would be 5273 K (which is just about 5 Mb).

File Format

One other factor—file format—can also affect the file size of bitmapped image files (we discuss these in detail in Chapter 16, *File Formats*). Storing an image as a TIFF file creates a file size different from one stored as a JPEG or EPS file, even if the dimensions and bit depth are the same. Why? Because the EPS file typically includes a preview image over and above the image stored in the file. JPEG always compresses files a bit, and TIFF and JPEG 2000 files can use built-in compression (see Chapter 17, *Compression*), making files smaller. And other file formats include similar additions or compression methods to suit different needs.

Plus, when you're saving bitmapped images in EPS format, there's one other consideration: binary versus ASCII encoding. Binary-encoded bitmaps are half the size of ASCII-encoded bitmaps. ASCII encoding is sometimes necessary for passing data over old networks or ancient modems.

Implications of File Size

This section describes the problems posed by large bitmapped image files. For advice on reducing file size, see Chapter 11, *Image Resolution*.

Storage and transmission. Hard disk storage is absurdly cheap. (A Dilbert cartoon shows Alice offering Mordac, the preventer of information services, a quarter to double her enormous storage allotment.) Where file size becomes an issue is when you transmit files, even over fast links, and when you exchange files using removable or write-once media. As David's grandmother always says, "Smaller is better."

Memory. With modern operating systems (Mac OS X and Windows XP or later), you don't need a lot of RAM to open an image. You can certainly place images on pages regardless of how much RAM you have. But as with most computation, more memory often speeds the task. If you're working routinely with many multi-megabyte files, you want to have several hundred megabytes available for your image-editing program. If the program can load the entire image in progress into memory, every task is faster.

When we wrote the first edition of the book, a few megabytes was a lot. The second edition, we advised at least 32 Mb, if you can even believe that. Today, 256 Mb is a realistic minimum, but 512 Mb to 1 Gb of RAM ($50 to $100 at today's prices) is a terrific investment to offset the amount of time you wait for operations to complete.

Printing. The biggest problem with big files is printing. You have to transmit the files over some kind of cable or network (USB, FireWire, Ethernet, whatever), and the printer or imagesetter has to digest all the information. At best, big files make you wait for output. At worst, you incur additional imagesetting charges for slow output—or the files won't print at all. Keep files small to avoid all these problems.

Bit, Bit, Array!

You now understand the fundamental building blocks of images: bits forming bitmaps. In the next chapter, we explain how bits and scale are related in bitmaps, and how to control image resolution.

11

Image Resolution

SCANNING, SCALING, AND RESAMPLING

We now arrive at what may be the most misunderstood topic in electronic publishing: resolution. The word *resolution* comes up in conversation—directly or indirectly—so often that you'd think it was a synonym for money. In some ways it is: if you don't understand resolution in all its different forms, you can't be efficient in your work; and if you aren't efficient in your work, you can't make money in this business.

The word *resolution* is used in so many different contexts that people quickly get confused about what it means. There's the resolution of an image, of an imagesetter, of a scanner, and so on. In this chapter we want to solidify your understanding of scanned image resolution in all its incarnations. Just remember what we keep saying: It's not as hard as it sometimes seems.

They're All Just Dots

Resolution describes a grid of dots that are assigned or mapped to a given physical or unit space typically measured in inches or centimeters. You can't have resolution without a measurement of how many dots per unit. It's as simple as that.

Most people use the word *dot* to mean many things: a printer dot, an on-screen pixel, a value for the area represented by each scanner sample, and so forth. In the following list, we've defined our terminology for dot, spot, pixel, and sample to make it simpler to understand exactly what we're talking about, and you can use **Table 11-1** as a quick reference.

▶ *Dots.* Printer resolution is measured in dots per inch (dpi). These are actual dots created by a laser printer or imagesetter.

Table 11-1 Where the terminology fits into the scanning process

Scanning	Final output		
Scanner units	**Output type**	**Device units**	**Device screening units**
Samples	Press	Dot	Halftone spot or line
	On-screen	Pixel	none
	Film recorder	Res (samples/mm)	n/a

▶ *Samples.* For scanned images or bit-mapped images, we talk about samples per inch (spi). A sample is a measurement of tone or color at a given place. Many people will insist that image resolution should be specified in dpi rather than spi, but you can look them right in the eye and say, "There are no dots in an image; just samples."

▶ *Pixels.* For display resolution, it's pixels per inch (ppi). A pixel (or "picture element") is a single x,y coordinate on a monitor that can represent any one of from 1 to 16 million different values. Adobe Photoshop uses ppi instead of spi for image resolution, and although Photoshop is the standard in image-editing tools, we aren't bowing to its terminology.

▶ *Spots and lines.* We talk about halftones themselves by using the term *spot*: the shape made up of printer dots that creates the halftone value. (We examine spots in much greater detail throughout Part 5, *Halftones,* but discuss them specifically in Chapter 19, *Dots, Spots, and Halftones.*) Halftones are measured in lines per inch (lpi).

▶ *Res.* Some service bureaus may use the term *res* (pronounced rez) to refer to the resolution of a scanned image. Res is another word for samples per millimeter. Scanner operators often scan at "res 12," meaning 12 samples per millimeter or 304 spi (25.4 mm to the inch).

By using these separate terms, each of which has a specific meaning, you'll always know when we're talking about a monitor display or a scanned image.

Resolving Resolutions

If there's one set of distinctions we'd like you to learn in this chapter, it's the differences between *sampling resolution, image resolution, effective resolution,* and *device resolution.* Just because a scanner scans an image at 200 spi doesn't mean that the resolution of the image that's saved, or even printed, will be 200 spi. The resolution can be affected if you scale or resample it at any point in the process.

Don't worry about always having to keep four different resolutions straight in your head—if you scan, edit, and output an image without changing its original dimensions, the values for the first three types of resolution are the same. But confusion can set in when image size changes during the process. That's when these terms can help you sort it all out.

Sampling resolution. This is the resolution at which the scanner samples the original. It's defined and limited by the scanner hardware, and you control it using your scanning software.

Image resolution. When you save the scanned image from your scanning software or image editor, the software writes the image's resolution into the file itself. (A very few older file formats don't include

The calculation for effective resolution can seem counterintuitive, but remember that you have to square the spi measurement to obtain the actual number of pixels in a given area. The spi number is linear, but image data is represented as the area on a two-dimensional surface. So 200 by 200 spi times 6 by 9 inches is 2.16 million pixels, the same as 300 by 300 spi times 4 by 6 inches.

the resolution information, but it's unlikely you will encounter them.) If you didn't resize or resample the image after scanning, the image resolution remains the same as the sampling resolution. For example, if you scan a 4-by-6–inch image at 300 spi and 100 percent scaling, then use Photoshop to scale it down by 50 percent (without resampling), and then save the image, the image resolution becomes 600 spi.

Effective resolution. This is the resolution of an image at its final output dimensions. Effective resolution differs from image resolution only when you scale an image without resampling its data (**Figure 11-1**). This makes the same number of samples cover a different area.

One example is when you scale an image in a page-layout program: If you take the 4-by-6–inch, 300-spi scan from the previous example, place it into InDesign, for instance, and scale it up to cover 50 percent more area on the page to 6 by

9 inches, its effective resolution becomes 200 spi, or one half the number of pixels in the same area. Effective resolution is set by the size of the image in a particular document, not by the image itself.

If you scale up an image too far, its effective resolution drops below the value required for good quality. To help you avoid this problem, InDesign CS's Info palette has a wonderful feature that tells you both the image resolution (which it calls Actual ppi, or pixels per inch) and the effective resolution of a selected image on a page (**Figure 11-2**).

 Chapters 6 through 9 provide more specific recommendations for setting appropriate image resolutions for particular types of devices.

Device resolution. This number isn't part of the image at all, but is the resolution of the output device. For example, a monitor might be 72 dpi, and an imagesetter might be 2400 dpi.

Device resolution can be confusing because its relationship to an image's resolution depends on what kind of device it is. When creating Web graphics or other images for display on a computer monitor, you want each image pixel to correspond to a monitor pixel. But for very high-reso-

Figure 11-1
Sampling, image, effective, and device resolutions

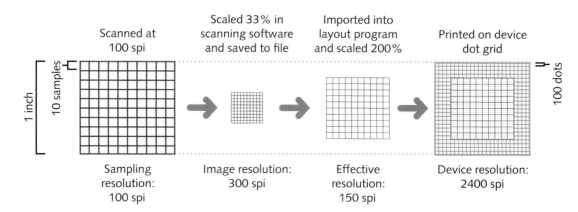

Scanned at 100 spi — Scaled 33% in scanning software and saved to file — Imported into layout program and scaled 200% — Printed on device dot grid

1 inch / 10 samples / 100 dots

Sampling resolution: 100 spi — Image resolution: 300 spi — Effective resolution: 150 spi — Device resolution: 2400 spi

Figure 11-2 Info palette in Adobe InDesign CS for a scaled-down image

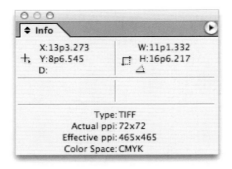

lution devices like imagesetters and photo printers, the image resolution shouldn't be anywhere near the output resolution because the output device uses all of the extra dots to build halftone spots or dither patterns, not image details.

In the previous section, we describe dots, samples, pixels, spots, lines, and res. Those terms correspond to the types of resolution we just covered. *Sample* is a unit related to sampling resolution and image resolution. *Spot* and *line* are units of measure for halftones, so the terms are mathematically related to device resolution. *Dots*, *pixels*, and *res* are device-specific terms for device resolution.

Scaling and Resampling

As mentioned previously, image resolution can be altered by scaling and resampling. It's important to understand the difference, so we've laid it all out for you here.

Scaling

First and foremost, when you place a scanned image on a page and scale it, you change the image's effective resolution (see **Figure 11-3**). As we note in Chapter 10, *What is a Bitmap?,* the grid's pixel dimensions stay the same. Let's say you have a 2-by-2–inch, 100-spi image. Reduce it to 50 percent, and you have a 1-by-1–inch, 200-spi image—the same number of samples packed into half the space or a quarter of the area.

If you specify a scaling percentage in the Print dialog box, you're further affecting resolution. If you enlarge to 200 percent, for instance, you're reducing the resolution by a factor of two.

Resampling

You can resize a bitmap while maintaining its resolution. Or you can change a bitmap's resolution without changing its size. This process is called *resampling*, and it's accomplished by using an image-editing program.

The best way to explain resampling is to show you Photoshop's Image Size dialog box (**Figure 11-4**). With Resample Image checked, when you enter new values for Width and Height under Pixel Dimensions, the file size changes but Print Size stays constant.

When you reduce the resolution of a bitmap, it's called *downsampling*. When you increase the resolution, it's called *interpolation*. In either case, there are more and less effective methods to perform these tasks without damaging an image.

Interpolation is the process of generating a sample point in a bitmap where there wasn't one before. Downsampling is similar, but it removes sample points throughout the image. Most resampling processes are very basic. A scanning or image-editing program might add a sample point and, to figure out what color it should be, just use the value of the sample next to the new one (*nearest neighbor*). If the software is slightly smarter, it'll compare the samples on either side and use the average between the two (*bilinear*). Sometimes this process gives you a good image, and sometimes it doesn't. The best kind of interpolation is *bicubic*, which looks at all four surrounding samples and applies their average value to the new sample point. This takes the longest, but yields the best quality with continuous tone images.

Figure 11-3 Scaling and resolution

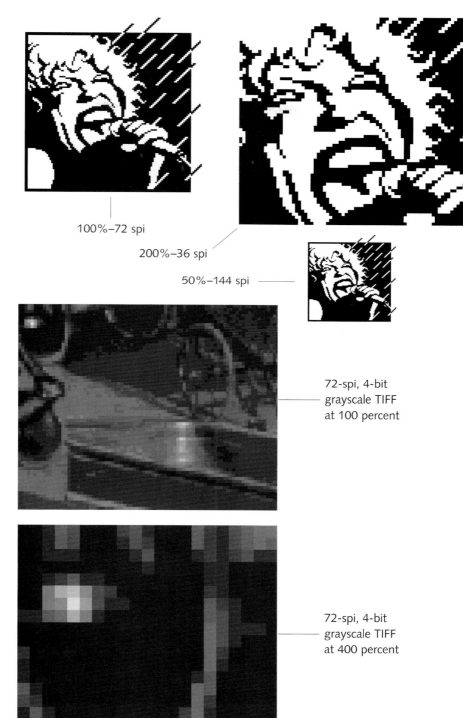

100%–72 spi

200%–36 spi

50%–144 spi

72-spi, 4-bit grayscale TIFF at 100 percent

72-spi, 4-bit grayscale TIFF at 400 percent

would. Because actual results depend on the image content, you might want to try each option when you're working with critical images.

The Limits of Interpolation

Unlike downsampling, which simply removes existing information (using more or less intelligent methods), interpolation is more problematic, because it attempts to add information that doesn't exist in the original image (**Figure 11-5**). While it can help reduce aliasing (aka *the jaggies*) in some situations, it can't add detail to an image if the detail isn't present in the original.

Alternative Interpolation Methods

Photoshop's long list of resampling options isn't the definitive list of what's available. When upsampling to a large scaling factor, some people claim that you'll get better results if you upsample in multiple steps. For example, if you want to enlarge an image eightfold, try upsampling by a factor of two through three iterations. Proponents of this method say that it minimizes the artifacts that upsampling can produce, but others say that you can do just as well using Photoshop's newer Bicubic Smoother option.

Some insist that fractal-math programs like Genuine Fractals can provide better, smoother upsampling than any of the methods within Photoshop. Again, others say they see no difference.

Figure 11-4
Photoshop's Image Size dialog box

Photoshop CS offers all three methods, and adds two of its own: Bicubic Smoother and Bicubic Sharper. These two options try to address limitations with bicubic resampling. When upsampling an image (such as for a photo enlargement), Bicubic Smoother may result in fewer artifacts than Bicubic. When downsampling an image (for instance, for the Web), Bicubic Sharper may blur the image less than Bicubic

Figure 11-5
Interpolation

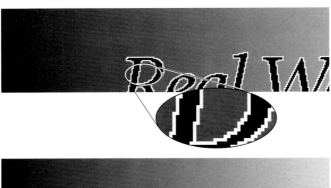

When you double the resolution, interpolation creates extra gray samples.

 You can download the Genuine Fractals trial version from **www.lizardtech.com** *and judge for yourself whether fractal resizing is better than incremental resampling or Photoshop's built-in options.*

Resolution and Quality

Armed with the information in this chapter, you can scan images at just the right resolution for your needs. Not so much that you have to run out and buy more hard disks, yet not so little that quality suffers.

For resolution advice that's more specific to particular output media, see chapters 6 through 9. Those chapters cover output-specific scanning and editing settings.

In the next few chapters we look at how to take the unpolished data you've scanned and sculpt it into that perfect final image you've had in mind from the time you put the original in the scanner.

PART 3

Image Correction

12

Tonal Correction

GETTING GREAT GRAYS

When you buy a new car, you make adjustments to it before driving it away. You first adjust the seat, then the mirrors, and you might even change the settings on the radio to the channels you listen to most often. When scanning images, you almost never just roll with what the scanner gives you by default. You adjust the picture's tones, sharpen the image, and along the way you might even change parts of the picture to suit your needs.

In this chapter, we discuss one of the first elements you want to adjust in your image: *tone*. You can think of tone as how the colors or gray levels throughout a picture relate to one another.

As we point out in Chapter 2, *Scanners*, many scanners have difficulty picking up detail in the darkest areas of prints and film. That means most of the desktop-created scans you see are either too dark, with no detail at all in shadow areas, or blown out, with white representing all the lighter tones, like light reflecting off a face.

In this chapter we play both ends off the middle: we want to increase detail in those trouble spots without washing out or filling in, while also brightening the image overall.

Visualizing Tonal Values

Most image-editing prorgams provide you with two effective tools for visualizing the tonal values in an image. One shows a histogram, which represents the distribution of samples across the tonal range, while

Figure 12-1
Histogram

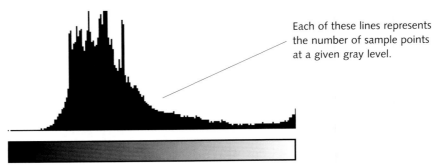

Each of these lines represents
the number of sample points
at a given gray level.

the other displays the relationship between input values (your starting point) and output values (the corrected image).

Histograms

Histograms are an extremely useful tool for looking at how gray levels are spread out through an image. A *histogram* is simply a relative or *normalized* chart of the percentage of samples in the bitmapped image that are set to each gray level (**Figure 12-1**). For example, a histogram can tell you that there are 10 sample points that are totally black, 34 sample points that have a gray level of 1 (out of 255 levels of gray), 40 sample points that have a gray level of 2, and so on.

By looking at the histogram of an image, you can quickly tell where the information in the image is concentrated—in shadow areas, in highlights, or in the midtones (**Figure 12-2**).

Gray-Map Curves

In order to change the tonal balance of an image, you need to adjust its gray levels. Different programs let you do this in different ways, but typically the mechanism you use is a *contrast* or *gray-map curve* (**Figure 12-3**). It *maps* grays to different gray values.

Perhaps the easiest way to understand a gray-map curve is to think about coffee or tea filters. When you pour water through a filter with coffee or tea in it, the water becomes flavored. You can use filters with images, too. A gray-map curve is a type of filter that you can pour an image through.

By looking at the gray map, you can actually figure out what will happen to an image when you apply that filter to it. Typically, the horizontal axis of the chart describes the levels of gray—from white to black—of the input image (the image that you start with). The vertical axis describes the levels of gray of the output image (the image you'll end up with).

A map or filter that shows a straight 45-degree line, like the one shown in **Figure 12-3** on the left, is called a *normal* contrast curve. With a 45-degree line, each input sample is left intact: it's a one-to-one relationship between input and output: the black pixels in the input image remain black; the 50-percent gray pixels remain that tint, and so on. Keep this filter in mind over the next sections.

Linear Correction, or, How to Ruin an Image

Linear correction is the most basic method of tonal correction. It keeps the line straight while altering the line's slope, hence the name *linear*. When you use the run-of-the-mill brightness and contrast controls found in most inexpensive image editors or pro-

A histogram has a fixed height, so the more samples there are, the more relative the chart is to the overall image size.

Figure 12-2
Various histograms

Low contrast; tonal compression

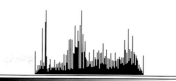

High contrast; expanded tonal range

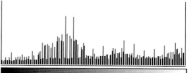

Darkened; histogram moves to the left

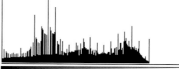

Linear corrections usually push dark
pixels to black and light pixels to white.

Lightened; histogram moves to
the right

Figure 12-3
Linear gray maps

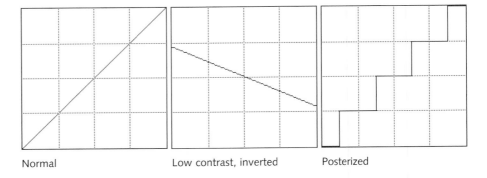

Normal   Low contrast, inverted   Posterized

grams that just happen to let you make basic changes to an image, you are making linear corrections. (Even if you can't see the graph in your application, that's what's happening behind the scenes).

As you'll see in the next few paragraphs, linear correction eliminates data in an unintelligent manner. We consider linear correction—the use of standard brightness and contrast controls—to be essentially worthless; but we'll explain how they work so you can see what we mean. You can affect linear correction in two ways: by moving the line up and down and by changing the slope of the line.

Brightness

The first linear correction we look at is adjusting brightness. In you take the line in our example in **Figure 12-3** and move the line straight up, you lighten the image (**Figure 12-4**). That's because each input sample point is converted to a lighter output value.

Depending on the program you use, moving a brightness control to a higher number or to the right pushes the line up, and to a lower number or to the left pushes the line down.

You might hear people talk about "linearizing" tones, which means to ensure that reproduction of tones progresses consistently from light to dark. Don't confuse this with linear correction.

For example, let's say we have a sample point that is 50-percent gray in the input image. When we pass it through the filter in **Figure 12-4** that sample point is converted into a lighter value (middle photo)—let's say 30-percent gray. Lowering the line has the opposite effect: it darkens the image (bottom photo). That same 50-percent sample point is changed to a darker value when it is passed through the filter.

As you can see in the histogram for the (lightened) image in **Figure 12-2**, brightness controls just shift all the values in the image up. Although brightening can make shadow detail easier to see, it doesn't increase the differentiation between subtly different values (which is what *really* increases detail in an image). And—this is the worst drawback of linear brightness adjustment—all the information at both ends of the histogram is lost. The highlights are literally pushed off the end of gray map—subtle tonal details in the highlights wash out to white. The shadows are completely pushed up out of the low end of the map, leaving no dark tones at all.

Contrast

Although changing the position of the line on the gray map filter changes brightness, changing the slope of the line alters the image's contrast. If you make the slope of the line steeper, you increase the contrast of the image (**Figure 12-5**). Gray levels below a certain level turn white and

Figure 12-4
Linear brightness
adjustment

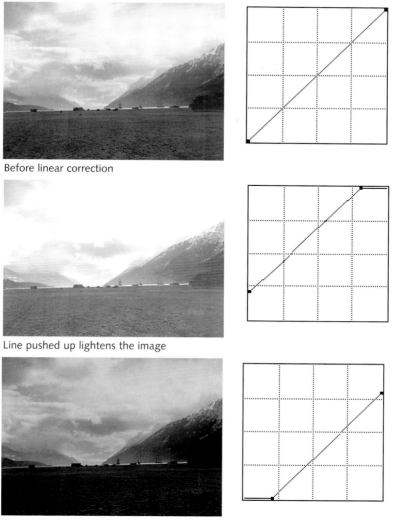

Before linear correction

Line pushed up lightens the image

Line pushed down darkens the image

above a certain level turn black. The subtle tones in between become solid bands with abrupt changes.

If you make the slope of the line less steep than the initial 45-degree angle, you decrease the contrast of the image. This is also called tone compression, because you're compressing the whole range of 256 gray levels into a smaller number of gray levels washing it out.

It depends on the software you're using, but typically contrast controls offer less (more washed out) or more (darker)

adjustments. Moving a contrast control to the left or more washed-out is like rotating the filter line to a shallower pitch. Moving the control to the right or darker rotates the line steeper.

Linear contrast adjustment is just as problematic as linear brightness adjustment, but in a different way. Increasing contrast does increase the difference between adjacent gray levels—improving detail in the midtones—but it lops off detail in both highlights *and* shadows. Decreasing contrast is almost never a very useful technique, unless you want to limit the range of highlights and shadows for reproduction reasons (see Chapter 22, *Reproducing Halftones*).

Nonlinear Correction, or, Correction Done Right

To achieve the kind of tonal correction you really need—by that we mean increasing shadow detail and brightening images without washing out highlight areas—you need to use *nonlinear correction* (**Figure 12-6**).

Nonlinear correction is not a panacea, however. It loses data just as linear correction does, but in a manner that preserves more detail that the eye can perceive. When you use nonlinear correction to bring out shadow detail, you lose some detail in the highlights: the curve is flatter, which makes a range of highlight tones shrink to a much smaller range. Since the biggest problem with desktop scans is bringing out shadow detail, it's worth losing highlight detail in exchange for shadow detail.

Another problem to watch for with nonlinear correction is posterization in deep shadow areas in which smoothly gradated tones are changed into bands of solid tones. If the angle of the curve in shadow areas gets too steep, you start seeing distinct jumps from one gray level to another—especially in areas of smooth tonal gradation.

Methods of Nonlinear Correction

Different graphics programs offer different methods for nonlinear correction—from drawing a curve to moving sliders.

Figure 12-5
Linear contrast adjustment

Steeper slope, higher contrast

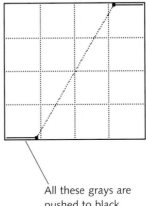

All these grays are pushed to black.

Shallower slope, less contrast

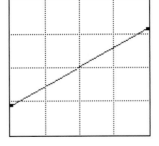

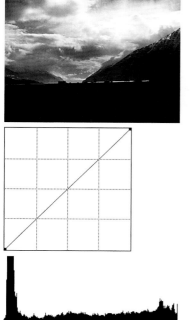

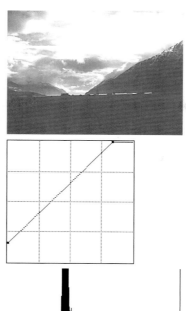

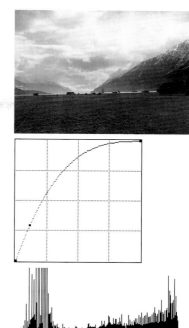

Uncorrected. As scanned, the image is very dark overall. There is no visible detail in the shadow areas—or well into the midtones, for that matter.

Linear brightness adjustment. This method simply pushes all the values up without increasing the differentiation between samples. All detail in the highlights is gone—pushed to white—but shadow detail is not enhanced much.

Nonlinear adjustment. The bars in the histogram are spread out increasing the difference between samples. This increases visible detail in the shadows and midtones with only minor loss of highlight detail.

Figure 12-6
Nonlinear tonal correction

Drawing Curves

One nonlinear approach is the simple pencil-and-graph tools in programs such as Adobe Photoshop CS (**Figure 12-7**). However, the inability to control the curve numerically makes it difficult or impossible to predict or repeat results with precision.

It's also quite difficult to draw a decent curve with the little pencil (though the option offered in some programs to smooth your coarsely drawn line can help solve this problem). A curve that isn't smooth can increase the risk of posterization. We recommend you walk, or run, away from this method.

Figure 12-7
Pencil-like curve tools

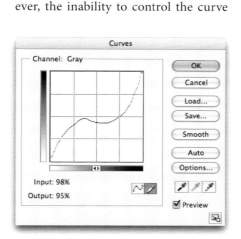

Adjusting Curves' Control Points

Most page-layout or image-editing programs let you move control points on a curve that represent input and output values. It's more like working in a drawing program than a painting program. In the better implemented of these techniques—

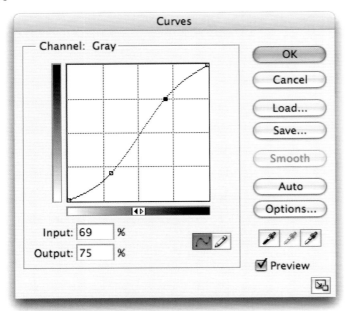

Figure 12-8
Control-point
curves

Pay attention to the gradients next to the curve graph that indicate light and dark. For example, in Photoshop, the graph goes from dark (0) to light (255) for RGB images, but the graph goes from light (0) to dark (100%) for CMYK and grayscale images.

Most programs also allow you to clip the upper and lower output levels, but some require values be entered manually; others use a separate image-control dialog box.

Photoshop adjustment. To adjust the tonal range of grayscale and color scans in Photoshop, we provide you with the following steps (**Figure 12-9**); these same steps apply to Corel Photo-Paint, Picture Publisher, and others.

▶ Select the Image menu, choose the Adjustments submenu, and then choose the Levels dialog box.

▶ Encompass the majority of the data on the histogram with the left and right input sliders. (See "Tone Clipping," below, for a useful technique for adjusting these sliders.)

▶ If you're preparing the image for a press, you may need to adjust the output levels so that tints and lines are within the range that can be reproduced on press (see Chapter 22, *Reproducing Halftones*). To find out which output levels work for different paper stocks, see "Keeping Tints and Lines Printable" in Chapter 6, *Scanning for Prepress*.

▶ Move the center input slider or control point (sometimes called the midtone or gamma value) to the left until the image looks about right on screen. We usually bump this up to at least 1.5. Once it looks just about right, bump it up a little more if the image will be be printed on a press. Scans look lighter on monitors (which are actually projecting light) than they

Photoshop's, for instance—you can see and precisely alter the numeric values associated with control points as you select or move them (**Figure 12-8**).

Adjusting Input and Output Sliders
Photoshop used to be one of the few image-editing programs that displayed a histogram and let you drag sliders to modify it. Virtually all image-editing programs now offer this feature, although some call it Image or Histogram Equalization. Some programs go a step further and show an overlay with the before and after histograms, or a sidebar with the resulting gray map you created with the sliders.

Whatever the program or name of the feature, we like this technique the best. It's fast, it's easy, and it's precise. Here are ways to apply it.

The general adjustment approach. In all of the programs that offer a histogram approach, you can use two or three sliders, which represent the black point, midtone point, and white point of the image data. (Some programs label these shadow, midtone, and highlight.)

Figure 12-9
Using Photoshop's
Levels dialog box

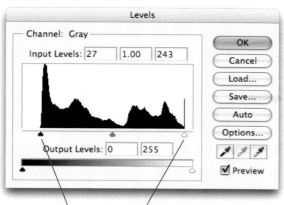

Move the left and right sliders to encompass the bulk of
the information in the scan.

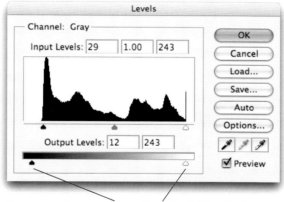

If necessary for press, move the output sliders to the
values specified in Table 7-1 (or type in the values).

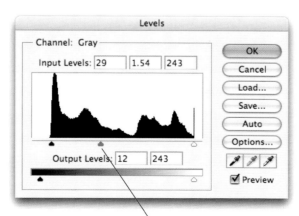

Move the center input slider to the left to brighten the
image and bring out shadow detail.

do on paper (which relies on reflected light). You'll almost never make an image too light using this method. But for more accurate previews, make corrections using a calibrated monitor and while soft-proofing the specific output device you're going to use (see Chapter 13, *Getting Good Color*). Always keep an eye out for posterization in the deep shadow areas.

Equalize

You often find an equalize or auto-balance setting in image-editing programs, sometimes in the same dialog box where you find the histogram and input sliders. Typically, these settings just evenly spread tonal values across the entire range. We find these settings almost totally useless. The point of nonlinear controls is to make a value judgment about where the upper, middle, and lower levels belong.

Tracking Your Tones

Photoshop's Levels dialog box includes a built-in histogram that shows how the tonal distribution changes as you edit. However, up through Photoshop 7 there was no way to view a live histogram as you worked in the Curves dialog box. But starting with Photoshop CS, Adobe makes the histogram available as a palette that updates as you work in the Curves dialog box. We recommend that you leave the Histogram palette open and keep an eye on it whenever you make changes that affect an image's overall distribution of tones.

Tone Clipping

One of the most useful tools for tonal adjustment we've seen is the tone-clipping display in Photoshop (**Figure 12-10**). This display shows you which samples in an image are getting clipped to the tonal edges—going all black or all white.

Using the tone-clipping display, you can make sensible judgments about what information is being lost and how important it

is. For example, your thinking might go like this: "Well, that shiny area over there is getting clipped to white, but it doesn't matter much because it's not central to the photo. I'll bring the slider in a bit more because I don't care if I lose detail there, and I can bring out more shadow detail by losing the information in that unimportant highlight area."

To use Photoshop's tone clipping display, hold down Option (Macintosh) or Alt (PC) while dragging the left and right input sliders in the Levels dialog box. (For more on clipping, see "Color Management Systems" in Chapter 13, *Getting Good Color*.)

Cumulative Corrections

As we mentioned earlier, making tonal corrections always involves some data loss in your picture. With linear adjustment, you lose detail in highlights and shadows (they go all white or all black). With nonlinear adjustment, you lose detail mainly in the highlights, because the curve is flatter in that area, but the eye distinguishes less detail, so the loss is less important.

Whatever correction method you use, remember that multiple corrections increase the data loss. So if you use your scanning software's adjustment tools to correct an image, then use Photoshop's Levels dialog box to further adjust it, you lose data twice. For this reason, avoid the temptation to correct a bad adjustment by making another correction. To avoid the cumulative corrections syndrome, you have several strategies at your disposal:

Adjustment layers. Use Photoshop's Adjustment Layers feature to keep adjustments on a layer apart from the actual image. You can see their effect on screen, but the adjustments aren't actually applied until you flatten the layers or print the image. That means you can change the adjustment layer's settings repeatedly, and the main image won't be modified until output time. However, it still pays to be efficient—three adjustment layers stacked on the same image will still apply three sequential changes, which in some cases cause slightly more data loss than one adjustment layer.

16-bit mode. Although an 8-bit image will suffer from just a few adjustment steps, a 16-bit image can withstand a lot more tonal abuse before posterization and artifacts set in. This is because a 16-bit image can potentially contain 65,536 levels per channel to start with, while an 8-bit image can only contain 256 levels. Of course, you do pay a price in that 16-bit images are correspondingly larger and slower to work with.

Undo and History. Use your image-editing program's undo or Photoshop's History palette to back up to the step before your mistake, and then redo the adjustment. If you want to compare different corrections made at very different times during a session, you can use Photoshop's Snapshot feature to keep a History palette snapshot of each version, and keep the one you want. But we think adjustment layers are easier. We now do almost all our tonal manipulations in adjustment layers, and hardly ever use Levels or Curves directly on the image unless we're working in 16-bit mode.

Keeping in Tone

Almost every image that you scan will need to be adjusted in a number of ways including tonal correction. Without this correction, your scans will almost always be too dark and too muddy. Of course, as we've stated repeatedly throughout this chapter, you want to keep as much image data as you can while you're making corrections (an image's data is its *sine qua non;* when you lose the data, you've just got a pile of dirt left).

Figure 12-10
Photoshop's tone clipping display

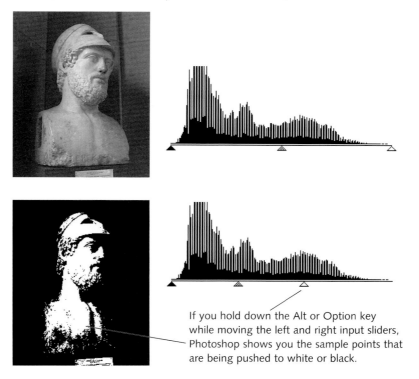

If you hold down the Alt or Option key while moving the left and right input sliders, Photoshop shows you the sample points that are being pushed to white or black.

In the next chapter, we talk about applying these lessons to color images, as well as setting up your system to do color corrections. And we address color management, which solves more and more woes in the workflow.

13

Getting Good Color

PAINTING BY THE NUMBERS

If you've never done color correction, it's unlikely you will master making professional changes to color images overnight—or even this month. Experts spend decades developing the visual acuity necessary to perfect the kinds of corrections we describe in this chapter.

Color guru Dan Margulis performs an impressive demonstration in which he loads an uncorrected color image on his monitor, switches the display to grayscale, does his color correction "by the numbers" (working with color value readouts), and then switches back to color display. And the correction is great. Dan makes it look easy: he can do a perfect correction quickly because he's spent years discovering the quickest, best methods.

But don't despair! While it still takes years to become a true color guru, the lat-est color-correction features in programs like Photoshop can help you reach a competent level of color quality much more quickly and easily than you would have in the pre-computer age when color correction involved tedious darkroom work with toxic chemicals, timers, and sheets of film.

Today's desktop technology significantly reduces the drudgery and increases your control of color correction, and boy, are we ever we glad about that. Some of the time-saving color features we discuss in this chapter include the Info palette in Photoshop (depicted much later in the chapter in **Figure 13-20**), which you can use to inspect color values anywhere in an image as Dan Margulis would; and features like Levels and Curves, which are essential for correcting colors like a champ.

However, in the production process from camera to final output, color correction must overcome a major challenge: each device reproduces color differently. For example, there's the color range and fidelity the camera film is able to record, the color range and fidelity the scanner can capture, the color range and fidelity your monitor can actually display, and the color range and fidelity that your printer, proofing device, press, or output device can reproduce. Some devices reproduce fewer colors than others and some distort the colors involved. Even when two devices reproduce the same number of colors, they might not reproduce the same set of colors.

Color management is a technology that mediates the color differences between devices so that you spend less of your own time doing so, while also providing a stable visual reference for your color corrections. Color management augments the Info palette and the screen display so that you can more easily anticipate how an image's color values will change when output to any medium.

In this chapter, we discuss color fundamentals, introduce color management as it relates to scanning, and cover some of the more frequently used color correction techniques.

Each of the areas covered in this chapter have entire sections or chapters devoted to them in Real World Adobe Photoshop, *a book by David and his colleague Bruce Fraser. Because of their focus on Photoshop, image data, and color—though grayscale images aren't avoided—they devote several chapters to issues surrounding color correction and color management. Bruce goes into even more detail about color management in* Real World Color Management.

Declaring (In)dependence

When you work with digital color, you have to discard the notion that what you *see* is what you *get*—wysiwyg. Unless you're using a very expensive monitor combined with a color-managed system, what you see on screen is a *device-dependent* view into the colors that make up an image.

It's easy to get an example of this. Walk into any consumer electronics store and look at the wall of televisions showing the same program. No two the same, eh? Computer monitors are better calibrated and more consistent than television sets, but the principle is the same: Each TV displays the same data in different ways.

You can store color in a way that is independent of a specific device; this image data represents absolute color, which is similar to color you can measure with a colorimeter. We call this *device-independent* color. Device-independent color is converted to device-dependent color via a table that represents the differences between the specific device's method of representing a set of colors, and the absolute, independent model of color.

But image data have to represent some physical properties, because images are displayed, printed, or scanned in the physical world. This representation is called *modeling*. A *color model* pinpoints each value in image data to a specific location in a *color space*, which is a mathematical representation of the range of a real-world color device. The color space also helps visualize the components that combine to make a given color.

The big difference in color models is between LAB, which describes a color objectively but doesn't identify how to represent it on a monitor or printer, and RGB and CMYK, which describe how to represent a color, but don't actually identify what the color looks like. HSB, HSL, and similar models are yet more ways to represent color more intuitively; they have neither a one-to-one relationship with how the information is stored nor a perceptual basis. Because LAB represents colors objectively, it's the color model used as an intermediary step for translating colors between all of the other color models.

The distinction between color models and color spaces is subtle but important. In the real world, a color model such as CMYK isn't specific enough. The press at the printing plant and the inkjet printer on your desk may both use CMYK inks, but the chemistry of each device's inks is totally different, so the colors produced by each set of inks occupies different color spaces within the larger CMYK color model. Similarly, your computer monitor and your TV are both RGB devices, but each represents a different color space within the RGB color model.

RGB

Most monitors use a combination of red, green, and blue phosphors or LCD filters to show color. In addition, all scanners use RGB scanning sensors, even scanners that produce a CMYK image. So it seems a natural consequence that we should store image data using the RGB color model by using its three channels, one for each of those colors with a value from 0 to 255 (or to 65,535 for 48-bit RGB) representing a point on each color axis that combine to form a color (**Figure 13-1**).

CMYK

CMYK color values correspond directly to the physical inks, dyes, and waxes used to create color in offset printing and digital color printing.

Traditionally, images scanned for a press were saved in the CMYK color model and edited for the press on which the images were printed. This still makes sense when images will only be printed on one CMYK device or on CMYK devices that all follow the same standard (such as a Pressmatch). CMYK is a targeted, highly device-dependent final transformation.

We don't recommend doing the bulk of your image editing in CMYK unless it's required by your service bureau or commercial printer. CMYK has several limitations:

▶ Some of the color correction tools we describe later in this chapter are disabled in Photoshop and other programs when working in CMYK.

Figure 13-1 RGB color model

The standard RGB model can be conceived as a cube within which all combinations of red, green, and blue mix. It's not a particularly intuitive way to think about color, but it is the way in which computers—and TVs—represent it.

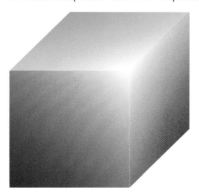

► CMYK color spaces generally cover fewer colors than RGB and LAB color spaces. This makes CMYK images less than ideal for reuse in RGB media such as the Web. Preserving cross-media color quality is more likely when you start with RGB images and create versions for RGB and CMYK media (as shown in the scenarios in **Figure 13-5**).

► A scan can take up more disk space as a CMYK image than as an RGB image, because the CMYK image must store four channels of information instead of three.

Working in RGB and saving a final-stage image in that mode lets you retarget your images to different presses, color printers, and alternative output devices. (Of course, if someone gives you a CMYK image and doesn't have a better-quality RGB original, you just have to do the best you can with it.)

A visual model of CMYK is impossible to depict because hue and brightness are actually the results of the interaction of cyan, magenta, and yellow inks. Black is added merely to make up for defects in pigments and the limitations of printing ink over ink on press.

LAB

Another way of looking at color is the LAB color space, which many professional image-editing programs support. LAB stores color in three channels, as does RGB. But RGB has three color channels, whereas LAB has a single channel for luminance or tonal values (L) and two channels of color information (A and B) (**Figure 13-2**). The color channels correspond to a scale, rather than a single color. A is a continuum from green to red, while B is a range from blue to yellow. The midpoint values for A and B correspond to neutral grays.

The idea behind LAB is that every step—each increase in a single channel's numeric value—represents the same perceptual distance as every other step. RGB colors are all bunched together, so a single number (or step) difference in the red channel might be imperceptible; but the same difference in the luminosity channel of LAB is identifiable. LAB is tied to measurable, physical properties, so that it can be used as an independent reference by which deviation from objective reality can be measured. Another advantage of LAB is that luminance is stored apart from color, so it's easier to make tonal changes that don't cause color shifts as compared to RGB, which does.

LAB might appear to be a perfect environment in which to work, but it isn't. One limitation is that it takes a while to get used to color-correcting along LAB's red/green and blue/yellow axes. Another limitation of LAB is that it isn't ideal for editing 8-bit

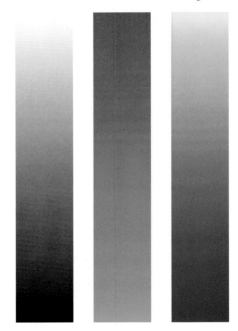

The LAB model split lightness into one channel (L, left) and uses one channel each with a spectrum from red to green (A, middle) and yellow to blue (B, right).

Figure 13-2 LAB color model

images—LAB is so large that the 256 levels available in 8-bit color are spread out far more than in spaces like CMYK and Adobe RGB. Small adjustments are more likely to create big changes, which increases the risk of posterization (banding). You can get around this limitation by scanning and editing an image at 16 bits per channel so that the image can take advantage of 16-bit color's 65,536 potential levels.

Because of these challenges, LAB is used less as an editing space and more as an intermediate color space for transferring colors among different device-dependent spaces (for example, from the scanner's color space to the monitor's to the printer's). LAB is big enough to handle all color spaces without dropping colors.

HSB

The Hue-Saturation-Brightness model (sometimes called HSL, where L is for Lightness) is a method of breaking up color into three separate visual components.

Figure 13-3 HSB color model

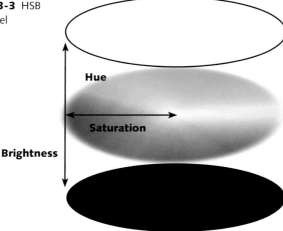

The HSB (Hue-Saturation-Brightness) model puts hue on a color wheel where the spectrum runs around the perimeter. Moving in towards the center of the circle decreases saturation, while moving up and down changes the brightness.

Hue is the actual color on a spectrum. Saturation is the intensity of that color from 100-percent white to 100-percent of the hue. And brightness or lightness is a measure of how much black is added to the color, from 0 to 100 percent.

You can visualize this model as a cylinder (**Figure 13-3**). The perimeter represents 100-percent saturated hues; the spectrum is wrapped around the cylinder; and the core is pure white. Moving outward from the center to the edge increases saturation. Moving up and down changes the amount of black. Walking around the core on a single slice of the cylinder changes the point on the spectrum or the hue.

HSB in practice isn't a perfect cylinder; there are combinations of HSB that can't be mapped to RGB, making it hard to use for correction. But it's a good tool to use to identify which aspect of color to change.

Color Management Systems

At the outset of this chapter, we talked about how hard it is to have color travel along a production workflow—from scanner to monitor to final output—and keep it consistent because each device perceives colors differently. Color management systems offer a solution by providing an objective frame of reference against which all devices can be measured.

What's in a CMS

A color management system (CMS) comprises several parts: a reference color space, a set of profiles that describe the color space of each device, and an engine that applies these profiles against image data at each step of the workflow. Some CMS implementations also let you specify which color spaces to use by default for each color model; this is sometimes called a *working space*. In Photoshop, CMS setup controls appear in the Color Settings dialog box (see "Making Color Corrections"). Higher-quality scanning software may also include similar controls, as we mention in Chapter 5, *How to Read Your Scanning Software*. Some CMS implementations also have components that let you inspect, build, or edit profiles.

Reference color space. The reference color space is typically defined by CIE (Commission Internationale de l'Eclairage), which we describe in Chapter 10, *What is a Bitmap?* The LAB color space is a reference color space, thanks to its ability to faithfully preserve other color spaces. The CIE or CIE-derived color spaces are all references based on an objective notion of color; they're all device-independent. The LAB and similar color spaces are perceptual in nature, but it's not necessary to have a reference color space that has that property to use it as a reference.

Profiles. Profiles are descriptions of how a given device varies from the reference color space. Some profiles are generic and describe the general characteristics of a specific device (like "all Trinitron-based monitors act like this"). Others are generated specifically for a given device (like "the specific monitor you bought acts like this"), which we describe a little later. The more specific your profile, the better chance that a CMS will work well for you, especially with less-expensive equipment not manufactured to as precise tolerances as the pricey gear. Since the previous edition of this book, there's been an explosion of products you can use to profile your own monitor, scanner, and printer, and their prices have dramatically fallen too. We expand on this in the "Calibration and Profiling" topic later in this chapter.

Engine. The CMS engine uses CMS profiles to correctly adjust images when they're scanned, displayed, or printed. In Mac OS X, the ColorSync color management system calls the engine a CMM, or color matching method. Each CMS uses different algorithms to reconcile colors. Adobe products use the Adobe Color Engine (ACE) by default.

Working spaces. Photoshop's implementation of color management includes an option for *working spaces*—the default color spaces in which you work (there's one for each color model). For example, if you open an image without a color space, you'll edit it in the current working space. It's best to use a set of working spaces that accommodate your final output. The Photoshop Color Settings dialog box makes this easy by listing predefined settings by media type; you select a Settings name corresponding to your output and the working space is set automatically.

Why not just assign the biggest possible space that encompasses all the colors you need? As we mentioned in the LAB discussion above, large color spaces are problematic when editing 8-bit color images. While different working spaces work best for different media (Adobe RGB for prepress images versus sRGB for Web images), you don't necessarily need to worry about the effects of changing the working space. Photoshop lets each image maintain its own working space, so as long as the Color Management Policies in the Color Settings dialog box are set to Preserve Embedded

 When working in 8-bit RGB, the generally accepted working space choices are Adobe RGB for printed output (including for press CMYK, which an image is converted to later), and sRGB for on-screen output; for more detailed guidelines see chapters 6 through 9.

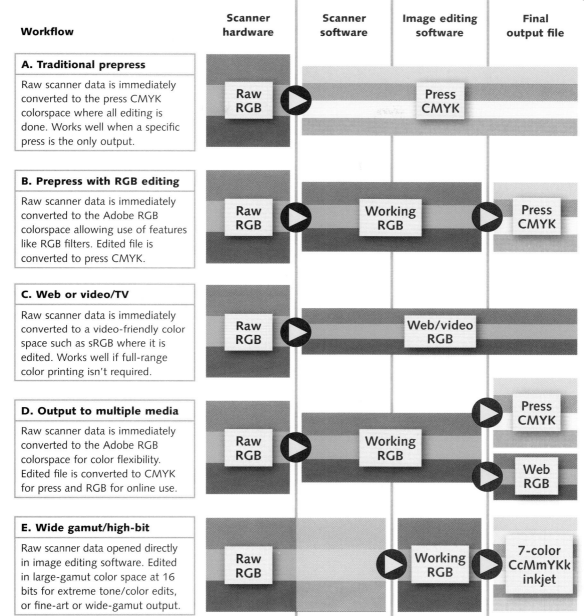

Figure 13-4
Color space conversions for various workflows

Gamut Mapping

Profiles, color in existing images won't be damaged by changing the working space.

Part of the problem in using color on different devices is that each device has a certain range of colors it can represent. This range is called the *gamut*. When converting an image from one color space to another, a CMS has to have a way to handle colors from the original color space that are not within the gamut of the new color space, such as when converting from a scanner's color space to an offset press color space. Color space conversions happen all the time; **Figure 13-4** can help you identify

Figure 13-5
Examining clipped colors in the Mac OS X ColorSync Utility

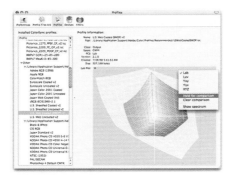

You can use the ColorSync Utility to compare the gamuts of two profiles. In the default view (looking down the lightness axis from maximum lightness), SWOP CMYK appears to be completely within the Adobe RGB color space.

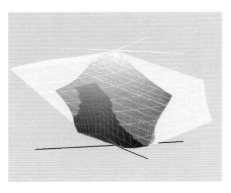

Rotating the LAB plot in 3-D (rotating the lightness axis to vertical) reveals that some darker SWOP blues and greens actually exist outside the Adobe RGB color space.

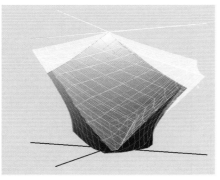

Rotating again around the lightness axis shows that some darker SWOP reds and magentas are also outside the Adobe RGB color space.

when they happen and what choices you need to make.

But it's not just a case of scaling one gamut to another. Gamuts have different shapes, too, and they're three-dimensional. Mapping one gamut to another is a more complex dilemma than simply pushing a square peg into a round hole—it's more like fitting a soccer ball into a mailbox.

If you use Mac OS X 10.3 (Panther) or later, you can use its built-in ColorSync Utility to get a more complete 3-D pic-

ture of how two gamuts match up (**Figure 13-5**). In the list on the left, select a profile representing your larger gamut, then Control-click the plot and select Hold for Comparison from the context menu. Then select the profile of your smaller gamut from the list on the left. The default view looks "down" the lightness axis from the top (maximum lightness). To see which colors clip at other lightness levels, drag the plot to rotate the comparison—it can be quite revealing.

Nevertheless, those geniuses known as color scientists figured out how to make practical sense out of such a seemingly impossible dilemma. The general technique of moving these out-of-gamut colors around is called *gamut mapping*. The automatic methods built into color management systems (*rendering intents*, described soon) use some variation on the methods described in the following list and shown in **Figure 13-6**. But if you manually edit image colors, you can use any combination of these methods.

Clipping the gamut. With gamut clipping, source colors outside the target gamut are just replaced with the nearest value in the target's gamut. You lose any differentiation between colors that exist outside the target gamut, so large areas of out-of-gamut colors may look flat. This is a reasonable method when there aren't many significant colors outside the target gamut, and if there are noticeable out-of-gamut colors, you can manually desaturate just those colors so that you have control over how they shift.

Figure 13-6 *is an extremely simplified illustration of how gamut mapping works. In practice, the color handling is much more complex and in three dimensions.*

Compressing the gamut. Gamut compression takes the entire tonal range in the source image and squeezes it to fit in the target device's gamut. The relationship between colors and tones is preserved, but the fidelity can be off. However, it makes the image have much the same feel as the original and is often used for photographic images. Our eyes are very forgiving, and we value the relativity of colors more than "absolute" color.

Adjusting saturation. When moving a smaller gamut into a larger one, you can increase saturation to make better use of the larger gamut. When moving a larger gamut into a smaller one, you can desaturate specific colors to keep the most saturated colors from clipping. However, you risk creating undesirable or unrealistic

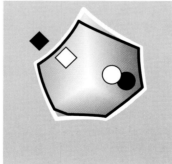

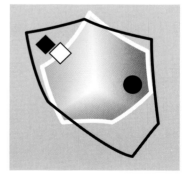

Before gamut mapping, one ColorMatch RGB color (represented by the diamond) is outside the SWOP CMYK gamut, and another color (the circle) is inside.

Compressing the ColorMatch RGB gamut fits all its colors inside the SWOP CMYK gamut, but both colors must shift. Their new locations are shown in white.

Clipping the gamut doesn't shift the ColorMatch RGB color (circle) that's inside the SWOP CMYK gamut. But the color outside the SWOP gamut (the diamond) can only be reproduced by the closest color in the SWOP gamut.

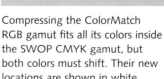

Figure 13-6 Clipping vs. compressing. Black outline is ColorMatch RGB, white outline is SWOP CMYK.

changes in color or tone. The best way to handle your out-of-gamut colors is not by manually adjusting them but rather by using the appropriate rendering intent.

Rendering Intents

The history of color correction is littered with the trials and errors of production people attempting to manually map RGB colors to CMYK before the era of color management. Now you can take advantage of gamut-mapping features that color management gives you without extra effort. They are called *rendering intents*. Rendering intents come into play when you convert to a color space that doesn't contain all of the colors in the source gamut. While this can be a manual conversion, remember that image color needs to be converted when going from your computer to the printer, which is why Photoshop includes rendering intent choices in its Print with Preview dialog box (**Figure 13-13**).

While rendering intents are far from perfect, they can save you a lot of time compared to the older methods. Apple ColorSync and the Adobe Color Engine provide the same set of rendering intents that are often presented as options when you use a CMS to convert color. The usual names for rendering intents are Saturation, Perceptual, Absolute Colorimetric, and Relative Colorimetric.

 We cover intents only briefly here, because of their complexity; they're more thoroughly covered in books like Real World Color Management.

Perceptual. The Perceptual rendering intent tries to maintain the integrity of the image so that it "looks good" as far as the human visual system is concerned. This type of gamut mapping can cause many colors to change, but it maintains the perceptual relationships among the colors. Perceptual rendering maintains color relationships by compressing a larger source gamut into a smaller target gamut rather than by clipping the larger gamut. But when the gamuts of two color spaces are quite different, you may see more compression and distortion of colors than you'd like.

You should use Perceptual rendering when important image detail is represented by out-of-gamut colors. If you first try Relative Colometric, described below, and you lose image detail, then Perceptual might preserve those details more effectively.

Absolute Colorimetric. The Absolute Colorimetric rendering intent maintains the color values of any image colors that also exist in the target gamut. But colors outside the gamut are clipped, and if the target medium has a different color balance and highlight value (also called the *white point*), Absolute Colorimetric doesn't compensate for that. This can be useful when you're proofing a different paper stock because the output will represent the paper color. Outside of proofing, you should use Relative Colorimetric or Perceptual.

Relative Colorimetric. The Relative Colorimetric rendering intent behaves the same way Absolute Colorimetric does, except that it adjusts for the white points of the image gamut and the target gamut. For example, if you're printing on paper that's a little on the warm side, Relative Colorimetric's white point adjustment can compensate so that the image doesn't appear too warm when printed on the paper (assuming you use an accurate profile of the paper and inks). The down side is that colors outside of the target gamut are still clipped. The way you'll see this is that colors that you saw as a saturated but smooth gradient on your monitor will be smashed into a single flat color, and the point at which the color blocks up (where tones that should be separate merge into one) is where the limit of the target gamut—color literally hits the wall.

Relative Colorimetric is preferred by many who convert RGB to CMYK and by many photographers, for the same reason: It works better for photos than Saturation and Absolute Colorimetric, and it won't change the in-gamut colors like Perceptual can. So how do the proponents of Relative Colorimetric deal with out-of-gamut colors? By manually desaturating out-of-gamut colors to precisely control how they're brought into the target gamut.

Saturation. The Saturation rendering intent gives priority to preserving the saturation. While this is generally used for synthetic graphics like business graphs, Saturation can, in some cases, help preserve details in out-of-gamut colors. Saturation may be a useful alternative to the Perceptual rendering intent when Perceptual reduces saturation too much. However, in general, Relative Colorimetric or Perceptual creates better-looking images.

Sneak Previews

By now, you might be wondering how you can know which colors are in the target gamut and which ones aren't. An obvious idea is to watch the numbers in Photoshop's Info palette (**Figure 13-20**), but no visually-oriented person wants to work that way. Fortunately, programs that have thorough color management support provide a feature called "soft-proofing," which is a very valuable way to see how the actual output will look.

In Photoshop, you can see which colors are out of range by defining your target gamut using Photoshop's Proof Setup feature from the View menu, then turning on Photoshop's Gamut Warning from the View menu to visually mark the source colors that fall outside the gamut you're

soft-proofing. To see how the image will look using the currently active Proof Setup profile, turn on the Proof Colors option from the View menu.

If you want to see the exact change in color values between the working space and the proof space, set an Info palette color readout to Proof Color. You do this by clicking an eyedropper icon in the Info palette; a pop-up menu appears containing multiple readout options. Proof Color readouts appear in italics.

 Photoshop lets you open multiple windows for the same document each with different view settings (Window menu, Arrange, New Window item). You could open three windows for an image: leave one in normal view, set the second to Gamut Warning view, and the third to Proof Colors view. As you edit colors, you immediately see how well your adjustments are working.

Setting up Color Management

Color management works right only when it's set up right. Different systems have different methods, but in this section we outline what you can do to improve and calibrate color inside and outside a CMS for each part of the workflow.

Calibration and Profiling

There's a classic Monty Python skit where a man walks into a department store to buy a bed, but he's confused because the first salesman he talks to tells him the bed he wants is 60 feet wide. That's when a second salesman informs the man that the first salesman always multiplies numbers by 10, meaning the bed is actually six feet wide. When the second salesman tells the customer that the same bed is two feet long, the first salesman tells the customer that the second salesman's numbers are always one-third of the actual number. Naturally, the customer's head begins to spin, and they all wind up singing while standing in a tea chest.

Strangely, that 30-year-old skit is a reasonable analogy for devices that operate without a CMS. Like uncalibrated devices, none of the salesmen communicates using the established numerical standard, so it's an ongoing challenge to determine the deviations from the standard and then compensate for them.

The terms *calibration* and *profiling* are widely misunderstood (for one thing, they're not interchangeable). Not all devices can be calibrated, but most devices can be profiled. This is because calibration involves altering a device's behavior, while profiling only describes the device without altering it.

Let's talk about what it would mean to calibrate and profile the salesmen.

If the salesmen were calibrated, all of them would state numbers that match the counting system everybody else uses— were they to say 60 feet, they would mean 60 feet, not six feet.

The salesmen are already profiled, because the customer was told exactly how far off the salesmen's numbers are. The profile of the first salesman is that his numbers are 10 times the actual number, so it's possible to use that profile to determine what the actual number is—just divide his numbers by 10. But if the profile was inaccurate, the customer wouldn't be able to determine an accurate number, and might not even know that the number he has is wrong. That's why accurately measured profiles are important.

And so it is with your color devices. The first step in setting up devices is calibrating them to a standard, as closely as is possible.

The second step is profiling the devices, so that you end up with profiles that either tell the color management system that the devices are calibrated, or else they indicate exactly how far off they are. With this information, the color management system can reconcile color differences throughout the workflow. Color management can't fix everything on its own, but it can reduce your guesswork so dramatically that it's more than worth the trouble. There are several products that let you create profiles for your monitor, scanner, printer, or all three. Two companies that supply a range of profiling devices are Colorvision (`www.colorvision.com`) and GretagMacbeth (`www.gretagmacbeth.com`).

 You'll often encounter the term characterization, *which is a widely used term for profiling. We think the term* profiling *is easier to understand.*

 It's useful to know that some color management documentation includes profiling steps in the process they call calibration. That's reasonable, because you're usually going to profile right after you calibrate, but keep in mind that calibration is actually different than profiling.

Monitors

You calibrate a monitor by setting its controls to the color standard you want to use, which can include a brightness level and white point. But you don't know if the monitor is really operating at those specifications until you profile it. You need to know what gamma and color temperature standard you want to use before you calibrate and profile, because the calibration and profiling hardware and software will ask you what your standard is.

Calibrating a Monitor

When calibrating a monitor, one of the characteristics you can adjust is *gamma*—the midtone value on a nonlinear tone curve. A gamma of 1.8 is typical for prepress work, whereas 2.2 works well for multimedia or other on-screen image displays. Gamma 1.8 matches the default Mac OS gamma, whereas 2.2 matches the default Windows gamma and the gamma of televisions. A gamma change is similar to moving the midpoint in a curves dialog box (**Figure 13-7**) or the middle slider in a levels dialog box.

 Monitor gamma doesn't affect the gamma stored in images; monitor gamma only changes how you view images, particularly shadow detail.

Monitors also have color temperature characteristics that affect how colors get displayed. Color temperature is a measure of the color of emitted light from red to blue (corresponding to the colors emitted by a theoretical "black body" object heated to various temperatures). Many CRT mon-

itors let you adjust the color temperature, but color temperature is not adjustable on LCD monitors. Color temperature is measured in degrees Kelvin and abbreviated as K—not to be confused with K standing for kilobyte used to measure memory or hard disk storage. Graphics professionals tend to set their monitors so that white is 6500° K or sometimes 5000° K. These color temperatures are also known as the D65 and D50 standards, respectively. Color temperature matters because it affects your color perception—if you ever try on clothing in a dressing room with incandescent lighting (around 2800° K) and then notice that its color looks quite different in daylight (around 5500-6500° K), you know what we mean.

Profiling a Monitor

The preferred method of profiling a monitor is to use a *colorimeter*—a piece of hardware that is attached to the surface of the monitor and measures color. These have been around for years, but they only really became valuable when they were able to generate a standard monitor profile from their measurements so that you could integrate the data into a color management system.

 If you want to profile an LCD, make sure you use a colorimeter made for LCDs, because the sensors are different and the suction cups on the older colorimeters can damage the LCD surface.

Using Operating System Calibration

You can also calibrate and profile a monitor using the Display Calibrator on Mac OS X (part of the Displays system preference; **Figure 13-8**), or you can use Adobe Gamma in Windows (**Figure 13-9**) if you have an Adobe product that installed

Figure 13-7
Gamma

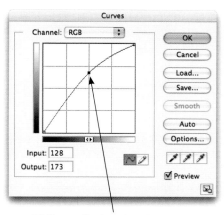

Midtone adjustment on tone curve

Chapter 13: Getting Good Color

Figure 13-8
Simple monitor
calibration in
Mac OS

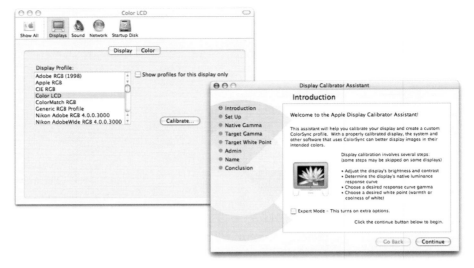

Figure 13-9
Simple monitor
calibration in
Windows

Adobe Gamma. Using one of these software programs is considered a *visual* method of calibrating and profiling, and it is nowhere near as accurate as using a colorimeter. If you're serious about color, buy the calibration hardware. If you have multiple monitors, you have to profile each of them individually, but you only have to profile the monitors you use for color-critical viewing. If you use a graphics card that supports multiple monitors, make sure it allows each monitor to use its own profile—support for this can be spotty, particularly on Windows.

Lighting Your Work Area
You can improve the usefulness of a monitor as a soft-proofing device if you light your work area using incandescent or fluorescent lights of the same color temperature you used to calibrate and profile your monitor; you can find temperature-specific bulbs at professional photographer stores. It's also a good idea to reduce ambient light in your working environment and equip it with neutrally colored walls and furniture.

Glenn worked in a facility where all monitors, lights, and viewing stands were tuned to 5500° K, and blackout shades and monitor hoods kept out extraneous light of other colors. This allowed him and his co-workers to entirely eliminate one variable in correction.

Scanners
Different systems have different methods of measuring scanner information. But the typical process is to place a target on the scanner like the one in **Figure 13-10**, capture it with all adjustments (such as sharpening or tonal correction) turned off, and read it into a package that "knows" what the correct values should be and then makes a profile that describes the differences.

The target is generally an industry-standard IT8.7, which has several hundred color and tonal values on it. Kodak's version is the Q60, which also includes a photographic image as part of the target. Similar targets are available for film scanners.

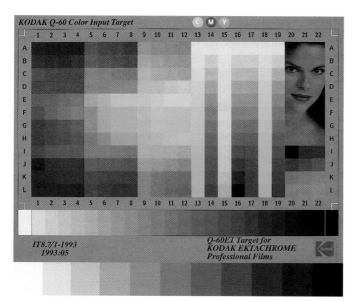

Figure 13-10 A target for profiling scanners

Many scanners now have a calibration pass they perform before each scan; this is sometimes configurable, but we recommend leaving it on for all serious scans. These scanners have a small area outside of the scanner bed that you need to keep clean. It performs a self-test in that area. Make sure the scanner has completed its calibration pass before profiling it.

Color Printers

Color printers usually come with manufacturer-supplied (often called *canned*) profiles that represent a typical or average printer of that model. But as you know by now, individual color devices can vary considerably from the assumptions made by the canned profiles, so imaging professionals recommend having a custom profile made.

You can buy software for most systems that will allow you to print out a standard target that looks similar to a scanner profiling target, scan it in through an already calibrated scanner, and build a custom profile for your specific device. You can even download targets from online services like `chromix.com` and `profilecity.com` and send

them your print of the target; they then send you a professionally made profile. If you're using a color printer for proofing or for final prints, it's probably worth going through this process to make full use of the CMS.

Presses and Proofing

Offset printers have never liked desktop color separation because only they really know the characteristics of their printing presses and digital and film-based proofers. However, with an output test of a target and a colorimeter, you can create a profile for a specific press and set of conditions. Bruce and David did this for *Real World Photoshop*, actually getting a four-color test run off in order to match colors. They were very pleased with the result, but you should anticipate this extra step and cost if you plan to introduce it into your workflow.

One potential problem with attempting to profile a press is that a press can be a moving target. Press conditions can change because ink flow and other settings are normally tweaked throughout the day. Another option is to use a proofing standard, such as Kodak Approval, as the target CMYK profile. Because part of a press operator's job is to match the proof, and because the proof isn't a moving target, the proof can often be a more reasonable and less expensive target to profile.

Computer-to-plate (CTP) technology provides a more direct route to the press, but removes the ability to see proofs from film. Because the electronic files are imaged directly to the printing plates, there is no film available from which a proof can be made.

Using Profiles

Once you have accurate profiles, you can use them with your scanning software, your image editor, your page-layout program, and any other color-management-savvy tools in your arsenal. However, because color-management terminology can be confusing, we provide a quick guide that can help you figure out what goes where and why.

The most important distinction to understand is between the device-specific profiles (monitor, scanner, printer) and the working space profiles (profiles good for editing, like Adobe RGB or sRGB). With few exceptions, you shouldn't use device-specific profiles for editing. A good editing color space is gray-balanced; this allows you to avoid adding a color cast when adjusting colors. But device profiles aren't tailored to avoiding color cast, but rather to representing a device's ability to produce color.

The main exception to this rule is editing CMYK images. A CMYK image using a profile like "U. S. Web Coated SWOP v2" can be considered device-specific, but it's perfectly acceptable to edit in this color space because it is the traditional editing space for the North American prepress industry.

Assigning vs. Converting

There's a significant difference between assigning profiles to images and converting images using profiles. You need to understand the difference when deciding which Photoshop command to use (**Figure 13-11**).

Assigning a profile is also called "tagging." When you assign a profile, other programs use the profile to interpret that image's colors, but the image's colors aren't permanently locked into the gamut of the profile. Programs that open the image simply interpret the colors the way the profile tells them to.

Converting actually changes the colors in the image. If the gamut you convert to is smaller than the original gamut, you permanently limit the image to the smaller gamut.

It's a difficult distinction, so here's an analogy. When you watch old reruns of the original Star Trek, you treat actor William Shatner as a starship captain, because that's the role the show *assigns* to him through his character's profile. He isn't really a starship captain, but the only way for you to correctly understand the show is to presume that he is one. What would it mean for William Shatner to be *converted* using his profile? He'd have to become a starship captain in real life, and he would no longer be an actor (as happened to Tim Allen as the fake-but-then-forced-to-be-real captain in *Galaxy Quest*)—converting is a fundamental change.

Monitor Profile

The monitor profile describes a specific monitor, and its main purpose in a scanning workflow is to take your monitor's idiosyncrasies into account when displaying your scans. This does not and should not affect the color values actually stored in the scan. Therefore, the only time you need to choose your monitor profile is when a program specifically asks for it—the option may be labeled "monitor profile" or "display profile" in your scanning software or image editor.

Don't be puzzled if image colors look the same after converting between profiles. This is exactly how it's supposed to work—the more the converted version looks like the original, the more successful the conversion. (Color shifts can be hard to avoid when converting to a color space of a smaller size or different shape.) You may see color changes when assigning a different profile, because you're changing the assumptions used to interpret the color values. In short: converting changes the color values but not the color interpretation, while assigning changes the interpretation but not the values.

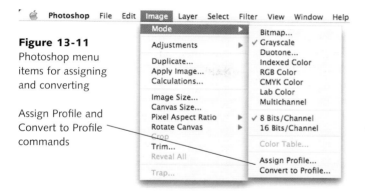

Figure 13-11
Photoshop menu items for assigning and converting

Assign Profile and Convert to Profile commands

You shouldn't convert scans to the monitor profile or assign the monitor profile to a scan. The monitor profile doesn't describe the scanner's color space, and the device-specific monitor color space isn't ideal for editing.

Scanner Profile

The scanner profile describes a specific scanner, and its main purpose is to help make a faithful conversion from the scanner's color space to your working color space, where you'll edit the image. Some manufacturers provide a generalized profile for their scanner models, but as with monitors, canned profiles don't usually match your specific unit exactly. As with monitors, it's better to use profiling software to create a profile for your particular scanner.

Usually, you want to set up your scanning software so that it uses the scanner profile as the starting point for accurately converting scans to your preferred working space, such as Adobe RGB, sRGB, or SWOP CMYK. That way, when you open the scan in your image editor, the image is already in a good color space for editing.

Another way to use a scanner profile is to apply the profile using your image editor. You might have to resort to this if your scanning software doesn't work with profiles. (You can still use other software programs to profile a scanner that doesn't support color management—this is actual-

ly one reason you'd have to use your image editor to apply the scanner profile.) The problem with doing the conversions in the image editor is that you have to convert every scan; if the scanning software can take care of it, every image's color space is ready to go when you open it in your image editor.

If you do apply a scanner profile outside of the scanning software, do so before you start editing the image, then immediately convert the scanned image to your working space.

If your scanning software doesn't support color management and you don't have a scanner profile, open the scan in your image editor and immediately save it with the working space profile embedded. There's no scanner profile to work with in this case, but your subsequent corrections can at least be referenced against the working space, and that's usually better than if the image wasn't tagged at all.

 Don't use the scanner profile as an editing color space; it's a device-specific color space that isn't ideal for editing.

Printer Profile

The printer profile describes a specific output device, and its main purpose in a scanning workflow is to let your programs (or the printer driver) accurately compensate for the way the printer represents color. A good printer profile is customized for the printer, ink, and paper you're using, because all three of these variables can change the look of the print.

There are typically three ways to use the printer profile:

Convert the scan to the printer profile.
You can use your image editor's profile conversion feature to convert the scan into the color space of the printer and media (**Fig-**

ure 13-12). If you save the converted image, this method permanently alters and locks the image colors into the output gamut, discarding or compressing any colors that don't fit. This can make it hard to print the image well on another type of printer; keep in mind that you will probably switch printers every few years. For more media flexibility, use one of the following methods instead.

Figure 13-12
Converting to a printer profile in Photoshop

Apply the profile using the program you're printing from. High-end programs like Photoshop can apply a selected printer profile to an image as it prints. This doesn't permanently alter the image colors because it's applied on the way to the printer. In Photoshop, use the Print with Preview command (**Figure 13-13**).

Figure 13-13
Applying a profile in Photoshop's Print with Preview dialog box

Apply the profile using the printer driver. Some printer drivers let you select a profile to apply to the image data as it comes through the driver. In this case, you don't use any of the conversion features in your graphics program to apply the printer profile—you let the printer driver do all the work.

The one thing you must avoid is over-color-managing your output. You only want to apply the printer profile using one method, and not again through any other method. If you manually convert a scan to the printer profile before printing, don't apply the printer profile when you print, and don't apply a printer profile in the printer driver. For example, in the Epson printer driver you would select No Color Adjustment (**Figure 13-14**). If the output colors look very wrong, make sure you haven't applied the printer profile in multiple places.

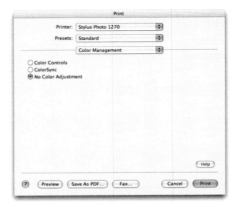

Figure 13-14 Making sure Epson printer driver color management is off

Missing or Mismatched Profiles

If Photoshop displays the Missing Profile dialog box, a scan has no profile embedded in it (it isn't tagged). If you see the Profile Mismatch dialog box, it means the color space of the scan doesn't match your working space (your default editing space). Both dialog boxes can be rather baffling even for those of us who think we know what we're doing, so here's a quick explanation for them.

In the Missing Profile dialog box (**Figure 13-15**), you have three choices:

Leave as is (don't color manage). Choose this when you don't want to interpret the

Figure 13-15
Photoshop's Missing
Profile dialog box

colors using any profile, and you don't want to assign a profile to it. This can be a reasonable choice for images that were scanned into CMYK for a non-color-managed prepress workflow, and are already set up for the press conditions by the scanning software or other image editor.

Assign working RGB. Choose this when you know that the scan was scanned into the same color space currently set as the working space in Photoshop, and you want to assign that profile as you open the scan.

Assign profile. Choose this when you know that a scan was scanned into a color space that's different from Photoshop's working space, and you know which color space it is. If you want to keep the image in that color space, don't select "and then convert document to working RGB." For example, if your working space is Adobe RGB and you don't want to change it, but you need to work on one sRGB scan headed for the Web, you wouldn't check the box.

In the Profile Mismatch dialog box (**Figure 13-16**), you have three choices:

Use the embedded profile (instead of the working space). Choose this when you want to keep the scan in the color space indicated by the profile that's embedded in it (usually by the scanning software).

Convert document's colors to the working space. Choose this when you want to change the scan from its current color space to your working space. For example, you have an image that was scanned in EktaSpace for archiving, but you need to use it in a prepress workflow built around Adobe RGB images.

Discard the embedded profile (don't color manage). Choose this when the scan shouldn't have a profile embedded

More Color Management Information

Believe it or not, we only had enough room to scratch the surface of color management—we could have written a 500-page book on color management alone. Fortunately, that book's already been written very well by Bruce Fraser, Chris Murphy, and Fred Bunting in their weighty tome, *Real World Color Management*.

A wealth of additional color management information is also available from the Web sites listed here.

Profiling hardware and software

▶ Monaco Systems (www.monacosystems.com)

▶ GretagMacbeth (www.gretagmacbeth.com)

▶ Colorvision (www.colorvision.com)

▶ Integrated Color Solutions (www.icscolor.com)

Information and training

▶ Color Remedies (www.colorremedies.com)

▶ Digital Dog (www.digitaldog.net)

Profiling services

▶ Profile City (www.icscolor.com)

▶ Dry Creek Photo (www.drycreekphoto.com)

Figure 13-16
Photoshop's Profile Mismatch dialog box

in it. The example for this option is much like the one described for the Leave As Is (Don't Color Manage) option for the Missing Profile dialog box discussed earlier.

Making Color Corrections

Now that you've been introduced to the parameters surrounding color spaces, here's some advice about reasonable changes you can make to color images to dramatically improve their quality (**Figure 13-17**).

Goals

Your goals for color correction need to be defined up front. Are you trying to make the image match as close as possible to a reference print? Or do you have a pre-defined idea of what the color composition should like? Are you also trying to match the balance, cast, and saturation in images supplied to you from other sources, or the color scheme of an existing lay-

out or book? Color correction isn't about making an image look unlike the original, but about targeting your specific need and keeping it realistic.

 We're not talking about special effects here. Most image-editing programs now come with so many filters and effects that we have to lie down after reviewing the menus.

Here are the primary goals to pursue with color correction.

Remove color casts. A *neutral* color contains equal components from all RGB color channels, or a little more cyan than equal amounts of yellow and magenta in CMYK. Where these values are out of balance, you have a *color cast*; where you should have a straight gray, a disproportionate amount of one or more colors tints

Figure 13-17
Color-correcting
a scan

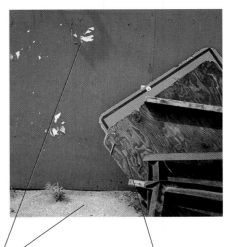

Whites aren't white

Overall color cast
is most obvious in
gray concrete

Shadows are too
light

Not enough
contrast; tones and
colors are dull

1. Highlights, shadows, and
neutral midtones are set using
Auto Color options in Levels
dialog box, improving overall
contrast and color.

2. Overall lightness and
contrast is fine-tuned
with curves.

that part of the tonal range or the entire image. Try scanning the same black-and-white image twice—once as grayscale and again in color. Check the Info palette for each and you'll probably see a slight color shift that can occur when trying to achieve these neutrals.

Sometimes it will be hard to find neutrals in an image, especially pictures with high color saturation—they may not exist at all. Our suggestion is to always scan a neutral gray wedge so that you can use one of the techniques described in "Methods" below, to help you find a neutral at many different tonal levels.

You don't always need to remove all color casts. Some are effects introduced by photographers through lighting or lens filters, a color tint that's natural to a scene (you don't want to neutralize an orange sunset) or choice of film (different films have different color properties). It's best if you have a print of an image you're working on so you know what's supposed to be neutral and what's not. If that's not possible, look for flesh tones, green grass, blue sky, or brown wood: these *memory colors* can help you make corrections in the absence of other information.

Change saturation. Scanners do a great job of capturing a larger range of color than any color output device can render. When you desaturate an image, you're reducing the intensity of particular hues in the image.

(See "HSB" above.) Sometimes, however, an image is washed out—the hues are blanched and need to be boosted. Reducing saturation can make an image reproducible; increasing it can sometimes make it "pop" and appear vibrant.

Non-CMS Setup

If you're operating in a CMYK prepress workflow that doesn't use color management, you may need to make a few changes in Photoshop before doing CMYK color corrections.

Monitor. Even if you're not using color management, using a monitor that's calibrated and profiled helps you produce images for print and screen that more closely match what you're seeing. See the monitor calibration guidelines covered earlier.

Color Settings. In Photoshop, the Color Settings dialog box (**Figure 13-18**) lets you choose a preset that fits the environment you're working in, whether it's fully color managed, not color managed, or somewhere in between. The presets are in the Settings pop-up menu.

Printing inks. If you need to customize the printing inks setup, click the CMYK popup menu and choose Custom CMYK. In the Custom CMYK dialog box, you can choose a pre-built table that describes the color characteristics of the printer or press you're heading to (**Figure 13-19**). Even without a CMS, it's possible to create your own tables by taking measurements and entering values by selecting Custom from the Ink Colors popup menu. You can import a file with these values supplied by an output device manufacturer or a printer for its particular press. Typically, we select SWOP for coated, uncoated, or newsprint stocks unless we know we're headed for a different kind of paper or press.

Figure 13-18
Color Settings
dialog box

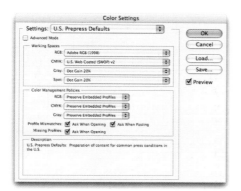

Figure 13-19
Custom CMYK
dialog box

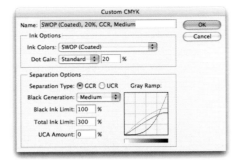

Separation. Also in the Custom CMYK dialog box, the Separation Setup options let you choose the method by which black is added into the process-color equation and CMY are subtracted to replace neutral grays or areas where cyan, magenta, and yellow add up to black in an ideal world (the bottom of **Figure 13-19**). These two methods are called gray component replacement (GCR) and undercolor

Figure 13-20
Info palette

Actual color

Proof color

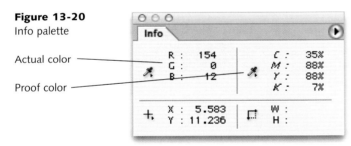

Proofing for Prepress

If you're heading for prepress output, and if you've set everything up as we discussed in previous sections, in Photoshop you can select the View menu's Proof Setup submenu, and then choose Working CMYK. This offers some predictive ability as to how the colors will look after coming off the press. The image is stored as RGB, but the CMYK changes are looked up and displayed as you make them.

Another option for prepress images is to make sure that the Photoshop Info palette (**Figure 13-20**) is displayed with one of the panels showing CMYK values (click an eyedropper on the Info palette to change the color model for the displayed values). If you become familiar with typical color values that produce good output for areas like flesh tones or blue skies, you can sample values to make sure your changes make sense.

removal (UCR), and we explain them in additional depth in Chapter 22, *Reproducing Halftones*.

Methods

Many programs supply dozens of methods of adjusting color images, but we suggest you look at just six categories. You can obtain best results with the following corrections by working in RGB if that's where your source image came from.

Levels and Curves

In the previous chapter, we cover how levels and curves are edited to create nonlinear corrections to grayscale images. Fortunately, both options are available for color correction as well. Levels and curves apply corrections on RGB data, which means that you are simultaneously changing hue, saturation, and brightness.

In Levels for each channel, move the black and white sliders so that they encompass the majority of the histogram. If this sounds like what we describe in Chapter 12 for correcting grayscale images, it is: Color correction essentially involves the optimization of each color channel.

In Photoshop, the midtone slider in Levels and the point adjustments in Curves give you the ability to remove slight color casts. In Levels, you can adjust an entire cast away by moving the midtone slider in a particular channel. In Curves, you can drag individual points in separate tonal ranges on individual channels to remove casts that might appear on just part of the scale. As you make color corrections, you can use the Proof Colors command and the numbers in the Info palette as reality checks.

Auto Color

The Auto Color command in Photoshop can be a quick and convenient way to correct images that should have a fairly typical color balance—particularly if you quickly become lost or confused when making manual levels and curves adjustments.

Figure 13-21
Auto Color
Correction Options
dialog box

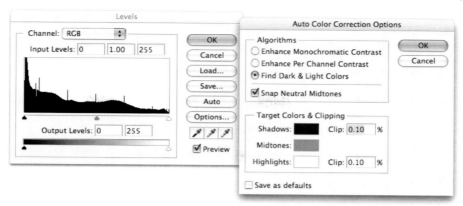

Although you can choose Auto Color (in the Image menu's Adjustments submenu), these changes are more precisely controlled through the Levels dialog box (**Figure 13-21**). A good starting point is to select the Find Dark & Light Colors and Snap Neutral Midtones options. Next, fine-tune the Clipping values—it's usually good to start at zero and move up from there in small increments. We use the up arrow and down arrow keys to make these fine changes. Then back off when the image starts to lose highlight or shadow detail.

As an alternative, you can also click the Shadows and Highlights boxes to set their target values with eyedroppers. If the adjustments so far have not corrected the color balance, click the Midtones swatch and adjust the values; equal values in all three RGB channels neutralize a typical image.

When you click OK, Photoshop might ask you if you want to save the current settings as the defaults. You can do so if you're going to work on more images that will need similar corrections. It's a good idea to save defaults that have Find Dark & Light colors selected and Snap Neutral Midtones turned on, because you're going to want those options to be on for most images. Default clipping values should be set to between 0.0% and 0.5% as a starting point.

Using Auto Color may not take care of every color problem, but if neutral shad-ows, midtones, and highlights existed in the original subject of the image, Auto Color can quickly provide you with a huge head start compared to other methods.

Avoiding Master Sliders

In both Levels and Curves, you can edit by channel or by using a master setting for all channels. (Most image-editing applications handle this the same way.) Although it's tempting to make overall corrections by dragging the master sliders (or curve points), you get higher quality by adjusting each channel individually. In Photoshop, instead of using the master input and output sliders use the Clipping setting in the Auto Color option in the Levels or Curves dialog box as we described earlier. Master sliders don't account for the possibility of different minimum and maximum levels in each channel, so there's more chance of clipping channel values unevenly (**Figure 13-22**), which can result in unbalanced color.

The Clipping setting uses a more intelligent approach of using each channel's own lightest and darkest values as starting points. If you do corrections in your scanning software, you might also check it to see if it has a per-channel auto clipping option that you can use.

Eyedroppers

The eyedropper tool appears in many image-editing programs' nonlinear cor-

Figure 13-22
Comparing master sliders to Auto Color clipping

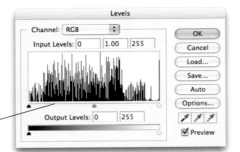

Master sliders and image's original histogram

Master sliders (above) clip individual channel tonal ranges inconsistently (below)

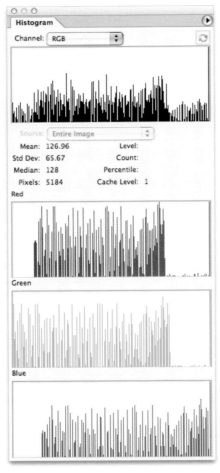

Auto Color clipping optimizes tonal range of individual channels (below)

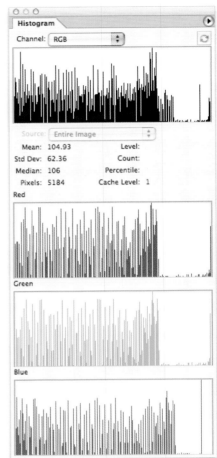

rections, allowing you to select values directly from an image. You can use curves, points, and sliders to adjust these values after you've sampled them, but it allows you the flexibility of making visual decisions about where you're correcting.

Corel Photo-Paint's Sample/Target Balance dialog box is the most intuitive we've seen, because it displays the starting points, target samples, and histograms in the same window (**Figure 13-23**). Photoshop's Levels and Curves dialog boxes offers the eyedroppers, but there's no representation of input and output samples.

If you've done what we suggest under "Goals," above, and scanned a gray wedge along with your image, you can use the midtone eyedropper to find a midtone-point gray with a single click.

In Photoshop, the gray eyedropper allows you to select a value without affect-

Figure 13-23
Corel Photo-Paint's
Sample/Target
Balance dialog box

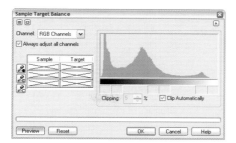

Figure 13-24
Hue/Saturation
dialog box

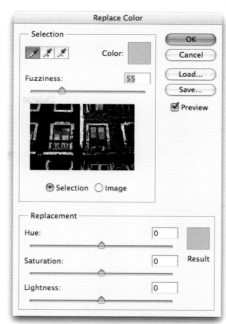

ing the tone or brightness, just the hue and saturation. As we suggested earlier, leave your information palette open while working on color; you can then hover over areas with the eyedropper to examine the values in each color channel and choose which ones to sample.

Hue/Saturation
Because the tonal correction tools move a color around on the lightness scale, the hue/saturation control—found in most image-editing programs—allows you to make moves by hue or overall in any combination of hue, saturation, and lightness (**Figure 13-24**).

Hue/Saturation in Photoshop offers the three primary emitted colors and their reflective counterparts, plus lightness. You can drag the sliders to make small or large adjustments from the color's starting point. It's a great way to increase or decrease saturation by hue or to fix an overall color shift without changing tone or saturation.

Replace and Selective Color
Replace and selective color allow you to do a kind of search-and-replace function in an image. You can use replace color to select

Figure 13-25 Replace Color dialog box

specific colors wherever they appear in an image—or more than one depending on the way the control is implemented—and make adjustments of the kind found in the Hue/Saturation control (**Figure 13-25**).

Selective color lets you make shifts from any point on the color wheel towards or away from any of the reflective color complements (cyan, magenta, and yellow) and black. This is the subtlest tool for making changes in overall hue. It's recommended for making changes in CMYK separations, but it's a finely graduated tool for doing small color changes in RGB as well (**Figure 13-26**).

Other Features
There are other features available in Photoshop for editing a color image, like Color Balance, Variations, and Desaturate. However, none of these tools provides you with anything but arbitrary sliders. Typically, we avoid using these tools unless we have a specifically tricky image or special effect.

Figure 13-26
Selective Color
dialog box

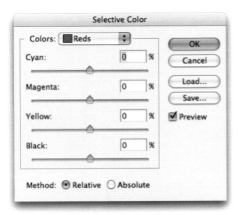

Color Me Corrected

As you can see, you have to keep a close eye on any scanned image as you walk it ever closer to the press or output bin. But the corrections we suggest in this chapter should give you practical tools to produce scans every bit as good as those formerly available for $50 to $200 apiece at color houses. And you avoid all that nasty stripping tape as well.

14

Freshening Up

REMOVING SCRATCHES AND DEFECTS

Since the previous edition of this book in 1998, scanners and their accompanying software have tackled more of the problems that bedevil a scanned image while its source is still in the hopper or on the flatbed. Several years ago, everybody assumed that a scratched, dirty, or badly exposed frame was automatically going to cost hours in retouching time.

Newer scanners are much better at cleaning up originals that are damaged or otherwise not ideal. Whenever possible, we recommend that you take advantage of the defect-removal features of your scanner. We cover these features in Chapter 5, *How to Read Your Scanning Software*. If your scanner's defect-removal features don't include everything you need to make a perfect scan, or if defect removal doesn't work with your originals for some reason

(you're scanning silver-based black-and-white film, for example), you can draw upon the ideas in this chapter.

Fixing Local Exposure Problems

In Chapter 12, *Tonal Correction*, we talk about correcting tones throughout an entire image. But if some parts of a scan need special attention, you may need to apply some of the following manual techniques using your image editor.

Shadow/Highlight command. Available in Photoshop CS, the Shadow/Highlight feature (**Figure 14-1**) brings out highlight and shadow detail in a much faster way than the usual manual methods. In many cases, all you have to do is adjust the bal-

Figure 14-1 Applying Shadow/Highlight settings: original at top, and after applying Shadow/Highlight at bottom

ance between the Shadow and Highlight enhancement values. If there are still specific areas to address, you can use one of the other methods we describe below.

Dodge and Burn tools. You can lighten dark areas with the Dodge tool or darken light areas with the Burn tool, but the effect can be harder to control than with the methods that follow.

History Brush. Some Photoshop wizards prefer to correct exposure using the History Brush together with the Screen and Multiply modes. For example, to lighten a dark area, select the History Brush tool, set the source of the tool to the current state in the History palette, set the History Brush blending mode to Screen in the Options bar at the top of the screen, and paint the areas that are too dark (**Figure 14-2**). To darken light areas, use the same technique, but set the tool's blending mode to Multiply.

Curves adjustment layer. We talk about Photoshop adjustment layers in Chapter 12, *Tonal Correction*, but that is in the context of overall adjustments. To use an adjustment layer to fix a specific problem area, you can use the adjustment layer as a mask.

For example, if an area of a scan is too light, add a Curves or Levels adjustment layer that corrects it; for now, don't worry that it changes the rest of the image. Next, fill the adjustment layer with black to hide its effect. To do this using a shortcut, select the adjustment layer in the Layers palette, press D to set the foreground/background colors to their defaults (white foreground and black background for an adjustment layer), and then press Command-Delete/ Control-Backspace to fill the adjustment layer with the background color, which should be black as a result of pressing D. This will appear to remove the adjustment, but it's actually hidden because an adjustment layer is really a mask. Now select the

Figure 14-2 Dodging with the History brush: original image at top; after painting with History Brush in Screen mode at bottom

brush tool, make sure the foreground color is white, and paint the areas where you want to apply the adjustment layer (**Figure 14-3**).

As we describe earlier, the advantage of painting into masks like the adjustment layer is that you can reverse the effect by painting the opposite tone into the mask (black instead of white, or vice versa).

Removing Rotation and Distortion

Despite your best efforts, you may discover that some scans come in slightly crooked, even if you followed our tips for straight scanning in Chapter 3, *Getting Your Originals Ready to Scan*. Other scans might suffer from problems other than simple rotation. For example, a photo of a building might be distorted into a trapezoidal shape. Fortunately, there are a few quick ways to set things straight.

Straightening an image. It's easy to rotate an image, but not easy to know exactly how much to rotate it. In Photoshop, you can get help from the Measure tool. Select the Measure tool and drag it along an edge that should be straight. Then choose Arbitrary from the Image menu's Rotate Canvas submenu. The Arbitrary command recognizes the angle of the line you drew (**Figure 14-4**) and enters the proper settings to make it vertical, so that in most cases all you have to do is click OK. You can then display the grid—choose the View menu's Show Grid option—to see if your horizontal and vertical lines are straight.

Removing distortion. If rectangular shapes in your scan are distorted and look like trapezoids, it's usually because the original photograph was taken at an angle instead of straight on. You can correct this problem using Photoshop's Free Transform command. If you haven't cropped the image yet, you can also remove distortions by using the Crop tool.

▶ To remove distortion using the Free Transform command, first turn on the grid. If the scan is labeled "Back-

Figure 14-3
Burning with
an adjustment
layer: original
image at top;
adjustment layer
added to image;
after painting in
adjustment layer at
bottom

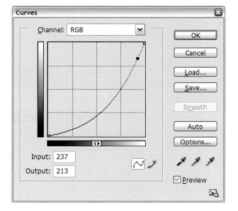

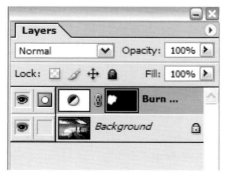

ground" and locked in the Layers palette, Option/Alt-double-click the layer to unlock it. Choose Free Transform from the Edit menu, and Command/Control-drag any of the corner handles of the free transformation box to align horizontals and verticals to the grid (**Figure 14-5**). When you're done, press Return or Enter.

► To remove distortion using the Crop tool, first select the crop tool and draw a standard crop rectangle. Then—and this is the important point—check the Perspective box that appears in the options bar after dragging the initial crop rectangle. Now you can drag any of the corner handles of the free transformation box to align the sides of the box with lines in the scan that should be horizontal or vertical (**Figure 14-6**). When you're done, press Return or Enter, and Photoshop will straighten the picture.

Using either method, you may find it easier to Command/Control-Shift-drag corner handles; this will constrain dragging along either the horizontal or vertical axis so that you don't introduce more distortions.

Correcting nonlinear distortions. Some scans contain distortions that you can't correct using Photoshop's built-in tools because they're curved, like the barrel distortions caused by camera lenses. To correct these distortions, you usually need a plug-in such as Andromeda Software's LensDoc. Andromeda makes many other useful plug-ins as well; they are all worth checking out at **www.andromeda.com**.

Removing Dust and Scratches

At first glance, there would seem to be two approaches to eliminating dust and scratches after scanning. One is to run a

Figure 14-4
Picking up a rotation angle from the Measure tool

Close-up of measure line

Applying Overall Defect Removal

There are seemingly endless ways to attack dust and scratches in an image. Most also remove useful details as well, but we'll

filter that attempts to detect and remove dust and scratches across the entire image. Another is to grab a tool and attack each defect manually—a chore often referred to as "dust-busting" after the trademarked portable vacuum cleaner.

However, the problem with the filter method is that it tends to be a blunt instrument that also kills details and textures that you want to keep. And the problem with manual dust-busting is that it's tedious and can take a lot of time if there are numerous spots or long scratches all over the scan.

A third, more effective approach combines both methods: First, run a filter that quickly repairs defects. Second, use a tool or technique to accept or deny any of the automatic corrections. Now let's get into the details of how this approach works.

Figure 14-5 Using the Free Transform command to remove distortion

Figure 14-6 Using the Crop tool to remove distortion: check Perspective after drawing rectangle, drag to match perspective, and view corrected image

Figure 14-7 Photoshop Dust & Scratches filter: original image (top) adjusted with filter (bottom)

deal with that dilemma in the next section. Here are effective ways to start:

Dust and Scratches filter. In Photoshop, dig down in the Filter menu's Noise submenu for Dust & Scratches. In Corel Photo-Paint, choose Dust and Scratch from the Image menu's Correction submenu (**Figure 14-7**). Start with low settings, increasing them as needed. The general rule is to back off before the image loses too much detail. But this is a basic type of filter that has a tendency to blur images before removing a useful number of defects.

Polaroid Dust and Scratch filter. Polaroid's free Dust & Scratch filter (**Figure 14-8**) has its fans because it has a few more options than the filters built into most image editors. In particular, you can manually identify defects or protect areas that don't have defects. You can use Polaroid's filter as a Photoshop plug-in or as a stand-alone application. You can download the Polaroid software from **www.polaroid.com/service/software/poladsr/poladsr.html**

Despeckle filter. In Photoshop, the Despeckle filter, found in the Filter menu's Noise submenu, is useful for removing numerous tiny spots, especially if they resemble noise.

Median filter. Try the Median filter as an alternative to a dust and scratches filter. In Photoshop, choose Median from the Filter menu's Noise submenu; in Corel Photo-Paint choose Noise Median from the Effects menu.

Handling Specific Areas

There are two strategies to fine-tuning the effect of a filter, and both rely on techniques that restore an unfiltered version of the image. If the filter helps more areas than it hurts, you can start from the filtered copy and restore specific unfiltered areas. If the filter hurts more areas than it helps, you can start from the unfiltered version and restore specific filtered areas.

You can create the filtered and unfiltered versions of the image in several ways. The method you use should simply be the one you're most comfortable with.

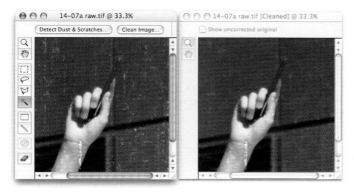

Figure 14-8
Polaroid Dust & Scratches filter

History/Undo brush. You can use Photoshop's History brush or Corel Photo-Paint's Undo brush to restore an earlier version of the image. For example, it's common for dust-removal software to remove specular highlights that you want to keep. After filtering the image, select the History brush in Photoshop, set the History brush source to the step before you filtered the image, and paint in the unfiltered areas you want to restore (**Figure 14-9**). In Photo-Paint, you don't have to set a source step, because you can only paint from the previous step (which in this case contains the unfiltered scan).

Multiple layers. For a bit more flexibility, you can duplicate a layer before you filter it, so that the duplicates are stacked on top

of each other. If you want to apply the filter to specific areas, you can filter the lower layer, then erase the upper, original layer to reveal filtered areas (**Figure 14-10**).

Layer masks. The great thing about using layer masks (called *clip masks* in Photo-Paint) is that any mistakes you make are reversible. But working with layer masks is a rather advanced skill. A layer mask is an *alpha channel* that's attached to a specific layer; an alpha channel uses grayscale values to control transparency. Black areas of the mask create transparent areas on the mask's layer, so that you can see through to the layer under it. White areas are completely opaque. Gray areas have partial opacity.

Let's say you have an unfiltered layer with a filtered layer on top of it. If you add a layer mask to the filtered layer, you can paint on the layer mask in black when you want the unfiltered layer to be visible (**Figure 14-11**). How is this better than simply erasing the top layer? When you erase pixels on a layer, they're gone forever (once the erasure step rolls off the History or Undo palette). When you make a layer transparent with a mask by painting black into the mask, you can make any area solid and visible again by painting white, or partially restore it by painting a shade of gray. If you're comfortable using layer masks, it is to your benefit because they certainly give you the most control.

Hand-to-Hand Dust-Busting
If you don't want to run a filter over an entire scan in Photoshop, you can remove each defect individually by using the Rubber Stamp or Healing Brush tools. Corel Photo-Paint's Clone tool is essentially the same as Photoshop's Rubber Stamp tool.

The Rubber Stamp and Healing Brush tools work in a similar way. First, you sample an undamaged area of the image by Option/Alt-clicking the area with the tool.

Figure 14-9
Using the History brush to restore unfiltered areas (top) and restoring specular highlights in metal pen clip (bottom)

Figure 14-10
Erasing areas of an unfiltered original (upper layer) to reveal the filtered duplicate layer (lower)

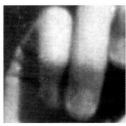

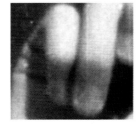

Figure 14-11
Painting white in a layer mask to apply filtered areas

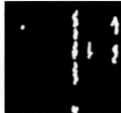

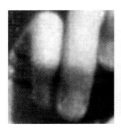

Figure 14-12
Using the Healing Brush to fix scratches

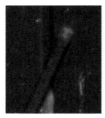

Second, you paint over a defect (**Figure 14-12**). The difference between the tools is that the Rubber Stamp paints exactly what you picked up, whereas the Healing Brush uses a bit of intelligence to try and match the underlying texture so that the results are more seamless. Photoshop's Patch tool is the Healing Brush's complement—instead of painting a source onto a destination, you select an area and drag it to the part of the image that you want to use as a source. If you're familiar with the Rubber Stamp tool, the Healing Brush will be a little more intuitive than the Patch tool.

Out of the Fixer

The techniques in this chapter help you handle most of the basic problems that bedevil a new scan. If you have images that need more help, you may want to consult books that delve more deeply into image correction and defect removal.

We can think of two books that provide many more alternatives than the methods we had space to cover in this chapter. *Photoshop Restoration and Retouching* by Katrin Eismann and Doug Nelson (Peachpit Press) is a wonderful book that covers techniques like restoring old photographs, removing dust and mold, and performing digital makeovers for portraits. And of course, *Real World Adobe Photoshop*, co-authored by David with Bruce Fraser. It provides deep coverage of topics like masking, adjustment layers, and history techniques.

15

A Sharper Image

GETTING RID OF THE BLURRIES

How do we recognize where one shape stops and another one starts? Our brain has specialized parts that process optical data, and one set of neurons is devoted to identifying adjacent areas of high contrast. The higher the contrast, the more we perceive an edge. Perhaps this was once a survival mechanism, especially in foggy climates, but today it just keeps most of us from walking into doors.

A good photographic print *pops* when you look at it: there are depth and contrast to a print that make it seem real. Images reproduced directly off a scanner without correction look flat and blurry. You have to take the scanned image and increase contrast at the edges of shapes so that you see the image as sharply and crisply as a photographic print—and the world around us. Fortunately, computers are good at rec-

ognizing edges: pixels next to each other that have a tonal difference.

Scans almost always require sharpening because of something we discuss at length in Chapter 2, *Scanners*. Because scanners can't easily distinguish the darkest (or densest) tones, so the contrast and sharpness at edges can be lost.

Averaging also affects an image: a scanner might capture a sample directly on an edge, so it is half black and half white; the sample then gets averaged to 50 percent, not captured as one side of the edge or the other.

When you limit an image's output values as we describe in Chapter 12, *Tonal Correction*, you make it possible to reproduce its lightest and darkest tones on an offset press. However, the resulting reduction in tonal range makes it less likely that

Chapter 15: A Sharper Image

Figure 15-1 How sharpening works

Unsharpened

Sharpened

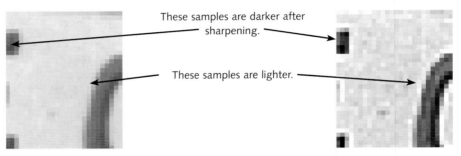

These samples are darker after sharpening.

These samples are lighter.

an image will pop. Scanning at a higher resolution doesn't help: more data of the same kind won't increase clarity, and usually it's just wasted information.

Almost all image-editing software, like Photoshop, have simple and complex sharpening filters that do edge detection and increase contrast. The simple ones in Photoshop are called Sharpen, Sharpen More, and Sharpen Edges. These don't allow you the kind of control that's needed for doing professional work; for that, you need unsharp masking.

All sharpening tools do one thing: emphasize difference, which helps our eyes pick out detail. Sharpening increases differences where they count (**Figure 15-1**).

When to Sharpen

The question of when to sharpen can come up simply because sharpening controls appear in multiple places. You see them in your scanning software and in your image editor. To understand when you

should sharpen, it helps to know the two reasons for sharpening.

Restoring original sharpness. The first reason is to restore the sharpness of the original. Along with the averaging issues we mentioned earlier, the image sensors currently used in scanners and digital cameras simply don't capture all of the detail in the original. For example, each green sensor is grouped with a red and blue sensor, so there's a gap between green sensors where green isn't recorded. This means there is quite a bit of green that never gets recorded, and the same situation exists for red and blue as well. These gaps help cause the slight loss of sharpness that results from digital image capture. If you apply sharpening to correct for this loss, it should happen in hardware or software right after the image is captured.

Optimizing for output. The second reason to sharpen is to boost apparent sharpness as much as the final output medium allows.

However, the correct settings are highly specific to the final medium, particularly image dimensions and image resolution, which means that output-related sharpening should be applied as one of the final steps of the editing process.

Keeping those two reasons for sharpening in mind, and the fact that one sharpening technique is applied at the beginning of the process and the other at the end, the question of when to sharpen becomes easier to answer:

▶ If you know that you'll need to work with the image further in your image-editing software, you can simply not sharpen at all in the scanning software, waiting until you've finalized the image in your image editor. Or, you can apply very slight sharpening in the scanning software—just enough to correct for the slight loss of sharpness caused by digital image capture. But you need to make sure you aren't introducing visible artifacts that might be amplified by later image editing.

▶ If you don't plan to edit the image further in an image editor, you can apply full, final sharpening settings in the scanning software. Just be aware of the consequences of locking down sharpening early in the process. For example, if you produce 300 spi, 5-by-7–inch prepress images straight from your scanning software, the sharpening settings will be locked into that combination of resolution or dimensions, so

changing the resolution or dimensions of the image later may result in an inappropriate level of sharpening.

Unsharp Masking

The method of choice for sharpening scanned photographs is called (somewhat oxymoronically) *unsharp masking* (USM). With its roots in the darkroom and its genesis in high-end prepress systems, unsharp masking provides controls that let you adjust sharpening for particular situations.

Unsharp masking works by combining a slightly blurry (unsharp) version of an image with the original. This combination results in sharp details in high-contrast areas (the edges, where adjacent light and dark samples are markedly different), without creating tonal shifts in low-contrast areas (areas of smooth gradation, where rapid tonal shifts would destroy the subtle transitions).

Since it increases the contrast in many areas of an image, unsharp masking also tends to increase the overall appearance of contrast.

How Unsharp Masking Works

How does combining a blurry version with the original make for a sharper image? We knew you'd ask that, so we prepared ourselves. Here's the skinny: **Figure 15-2** shows a simple situation—a jump in tonal value from 40 to 60 percent.

When you apply a blurring filter to the image (in our example, we've used a Gaussian blur filter), you get what you see in **Figure 15-3**. The values ramp up from 40 to 60 percent in a smooth transition. Note that this is an intentionally low-resolution bitmap we're working with, so it shows the effects clearly.

The USM filter does some clever if/then calculations. If the sample in the blurred

Figure 15-2 40-to 60-percent tonal jump

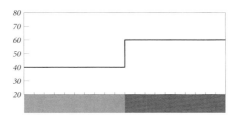

Figure 15-3 After Gaussian blur

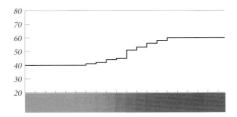

Unsharpened   Oversharpened

Figure 15-5 The "halo" effect of unsharp masking

image is darker than the same sample in the original, it makes that sample lighter by an amount equal to the difference. If the sample in the blurred version is lighter, it does the opposite (**Figure 15-4**).

The key things to notice in this figure are the "blips" on either side of the tonal shift. By accentuating the adjacent light and dark areas, unsharp masking gives the impression of sharpness. Too much, and you get the *halo effect* (**Figure 15-5**). When it's pronounced, the halo effect is a problem, but it's an integral part of how sharpening works. In the next section, we tell you how to avoid pronounced halos.

Problems with Unsharp Masking

When used improperly or excessively, unsharp masking can make an image look artificial or bizarre, and it can accentuate problems in the original image or the scan. Let's look at the four problems that result.

Halos. The blips that appear on either side of tonal shifts with unsharp masking can turn into a too-obvious halo, giving the image an artificial look. In excess, it can make an image look blurrier as well. This is especially a problem when the halo is too wide, though it's also a problem if the

Figure 15-4 After unsharp masking

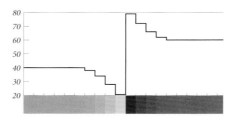

blips are too light or too dark—in other words, if they're too different from their surroundings (**Figure 15-6**).

Figure 15-6 Artificial look due to halos from unsharp masking

Aliasing. Hard diagonal edges—like a dark building against a light sky—often display aliasing (the *jaggies*) after applying unsharp masking (**Figure 15-7**). Aliasing becomes significant when an image's effective resolution is less than two times the screen frequency (the lower the resolution, the more potential aliasing).

Speckling and mottling. Scanned images often contain a few random sample points that don't match their surroundings. This may be due to a noisy scan, irregularities in the original image, or simply the con-

Figure 15-7
Resolution,
sharpening,
and aliasing

300 dpi,
unsharpened

300 dpi,
sharpened

Aliasing is a danger
at lower resolutions,
visible in the ships'
rigging.

200 dpi,
sharpened

150 dpi,
sharpened

tent of the image. At the finest levels of optical resolution, it can even be caused by the scanner picking up the grain of the film. (This is mainly a problem when you scan high-speed, coarsely grained film on high-resolution drum and slide scanners; or, when you scale an image up significantly.) Sharpening can accentuate those irregularities, resulting in a number of problems—especially with lower-resolution scans.

The most immediately noticeable problem is speckling—usually light pixels in otherwise dark areas. This is especially a problem with low-quality scans that have a lot of noise. You can get rid of speckling to some extent by running a despeckle filter before sharpening.

A less obvious but equally problematic result of sharpening is mottling—often causing people to look like they have bad complexions. It can also destroy the impression of smooth gradations; for instance, in a photograph of a sand dune.

Content-related problems. There are many other sharpening problems that are con-

tent-related, and that you need to watch for on an image-by-image basis. For example, sharpening can accentuate the highlights in someone's hair, introducing a case of premature gray. And, in heavy doses, it can give the impression of buck teeth. Watch out for embarrassing accentuation; it's the stuff that caricatures are made of.

Unsharp Masking in Photoshop

Okay, let's get to the juice of the chapter: how to use Photoshop's Unsharp Mask filter while avoiding the four problems above. Photoshop offers the most complete unsharp masking controls we've seen on the desktop. By explaining those controls, we can provide detailed suggestions on how to control the sharpening process. Some other programs offer similar, sometimes identical controls, so you can apply these lessons to those programs as well.

Photoshop's Unsharp Mask filter has three variables: Radius, Amount, and Threshold (**Figure 15-8**), discussed in turn next. Each increases or decreases sharpening in different areas and situations.

As you're reading through this section, refer to **Figure 15-9** a little later in this chapter due to the large number of figures; that figure illustrates the same image sharpened with many different combinations of Unsharp Mask settings.

Radius. The first step in properly using unsharp masking is determining the Radius value. Once you've set Radius, you can go on to adjust the other settings relative to that.

The Radius setting controls how many samples wide the blips are on each side of an edge. Large values make for wide blips (big halos with lots of sample points involved); small values make smaller blips. The size of the sharpening-induced halo affects how sharp an image looks (a larger radius means

Figure 15-8
Photoshop's
Unsharp Mask
dialog box

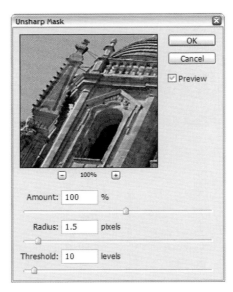

more sharpening). And in excess, it causes most sharpening-related problems.

Even though Radius is measured in pixels, the relationship between Radius pixels and image pixels is complex. A Radius value of 1.0 results in blips about one sample wide. A value of 2.0 gives you about four samples on either side of the blip. So what Radius value should you set? Start with resolution divided by 200. For a 200-spi scan, use a Radius setting of 1.0. For a 300-spi scan, use a Radius setting of 1.5. This ratio results in a halo of $\frac{1}{50}$ inch—$\frac{1}{100}$ inch for each blip. It provides the sharpening effect without looking artificial. Images with fine details require a smaller Radius; coarse details require a larger Radius.

Amount. We like to think of the Amount setting as the volume, or amplitude, control. It adjusts how intense the blips are on each side of a tonal shift—in other words, how

*Overly large Radius settings are the prime culprits in producing the ugly oversharpened look that stands out so markedly, so be sure not to increase this setting too much. The images with a Radius of 2.0 shown in **Figure 15-9** make this clear.*

much the tonal differences are accentuated. Large values make for big blips (large tonal differences where edges meet); small values make for less significant blips. We're not talking about the width of the halos here—just the *amount* of tonal difference between adjacent samples.

If you use the settings provided earlier for Radius, an Amount setting of 200 percent is a good choice, or at least a good starting point. If the Amount value is set too high, you can get the kind of artificial look we mentioned in the Radius section. It's not much of a problem if you keep the Radius setting low, but if you increase both the Radius *and* Amount values, images go weird very quickly.

Also be aware that as you increase the Amount setting, you start to reach a point of diminishing returns. The blips around big tonal shifts end up going all the way to white and to black (a problem in itself, because the white blips in particular show up as noticeable artifacts), so increasing the amount has no further effect in those areas. Since those areas of large tonal shifts are the ones you most want to accentuate to give the effect of sharpness, and since you can't accentuate them beyond black and white, increasing the Amount setting beyond a certain point is fruitless.

Large values in the Amount field can also accentuate the problems with noise and mottling as we mentioned earlier, but you can avoid these problems by using the Threshold value, which we discuss next.

Threshold. The Threshold value specifies how many tonal steps apart, on a scale of 0 to 255, that adjacent samples have to be before the filter adjusts them. If Threshold is set to 3, for instance, and the values of adjacent sample points are 122 and 124 (a difference of two), they're unaffected by sharpening. So low-contrast areas—those with smooth gradations—aren't affected; the gradations stay smooth.

Billboard Sharpening

The one situation where you might want to use a larger Radius setting is for large images that people will never look at up close—like billboards and (some) posters. In this case, you may need a larger Radius to make the sharpness really pop at the intended viewing distance ($\frac{1}{100}$ inch ain't much at 100 feet). In that case, try this formula to determine an appropriate Radius setting:

```
Viewing Distance (inches) × Resolution (spi) × .0004 =
Radius setting
```

This formula is based on some theories about the eye's sensitivity to cycles of amplitude modulation over a given viewing arc (we love throwing around big words like that). We haven't had the chance to test this on a billboard, so we suggest you use it as a starting point, and with a pinch (if not a bag) of salt. You might try a small (tabloid-size) area first, and place it far away to see how it looks.

The Threshold setting is the key to avoiding mottling, speckling, and artifact-related problems that sharpening can cause. This setting causes the filter to ignore those slightly-out-of-place pixels, rather than accentuating them. This is especially important for smooth natural tones as in an image that has a solid blue sky in the background.

Low Threshold values result in an overall sharper-looking image because fewer areas are excluded. High values result in less sharpening. We recommend a setting of 3 or 4 for most images. Settings of 10 and higher aren't advisable, because they exclude so many areas and reduce sharpening to near invisibility.

Color Sharpening

While it's easy enough to play with the values and settings we suggest in the previous sections, additional techniques can dramatically improve your ability to use unsharp masking with color images.

The eye perceives differences in luminance—tonal values—much more readily than differences in chrominance—color variation. If you could sharpen the luminance separately from the chrominance, you'd be able to achieve the same sharpening results at lower sharpening values.

However, in RGB color space, color and luminance are lumped together. This lumping together has an unpleasant side effect—color fringing can appear at sharpened edges. No need to worry, because there are easy ways to sharpen just luminance and not chrominance. Let's look at two techniques.

LAB color space. Photoshop and several other programs support the LAB color space, which stores a color image as a channel of luminance (L) and two channels of color information (A and B); see Chapter 13, *Getting Good Color*, for a full explanation.

In LAB mode, it's easy to sharpen just the tonal information without disturbing color details. All you have to do is select the L channel in the Channels palette before running the Unsharp Mask command. One reason to do this is to avoid oversaturating color images. When you increase the contrast in a color image, you increase the saturation in colors that are on the "high" side of an edge (**Figure 15-9**).

You should avoid going back and forth between RGB and LAB, because values are lost and compressed during the conversion. If your final step is CMYK conversion, you can switch once from RGB to LAB, applying sharpening, and then convert to CMYK.

If your job will eventually be printed as CMYK, you can also choose to change the mode from RGB to CMYK and then sharpen just the K channel, since that channel carries most of the brightness information in CMYK. This is a good technique if you don't need to do any more editing in RGB. Don't return to RGB from CMYK, or the image may lose colors.

Figure 15-9
Sharpening with
luminosity

The original image needs a relatively high amount of sharpening.

Sharpening in RGB improves the image, but color fringing creeps into the contrasty area around the embroidery and emphasizes color noise or grain in the white cloth. The enhanced edge contrast also pushes some colors outside the output color gamut.

Applying the Fade command with Luminosity applies the previous sharpening values to lightness but not color, leaving colors at their original values and minimizing color fringing.

Luminosity blending mode. You can avoid the side trip to LAB color space by fading the sharpening effect with Luminosity mode. To do this, apply the Unsharp Mask filter, then immediately choose Fade Unsharp Mask from the Edit menu. Choose Luminosity from the popup menu, specify an Opacity value if you want to reduce the effect, and click OK (**Figure 15-9**, bottom).

The results of applying a luminosity fade are nearly the same as sharpening the LAB color space's L channel. If you compare the two, you'll probably only see very subtle differences in the results.

Sharpening Specific Areas

Sometimes the sharpening settings that work for most of an image don't work for all of the image. There may be areas that appear over- or under-sharpened. You can control the amount of sharpening in each area by using the techniques in this section.

You can also use the techniques to control local exposure and defect removal, which we describe in Chapter 14, *Freshening Up*. You can apply different amounts of sharpening to duplicate layers of the same scan and then use the erase tool, layer masks, or the history/undo brush to paint in more or less sharpening anywhere in the image.

Selections

As with any filter, you don't have to arbitrarily select the whole image. You can manually select an area—or use one of many tools to select by color or tone—and sharpen just that bit. This method is sometimes used to sharpen the eyes in a face without disturbing flatter facial tones; it's also used to sharpen faces in a crowd.

If you have an image with a relatively flat or even-colored background, you would normally set the Threshold value to 2 or 3

Figure 15-10
Sharpening
selectively

The original image (top) has a strong figure in the center of the picture, while the background is a little out of the depth of field and blurred. The face to the right of the central figure could distract from the overall composition if it were as sharp as the foreground figure.

Sharpening the whole image (middle) makes the out-of-focus background noisy and too crisp. It also brings into sharper focus the face to the right of the central figure.

Sharpening just the central figure's face (bottom) helps keep attention in the right spot and reduces noise. The face is sharpened with Threshold set to 3.

to avoid mottling in the flat colors. However, you might simultaneously have a subject in the foreground that needs a Threshold of 0 or 1. The solution is to select the background you want to preserve using Photoshop's selection tools, invert the selection, choose the Feather command on the Select menu to soften the selection (try a small value like 3 pixels), and just sharpen your foreground subject (**Figure 15-10**).

Facial Care

We scrutinize faces, even in photographs, more carefully than anything else—it's an automatic reaction. So if you sharpen photographs with people in them, especially close-ups of faces or mug shots, it's a good idea to increase the Threshold value. The plane of a face has many subtle transitions, and a low Threshold will create artifacts all over a face. Set the Threshold high and the Radius small, and you'll get the best results (**Figure 15-11**). If you combine this technique with selections in particularly difficult images, you will get much better results over an entire image.

Running the Numbers

We used to get incredibly frustrated using the documentation of Photoshop's Unsharp Mask filter, which used to provide information like "If you'd like to enter 1 in the Radius field, enter 1." However, the manuals have improved to the point that they explain each setting and suggest how to approximate your needs. And, after slogging through endless trial and error attempts—on screen and on output—to develop simple formulas we can use for sharpening, we provide you with some practical settings in **Figure 15-12**. They make our lives much simpler; we hope they will do the same for you.

Figure 15-11
Sharpening faces

The original,
unsharpened image

The image sharpened with Threshold at 0

The image sharpened with Threshold at 5

Taking the unsharpened image above and applying the Unsharp Mask filter with Threshold set to 0 results in a grainy facial texture.

Setting Threshold to 5 results in less pixelization in the face, although the background stays a little fuzzier.

Figure 15-12
Various settings
for Photoshop's
Unsharp Mask filter

200-spi image
133-lpi screen

Unsharpened

Optimal sharpening:
Amount: 200 Radius: 1 Threshold: 3

Figure 15-12
Various settings
for Photoshop's
Unsharp Mask
filter, *continued*

200-spi image
133-lpi screen

Amount: 75 Radius: 2 Threshold: 3

Amount: 125 Radius: 1 Threshold: 3

Amount: 100 Radius: 2 Threshold: 3

Amount: 150 Radius: 1 Threshold: 3

Amount: 125 Radius: 2 Threshold: 3

Amount: 175 Radius: 1 Threshold: 3

Amount: 150 Radius: 2 Threshold: 3

Amount: 200 Radius: 1 Threshold: 3

PART 4

Storing Images

16

File Formats

WHICH ONE AND WHY

Why are there so many languages in the world? Because each culture seems to have its set of messages that need to be conveyed, and each language doesn't contain the same set of concepts. Likewise, when you look at a laundry list of file formats, like JPEG, GIF, TIFF, and EPS, you ask yourself: why so many? Because each has its own idiom that lets it serve a particular message best.

When we talk about file formats, we're referring to how a graphic image is stored on a disk. How it's stored determines what programs can open ("read") the graphic, and what you can do with the file once it's opened. If you say a program can read a given format, you may mean one of two things. The program may be able to place the image on a page and print it, or it may be able to open the file and actually edit it.

This chapter is one of the longest in the book by far because of the interrelated scope of what's covered. We introduce you first to the major split in what's stored in file: bitmapped and object-oriented images. We then walk through the details of the major file formats for each kind of data, including some that combine both bitmaps and objects. We then talk about deprecated and outdated formats you still might encounter, and conclude by showing you a magic trick: how different platforms identify image types.

It's time to pull out your acronym decoder, and learn the nitty gritty.

Bitmaps and Objects

Before we dive into file formats, we need to explain an important distinction between bitmapped and object-oriented graphics.

Most file formats are designed to handle only either kind of graphics, but a few can handle both. Let's examine this distinction before discussing individual formats.

Bitmapped graphics. Bitmapped images are just big grids of pixels, as we explain in the previous few chapters. To do something useful with a bitmap, the file format needs to contain information on dimensions, resolution, bit depth, color model, and compression.

Bitmaps come from three primary sources: scanners, painting and image-processing programs (such as Photoshop, Photo-Paint, DeBabelizer and so on), and screen-capture programs (HyperSnap, SnagIt, SnapzPro, and a host of others). If you create a graphic with any of these tools, the result is a bitmap.

Object-oriented graphics. Object-oriented files are typically more complex. Instead of describing a rectangle with a bunch of dots, object-oriented graphics use an instruction such as, "Draw a rectangle this big and put it at such-and-such place on the page." These images can include lines, boxes, circles, curves, polygons, and text blocks, and all those items can have a variety of attributes—line weight, type formatting, fill color, graduated fills, *et al., ad nauseam.*

You can scale object-oriented graphics to almost any size, large or small, without distorting their appearance. The interpreter that understands the object language always draws the details of the object at the resolution of the printer it's outputting to. Unlike a bitmap that contains a fixed

You can almost always place an object-oriented graphic on your page and print it, but it's not always certain that you will be able to edit it. Some formats use too many compound objects or pure PostScript code, which makes them difficult to manipulate visually.

amount of image data and which looks blurry when enlarged, an object-oriented file contains just shapes that don't have a particular size—although you usually design them to reproduce at a fixed size.

Object-oriented graphics come from two primary sources: drawing programs (Macromedia FreeHand, CorelDraw, and Adobe Illustrator, to name the big ones) and computer-aided design (CAD) programs. You also might export object-oriented graphics from a graphing program or a spreadsheet with a graphing module.

Object-oriented graphics are also called *draw graphics* or *vector graphics.*

Bitmaps qua objects. As it turns out, the distinction between bitmaps and objects is slightly fuzzy, because object-oriented files can include bitmaps as objects in their own right; they just usually don't allow you to make any changes to them. If you're creating an illustration in Illustrator, for instance, you can include a TIFF or other bitmapped image as one of the objects in the illustration.

If you include a bitmap as an object in an illustration, you may not be able to edit that bitmap. You can place it, rotate it, or twist it around, but you can't modify the actual image. Some programs, however, such as ACD Systems's Canvas, have object-oriented *and* bitmapped layers, which allow you to jump back and forth between models. And PDF files almost always include both bitmapped and object-oriented graphics without any fuss about which kind is which.

Bitmap-only object-oriented files. An object-oriented file can also include a bitmap as its *only* object. In this situation, the file is essentially a bitmapped graphic file, and depending on the file format, you may be able to open the bitmap for editing in a painting or image-processing application. Photoshop EPS files are an example of a bitmap-only object-oriented file, although we're seeing more and more PDF documents that are nothing but a scan.

Bitmapped File Formats

When the first edition of this book appeared, folks were still arguing over which bitmapped file formats to use—and even how to pronounce them. The disputes have long since been settled: TIFF, EPS, GIF, JPEG, and PNG rule the day. These formats each have a specialty, making them distinct from each other. All five formats have compression options, but each treats color and tonal fidelity differently. In **Table 16-1**, we compare some basic features of each format, and compare them to Photo CD, a relatively common way to convert images directly from photographic film into digital files without a scanner. If you don't understand all the terms listed in the table, don't worry—by the end of the chapter, you will.

Tagged Image File Format (TIFF)

The Tagged Image File Format (TIFF) is the most widely used, industry-standard bitmap file format. A TIFF bitmap can be of any dimensions and any resolution (at least we haven't heard of any limits). It can have theoretically unlimited bit depth, but most software reads or writes some standard sizes: 1 to 8, 24, 32 (for CMYK), or 48 (for RGB) bits per sample. TIFF can encode grayscale, RGB, indexed-color, or CMYK color models. It can be saved in compressed and uncompressed formats.

Table 16-1 Major bitmap formats compared

Format	Compression	Displays in browser	Bit depths	Color	Interlacing	Metadata[1]	Transparency
TIFF	Lossless	No	1–8, 24, 32, 48	Indexed, gray, RGB, CMYK	No	Yes	Alpha channel
EPS	Lossless or lossy	No	same as TIFF	Gray, RGB, CMYK	No	Yes	Only in bilevel mode
GIF	Lossless	Yes	1–8	Indexed	Yes	Yes	One color
JPEG	Lossy	Yes	8, 24, 32	Gray, RGB, CMYK	Yes[2]	No[3]	None
JPEG 2000	Lossy or lossless	Yes[4]	8, 24, 32	Gray, LAB, CMYK	Yes[2]	Yes	Alpha channel
PNG	Lossless	Yes[4]	1–8, 16, 24, 32, 48	Indexed, Gray, RGB	Yes	Yes	One color or alpha channel
Photo CD	Lossy	Yes[5]	24	PhotoYCC[6]	No	Yes	None

[1]Stores information in text form about the image in a way that image-editing programs can read and/or modify. [2]Multiple settings for interlacing. [3]Photoshop supports this, but the basic image data format used for JPEG doesn't. [4]Browser support varies. [5]Requires third-party plug-in for all browsers at this writing. [6]PhotoYCC is a Kodak-only colorspace that's similar to LAB in how it stores color.

Almost every program that works with bitmaps can handle TIFF files—whether for placing, printing, correcting, or editing the bitmap.

TIFF sounds like the ideal bitmapped file format, and it's pretty close. Several years ago, there were problems in converting TIFF files between different programs and different platforms, but those issues disappeared for all major software vendors, and virtually all other image-manipulating software. There are very rare times when you have to open an older TIFF in a graphics converter and then export it from that program in order to make it fully compatible with newer software.

Here's some background on the choices you face when saving TIFF files in most programs; this information can also help you debug problems you might encounter with archived files from the depths of time (late '80s and early '90s) or those created by people who aren't quite familiar with a program.

Gulliver's samples. A holdup that used to catch production people was the Lilliputian problem of TIFF files: you would try to open a file on a Mac and it would tell you the file was stored in an "IBM PC" format, or vice versa. A TIFF file can store its multi-byte samples in one of two ways because some computers look at bytes that make up a sample from left to right; others, from right to left.

Nerds call the left-to-right byte ordering "big-endian" (because the big end, or digits representing higher units, are read first); right-to-left byte ordering is "little-endian" (the lower-unit digits are read first). IBM processors that power the Macintosh prefer big-endian, while Intel PCs running Windows and Linux are little-endian.

The terminology comes from Jonathan Swift's *Gulliver's Travels* in which the Lilliputians war absurdly over what end to eat a soft-boiled egg from, and is another example of why programmers need more sun. (A programmer who nicely vetted this chapter for us suggested that computer-book authors just need a better sense of the absurd.)

Nowadays, the Lilliputians' wars are forgotten and every major image-editing program that can open and save TIFFs can read either kind of byte ordering without a hitch; the TIFFs actually have a key at the beginning of the file that tells an application what order they're stored in. Other image formats hide this ordering from users, and just cope without a word. (You can also see some low-level information about these keys later in **Table 16-3**.)

When you choose IBM PC or Macintosh from Photoshop's Save As dialog for TIFFs (**Figure 16-1**), you're choosing the byte order. If you ever encounter a problem image, open the file on the platform it was created on and save it with the setting for the platform you're moving the file to. However, most current programs can read either byte order without a problem.

Color models. TIFF's specification allows for CMYK color as well as RGB. This means you can separate an image into the

Figure 16-1 Photoshop's Save As dialog box for TIFF files

four process colors, and save that preseparated image in a TIFF file. (If that last part was meaningless to you, see Chapter 13, *Getting Good Color*.) When you place that file in a page-layout program or the like, no further separation is required. The program can simply extract the cyan channel when it's printing the cyan plate, the magenta channel when it's printing the magenta plate, and so on.

Compression. You can save TIFFs with LZW compression—we discuss what LZW is and why it can be a good thing in Chapter 17, *Compression*—but you don't have to use it. Fortunately, LZW compression is lossless, meaning that the image data doesn't degrade when you save the file. Photoshop can also compress TIFFs using ZIP compression (discussed in the next chapter, also), but this addition is relatively new; some programs may not work well with ZIP-compressed TIFFs.

PostScript extras. There is no facility for including halftone screening instructions in a TIFF file. Screening is controlled by the program from which the TIFF is printed. If you want to save a bitmap with screening instructions, use EPS.

TIFFs can handle a clipping path, however; both QuarkXPress and Adobe InDesign can read the path and properly trim out a background.

Layers. TIFF—like most other bitmap file formats—didn't support layers in its earliest form, but recent versions of Photoshop can save TIFF files that include layers. While TIFF layer support is convenient, it's a relatively new extension of the TIFF format; older programs or devices may not understand TIFF layers and might produce unexpected results like skipping over the layer data. When in doubt, save a TIFF without the layer data (flatten it).

See "Encapsulated PostScript" later in this chapter for a description of clipping paths.

Transparency. A TIFF file can also include transparent areas (that checkerboard background pattern in Photoshop). However, most programs (like QuarkXPress) ignore the transparency and just give the image a white background. Adobe InDesign preserves image transparency, so you don't need a clipping path. A TIFF can also include vector paths or alpha channels, which some programs can convert into hard-edged clipping paths.

Pronunciation. TIFF is pronounced *tiff*. It's straightforward, but wait until the next entry.

Graphics Interchange Format (GIF)

We barely mentioned GIF in the first edition because in 1993 it was used almost exclusively by CompuServe users to send low-quality images to each other. Now, almost everyone on the planet knows that GIF is one of the World Wide Web's standard graphic formats.

The GIF file format was originally developed in 1987 ("GIF87a") and revised in 1989 ("GIF89a")—unfortunately, not every program upgraded its support to the later version. The main visible difference is that GIF89a added a transparency color (see "Transparency" in Chapter 7, *Scanning for*

TIFF can also store indexed-color bitmaps, but almost no one ever uses it for this; we prefer to use GIF for indexed-color images. The PNG format offers the same choice of indexed or RGB color with its own unique advantages, which we describe later in this section.

the Web and Video). In fact, Adobe didn't even initially update Photoshop until 1996 (via the "GIF89a Export" plug-in).

Our advice: don't use the GIF format for any kind of high-resolution color output for printing; the color fidelity is too poor and the images almost always appear posterized.

Here are the salient characteristics of the GIF format.

Color model. GIF files can contain a maximum of 256 different colors, which are stored in a palette that is part of the GIF file itself (**Figure 16-2**). It's called an indexed color palette because the colors in the image data aren't directly represented by RGB values. Instead, the image data comprises single-byte values that correspond to entries in a color palette, just like entries in a two-column spreadsheet. The single-byte value is paired with a full, 24-bit (3-byte) RGB value in the palette. This saves a lot of space but still allows you to specify an actual color for samples to be translated back into when the file is displayed.

Figure 16-2
A sample GIF colormap in Photoshop (which calls it Color Table)

GIF image data and the indexed color palette are editable in virtually every image-manipulation program. You don't have to use all 256 colors: GIF palettes can represent anywhere from 1 to 256 colors using from 1 to 8 bits for the index value. And the fewer colors in the palette (or *colormap*), the better the built-in compression works and the more consistent the display across different browsers and platforms. (Again, see Chapter 7, *Scanning for the Web and Video*, for details on reducing the color palette and other GIF-related issues.)

Compression. GIF uses lossless compression that can't be turned off (you wouldn't want to) and can substantially reduce file size. Compression depends entirely on image content; images with mostly flat colors—solid fields of color—can be reduced to one-tenth (or even one-hundredth) the size, while natural images (scans of photographs) often compress very poorly. (We talk about this compression more in depth in Chapter 17, *Compression*.)

Resolution. GIF was designed for screen display so the format assumes each image pixel corresponds to a screen pixel: GIF stores no information mapping pixels to scale. Photoshop always opens GIF images at 72 dpi, but that's not because the file contains that information: it's because Photoshop makes that assumption for GIF files.

Pronunciation. Discussions on how to pronounce GIF have resulted in fistfights. The guy who actually wrote the format, Steve Wilhite, apparently said the "g" as "j" as in "jelly," and often uttered the line, "Choosy programmers choose jiff" (if you're not up on American television advertising from 20 years ago, just smile and nod appreciatively). However, many well-meaning and gifted professionals say the "g" like in "gift." We tend to just say, "Ummm ...you know... *that* format."

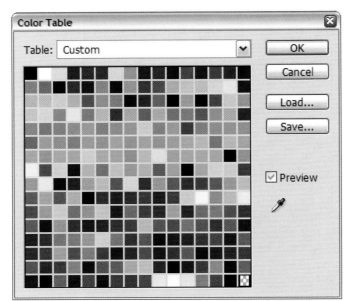

Color Table

Table: Custom

OK
Cancel
Load...
Save...

☑ Preview

JPEG

The JPEG file format—known as the Joint Photographic Experts Group standard by those wishing to be excessively obscure—has risen to prominence as the compressed file format of choice for both print and Web publishing.

JPEGs lose quality each time they're saved, due to the format's lossy compression scheme (we explain why in Chapter 17, *Compression*). For this reason, you don't want to save multiple generations of an image. Typically, you should only save an image in the JPEG format as the last stage in the production process.

JPEG is useful as a method of reducing a file's size enough to fit on a disk or send over a modem line because you can compress natural, scanned images significantly (often to less than 5 percent of their original size). This is why JPEG images are used so often on the Internet. JPEG files are also frequently created for proofing purposes so that someone can look at a final illustration on screen without requiring large source files, though the PDF file format is quickly replacing this function. (PDFs, in fact, allow JPEG compression as one of many methods of reducing image sizes.)

Here's more on what you need to know about JPEG files.

Image format. Although we call the format a JPEG file, the JPEG-compressed data is actually stored inside another format, rarely mentioned, but worth pointing out. The JPEG spec defines the image's compression and the JFIF (JPEG File Interchange Format) packages JPEG data with the image's color model, resolution, and file descriptions, like photographer or keywords. You rarely see the name JFIF except in more obscure or technical image-editing programs, and there are other rare ways to wrap JPEG data using a format like JFIF.

Color models. JPEG allows bitmaps 8, 24, and 32 bits deep to be stored with variable compression (from high compression and lousy quality, to low compression and high quality). The original JFIF wrapper spec only allows 8-bit grayscale and 24-bit RGB images, but Adobe "hacked" the format to handle 32-bit CMYK data as well. If you decide to use CMYK JPEG, make sure both your service bureau and your page-layout program support this format.

Pronunciation. Say "jay-peg" and you're set.

JPEG 2000

The JPEG 2000 file format is the latest incarnation of the JPEG file format. JPEG 2000 and JPEG have important differences and aren't compatible with one another. Save a file as JPEG 2000, and a program that can only read and handle JPEG can't open it without an update or a plug-in. When writing this edition of the book, many software firms had updated their software, including Adobe with Photoshop CS and other members of the Creative Suite of applications. Let's run through this format's particulars.

Compression. JPEG 2000 makes use of *wavelet* compression, which provides improved quality at the same compressed file sizes as the conventional JPEG format. JPEG 2000 also supports lossless compression, whereas JPEG only provides lossy compression.

Alpha Channels. Conventional JPEG doesn't support alpha channel transparency, but JPEG 2000 does.

Metadata. JPEG 2000 provides for the inclusion of metadata, such as exposure, lens, and other shooting information about a particular digital photograph.

Wavelets are an interesting mathematical structure in which information is deconstructed into differences that can be more easily compressed. It was the hot, new math of the 1990s.

Portable Network Graphics (PNG)

The genesis of the PNG file format was brought about by the controversy over the LZW compression algorithm used to compress GIF images. In 1995, when the patent holder, Unisys, belatedly started to demand its dues, software developers started balking at this extra cost. This camp stated that, had they known that GIF would require licensing fees, they would have developed their own, free format.

They then put their money—or principles, rather—where their mouths were and developed a specification that could describe rich, deep, complex images better than GIF. These folks came up with the PNG file format.

PNG has key features that make it akin to GIF: it uses lossless compression, can interlace images, is displayable in browser windows, and can use an indexed color palette of up to 256 colors. However, PNG has incredibly powerful features found together in no other image format meant for the Web or not. (See Chapter 7, *Scanning for the Web and Video*, for the Web-related features.)

There were many debates over whether Unisys could legitimately collect fees for LZW, because it was a hardware patent, not a software patent. However, companies ponied up rather than challenge it in court. Unisys's patent expired in 2003, rendering the issue moot for future compression libraries. Meanwhile, open-source developers have created alternate, patent-free, more efficient compression algorithms, including zlib.

We hate to predict the future—it's so easy to be wrong where technology is concerned. (The previous edition of this book covered the FlashPix format like it was going to take over the world.) But PNG never caught fire as much as we expected. However, it is quite widely used and supported. It didn't replace GIF, but many sites chose it to avoid patent issues, and many software developers—especially in the free and open-source world—opted for PNG to avoid licensing fees.

Let's walk through details of what PNG can store and in which programs it can be used.

Color models. PNG can store either deep bitmaps (from 1 to 16 bits for grayscale and 24 or 48 for RGB) or an indexed color map. You have to choose one or the other, but you get the best of either JPEG-like deep color without compression, or GIF-like indexing to control how colors display on low-bit-depth monitors. The format was designed for the Web, so there's no support in the specification for CMYK.

Support. The biggest problem with PNG files today is inconsistent browser support. While the current versions of major Web browsers support PNG, they don't always support all of PNG's features. Most notably, Microsoft Internet Explorer for Windows 6.0—the current version (as of this writing) of the most widely used Web browser—doesn't properly render PNG-24 alpha channels. If you have to use PNG, you may want to verify that it works with the browsers your audience will use; otherwise, you may want to use GIF or JPEG instead.

Pronunciation. The folks who developed PNG weren't going to lead people down the same path as GIF, so the PNG specification spells it out for you: "PNG is pronounced 'ping.'"

Photo CD

"Gramma wants a Photo CD player for Hanukkah."

This scenario must have been the hallucination of some Eastman Kodak Company marketing executive when he or she was sold the idea that dedicated Photo CD players would be a consumer technology that people would use to view snapshots on their televisions. Glenn actually worked at the Kodak Center for Creative Imaging during Photo CD's introductory period and beyond, giving dozens of talks and demonstrations of Photo CD. He walked away convinced that it was doomed as a mass-market product—but that it could be extremely useful for professionals.

During Photo CD's brief peak, the format enjoyed some popularity with desktop publishers and professional photographers who decided that the price and quality were right. At the time, storage was expensive and good scans were dear. Photo CD offered scans that were nearly as good as drum scans—but much cheaper—stored on archival media for selective retrieval.

When scanners and CD writers reached the point where they were cheap enough, fast enough, good enough, and easy enough to use, fewer people felt they needed to pay to send their film out to be scanned, and thus began the decline of Photo CD. But the Photo CD market hasn't completely dried up and blown away. Photo CD scanning services are still available from many photo labs and within businesses where in-house Photo CD workstations bought years ago still make great scans.

There is also an ongoing need to open the millions of images that were archived to Photo CDs. Many of the "non-standard" aspects of Photo CD seemed strange at the time, like the choice of a device-independent color space and the use of color space profiles. Now that device-independent color, cross-media repurposing, and color-managed workflows are common,

we can see that the choices behind Photo CD were forward-looking attempts by Kodak's color scientists and engineers to future-proof the format.

Photo CD went out of favor not from technological obsolescence, but because of factors Kodak couldn't control: Moore's Law and the economies of scale in mass producing scanners, optical disc writers (CD and DVD), and hard drives.

Color models. Are Photo CD scans stored as RGB or CMYK? Answer: Neither! Photo CD uses a color space called PhotoYCC, which isn't mentioned elsewhere in this book. PhotoYCC is like the LAB color space mentioned in Chapter 13, *Getting Good Color*. PhotoYCC stores luminosity (the Y channel) separately from color (the two C channels). The decision to use such a device-independent color space was made so that Photo CD scans could take full advantage of the color gamuts of TV screens, printing presses, and output devices not yet invented. You convert a Photo CD image to RGB or CMYK when you open it, as we describe in "Opening Photo CD Scans," later in this chapter.

Compression and color fidelity. Photo CD stores data in an interesting interleaved format—see "Resolution," next—which reduces the necessary data for images above a base resolution by discarding a good hunk of the color information. It doesn't transform color like JPEG; it just throws it away selectively. It's lossy, but not very lossy (see Chapter 17, *Compression*). Fidelity can suffer at its higher resolutions.

Instead of remembering all three channels of the image at every resolution, Photo CD retains all the luminosity information and throws away almost 60 percent of the color information for the resolutions above its base resolution. That means that the resolutions above the base in each image contain progressively less color information.

The biggest problem is that colors don't show as much variation and can seem flat in the highest-resolution images.

Resolution. Photo CD comes in both its original flavor, now known as Photo CD Master, and a higher-resolution version called Pro Photo CD. The master format stores approximately 100 color images, or about 150 grayscale images (made from so-called black-and-white film). Each image is encoded into a single file Kodak calls an Image Pac, because it actually contains five different resolutions of the file (**Table 16-2**). Pro Photo CD stores fewer images on a CD because it adds a sixth resolution's components as a separate file. The last two columns of the table suggest output sizes for different resolutions at different frequencies using a decent 1.5:1 resolution-to-frequency ratio.

The Base image fits on a regular TV set, which can display between 400 and 500 pixels vertically. Base*4 was geared toward future HDTV (high-definition television) displays.

Pro Photo CD will let you use images at Base*64, or four times the size of Photo CD Master. One of these images, when acquired, is 72 Mb. Typically, you won't need this kind of image unless you're doing large-format, high-frequency images such as tabloid magazine covers. You could easily print a full 11-by-17–inch page with a bleed at 150 lpi using the Base*64 image.

Or you might need it if you need to capture a very small detail of a larger picture, such as one face in the middle of a college class photo. (Of course, as we discuss in Chapter 2, *Scanners*, when you blow up 35mm film that big, you start seeing the film's actual grain, so Pro Photo CD is better suited to larger film formats.)

Ordering Photo CD scans. Photo CD scans may be an attractive option if you need a lot of quality scans done quickly, and you don't have the equipment, staff, or time to do it. Photo CD scans can be made from consumer 35mm film up to 4-by-5–inch transparencies that professionals prefer for studio shots. The original Photo CD master format handles only 35mm film and the Advanced Photo System (APS) format that Kodak markets as Advantix; Pro Photo CD handles the larger film sizes.

For slide film and more exacting professional work, both Kodak—in white papers on its Web site—and experts such as Bruce Fraser recommend asking your Photo CD service provider to do a little custom work on the defaults for best results with film positives. Ask them to use Universal Film Terms to avoid correcting what you've worked to achieve. Selecting a Universal Film Term turns the Scene Balancing Algorithm (SBA) off. If turning it entirely off doesn't help, your Photo CD service provider will need to experiment to achieve better results.

Table 16-2 Image Pac resolutions for Photo CD Master and Pro with output sizes

Format name	Dimensions	Acquired size	133 lpi (inches)	150 lpi (inches)
Base*64	4096×6144	72 Mb	20.5×31	18×27
Base*16	2048×3072	18 Mb	10×15.5	9×13.5
Base*4	1024×1536	4.5 Mb	5×7.5	4.5×7
Base	512×768	1.1 Mb	2.5×3.8	2.3×3.5
Base/4	256×384	288 K	1.3×2	1.1×1.7
Base/16	128×192	72 K	N/A	N/A

To get maximum quality from a Photo CD scan, you could turn to scanning-software veteran Laser-Soft Imaging, which offers SilverFast Photo CD (www.lasersoft.com), a program dedicated to getting the most from Photo CD files.

Opening Photo CD scans. As mentioned earlier, Photo CD scans are stored in a proprietary Kodak format that you can't use in other programs without a conversion of some sort. You can convert Photo CD scans to a more standard format using an image editor like Photoshop; most image editors have shrinkwrapped support—an external plug-in is rarely needed.

In Mac OS X, iPhoto 1.1.1 and later can directly read images from Photo CD discs, importing the scans at their highest resolution only. However, you may need to use Photoshop, GraphicConverter, or other software to open Photo CD scans that aren't on a Photo CD disc (for example, Photo CD scans copied to a hard disk). In Mac OS 9, direct support for Photo CD on the desktop is provided by Apple QuickTime.

Windows XP can mount a Photo CD as a regular CD (which it is), but it can't show thumbnails or previews of Photo CD scans, as it can for other file formats. You'll need other software like Photoshop, Photo-Paint, or PhotoImpact to actually preview and open Photo CD scans.

Once you've opened the Photo CD image, confirm that it's in your standard color space (such as Adobe RGB), converting it if necessary. Then you can save the image in a standard format and work with it as if you scanned it yourself.

Some Photo CD workstation settings are optimized for television display, so you may need to decrease saturation a bit and adjust the tonal range to compensate, or you can ask the service provider to turn off or reduce the effect of its Photo CD SBA. Also, Photo CD images are not sharpened at all, so as with other scans, you'll need to take that step before creating final output.

Object-Oriented File Formats

As we mention earlier, object-oriented file formats need to store a much wider variety of information than bitmapped formats. Given that variety, it's not surprising that there isn't a good industry standard object-oriented file format that can be edited by a wide range of programs and printed to any printer.

Bear in mind that you can use some of these object-oriented file formats as bitmap-only formats as well. This means that a painting or image-processing application can open the file for editing.

Exchanging Objects

While there's no universal format for exchanging object-oriented files, Adobe Portable Document Format (PDF) is arguably the strongest contender. This means that you can build a page in QuarkXPress, export the page to PDF, and then open the results in Illustrator, which can edit the individual objects in PDF files. From there, you can export to other formats.

This isn't to say that it's a two-way road. Many applications can create and import PDF documents—especially on Mac OS X, where Apple built the operating system's Quartz graphics around PDF—but few programs can edit vector objects in a PDF file. If you have a program that can edit objects, PDF allows for the transfer of objects that would otherwise be impossible. If you need to retrieve vector graphics from a file, but the file was made by an application that doesn't export any compatible graphics formats, you can use Adobe Acrobat to convert it to PDF (or simply print it to PDF using Mac OS X) and then import the resulting PDF into Illustrator or Free-Hand to edit its objects.

Illustrator 1.1 used to be the *lingua franca* of object-oriented programs; many programs would save and open in that format for interchanging files. Some still do, and in a pinch, it's a great choice. But as vector drawing programs have advanced, some of them use features that can't be stored in the relatively basic Illustrator 1.1 format—another good reason to use PDF.

Encapsulated PostScript (EPS)

Encapsulated PostScript files contain pure PostScript code wrapped (*encapsulated*) with some information about the file and, optionally, a bitmap preview often at a low resolution used for placing the image in a page-layout program. It's used to take type and images and convert them into an intermediate language that a laser printer or imagesetter converts into bitmapped images and then prints onto paper or exposes onto film.

For many years, print designers habitually turned to EPS as a simple way to transfer both bitmapped images (which can be printed as part of a PostScript stream) and object-oriented graphics among programs that otherwise had no straightforward interchange format. For instance, taking an Illustrator file into Quark was best accomplished with EPS.

If you're not creating printed pieces you may find EPS to be less useful, because EPS works best when your output device is a PostScript printer and you don't want to edit the graphics, even to adjust their tonal values. The traditional role of EPS has been gradually eroded by the spread of PDF as a more editable, inclusive, and flexible format for graphics and layouts.

At its lowest level, an EPS file is just a bunch of text commands that a PostScript interpreter understands. However, it can take different forms, including binary or ASCII, with or without a preview, and with an optional clipping path.

Binary versus ASCII. You may never need to choose anything but Binary (often the default), but the choice of Binary or ASCII is often offered when you export an EPS file from Illustrator and other programs. The historical reason for this choice was to avoid problems that cropped up when transferring images over serial cables, onto network file servers, or to a commercial online service. Sometimes binary encoding would get garbled or cause wacky file server behavior.

Binary encoding uses all eight bits in a single byte, while ASCII encoding requires two to do the same job. ASCII sends an identical data stream as binary data, just recorded in a less efficient way. Use binary unless you have odd problems crop up; then try ASCII. Then call a nerd.

EPS without preview image. In their simplest form, EPS files are made up of PostScript code that conforms to a few document-structuring conventions defined by Adobe (creator of PostScript). For example,

Printing an EPS without Hardware PostScript

If you don't have a printer with PostScript built into its hardware, you might find it hard to print an EPS graphic at full resolution. Here are three alternatives.

▶ Open the graphic in an Adobe Creative Suite application. Photoshop, InDesign, Illustrator, and Acrobat can interpret EPS and PostScript directly. It's a neat trick, avoiding other intermediate steps.

▶ Use a standalone software PostScript interpreter, which creates a bitmap output on your computer, which is then sent to your printer at a resolution optimized for one of its modes. Consider the PostScript version of Colorbyte Software's ImagePrint (**www.colorbytesoftware.com**) or Ghost-Script (**www.cs.wisc.edu/~ghost/**).

▶ Open the graphic in Mac OS X 10.3 using the free, included Preview application. Mac OS X uses PDF as its screen display model, which means it's interpreting PostScript all the time. The Preview application uses the Mac OS X display engine to process EPS, PostScript, or PDF files.

In certain programs, you see the highest-resolution or best-rendered version of an EPS graphic only when you have a special preview mode enabled. In InDesign, for instance, choose High-Quality Display from the Display Performance submenu on the View menu.

certain commands can't be used, and there are some comments in the file that specify the file name, creator, and so on.

If you place one of these files on a page in software that only reads EPS previews and not the EPS code, you probably won't see the graphic, you'll just see a gray box and some of the comments (**Figure 16-3**, upper left). When you print to a PostScript printer, however, the graphic will appear in all its glory.

Also, as we noted above, most Adobe software and the Mac OS X Preview software will render a preview using a software-based PostScript interpreter. Not only that, but they can also render an EPS file at full resolution as far in as you can zoom, which is much superior to looking at its screen-resolution preview.

EPS with preview image. The most common form of EPS has a low-resolution screen-preview image built in. When you place one of these files on a page, the computer shows you the low-res image (**Figure 16-3**, upper right), and when you print it, the computer uses the PostScript code. (If you don't have a PostScript printer, what prints out is the low-res preview, which is not terribly useful except for simple proofing.)

Photoshop has the richest set of preview options. On the Macintosh, it can save an EPS with one of three Macintosh previews (1-bit, 8-bit, or JPEG); on both Mac and Windows it can include either a 1-bit or 8-bit TIFF preview. (In other image-editing programs, like Ulead PhotoImpact, the options for previews aren't quite as varied; see **Figure 16-4**.)

EPS file previews can potentially be confusing, because in some cases the preview doesn't match the actual content. If a high-resolution color EPS file is saved with a 1-bit preview, you see a grainy black-and-white preview. It's up to you—or the person who sent it to you—to know that the preview is not what the file really looks like. For this reason, EPS files are generally easiest to work with in programs that can interpret them directly and display them smoothly, such as the programs in the Adobe Creative Suite (**Figure 16-3**, bottom).

Clipping path. Often, you'd like to mask the edge of an image so that you're not printing a rectangle. EPS has the ability to use a *clipping path*, which is just a PostScript outline that defines the image; the rest of the image is transparent. However, a clipping path can cause problems when you've defined too complex a path or are printing on an old laser printer or imagesetter RIP. The clipping path can be calculated at the full resolution of the output device—which can be thousands of dots per inch—and a "decision" has to be made about which pixels fall inside and which fall outside the path. The printer also has to handle the interface between the edge of the path and the image or text underneath.

Figure 16-3
EPS display in layout programs

EPS file with no preview

EPS file with low-res bitmap preview

EPS file with preview generated by InDesign

Typical Display

High Quality Display

Figure 16-4
Photoshop and
PhotoImpact's
approaches to
saving previews
with EPS files

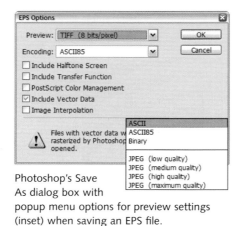

Photoshop's Save
As dialog box with
popup menu options for preview settings
(inset) when saving an EPS file.

PhotoImpact's EPS
saving options

However, by setting *flatness*, a measure of how closely to calculate a curve against the output resolution, you can eliminate almost all problems that result from too complex a path. Flatness is an option that appears in almost all DTP (desktop publishing) programs that handle PostScript paths. Some, like Macromedia FreeHand, let you set flatness per object; others have a setting in the Page Setup or Print dialog boxes nested a level or two deep.

 David prefers to set flatness to 3 or 4. It sacrifices a little bit of smoothness in curves, but it dramatically reduces processing time on older machines, and it's unnoticeable.

Desktop Color Separation (DCS). The DCS specification was developed by Quark, Inc., for use in process-color work, though

InDesign can handle it, too. A DCS image is an EPS format that consists of five parts: a low-resolution screen preview, plus cyan, magenta, yellow, and black layers. Support for DCS is generally found only in professional image editors and layout programs.

DCS version 1.0 is made up of five files—the low-resolution version that you place on a page, which contains pointers to four data files. These are sometimes called five-file DCS or EPS-5 files. The DCS version 2.0 format can contain all the information in a single file. Plus, DCS 2.0 files can contain more than just four process colors; you can have a number of spot colors included as well, or even High-Fidelity or Hi-Fi color separations (see Chapter 26, *Stochastic Screening*, and Chapter 28, *When Grids Collide*, for more on Hi-Fi).

 The primary limitation of DCS is that it's pre-separated like a CMYK scan, which means it's tied to a specific set of output conditions.

Acrobat Portable Document Format (PDF)

PDF is both a child of and big brother to EPS. Adobe introduced it as a paperless document file that could be created from PostScript output and pretty much exactly reproduce the original document. If you want to distribute a document over the Web that is as close as possible to the original—say, a graphics card's specification sheet—PDF is the easiest way. In fact, PDF has become an entrenched standard in the advertising industry.

It has built-in image compression (JPEG, LZW, ZIP, and CCITT), preserves the look of the original document, can be searched and indexed, and—with a simple plug-in—can even be viewed inside a Web browser window. The Adobe Reader software that displays PDFs is free (**www.adobe.com**).

PDF files can contain multiple pages, and each page can have different dimensions and be printed separately. This is a big advantage over EPS files, which can only represent a single page and can't be printed out without being placed on a page or rendered. (It's also a big advantage over PostScript files, which store multiple pages, but don't let you choose which pages to print.) Another huge advantage of PDF files is their ability to embed graphics and fonts inside the files along with color profiles and other printing details.

Creating PDF Files

As PDF usage has spread, it's become a lot easier to create PDF files. The mothership of PDF creation is the Acrobat Distiller program and the Adobe Acrobat package it comes with, which is available at various prices depending on the features you need. If you work with PDF all the time, Acrobat Standard is the minimum package to get. The pricier Acrobat Professional adds several features including the option to scan straight into PDF format and apply optical character recognition (OCR) to scans (as we describe in Chapter 9, *Scanning for the Office*).

You can also create PDF files from any of the programs in the Adobe Creative Suite (Photoshop, Illustrator, InDesign). If you use Mac OS X, basic PDF creation

Because you can generate a PDF in many different ways you can easily exclude settings or data needed for particular output device. To address this, the international standards body ISO created PDF/X-1a and PDF/X-3. These formats aren't variants on PDF, but rather a specific set of parameters to generate a PDF with the right settings to send out for reliable reproduction. Ad agencies and other major print vendors are requiring that PDF files submitted to them meet these standards. PDF/X-1a is PDF 1.3 (compatible with Acrobat 4) with all objects in CMYK format with no omitted OPI. PDF/X-3 can be CMYK or color-managed RGB.

If you're not satisfied with the quality of the PDF file created from a program, you may get better results creating PDF files using Adobe Acrobat instead.

is built into the operating system itself, and is actually used to draw what you see on screen. In Mac OS X, you can make a PDF straight from the Print dialog box of any program. However, the version of PDF created by Mac OS X may not be in sync with Adobe's current release of the PDF specification (at this writing, Adobe's version of PDF was newer than the PDF version produced by OS X).

PDF on the Web

If you save a PDF with the Save As Optimizes for Fast Web View preference checked in Acrobat 6 or later (look in the General panel of the Preferences dialog box), the file will be optimized for "page-at-a-time" download over the Internet. The PDF Web plug-in lets you view PDF files directly in major Web browsers, and an optimized PDF stores the text first, followed by graphics, and then the fonts (if needed). This way, you can read the text long before images arrive. PDF uses special serif and sans-serif fonts to emulate the correct text display by matching the size, spacing, line endings, and approximate look of the original fonts, even when the original fonts aren't available.

PDF for Prepress

PDF is an increasingly key format for prepress output, too. Distiller has an option to leave CMYK images in their original form; you can convert them to RGB if you're creating just an on-screen version. PDF is more reliable than raw PostScript or other compromises, compresses extremely well, and can be used without having anything like the original application around. It's also, needless to say, totally compatible with imagesetter PostScript interpreters. Some PostScript 3 RIPs allow direct output of PDFs without any intermediate step.

Fuhgettabout 'Em

We don't want to let you down and not mention golden-oldie file formats that are now deprecated—meaning, don't use 'em, don't accept 'em, forget about 'em entirely. (David and co-author Bruce Fraser refer to them as "unreasonable formats" in *Real World Adobe Photoshop*.)

Windows Wipeouts

In the bad old days—which continue 'til today for users of older programs and operating systems—PCX and BMP were what you used in Windows to handle bitmaps, and CGM (Computer Graphics Metafile) and WMF (Windows Metafile) were used for objects. Today, none of these four formats is really used except by older programs—ones that create files for use only in Windows or some built-in software that comes with Windows.

The best thing you can do with any outdated Windows file format is convert it immediately to a modern file format, like GIF, TIFF, JPEG, or EPS.

Oddball Macintosh Formats

The Mac has its share of items peculiar to it, and graphic file formats aren't an exception. Two of the most popular have been around as long as the Macintosh itself, though their use is rightly minimal for most purposes these days.

PICT. The PICT format is the original Mac-standard object-oriented file format. PICT was based on the QuickDraw screen-drawing language of the classic Mac OS. A PICT graphic can contain a bitmap as one of the objects in the file, or as its only object ("bitmap-only-PICTs"). Bitmap-only PICTs can be any size, resolution, and bit depth. Object-oriented PICTs, which have mostly disappeared from view, had strange problems with line widths and other irregularities when printed. We don't recommend using PICT these days unless you're creating multimedia work for pre-OS X Macs. PICTs are awfully difficult to open on other platforms.

Apple finally gave up on PICT as its default format: Now, in Mac OS X, the Quartz two-dimensional rendering model used for screen drawing relies on PDF.

MacPaint. The MacPaint format is ultimately the most basic of all graphic formats on the Macintosh. Paint files (more rarely called PNTG, or "pee-en-tee-gee," files) are black and white (1 bit per sample), 72 samples per inch, and 8 by 10 inches (576 by 720 dots). That's it. No more, no less.

Bad Ideas

Some vendors thought that developing their own, distinct file format was a good idea, despite growing industry consensus on other formats. RIFF (Raster Image File Format) was a TIFF competitor primarily supported by the company once known as Fractal Design software, which created Painter and ColorStudio—the world's greatest orphaned program. Quark-XPress used to place RIFF files, but since we haven't seen a RIFF file since 1993, we don't know if it still does.

The FlashPix file format we covered using over two pages in the second edition of this book in 1998—Glenn apologizes—was introduced as a standard with the support of several camera and imaging software vendors. But it, too, has fallen by the wayside. The FlashPix standard was maintained by Kodak, but you can't even find support for it on any Kodak digital cameras today.

File Types, Extensions, and Magic Numbers

The Macintosh, Windows, and Unix operating systems "see" files differently. Mac OS 9 and earlier use file types and file creators to track which program to open a given file in and which format the file uses. Windows still uses filename extensions—even though Windows 95 introduced long file names—and a Registry that records what these extensions mean. And Unix—including Mac OS X—can use "magic numbers" to identify a file type.

Windows

In the Windows world, everything is different. Although Windows 95 added "long filename support," every Windows (or DOS) file is still identified by a simple filename extension. Before Windows 95, the format was called "eight-dot-three" for the maximum filename length of eight characters, a period, and then three more characters. Now it would be "252-dot-three" (or more, since Windows no longer limits extensions to three characters).

The Windows Registry maintains a list of extensions and which programs they are mapped to. Unfortunately, until recently (and we believe this still goes on), many programs named their specific files using the same extensions, like ".doc". Newer programs tend to be better behaved and not overlap existing extensions.

The Registry is a nightmare to figure out, and books have been written on the subject (and millions of hours of sleep lost, too). But there's a simple way in Windows 95 and later versions to see a list of the extensions your particular system knows about. Double-click on "My Computer" on the desktop. Select the Tools menu, and then select Folder Options. Click on the File Types tab. You'll see a scrollable list of extensions and which programs they belong to (**Figure 16-5**). This is a lifesaver when you're trying to sort out what's going wrong.

Unix

Where do we get off bothering designers and photographers about Unix? Well, it's important because Mac OS X is now based on Unix, and the World Wide Web is largely run by Unix-based Web servers. The Mac hides most of this Unix complexity while modern Unix image-editing software (using the confusingly named "X Windows" windowing environment) can cope more readily with less explicit file format information, too. But it's great to understand how the sausage is made in a pinch.

Unix doesn't look at extensions or file types when it comes to identifying a file format. Unix instead looks at the first several bytes of data in a file, which is called—in the beard-and-suspenders-guru land of Unix—the file's *magic number*. These bytes usually contain enough information for the Unix system to guess what the file format is, and most image file formats are designed to have this kind of identification in place.

Figure 16-5 The list of extensions in the Windows XP Folder Options dialog box

Hardly efficient, but it works. (This information can also be helpful in repairing corrupted files with a disk file editor; see **Table 16-3**.)

In general, as long as you transfer the file as binary, or as Raw Data in some programs, and use the right capitalization in the file name, Unix shouldn't intervene. (See Chapter 7, *Scanning for the Web and Video*, for a full range of transfer tips.)

Another reason to mention this is that it looks like this is a trick Photoshop pulls on Mac and Windows boxes as well. Photoshop can identify most image files when you open them with the Open As file option, even if they lack an extension or file type. It looks like Photoshop has a little "magic" in it, too.

Mac OS

Mac OS 9 and earlier and Mac OS X differ in how they deal with the identification of files. Mac OS 9 and previous releases rely on special attributes; Mac OS X uses a variety of tricks.

Mac OS 9 and earlier. Every Macintosh file in Mac OS 9 and earlier has several attributes attached to it, including file type and creator. These are mysterious four-letter labels hidden inside each document that tell Mac OS 9 what sort of file it is and what program generated it. For example, when you double-click on a file, the Mac looks at the file's creator to determine which application to start up. If the creator code is **8BIM**, the creator is Photoshop, for instance.

If you move an image from another platform to Mac OS 9, you may not be able to open or place it, because the image may have been assigned a generic file type of **CODE** or **DATA** or some such, and the opening application is looking for **EPSF** or **TIFF** or the like. If the file seems to be unrecognizable, you should first check to see if the file has a standard and correct cross-platform filename extension (.tiff, .eps, .jpg). If it doesn't, add the right one. Then any previous version of Mac OS that contains the PC Exchange Control Panel can open it.

You can also view and change a file's hidden type and creator codes using various commercial, public-domain, and shareware programs. We recommend Bare Bones Software's venerable Super Get Info (**www.barebones.com/products/super/index.shtml**) for Mac OS X. On Mac OS versions up to 9.2.2, you can use Apple's free ResEdit utility.

Mac OS X. Mac OS X handles filename extensions in a way that tries to take advantage of the best features in Windows, Unix, and pre-Mac OS X versions, using both hidden codes and file extensions to determine which program should open a file.

Table 16-3 Image format magic numbers

Format	# of bytes	Start of file[1]	ASCII[2]
GIF87a	6	47 49 46 38 37 61	GIF87a
GIF89a	6	47 49 46 38 39 61	GIF89a
JPEG	3	ff d8 ff	...
PNG	8	89 50 4e 47 0d 0a 1a 0a	.PNG....
TIFF (big-endian)	4	4d 4d 00 2a	MM..
TIFF (little-endian)	4	49 49 2a 00	II..

[1]In hexadecimal, or base-16, numbering. [2]The characters at the start of file; periods represent non-ASCII.

Mac OS X can understand OS 9 creator information, but it doesn't add that information for new files. It can interpret file extensions if they're available. And it can read magic numbers.

Working with Files

Without a solid foundation in what kind of graphic files you're working with, it's almost impossible to be efficient in desktop publishing. You'll forever be banging into barriers and asking: Why can't I import this image into my illustration program? Why can't I edit this photograph in this program? Why can't I move this file format over to the Macintosh? Why can't I use tonal correction on this file? And so on.

However, now that you have some substantial information about bitmapped versus object-oriented images, and TIFFs versus EPS files, you can really start to fly. Our next few chapters go into more detail about bitmap images, particularly scanned images.

17

Compression

KEEPING FIDELITY AND CONSERVING SPACE

We're mighty old. So old that we remember when hard disk space was at a premium, and a 14.4 kilobits-per-second modem was state of the art. Thus, compression remains near and dear to our hearts, even as some of the prevailing reasons for it have become less critical.

In this chapter we provide an overview of the compression world: what it is, what it does, and generally how it does what it does. We also give you some guidelines for choosing between compression methods, depending on your needs and the techniques you're using.

Compression makes use of algorithms, which are descriptions of how to do a given mathematical or programming task, step-by-step. Compression algorithms describe a process by which raw data, like the bits

making up a TIFF image file, are transformed through a series of mathematical operations resulting in a smaller file.

The real trick, of course, is that later you want to take this compressed image and *decompress* it into what it was before. That's where the distinction between the two major kinds of image compression comes into play. The first question you have to ask with compression is, "Lossless or lossy?"

Lossless

If you compress an image using *lossless* compression and then decompress the resulting file, you have an identical image. No information is lost or changed in any way—guaranteed. It's like a kitchen sponge:

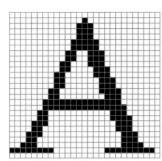

40 sample points of white
1 sample point of black
25 sample points of white
3 sample points of black
25 sample points of white
3 sample points of black
and so on...

Figure 17-1
Run Length
Encoding

you can squeeze the sponge down to a very small size, and when you let go, it reverts to its original form. We could illustrate this method by showing you two pictures—one before saving in a lossless format, and one after—but since they'd look identical, that would be kind of silly.

Lossless compression is available on the desktop in both Windows XP and Mac OS X 10.3 (Panther), and in programs like WinZIP and StuffIt Deluxe for archiving programs and data. Lossless compression is used to archive programs and data because you can't afford to mistake a single bit. It's also used for images in which you want to preserve the precise original scan warts and bumps intact.

There are several kinds of lossless compression; each is used in one or more major image file formats, which we discuss in Chapter 16, *File Formats*.

Run Length Encoding

One of the simplest forms of lossless compression for images is Run Length Encoding (RLE), which is an option you can select when saving into formats like TIFF and BMP. RLE works by looking for the same value multiple times in a row. For example, let's say you have a black-and-white bitmapped image of a cow. A program that compresses image data with RLE sees that the first 245 sample points in the image are white, followed by 80 black points, followed by 16 white points, and so on. The program can then compress that data by just recording those values: "245 white, 80 black, 16 white," and so on. (**Figure 17-1**).

This compresses a simple image down to almost nothing, and a complex image by just a little; in fact, if an image is complex enough (or has noise in flat color areas), RLE compression can make the file *bigger*!

LZW

LZW (Lempel-Ziv-Welch, named for its inventors) compresses data by looking for patterns throughout a file. These patterns, called *phrases*, are identified and stored in a table. The table has short tokens that correspond to these longer phrases. So if you had the word "ishkabibble" appearing 500 times in a text file and you apply LZW compression, "ishkabibble" would be replaced by a single number that might take only one or two bytes to represent. If you look that number up in the encoding table, you'd find "ishkabibble." (See **Figure 17-2** for an example with just nine substitutions.)

The standard implementations of TIFF and GIF use LZW compression

Figure 17-2
Partial LZW
compression
of text

Before phrase replacement
Of a certain knight that swore by his honour they were good pancakes, and swore by his honour the mustard was naught; now, I'll stand to it, the pancakes were naught and the mustard was good; and yet was not the knight forsworn.

After phrase replacement
Of a certain ❼ that ❽ by his ❺ they were ❸ ❹, ❷ ❽ by his ❺ ❶ ❻ was ❾; now, I'll stand to it, ❶ ❹ were ❾ ❷ ❶ ❻ was ❸; ❷ yet was not ❶ ❼ forsworn.

Phrase table

the	❶
and	❷
good	❸
pancakes	❹
honour	❺
mustard	❻
knight	❼
swore	❽
naught	❾

Deflate

After the flap about Unisys's ownership and licensing of the LZW patent—see "Portable Network Graphics (PNG)" in Chapter 16, *File Formats*—a number of rather clever people helped design software that could be used without any earlier patent claims. One algorithm is called *deflate*, and a common free implementation of deflate is the *zlib library*.

Deflate uses techniques similar to LZW to losslessly compress data, but the developers made every effort to ensure that the deflate algorithm wasn't covered by the now-expired LZW patents. The ZIP format for Acrobat—mentioned at right—uses the deflate method, as do PNG and some archival compression programs.

because it's an efficient way to represent patterns in color images even if there is some noise. Like RLE, it works best if you have areas of consistent, noise-free colors, but it works acceptably well with complex, photographic images, too.

Huffman and CCITT Encoding

We only mention Huffman and CCITT encoding because you might see the terms as compression options in programs and should know whether to choose them or not. Huffman encoding was invented way back in 1952, and it's used as part of a number of other compression schemes, like LZW and deflate (see the "deflate" sidebar for more information).

Huffman encoding is a technique that takes a set of symbols, like the letters in a text file, and analyzes them to figure out the frequency of each symbol. It then uses the fewest possible bits to represent the most frequently occurring symbols. For instance, E is the most common letter in English. In Huffman encoding, you might be able to represent E in as few as two bits (1 followed by 0) instead of the eight bits needed to signal E in ASCII, which is used to store and transmit virtually all text on and between computers.

CCITT (the abbreviation for the International Telegraph and Telephone Consultative Committee) encoding was developed for facsimile transmission and reception. There are several different standards, but you'll see the terms *Group 3* and *Group 4* most often. Huffman and CCITT encoding aren't interchangeable terms; CCITT encoding is a version of a narrow use of Huffman encoding.

CCITT is used for compression of black-and-white bitmaps. For instance, CCITT options are available for compressing monochrome images when you create PDF files using advanced tools like Acrobat or InDesign. In InDesign's Export PDF dialog box, there's a Compression panel in the Monochrome Images section from which you can choose CCITT Group 3 (identical to fax format), Group 4 (like fax format but without special control information, and the default option here), Run Length (same as RLE), and ZIP, a format that Adobe implemented using the deflate algorithm.

Neither Huffman nor CCITT are actual file formats; their algorithms are always used inside of other formats, like TIFF, EPS, or PDF.

Lossy

The second type of compression—*lossy*, a term that dates back to at least 1945, though it sounds like it was invented by software engineers—actually loses information in the process of squeezing the data. But it eliminates data in a very intelligent manner. It's like tightly folding a cotton shirt and packing it into a suitcase. If you really cram it in, you might save some room in your suitcase, but when you unfold the shirt, it doesn't look as good as it did before you compressed it.

Lossy algorithms start with notions encoded in them about what kinds of image information is most important. The most important information is retained even at the highest compression levels. The less important information can be dropped out depending on the quality level you choose. For instance, luminance information—or tonal values—is much more important than color information, because the eye is more sensitive to changes in tone. All lossy image compression methods store more luminosity data than data about hue or saturation.

By losing less important information, you can increase compression ratios enormously. Where an LZW-compressed TIFF might be 40 percent of its original size, the same file saved with lossy compression could be *two percent or less* of its original file size. Lossy compression methods typically give you a choice of how tight you want to pack the data. With low compression you get larger files and better quality. High compression yields lower quality and smaller files.

How much quality do you lose? It depends on the level of compression, the resolution of the image, and the content of the image. Lower quality means there are more artifacts in the image; *artifacts* are errors, such as grainy sample points, introduced by software.

Lossy compression is based on mathematical algorithms that are too complicated to include here (that's a nice way of saying we don't understand the math well enough ourselves).

Archives

When you're moving files around or storing them for later use, it can be useful to group them together as a single entity using a program that can handle one or more files—or even an entire directory structure of files and folders—and put them together in a single *archive* file.

Most file archiving software also applies compression as it adds files to the archive, making the archive's final size much smaller than its constituent elements.

StuffIt Deluxe and PkZIP are two popular archiving and compression programs, although there are dozens available. Mac OS X and Windows XP also provide built-in archiving using the ZIP compression standard, but it lacks flexibility.

An archive file includes the compressed version of each original file's data, and if you've added folders or directories, the location of files in the hierarchy.

You generally need to open a compressed archive in the same software that created it to access the folders and files within. Often, you can also use an application that's distributed for free by the archiving program's maker that is designed to just extract and decompress the entire set of files—not selectively choose individual files. For instance, StuffIt Deluxe has advanced features that allow you to open and manipulate individual files in an archive, but it's commercial software; StuffIt Expander is a free program for Mac and Windows that can just decompress and extract files.

Some compression programs can read other compression programs' files; for instance, WinZIP and StuffIt can both extract from the Unix "gzip" format. A few file-searching and virus-protection applications can see inside archives, but these are the exceptions, not the rule.

For day-to-day use of image files, compressed file formats, not compressed archives, are the best choice, since they can be read and written by the programs you use to edit and place them.

The main reason to archive compressed image files is simply for convenience in transferring or storing them, because compressed file formats already squeeze out most of the savings in file size.

JPEG and JPEG 2000

The most common lossy compression scheme is currently JPEG, which we discuss in Chapter 16, *File Formats*. As we note in that chapter, although JPEG could be implemented inside of all kinds of image data formats, it's usually used only with a very simple spec called JFIF, which can do 8-bit grayscale and 24-bit RGB. Adobe uses a variant of JFIF for its JPEG format, which was tweaked to handle 32-bit CMYK data as well (**Figure 17-3**). Similarly, JPEG 2000 compression can also be used within other image formats or as a standalone file contained inside its own optional JP2 spec.

Figure 17-3 JPEG compression compared with the original image

Original image with detail marked

Blown up from the original image

Blown up from a JPEG version saved with highest compression

JPEG Compression

The original JPEG spec uses several tricks to maximize compression. It first converts image data to a LAB-like color space (see Chapter 13, *Getting Good Color*). It then throws away half or three-quarters of the color information (depending on the implementation).

It next applies an algorithm (called DCT for Discrete Cosine Transform) that analyzes 8-by-8-pixel blocks in the file. For each block, it generates a series of numbers that represent features on a spectrum from coarse to fine. The first few numbers represent the overall color of the block and later numbers represent fine details. The spectrum of details is based on human perception, so the coarse details (or larger features) are most noticeable; the finest, least.

These DCT numbers don't correspond one-to-one with pixels, which is another reason JPEG is lossy; even when you save JPEG with the least compression, you still don't wind up with an exact representation of the original image.

In the next step of the process, based on whatever setting you've chosen for your JPEG image, more or fewer of the numbers that represent finer details are dropped out. If you choose better compression, only coarse details are retained, making the resulting image look speckled;

choose better quality and you retain more fine detail, with just minor color shifts in certain areas.

In the last step, JPEG uses Huffman encoding (see "Lossless," above, for an explanation of this algorithm) to most efficiently store the resulting, pretty arbitrary data. It's important to recognize that at the end of the JPEG compression process, you're left with data that really has no correspondence with the bitmap of your original image: it's pure math that has to be run back through the JPEG routine in the other direction to re-create a resemblance to your original image data.

JPEG 2000 Compression

JPEG 2000 employs a different form of lossy compression with an option for a lossless mode: *wavelets*. Wavelets are a mathematical representation of the difference between two sets of data: an original set (like an image) and a set that's half the original's size (like a downsampled image).

Take an image file and downsample it to 71 percent to get half the pixels (downsampling to 50 percent would result in half the dimensions, but not half the area or overall pixels). If you then blow it up to view it at 140 percent and look at it side by side with the original, you see that two pixels in the original now represent just one in the downsampled version.

Wavelet theory allows you to represent just the difference in data between those two resolutions. You can continue to downsample the data to some arbitrary point—although it could be down to just one value! Each of these differences can be stored more efficiently than the original data, because the differences are full of redundancy.

The lossy compression comes in at the point when you're deciding which and how many of these differences to store. One of the benefits of wavelet compression is perceptively less "blockiness" than JPEG, because the algorithm analyzes the entire image instead of analyzing subdivided areas of the image.

This kind of compression has two benefits: rapid viewing at many sizes without down- or upsampling, and substantial file-size reduction with less apparent loss than similar JPEG compression ratios.

Using JPEG Right

Here's a few tips on using JPEG the right way and for the right images:

▶ Images with hard, high-contrast, and angular areas are most likely to develop artifacts when you compress them using JPEG. For example, a yellow square on a green background in a lower-resolution image would look pretty miserable after compression.

▶ Compressing and decompressing images repeatedly can make images worse than just going through the process once. It's just like photocopying a photocopy. After the first few generations, your original image becomes unusable.

▶ If your image is somewhat grainy or impressionistic at the outset, lossy compression probably won't hurt it much at all, but applying lossy compression is also unlikely to compress this type of file very much.

▶ The flip side is that photographs with large, smooth areas compress very well with JPEG. Images with lots of detail are better compressed as an LZW TIFF.

New Math

Computer scientists are fascinated with compression. We're not precisely sure why, but they spend a lot of time writing about and creating new mathematical techniques for compressing data. In the 1990s, two techniques appeared (to us) to have great promise for image compression, although their subsequent adoptions differed from our expectations.

The newer form, *wavelet compression* eventually found its way into JPEG 2000. You can read more about it in that section earlier in the chapter.

But we actually had our eye on *fractals* when we wrote the first edition of this book in 1993. If you remember seeing those beautiful recursive images that seemed otherworldly and possibly recall the phrase *Mandelbrot set*, you know that fractals date back to the 1970s. It took high-powered computers to turn fractal math into reality.

Fractal math uses equations that can describe infinite recursion in which each shape is made up a finite copy of the same shapes at a smaller scale, which in turn are made up of the same shapes again and again.

Fractal math gets applied to the real world because any picture of a physical object or scene, such as a piece of wood or a landscape, has many identical patterns that appear at different sizes and orientations. Think of a leaf on a tree: there might be thousands of leaves, many of which are nearly identical in form, but not in size or location. Fractal compression identifies these patterns—it's best at doing so in natural scenes like that—and builds up a representation of an image that uses formulas to represent these patterns wherever they occur and in whatever transformation (rotation, scale, skew, and so on.)

Fractal compression is currently used for some purposes in specialized fields, but it never really came into wide use. Compared to JPEG, fractal compression is a patented process that requires royalty payments, and it doesn't compress as quickly as JPEG. Wavelet compression appears to have taken over in areas where fractal compression might otherwise have had success.

Small Is Beautiful

The whole idea of compression is to make a file on your hard disk take up less space. Although there are many ways to do this, keep in mind that you can always purchase another larger hard drive. Compression always takes extra time somewhere in the workflow process (while compressing and decompressing), and that can be a hassle. Small is beautiful (hey, no comments about our height), but fast and efficient is next to godliness.

18

Creating Master Images

KEEPING THE EXTRA BITS FOR LATER

Are your current scanning habits limiting the uses of your images in the future? When a scan is unnecessarily limited, it's hard to reuse in other media today, and it may not take full advantage of the improved output devices that are sure to appear in the future.

For many years, we focused on exactly the characteristics we needed to get an image onto a press, which was the only reason to scan an image in the mid-90s. To look good on press, a scanned image must print within the CMYK gamut and spot gain characteristics of a printing press.

After saving a scan in CMYK, prepress scanner operators would then act as digital sculptors, whittling away at the characteristics of an image that wouldn't work on press. The image would lose some saturation, particularly in blues, and the tonal

range would be restricted, but that's what was necessary to reproduce the scan well on press.

Now scans are often destined for multiple media, like print and Web and video. But if you need to use an image for both print and Web, the total color range of a CMYK image won't fully use the Web's RGB color gamut. The color of a CMYK original was trimmed for a reason that may not apply any more. Therefore, a full-gamut RGB scan would be easier to repurpose for press, multimedia, and wide-gamut printers. Using this line of reasoning, the best image to archive would be one that preserves the qualities of the original as much as possible.

Does this mean it's wrong to make images that only work for one purpose? No, but it depends on your goals. If you want to scan an image once and be able to use it in multiple ways, use the strategies we lay out in this chapter. But if you're scanning images that you'll only ever use in one way, like a specific issue of a printed magazine with no online equivalent, follow the conventional advice and base your scanning and editing decisions on your single type of final output. When you know that you'll only need to target one medium, you can save time because you don't need to worry about accommodating other media, and you can concentrate on optimizing the image for that medium alone.

In this chapter, we talk about scanning an original once in a way that makes it easier to reuse across today's media and on tomorrow's output devices.

Media-Dependent Workflow

The conventional workflow is easy to understand, and is the workflow around which most scanning software is designed (**Figure 18-1**). You scan your original using settings based on your final output medium. If you have really good scanning software, you might be able to produce a final image straight from that software, although it's more likely that the scan will have to make a stop in your image editor for fine-tuning. The disadvantage of this approach is that if you later want to use the image in other media, you usually have to scan the image again.

To use your scanned image in a single medium, use the following guidelines for the best results.

Resolution. Specify a resolution that produces the required level of quality at the final output dimensions of the scan, whether it's 300 dpi for a press or 96 dpi for the Web.

Color. Choose an output color space that accommodates the gamut of the target medium, but no larger. In many cases, you'll scan into Adobe RGB or sRGB.

Bit depth. Scan at 8 bits per channel, usually.

A media-dependent workflow typically uses the following settings:

File format. Scan directly to the file format required by the final medium (such as GIF for the Web), although it's more useful to scan to TIFF or Photoshop (PSD) format for high-quality editing.

Sharpening. Sharpen the image using the settings that make it look good at the final resolution and dimensions.

Correcting. Optimize the image's tonal range and color balance. Then adjust it for the final output medium by adjusting its gamut, saturation, and output levels.

Reusing an image that was scanned for a media-dependent workflow might not be a problem when you need to make a version of an image for a medium of lower quality. If you scan an image for prepress using Adobe RGB at 300 dpi, you'll be able to make an acceptable Web image from

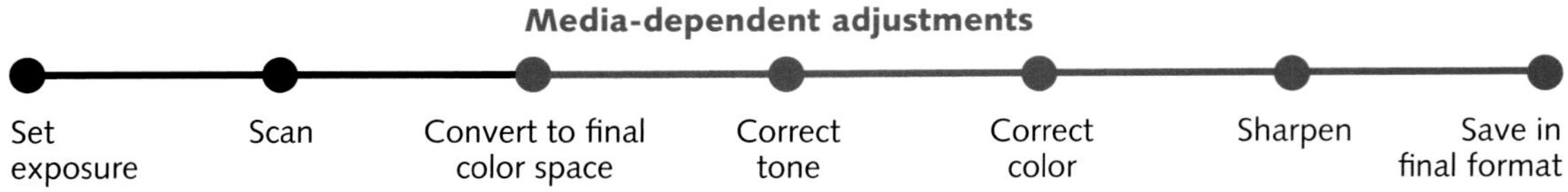

Figure 18-1
Conventional media-dependent workflow

Media-dependent adjustments

Set exposure — Scan — Convert to final color space — Correct tone — Correct color — Sharpen — Save in final format

that scan. But you wouldn't be able to reuse a Web-targeted scan for prepress because you simply don't have enough of the correct kind of image data.

Separating Input and Output

When you want to scan a media-independent master image, you need to know which scanning adjustments are media-independent; those are the only adjustments you want to apply to the master. Color balance and other adjustments related to fundamental image quality fall into this category because they can be carried out without knowing the final medium.

Once you have a good master, you make copies of it so you can apply media-dependent adjustments to the copies. You can tune each copy as much as you need to, keeping the master image locked away for future uses.

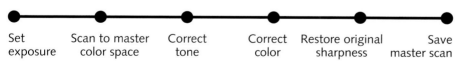 You might create a second sort of intermediate master file. For instance, our copy editor Don Sellers has created thousands of product shots for a culinary store. He has saved both master versions and high-resolution intermediate versions with the backgrounds removed so that a time-consuming step typical for their use doesn't have to be repeated.

Unfortunately, most scanning software doesn't make the distinction among different workflow goals very well. For instance, the level of sharpening that an image needs during a scan is different from the amount that it needs for a specific medium. But sharpening software typically provides just one sharpening control with no indication of its place in the workflow. **Figure 18-2** shows which adjustments are typically media-dependent.

So, one difference between media-dependent and media-independent workflows is the point in the process at which you apply the media-dependent adjustments. A media-independent workflow also adds an intermediate file—a master image—that you can draw from for media-dependent copies so that you don't have to scan and correct the image more than once. The media-independent workflow is more work, so choose it only if you need the flexibility.

A good analogy would be choosing between taking a local or express bus to get across town. A media-dependent workflow is like an express bus: If you only need to reach the express route's destination, you take the express because it's faster and more direct. A media-independent workflow is like the local bus: If you need to run some errands at stops that the express route skips, the local bus is the way to go. It might take a little longer, but you won't need to backtrack.

Capture stage—creating a master

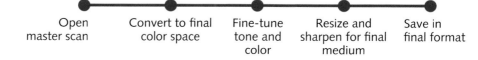

Set exposure — Scan to master color space — Correct tone — Correct color — Restore original sharpness — Save master scan

Figure 18-2
Input and output separated and collapsed

Output stage—adjusting for a specific medium

Open master scan — Convert to final color space — Fine-tune tone and color — Resize and sharpen for final medium — Save in final format

Media-Independent Workflow

A media-independent workflow produces a high-quality digital master you can use as a source for any medium (**Figure 18-3**). You apply media-specific settings to copies of the master to generate images that are tuned to each medium you target.

For best results in a media-independent workflow, follow these guidelines.

Resolution. Set the scanner to the highest resolution you're likely to need. If you think you might someday need an 8-by-10–inch color print but don't think you'll ever need anything bigger, set the resolution to 300 dpi at 8 by 10 inches. You can always *downsample*, or make a copy with a reduction in the amount of image data, for lower-resolution media such as the Web.

Determining the resolution you need may depend on how far into the future you're looking. If you want to scan once and use the master image for the next 100 years, test your scanning equipment by starting at its highest optical resolution and scan at lower and lower resolution until you start to see a difference. Otherwise, you may want to keep file size in mind and scan at the highest resolution that offers you the most flexibility.

Color. Set the scanner to a color space that can accommodate the largest color gamut you're likely to use. If you're scanning an image that will only be used for prepress and the Web, the Adobe RGB color space will be sufficient. When color quality is a priority, sRGB is too limited to be a sensible choice for a master image. On the other hand, if you anticipate sending the image to an output device with a gamut wider than a printing press (like a photo printer), you might want to scan into a larger color space such as EktaSpace RGB or ProPhoto RGB.

Bit depth. Pick an appropriate bit depth, which depends largely on the chosen color space. For color spaces like sRGB, 8 bits per channel is fine. However, if you are using a larger gamut like Adobe RGB, EktaSpace RGB, or ProPhoto RGB, 16 bits per channel is a good choice in order to prevent banding from appearing in colors and tones as you edit the image.

File format. Scan into a lossless file format like TIFF or PSD in order to preserve as much quality as possible. TIFF and PSD also accommodate features like Photoshop layers, which can be useful to store with a master image.

Sharpening. Sharpen only slightly, if at all. There really isn't much reason to apply sharpening to a master image, because sharpening settings are largely media-dependent. You might sharpen just enough to make up for the slight softening inherent in the scanner's analog-to-digital conversion. It's true that you'll eventually need to sharpen the image using settings appropriate for the final target medium, but in a media-independent workflow, you don't apply output-based sharpening to the master image—you apply it to a copy that you're optimizing for a specific medium.

Correcting. Clean up defects and optimize the image's tonal range and color balance… but stop there. When you create a master image, you need to create the ideal version of that image, without compromising it for any specific medium. If you're a professional photographer scanning high-quality slide film originals into 16-bit EktaSpace RGB files, correct your image in that space without worrying whether the colors will print. When you need a version of that image for a specific medium, you copy the master image and then adjust the copy's tones and colors to the range that the targeted output device can handle.

Figure 18-3
Media-independent
mastering workflow

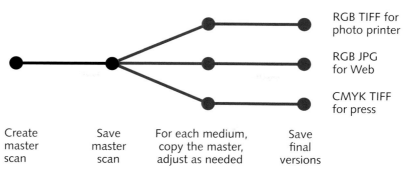

Media-independent workflow

RGB TIFF for
photo printer

RGB JPG
for Web

CMYK TIFF
for press

| Create master scan | Save master scan | For each medium, copy the master, adjust as needed | Save final versions |

The key to taking advantage of a media-independent, master-image-based workflow is understanding the flexibility that the master image gives you. Whereas the conventional, media-dependent scanning workflow has one input (the scan) and one output (the final medium), a media-independent workflow has two input/output paths. The master image is the hub—the end of the scanning path and the beginning of all possible output paths.

Once you have a master image, you can also archive it for future uses. We discuss archiving in Chapter 4, *Getting Your Computer Ready for Scans*.

Master of the Raster

The usual motivation for creating full-gamut master images is to retain flexibility for multiple media, but building an archive of well-scanned master images is also a form of future-proofing. Without having to rescan your images, you are ready to take advantage of exotic new printing processes with wider color gamuts, or of differently optimized versions of originals that are no longer available for rescanning. About the only reason you'll ever have for rescanning an image is if you get a higher quality scanner. And when you don't have to go back and redo your work, you can spend that time taking your work in cool new directions.

PART 5

Halftones

19

Dots, Spots, and Halftones

HOW HALFTONES WORK

When you look at a book of Georgia O'Keeffe prints, your first thought probably isn't, "Look how well they reproduced those colors!" But that's our reaction. It's what we think about all the time: how colors and tones are represented on a printed page using halftones.

No printing press—or inkjet or laser printer—can reproduce different tones; they can only print shapes in one solid color at a time. Presses and printers can lay down two, four, six, or more colors onto the same piece of paper but still just one at a time. That is, they might be able to print cyan, yellow, magenta, and black, but they can't directly reproduce the different shades of gray or gradations in color that you see in a photograph. That's where halftones come in.

Halftones are used in virtually every piece of printed material, and when they're done well, you don't even notice them. When you're looking at the O'Keeffe book, you may see colors, but those hues and tones aren't what they appear to be.

So what are you looking at?

The Spot's the Thing

In the late 19th century lithographers figured out that they could create a tint of a colored ink by breaking the color down into a whole bunch of little spots. They could make gray, for instance, by printing small black spots really close to each other. Our brain tries to make order out of chaos by telling us we're seeing a tone instead of black spots.

Figure 19-1
A halftoned photograph

This process of breaking a gray image into black spots is called halftoning. **Figure 19-1** shows an everyday halftone of a photograph, with a blown-up section showing the halftone spots.

Photographic Halftones

Traditionally, halftones were photomechanical reproductions. Someone put a piece of photosensitive paper behind a finely etched *screen* (originally made of glass, and later of acetate) and projected light through the photograph, which exposed the paper (**Figure 19-2**). The result was a pattern of evenly spaced spots of different sizes. Because of *diffraction*—the spreading of light after passing through a narrow

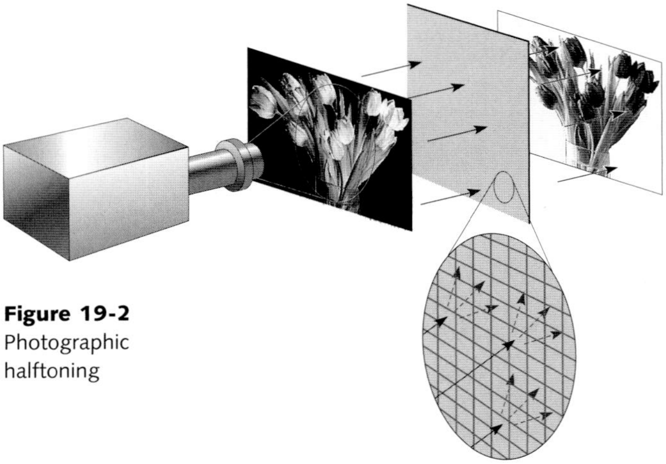

Figure 19-2
Photographic halftoning

aperture—the spots in dark areas were big (even overlapping), and the dots in light areas were small.

Tints and Tint Percentages

Bear in mind that this kind of halftoning wasn't just for photographs. Flat tint areas were made using the same method described earlier, except that light was projected directly through a screen rather than passing through a photographic negative first.

Tints are referred to in percentages. A light gray tint, where the halftone spots are a tenth of their full size, is a 10-percent tint. A medium gray area might be a 50-percent tint, and in a dark gray area—let's say a 90-percent tint—the spots are 90 percent of their full size. A 100-percent tint, of course, is black (**Figure 19-3**).

Figure 19-3 Tint percentages

Digital Halftones

Photographic halftones in our part of the world are generally limited to a vanishingly small number of older newspapers and magazines that haven't updated to digital techniques. Outside of North America, they're still used in quite a few places because the equipment is reliable, long-lasting, and involves labor—not constantly tweaked digital hardware.

Today, computers coupled with laser printers and imagesetters are the main tools used for creating halftones—though, of course, they don't use screens made of glass or plastic to make them. In order to understand how computers make halftones, we need to stop for a moment and look at how these devices make images in the first place.

Dots

As we say throughout the book, computers represent everything in ones and zeroes: on or off. Fortunately, this corresponds to offset printing and laser output: You can either have black or not—there's no in-between. When a laser printer is creating an image, it simply turns the laser on and off—on where the paper should be white, and off where it should be black. The dots that the laser creates are so small and close together that there's no space between adjacent dots—a row of them looks exactly like a line. An imagesetter works the same way with different effect: It uses light in the form of a laser turning on or off to expose a tiny dot on specially coated paper or film.

The dots that most desktop laser printers create are tiny. In fact, you can fit 600 of them next to each other along a single inch. That's why people call them 600-dpi (dots-per-inch) printers. Other printers— from higher-resolution laser printers to plate-exposing imagesetters—can create

even smaller dots, as fine as 1200, 2400, or even several thousand dpi.

Spots

But how can you make halftone spots larger and smaller when a laser printer's dots are all the same size? The solution is pretty simple. The computer groups together a bunch of dots into a single halftone cell, which we call a *halftone spot*. This cell is a square grid of dots, each of which can be turned on or off. To create a dark area (a large spot), lots of the dots are turned on; to create a light area (a small spot), only a few dots are turned on (**Figure 19-4**).

The important concept here is that the spacing of the halftone spots doesn't change. They're not closer together in dark areas. Only the number of dots turned on *within each cell* changes. The group of dots that are turned on is the halftone spot (**Figure 19-5**). We'll talk more about these spots and their shapes in the next chapter. (There is a way of creating digital output without halftones that involves arrangements in space instead of changes in size; it's called *stochastic screening*. We devote Chapter 26 to this subject.)

Figure 19-4 A representation of digital halftone cells

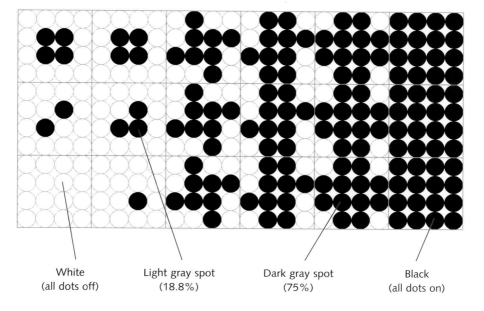

White
(all dots off)

Light gray spot
(18.8%)

Dark gray spot
(75%)

Black
(all dots on)

Figure 19-5
Halftone spots

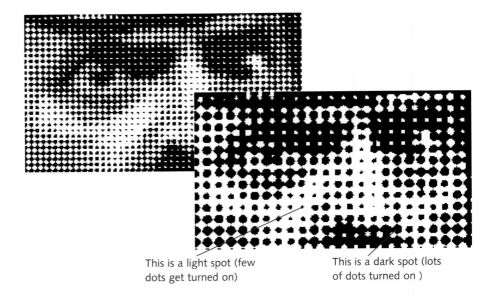

This is a light spot (few dots get turned on)

This is a dark spot (lots of dots turned on)

Halftones, Tints, and Screens

There's one other piece of terminology that we want to clarify before we end this chapter: *screening*. We mentioned above that the etched piece of glass or film that's used to create photographic halftones is called a screen. The process of creating the half-tone pattern is called screening. To confuse matters more, the pattern of dots that results from screening—the halftone pattern—is also called a screen.

The more you recognize halftones and how they're used and created, the more effective you can be in your own work. Next we look at some more details about halftoning: frequency, angle, and spot shape.

20

Frequency, Angle, and Spot Shape

WHAT MAKES A HALFTONE

If you go to David's house, he and his wife, Debbie, will certainly show off a quilt they received from a dear friend of theirs. This quilt is an intricate arrangement of different fabrics in a grid that close up seems like a lot of nice fabric patterns; when you stand back, it creates the image of a heart. Perhaps David likes it so much because it's a real-world halftone of sorts.

As we noted in the last chapter, halftones are made up of bunches of spots, some larger and some smaller. These spots fool the

eye into seeing grays and colors where only spots exist. Each spot is a group of dots in a grid or a *cell*. These halftones cells are arranged in a pattern with three primary attributes: frequency, angle, and spot shape. Let's look at each of these in turn.

Screen Frequency

Imagine eggs in an enormous egg carton. Each egg sits in its own place, with an equal distance to the eggs on the left and the right. If the egg carton were big enough, you wouldn't say it was a 6-egg carton or a 12-egg carton. Rather, you'd say there were 12 eggs per foot or 39 eggs per meter, or something like that. Each row is the same distance from the next row, so you could say that the "egg-per-foot" value (epf) is the number of rows of eggs per foot (**Figure 20-1**).

Figure 20-1 Eggs measurements

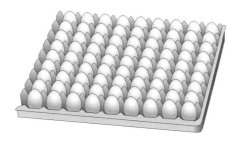

Figure 20-2
Screen frequency

20 lpi   75 lpi   130 lpi

Now let's look at halftones in the same way: You have a whole bunch of spots (eggs) that sit in rows of a big grid (egg carton). There are too many spots to count, so you simplify the problem by counting the number of spots—or rows of spots—per inch. This is called the frequency of the halftone, because it tells you how frequently spots occur within an inch.

The frequency is typically measured in lines per inch (lpi). Of course, in countries that use the metric system, it's measured in lines per centimeter (L/cm). Specifying screen frequency in lpi or L/cm confuses the issue slightly, because we're not really talking about lines here. We're actually talking about rows of spots. But if you keep that in mind, you won't go wrong.

People often talk about coarse and fine screens. The lower the screen frequency, the coarser the screen. That is, the cells are bigger and the image is rougher looking, and the dots are more visible and don't fool the eye as well. The higher the screen frequency, the finer the image, because the cells are really small (**Figure 20-2**).

Coarser screens are used in newspapers, because cheap newsprint can't reproduce a fine screen well; whereas exceedingly fine screens are found in books reproducing artwork printed on exquisite paper. (We talk about paper and screens in Chapter 22, *Reproducing Halftones*.)

Screen Angle

If we go back to our egg analogy, we see that the pattern of all those eggs not only has a frequency, but an angle as well. If you look at the eggs straight on, the rows of eggs are at an angle of zero degrees. If you turn the carton, the angle changes. Turn it to "1 o'clock" and the angle is at 30 degrees. Turn it to halfway between 1 and 2 o'clock, and the angle increases to 45 degrees (**Figure 20-3**).

Figure 20-3
Rotating eggs to demonstrate angles

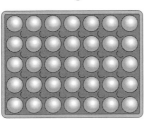
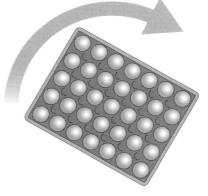
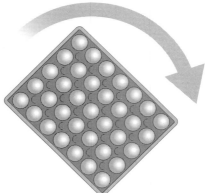

Figure 20-4
Halftone angles

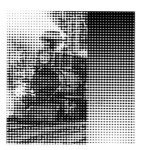  

0 degrees   15 degrees   45 degrees

You can rotate a halftone screen almost as easily as turning an egg carton, and the angle to which you align the rows of spots is called the screen angle. A standard screen angle is 45 degrees because it's the most traditional and least noticeable. It does the best job of fooling our eyes into seeing gray instead of a pattern of spots (**Figure 20-4**). However, there's another good reason to change the angle of a screen—to improve color separations (see Chapter 28, *When Grids Collide*).

Spot Shape

Figure 20-5
Gradations with differently shaped halftone spots (from top to bottom): round, line, square, and diamond

The final element of halftone screens is the spot shape. Until now, we've been talking primarily about round spots. But remember that these spots are made of tiny dots, and we can arrange the dots any way we want. So, our spots can be circles, squares, triangles, lines, or even little pictures of Barney the dinosaur (Figure 20-5).

You almost never notice the shape of a halftone spot unless the screen frequency is really low—think Roy Lichtenstein paintings. (In a 10-lpi halftone, there are 10 halftone cells per inch, so you can see the shape pretty easily; in a 133-lpi screen, each cell is so tiny—$\frac{1}{133}$ inch—that you can barely see what it looks like.) However, the spot shape can make a difference in the appearance of your halftones. For example, a square spot often results in a sharper, higher-contrast look—especially in midtones—while an elliptical dot (actually a rounded-corner diamond) results in smooth transitions in graduated blends. Typically, you don't have to worry about spot shape unless you're trying to achieve a special effect.

Eggs-cell-ent

There's more you should know about spot shapes, so we provide more detail in Chapter 25, *The Glorious Spot*. However, we do think it's important to point out sooner rather than later that the egg-in-a-carton metaphor breaks down at this point: you can't construct differently shaped eggs at home or in the office without lithographically minded chickens.

21

Frequency vs. Gray Levels

TRADE-OFFS IN DIGITAL HALFTONING

When a picture of China's president ran on the front page of *The New York Times* a few years ago, Glenn noticed something strange and pulled out his line-screen detector: The *Times* had accidentally run the photograph at such a high frequency that the image had a very high contrast and only a few tones in it.

In digital halftoning, there's an essential trade-off between screen frequency and gray levels: the more you have of one, the fewer you have of the other. In trying to achieve photographic effects, you can wind up with so few gray levels that the image looks somewhat like pop art.

Let's outline the problem first, and then take a little time to discuss why it's there and what you can do about it.

Screen Frequency, Gray Levels, and Output Resolution

Put succinctly, the halftone screen frequency has an inverse relationship to the number of gray levels possible at a given output resolution. Put more simply, the higher the screen frequency, the fewer levels of gray you can get at a given resolution. Reduce the screen frequency (or increase the output resolution), and you can get more levels of gray.

For example, on a typical 600-dpi desktop laser printer you can only get 33 different shades of gray (including black and white) in a 106-lpi halftone. If you make

Figure 21-1
Posterization

the halftone coarser—let's say 71 lpi, which is the lowest reasonable value for a good halftone on that printer—you can get 73 different shades of gray.

Posterization

When you don't have enough gray levels, the result is *posterization*—an obvious stair-stepping from one gray level to another, quite different, gray level—rather than a smooth transition. It's primarily a problem in graduated blends or halftones of photographs in which smooth transitions from white to black occur (**Figure 21-1**). Posterization can also be an interesting special effect at times—but only when you want it. (In the example in the introduction, the *Times* certainly didn't want it.)

Figure 21-2
Number of gray levels determined by number of dots comprising halftone spots

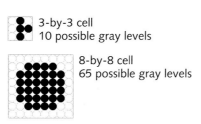
3-by-3 cell
10 possible gray levels

8-by-8 cell
65 possible gray levels

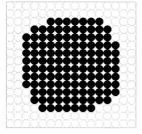
16-by-16 cell
257 possible gray levels

Scarcity of Dots

But why? Why should there be such a limitation on gray levels when halftoning is so flexible? It's because the number of possible gray levels is determined by the number of dots in a halftone cell (**Figure 21-2**). If a cell is made up of 25 dots, there are 26 possible gray levels (including white and black—all dots off and all dots on). If a cell is made up of 256 dots, there are 257 possible gray levels. The more dots per cell, the more possible gray levels.

The goal is to work with halftone cells that have lots of dots in them, so you have lots of available gray levels. Therein lies the essential problem of digital halftoning—there are only so many printer dots to work with. The finer the halftone screen, the fewer the number of dots there are in each halftone cell, and therefore the fewer levels of gray you have available (**Figure 21-3**).

You can determine the number of dots in a single halftone cell with simple arithmetic. If you divide the resolution of the printer by the screen frequency, you get the number of dots on one side of the halftone cell. Square this number (multiply it by itself) to find the total number of dots in the cell.

To figure out the total number of levels of gray you can get, just add one to the number of dots in the halftone cell. In other words, if each level of gray is created by

One inch

300 printer dots

4-by-4 cell
17 gray levels
75-line screen

6-by-6 cell
37 gray levels
50-line screen

10-by-10 cell
101 gray levels
30-line screen

Figure 21-3 Finer halftone screens contain fewer levels of gray

turning on an additional dot, you can get the same number of grays as there are dots in the cell, plus one. **Figure 21-4** portrays the trade-off graphically. For those of you who like formulas, here it is:

```
Gray levels = (output resolution ÷
screen frequency)² + 1
```

For example: Let's say you're printing a halftone at 133 lpi on an imagesetter with a resolution of 2400 dpi. Divide 2400 by 133 and you get 18. Multiply 18 by 18 and you get 324 dots in the halftone cell. Add one for white, and you see that you can get 325 tones.

You also can't cut a dot in half, so if you print a 75-lpi halftone on a 300-dpi printer,

 The original PostScript Level 1 and Level 2 page-description interpreters for printers could only render a maximum of 256 different halftone spot sizes in any given screen frequency. Anything over 256 levels of gray just renders as the next nearest tone. Newer printers with PostScript Level 3 can handle 4096 spot sizes.

 Some laser printers can print dots of different sizes; see "Variable Laser Dots," later in this chapter.

you would leap from 31-percent gray to 38-percent gray or five dots turned on to six dots turned on.

Also, there's a school of thought—propounded by Adobe Systems, the creator of PostScript, among others—that says the human eye can't perceive more than 256 levels of gray in a single visual field. (We live in Seattle, where the weather is gray, cloudy, foggy, and misty so often that we've developed the ability to discern *and name* more than 256 levels of gray.) What is certain is that job printing presses—those used for workaday brochures, posters, and books—can't reproduce more than 100 or so levels of gray.

Fine printers can often do much better because of the quality of materials, paper, and press conditions. If you're working on

Figure 21-4
Frequency tradeoffs for different resolution printers

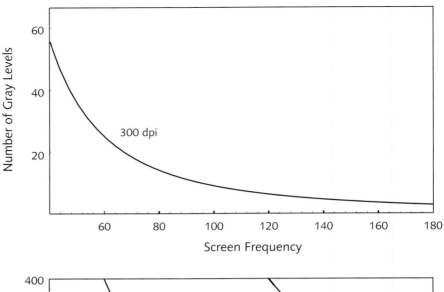

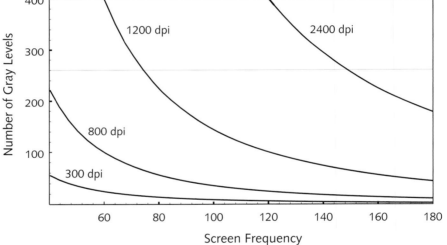

a project where subtlety at this degree of refinement counts, you'd better check with your service bureau as to what version of PostScript they're using.

The Rule of Sixteen

The practical limitation of 256 levels of gray means that you rarely need to do the calculations described in the previous section. Instead, you can simply focus on two questions: What is the highest (finest) screen frequency you can use, given the resolution of your printer? Or, what is the minimum-resolution printer you can use, given the screen frequency you're using?

The Rule of Sixteen gives you the answer to both these questions (it works because 16 is the square root of 256). You still have to do a little math, so don't put that calculator away too quickly. But this calculation is really easy. Here's the formula.

```
Maximum screen frequency = Output
resolution ÷ 16 or Required output
resolution = Screen frequency ÷ 16
```

For example, if you want to print a halftone at 150 lpi, multiply that value by 16 to find that you need a minimum of 2400 dpi to get 256 levels of gray. Or, if you know you'll be printing on a 1200-dpi printer, you can divide that value by 16 to find that you shouldn't print a halftone higher than 75 lpi.

Variable Laser Dots

Many of today's laser printers can create variable-size laser dots, which to some extent bypasses the essential trade-off of digital halftoning, providing more gray levels at a given screen frequency and output resolution. Because the laser dots can vary in size, there is more control over halftone spot size, hence more potential gray levels. Hewlett-Packard claims that its Resolution Enhancement Technology (RET) can produce 210 levels of gray at 106 lpi from a 600 dpi laser printer. Without RET, a printer would be able to achieve only 33 levels of gray using conventional halftoning. If you use an enhancement option be aware that

We've only seen variable-size dots in laser printers, not imagesetters or platesetters so this shouldn't affect your offset work.

the formulas provided earlier in this chapter won't apply because they're based on conventional halftoning.

Who Needs 256 Grays?

Many designers realize that some types of moderate-quality output, like newsprint, can't reproduce more than 100 to 150 levels of gray in scanned images. Graduated fills and some high-quality images almost always need 256 levels of gray (see Chapter 27, *Band Aid*). But if an image already has a lot of noise in it—or if you're printing on very absorbent paper—fewer gray levels might be fine for you.

By the way, if all your halftones are straight tints (no blends or photographs), then you probably don't have to worry about posterization and achieving 256 levels of gray. If you're producing a newsletter that has several 20-percent gray rectangles behind some type, you could easily print that document at 120 lpi, even on a 1200-dpi imagesetter. Sure, you can't get more than 101 shades of gray, but who cares? You're only using one shade of gray on your page!

22

Reproducing Halftones

SPOT VARIATION AND THE PRINTING PROCESS

Figure 22-1
Simulated spot variation
Top: Without spot variation
Bottom: With spot variation. Shadows get darker (almost to black); highlights get lighter (almost to white)

After all your hard work making a perfect halftone, you still have to contend with a printing press. Those thousands of tiny halftone spots spread out or shrink, depending on their size, the pressure of the offset cylinders, and (primarily) the absorbency and smoothness (or *calendarization*) of the paper. Sometimes they spread or shrink just a little, but sometimes they spread out so much that your image will look like the blob that ate Cincinnati (**Figure 22-1**). As dark tints fill in and become black, your nice photograph becomes a shot of the Black Lagoon.

The opposite problem also arises. The smallest spots tend to disappear. The tiny areas of ink don't adhere to the paper, or they get filled in during the process of creating lithographic negatives or plates. This makes the subtlest tones in a snow bank blow out to white or a 4-percent tint vanish entirely.

Spot Gain and Loss

The growth of halftone spots is traditionally called *dot gain*. This use of "dot" instead of "spot" is a holdover from conventional halftoning terminology, but we're going to call it *spot gain* to be consistent and avoid confusion. When small spots disappear and you lose the light tones they represent, you say they're *blown out* (as in the phrase, "This picture of Dr. Evil's head is solid white; all the highlights are blown out!"). We refer to the two problems together as *spot variation*.

Spot gain is measured in percentages: people talk about 5- or 10-percent spot gain. Be aware, however, that 5-percent spot gain doesn't mean that 10-percent spots become 15-percent spots. Spot gain percentages refer to the increase in area covered by a 50-percent spot. So with

10-percent spot gain, a 20-percent spot increases to 22 percent, and 50 percent spot increases to 60 percent.

It's also important to understand that because of this growth in area, spot variation is nonlinear. All the spots in an image don't just increase by 10 percent on press (which is the impression given by the term *dot gain*). Small spots become only slightly larger, midtone spots grow more, and spots in shadow areas start to overlap and thus have less surface area and suffer less from spot gain. Thus a graphical representation of dot gain across the tonal scale looks like a curve, not a line. If your software has a dialog box that lets you correct for spot gain by typing in a single percentage value, you should eye it with some suspicion.

High-Frequency Problems

Spot variation is more of a problem with high (also known as *fine*) screen frequencies printed on presses or plates that are unable to handle small spot size, or on uncoated or textured paper. The spaces between spots are smaller at fine screen frequencies, so they clog up with ink quickly. In light areas, the spots are also small, so they're more likely to disappear entirely.

If you work with a printer whose equipment and staff consistently reproduce screens of 175 lines per inch or higher, they know how to cope with these problems; avoid printers who aren't familiar with such high screens.

Reproducing Thin Lines

The *blow-out* problem happens somewhat differently with rules or lines that approach the width of the smallest halftone spots, as in line art, boxes, and *callouts*—lines that point to elements in an illustration. (We talk about scanning line art in Chapter 11, *Image Resolution*.)

For suggestions on setting screen frequency to control spot variation, see Chapter 23, Setting Screens.

The problem with lines is that it's immediately apparent to the eye when a line is a little broken up or missing pieces. Your optical processing center instantly recognizes when a few missing or lopsided spots are below the perceptual threshold.

With a scientific calculator, you can quickly calculate the size of the smallest safely reproducible spot and then figure out the associated thinnest line width you can use without fear of grottiness. In **Table 6-1** in Chapter 6, we provide you with upper and lower spot-size percentages for different kinds of paper.

Let's say you were printing to coated paper at 133 lpi with the output coming from a 2540-dpi imagesetter. Your minimum spot size should be 5 percent—lower than 5 percent, and the spot disappears or breaks up. Now there are 133 cells per inch and a 5-percent spot takes up 5 percent of the overall area. So the formula to determine the width of the spot is

$$\sqrt{((dpi/lpi)^2)} \times percentage$$

You divide the printer resolution by the screen frequency to get the number of dots on each side of a halftone cell. You square that to get the area, multiply by 0.05 to get a 5-percent spot's area, and then take the square root of the remaining number to get the length of the sides of a 5-percent spot. In this case, that's $(2540/133)^2 \times 0.05 = 18$, the square root of which is about 4 dots on a side or $^{17}/_{10,000}$ inch.

The recommendation we make is to be about 2.5 times larger than that smallest spot's width to ensure a crisp line. That's about $^{35}/_{10,000}$ inch, or about 0.3 points in pica measurement. Not coincidentally, this is the usual recommended "hairline" width.

For comparison, if we were doing the same output to rough, uncoated paper, a 10-percent minimum spot is recommended. That gives you about a $^{23}/_{10,000}$-inch spot or a ½-point minimum rule.

What Causes Spot Variation?

Spot variation arises for a number of reasons throughout the process of converting digital information into real, physical spots on paper (**Figure 22-2**). Many factors can affect the reproduction of halftones; all of them fall into the following categories:

▶ **Software settings**: including applications, drivers, and the color management system if used

▶ **Hardware conditions**: such as the laser voltage or press ink pressure, or settings such as density

▶ **Generational artifacts**: the side effects of making film copies before making plates

▶ **Press factors**: including how precisely the press is adjusted, and the absorptive properties of the output medium, such as coated or uncoated paper

An introduction to some common terminology is useful before we proceed to discuss each of these categories in more depth. Imagesetter output is usually called *lithographic film* or *lithographic paper*. It's called *lithographic* because it shares the same properties as offset lithography—it can only capture black and white, just as offset presses can only print a given ink color in a given location, or not. There's no tone in lithographic material, unlike photographic *contone* (*continuous-tone*) film and paper.

Paper, Film, and Plates

In the most typical kind of offset printing used worldwide, the printing plates are made by contacting film to a metal or plastic substrate coated with photosensitive material. In the early stages of digital imagesetting, output devices produced images on plain resin-coated paper from which the intermediate film stage was created, and that film was exposed onto plate material. As imagesetting matured, a digital printer output directly onto film, which was then contacted directly onto plates, removing the paper stage.

In the late 1990s, maturity was finally reached with computer-to-plate (CTP) technology, in which there are no intermediate analog steps between the data and the plate that's used on press. In fact, this book was composed electronically with halftones in place and dumped directly to plates. For some jobs, CTP doesn't provide enough control before reaching the press-check stage; but for many other jobs, it's faster, cheaper, and easier.

(We originally called this direct to plate until we realized that those initials would be confused with desktop publishing; the graphic arts industry has been using the now-standard CTP for a few years.)

The difference between film-to-plate and CTP is that *platesetters* directly expose plate material. In older processes that use paper and film (or just film), those extra steps are opportunities for unwanted spot gain to creep in.

Film is proofed using *bluelines* (blueprint-paper contact prints of negatives), which let you see tiny imperfections and fix errors. That's not possible using CTP, so printers that use CTP often provide calibrated inkjet output or special color proofs of part of the job to guarantee overall consistency.

Software Settings

Output settings you choose in image-editing or layout programs control the instructions sent to the imagesetter, platesetter, or other output device, so they obviously affect the spot size. Software settings that affect spot size include:

▶ Color management profiles, which often have spot gain information encoded in them

▶ Transfer functions that are either part of the information saved inside an EPS file or applied as a print option in Photoshop

▶ Printer media settings, which may be adjusted for the spot gain characteristics of different papers

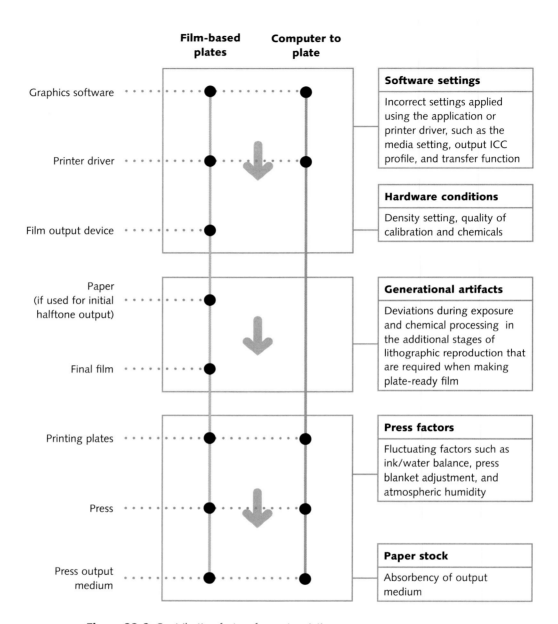

Figure 22-2 Contributing factors for spot variation

Hardware Conditions and Output Density

Density is a measure of the ability to absorb light passing through (film) or reflecting off (paper)—in other words, its opacity. (We go into the input side of density— how it relates to scanning—in "Dynamic Range and Bit Depth" in Chapter 2, *Scanners*.) You can measure this opacity with a densitometer, which can also measure halftone tint percentages. Any service bureau producing film output from an imagesetter must have a densitometer, or it can't calibrate its imagesetter correctly. When density is inconsistent or imprecise, highlights can blow out or shadows can plug up.

Density is measured on a decimal logarithmic scale, like the Richter scale for earthquakes. A graph depicting linear and logarithmic density values can be found in **Figure 2-1** in Chapter 2. A value of 4.0 means a 'quake (or density) that is 10 times greater than a value of 3.0. Lithographic film should have a density of roughly 3.5; lithographic paper should be around 1.7, but these are just guidelines. As with other printing variables, printers know what values work best on their systems.

An imagesetter is a complex beast that produces usable density only when its components are properly tuned. Hardware factors that can affect density include:

▶ **Density settings.** These are present on imagesetters and laser printers. Because this is a hardware setting, the density control may be available through the output device's front panel or as a knob you turn on a laser printer.

▶ **Precision of imagesetter calibration.** If you specify a 10-percent tint, you should get a 10-percent tint. A good test for a service bureau is to bring in a sample with tints, have the bureau run it out, and watch them check the tints on their densitometer. Percentages should be off by no more than 2 percent and should generally be as close as 1 percent. If you use color management, the ICC profile you use should account for the imagesetter's calibrated state.

▶ **Chemical quality and temperature control.** The main causes of improper density during processing are improper temperature and chemicals that aren't kept fresh. A service bureau using a "replenishing-bath" processor won't have these problems, because it introduces new chemicals at a constant rate and maintains them at an even temperature. The wash water should either be replenished through a feed from a water line or through a frequently changed tank.

 You can tell if wash water is stagnant, because your output will have traces of algae on it. True, and yucky.

Generational Artifacts from Lithographic Reproduction

When computer-to-plate isn't the best option for the job, the original output must be transformed into a printing plate using one or more additional steps; each of which can introduce spot variations. There may be film stripping involved, for instance, and the printer might require a single piece of composite film for platemaking. (CTP skips all of the intermediate film or paper generations, so you can just concentrate on the parameters of the press.)

If for some reason the printer can't use your original output directly, good practices can keep the number of generations down, minimizing spot variation during lithographic reproduction.

Output to film, not paper. Paper is more absorbent than film, so if you can keep paper out of the workflow, you'll avoid a major potential source of spot gain. (For laser printer output, you can use acetate.)

Provide film to specifications. If you follow your printer's specifications exactly (not providing a positive image when they require a negative), you can avoid intermediate generations that also introduce spot variations.

Overexpose when shooting from laser output. If you deliver paper laser output to the print shop, you might ask them to overexpose slightly when shooting film. Since they're creating negatives, overexposing causes white areas on your original to encroach slightly on the jaggedy-edged, toner-based spots, reducing the problem of spot gain. The worst that can happen is that highlight might wash out, but this may be preferable to the alternatives of spot gain and blocked shadows.

Press Factors

If too much or too little ink is used on the printing press, halftone spots tend to clog from spot gain, or blow out entirely. This can also happen if the ink/water balance is off. Similarly, any one of a number of problems with the printing press can throw off tonal values in the halftone.

For example, *spot doubling* (which looks a lot like severe spot gain) often happens if the press blankets are too loose. *Spot slur* occurs if the paper stretches too much or *skids* slightly across the impression cylinder. If you're working with a good printer, they should be catching these problems before you even see them.

Many minor variables—such as humidity—can also affect spot variation, but these are out of your control.

Controlling Ink

You can make a difference by controlling the overprinting ink on ink. That effect can result in dramatic spot gain, but using black replacement and rosette formation lets you reduce the amount of ink put down on paper.

Black replacement. In four-color process printing, you can literally put down 400 percent ink—100 percent each of cyan, magenta, yellow, and black. However, ink is both sticky and moist, and putting that much ink on paper on a printing press is a bad idea (the paper could buckle, stick to the rollers, or cause all kinds of trouble). Therefore, most color-separation software, including the routines in Photoshop, do *undercolor removal (UCR)* and *gray component replacement (GCR)* to remove various amounts of color and reduce the total ink percentage down to something reasonable (between 240 and 350 percent typically, depending on the press type, paper, and so on).

UCR replaces cyan, magenta, and yellow with black wherever they combine to form what should be black. In reality, those three colors have enough impurities to form muddy brown instead. GCR extends further into neutral areas where equal amounts of cyan, magenta, and yellow should combine to form grays; GCR replaces those with corresponding straight tints of black.

These techniques reduce the overall amount of ink on press. Printers may have a preference for one over the other; you may need to use GCR for a newsprint press that has a maximum of 240-percent ink coverage, for instance.

Rosette formation. There are different ways to formulate patterns in the different process color separations so they don't form unintentional patterning. In Chapter 28, *When Grids Collide*, we discuss what a rosette is—a pattern formed by the set of all the color separations—and how it works. For our purposes here, though, it's important to know that using an open-centered rosette minimizes the number of places where larger halftone spots overlap, reducing the overall spot gain from printing ink on top of ink.

If you use Adobe InDesign CS, you can use the Separations Preview palette to view the total ink coverage anywhere on your page, so that you can locate problems and make adjustments before committing to output.

Choosing Paper Stock

The area in which you have to be most aware of spot variation is in your choice of paper stock. You'll always encounter noticeable spot gain on uncoated stock, because the ink is absorbed into the porous paper. An extreme case of this is on newsprint, where spots can easily gain 35 percent.

Coated stock reduces spot gain considerably, because the paper isn't as porous. Super-slick paper, on the other hand, sometimes causes spot slur (which has an effect similar to spot gain) because it can slip slightly in the press. Once again, consult with your printer when choosing a paper stock.

We discuss paper stock in relation to screen frequency and spot gain in Chapter 23, *Setting Screens*.

Upper and Lower Tint Limits

There is one incredibly easy way to avoid most spot variation in extreme highlights and shadows: eliminate highlights and shadows entirely. If no tint in your publication is too light or too dark, the problems of spot gain are somewhat reduced, although still a lesser factor throughout the rest of the tonal range. We discuss how to manage clipping the top and bottom of the tonal range with scanned images

using tonal compression in Chapter 12, *Tonal Correction*.

If you aren't using color management, use the Levels dialog box in Photoshop to set each image's output levels to values suggested by your service bureau. **Table 6-1** in Chapter 6 provides typical values for some paper stocks. However, if you and your service bureau are using color management, you don't need to change the images—simply make sure the correct input and output profile are assigned, and the color management system will apply the tint limits automatically.

DTP vs. the Blob

You're probably getting the idea right about now that creating high-quality halftone images is much harder than the salesperson at the computer store told you. Spot variation is a major issue in scanning and halftoning, though it's one rarely focused on. Fortunately, it's also one that's surmountable.

Although proper attention to paper stock, calibration, and the other elements we discussed in this chapter will set you well on your way to creating excellent-looking halftones, one factor is so important in the discussion of spot variation that we've given it its own chapter: screen frequency. That's where we go next.

23

Setting Screens

FREQUENCY AND SPOT GAIN

Screen frequency is one of the most important factors you need to consider when working with halftones. We look at the trade-offs between screen frequency and number of gray levels in Chapter 21, *Frequency vs. Gray Levels*. In Chapter 22, *Reproducing Halftones,* we discuss the factors that cause spot variation. In this chapter, we look at how screen frequency affects spot variation.

The Problem with High Frequencies

As the screen frequency of a halftone increases, it becomes more susceptible to spot variation and muddiness. There are two reasons for this frustrating effect. First, because spot gain occurs at the edges of spots, when there are more spots per square inch, there's more spot gain happen-

ing (more spots mean more edges, which means more potential spot gain). Second, at higher frequencies the spots are so close together that any spot gain can fill in what tiny space there is between each spot.

But how do you know what screen frequency you can get away with? There's no hard-and-fast rule for this; rather, you need to take several factors into consideration.

Factors to Consider

Typically, unless you're trying to achieve some sort of special effect, you want to use the highest screen frequency you can. However, maximum screen frequency is dictated by many different factors. Generally, the rule is to ask your printing service what the proper screen frequency should be; but of course that doesn't always work. We're often reminded of the time we brought some artwork to a quick-print shop where the kid behind the counter thought screens were used to keep flies out.

The primary factors you need to consider when setting your halftone screen frequency are output resolution, output method, reproduction method, and paper stock.

Output Resolution

In Chapter 21, *Frequency vs. Gray Levels*, we explain the relationship between gray levels, screen frequency, and output resolution. If you adhere to The Rule of Sixteen—screen frequency should not exceed output resolution divided by 16—you'll always get a full complement of 256 gray levels.

You can use a higher resolution if you don't need all those gray levels; for instance, if you're printing just solid tints and no blends. Or, if the imagesetter you're printing to does "supercell screening" in which case it can make irregular cells that can simulate a higher number of spot sizes. You need to ask your service bureau or printer whether that will work.

Another option is to switch to a higher-resolution device; if you can't, you might output your scanned images and graduated fills—which require all 256 gray levels—at a lower screen frequency than your flat tints. That way you get a fine screen for type, lines, and boxes, and 256 gray levels for photographs and graduated fills (see Chapter 29, *Angle Strategies*).

Output Method

Output method refers to the sort of printer you're outputting your artwork on. If you're producing final artwork on any type of toner-based laser printer, don't expect to exceed 110 lpi, even if the printer prints at high resolutions; for best results, use 65 or 85 lpi. The ragged-edged spots that result

from toner-based devices are more prone to dot gain. On the other hand, the maximum screen frequency on an imagesetter or platesetter is limited only by its output resolution.

Output Medium

Whether you use paper, film, or plate material for your output makes a big difference in which screen frequency you use. If you're outputting to paper, you're limited to about a 110-line screen, because the photographic process of shooting lithographic negative film can't hold a screen much finer than that. If you want a higher screen frequency, you must output to film or to plates, which we recommend for almost every purpose anyway. (However, if you're outputting line art and text, or halftones below 100 lpi, a 600-dpi-or-higher resolution paper laser printer works well—and is much cheaper.)

Reproduction Method

Another factor in choosing a halftone screen frequency is the reproduction method that you're using. Different printing methods dictate different screen frequency settings. Here's a very quick overview of some common methods.

Offset printing. The limits on screen frequency particular to offset printing are dictated by the printer's press, the skill of the presspeople, and the paper stock you're using. Screen frequency can range from 75 lpi to as much as 300 lpi. Ask your printing rep for the proper frequency. We've seen small job printers with inexpensive, high-quality presses and computer-to-plate (filmless) output hold 133 to 150 lines perfectly.

Gravure. This printing method can hold a fine screen very accurately. If you're using gravure, you're probably working with a top-notch printer and don't need our advice to choose screen frequency. Ask your rep.

Quick printing with paper plates. Using this method, you'll almost always want to use 120-lpi screens or lower.

Photocopying. For photocopying, screen frequencies up to 100 lpi are possible, and 85 lpi is pretty safe, though we've seen scans clog up at even this low frequency. Try 75 lpi with scanned images. Some sophisticated photocopying systems, like Xerox's DocuTech, can output directly from Post-Script, allowing higher resolutions with perfect clarity. (See Chapter 9, *Scanning for the Office*, for more tips.)

Inkjets. Screen frequencies don't directly apply to desktop inkjets, because most of them don't render tones by specifying half-tone screens with numerical amounts. They generally use stochastic screens, which we discuss in Chapter 26, *Stochastic Screening*. For inkjet printers, the closest equivalent to screen frequency is the media type option you select in the printer driver software. The media type setting adjusts the size and spacing of printer dots to account for the spot gain of the media. Coated paper has

less spot gain, so coated paper media-type settings allow finer detail by laying down tinier dots and more closely spaced dot patterns.

Paper Stock

Perhaps the biggest consideration when choosing halftoning screen frequency is the paper stock you're using for printing. There are hundreds of different types of paper, each with its own amount of absorbency. However, the basic information to remember is that coated papers boast the least spot variation; uncoated papers create more spot variation because they're more absorbent; and newsprint sucks up ink like the Sahara sucks up rain water (printing newspapers has been compared to putting kerosene on toilet paper at 200 miles per hour).

 For more in-depth information on paper, consult International Paper Company's Pocket Pal.

Maximizing Your Frequencies

The name of the game is getting the best-looking images on your pages, right? But like any other game, this one also has its rules and regulations. To attain higher frequencies, you have to control the factors that affect spot gain. To preserve the number of gray levels as you raise the screen frequency, you must limit spot gain and raise the output resolution as well. When enough thought and care go into planning and executing your work, you can reach the level of quality you strive for.

You usually can't render halftone screens on an inkjet without sending it a pre-halftoned bitmap image or by using PostScript RIP software which turns images into bitmaps for you. If you use these methods and high-quality paper stock coated specifically for inkjet printers, the printer may be capable of screen frequencies comparable to those achievable by a good photocopier or laser printer.

24

Who Does the Halftone?

PRINTERS AND SOFTWARE

When you need to print a job, it's usually best to let a PostScript printer carry out halftoning for you. But in certain special situations, you might apply halftoning from your image-editing or layout software.

When you print to a PostScript output device, you almost never have to think about when the halftoning happens, or who does it, because PostScript manages it all for you. You simply build publications, specify tints, place scanned images, and then print. Your software's Print dialog box (**Figure 24-1**) may let you inspect and specify the halftone screen frequency, angles, and possibly the spot shapes available to you in the output device.

When your software prints via the operating system, it passes this information to the printer's PostScript interpreter, which applies your settings as it turns those grays into halftones. This method of halftoning

usually produces the best results with the least amount of work, particularly when you use a high-end imagesetter.

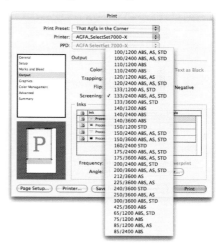

Figure 24-1 Choosing from a device's halftone options in Adobe InDesign CS

Halftoning in Software

There are times when it's advantageous or necessary for your software to do the halftoning prior to sending the job to the printer. Here are a few reasons why you might want the software do the halftoning:

▶ Your printer or raster image processor (RIP) doesn't support PostScript.

▶ You want to use unconventional halftoning settings for a special effect.

▶ You want a halftone effect to apply to individual objects, not to an entire publication.

▶ You want to use Photoshop to make the halftone.

▶ You're using a special RIP in place of the screening that's native to the output device, such as stochastic screening. (We discuss stochastic screening in Chapter 26.)

We've address how to deal with halftoning methods that aren't built into the printer in "What Overrides What," later in this chapter. That section can help you understand how your custom halftones interact with other types of halftoning that software and hardware may be trying to apply.

Halftoning on Non-PostScript Devices

Non-PostScript printers typically don't know *bubkes* about halftoning. That's because halftone dots aren't always the best solution for desktop printer output—halftoning is a process specifically designed for printing presses. Inkjet printers, like those made by Epson and Canon, generally use a dithered (or *stochastic*) screening technique because it tends to appear smoother and be more effective on the paper types used in those printers by consumers.

So if non-PostScript printers reproduce tones using methods that are better matched to them than halftoning, why would you want to make them use halftones? Well, that depends on your goal. If you're using a non-PostScript printer for final output and you want the best possible print it can make, it's probably best to let the printer use its built-in method of reproducing tones and colors.

However, it may make sense to force a non-PostScript printer to produce halftones when you're using that device to prepare materials for a medium where halftones are preferred. You might be making screens for printing silk-screened T-shirts, which generally use screen frequencies from 35 to 65 lines per inch, a range that a desktop printer can easily achieve. If the device is capable of high resolution, it may be acceptable to use it to create plates for moderate-quality press runs like business cards or newsletters.

To output halftones on a non-PostScript printer, you need a way to bypass or override the device's default screening and then replace it with halftone screens you create and send to the printer. You can generate your halftones using special third-party RIP software or by manually creating pre-halftoned bitmaps in a program like Photoshop (see "Halftoning Manually in Photoshop," later in this chapter).

When you create halftones manually, you may not achieve the same degree of precision and control that you'd enjoy using a true PostScript output device for halftones. This is due to the complex issues that affect the ability to achieve the exact screen ruling and angle you want. (We describe those issues in Chapter 21, *Frequency vs. Gray Levels*, and Chapter 29, *Angle Strategies*.)

Some non-PostScript desktop laser printers may reproduce tones using halftone dots. While the halftones may appear quite similar to PostScript halftoning, don't expect the results to match exactly what a PostScript printer would produce.

Halftones as Effects

Halftones are similar to the re-bar inside reinforced concrete: They are essential for holding up the building, but you're never supposed to see them. Yet an artist who likes to expose what's hidden might decide to use re-bar as the focal point of a sculpture.

You can take the same approach with halftones, blowing up halftone dots to give an image a Roy Liechtenstein pop-art look (**Figure 24-2**). This takes halftones across the line dividing production and art, using halftones as pure effects rather than as a way to structure image data for optimum reproduction. Unlike production halftones, you typically want to apply a halftone effect to specific images, not to everything in a publication.

Image editors like Photoshop normally have multiple options for applying a halftone effect. You can specify halftone options when applying a halftone effect filter or converting an image to a 1-bit bitmap. (For more effects, see the next chapter, *The Glorious Spot.*)

Figure 24-2 The Color Halftone filter in Photoshop CS: original image (left), with filter applied (right)

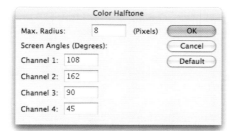

If you are working on a CMYK job, convert the image to CMYK before applying the Color Halftone filter so that the cyan, magenta, yellow, and black dots are on the correct channel from the get-go.

Halftoning Manually in Photoshop

Photoshop CS provides several ways for you to control the conversion of continuous tones to halftones. The options in the following list affect different stages of the imaging process, and specifying halftone settings in one place may override halftone settings you set somewhere else. We talk about this override hierarchy in the next section, "What Overrides What."

Print with Preview/Output options. You can specify halftone attributes using the Print with Preview dialog box (**Figure 24-3**). This is a useful option if you are printing a single image directly from Photoshop to an imagesetter or other PostScript output device. Save the image as an EPS file if you plan to import the image into another program and print it on a PostScript printer.

To change halftone settings, select Print with Preview from the File menu. Check the Show More Options box, then select Output from the popup menu. Click the Screen button, and then uncheck Use Printer's Default Screens. You can then specify the screen frequency, angle, and dot shape for each CMYK channel. If you click the Auto button, Photoshop works out the optimum screen frequency and angle for each channel.

Color Halftone filter. From the Filter menu, select Pixelate, and then select the Color Halftone filter. This filter gives you that 1960s pop-art look. In the Color Halftone dialog box Max. Radius refers to the size of the halftone dot in pixels (**Figure 24-3**). The default screen angles correspond to the traditional angles for color separations (see Chapter 28, *When Grids Collide*).

If the image is hard to recognize after applying the Color Halftone filter, select Undo, and try upsampling the image before applying the filter again.

Using Photoshop also allows you to use halftone effects for particular images in a document in which you want all of the other images and screen to use conventional halftones.

Figure 24-3
Halftone Screens options when printing from Photoshop CS

Bitmap mode conversion. This method works well for jobs that don't require color separation for two reasons: it only works on grayscale images, and the end result is always a 1-bit bitmap.

In Photoshop, choose the Image menu's Mode submenu, and then choose Bitmap. (If the Bitmap command isn't available, make sure the image is currently in 8-bit Grayscale mode.) In the Bitmap dialog box (**Figure 24-4**), enter an output resolution. For high-resolution devices, you don't need more than 1200–1440 dpi. Choose a value that divides evenly into the device resolution. Then from the Method pop-up menu,

The screen options in the Print dialog box are sensitive to interactions with the equipment you send it to—everything from the imagesetter's driver software to the idiosyncrasies of the screen frequencies and angles produced by a particular imagesetter. To make sure your custom settings produce the results you want, consult with your service bureau and run tests on the imagesetter before you run (and are billed for) the actual job.

choose Halftone Screen. In the Halftone Screen dialog box, specify a Frequency, Angle, and Shape.

This method is useful for creating halftones for black-and-white desktop laser printers or for special effects. Although this method won't preserve an image's original colors, you may be able to use your image editor or layout program to colorize the resulting halftoned bitmap or assign it to a spot color plate.

If you're working with an image that was originally in color and the bitmap version lacks definition, it may help to increase or otherwise adjust the contrast of the grayscale version before converting it to a bitmap.

What Overrides What

Whether or not you're a control freak, you're going to end up wanting to control your halftone screens at various stages of your work. You might want the picture of Aunt Jean to be a 45-degree, 40-lpi image; that photo of Uncle Izzy to be much coarser; and all the other tints on your page to have 133-lpi screens. So how do you go about controlling those screens, making sure the right screen comes out at the right part of the process?

The answer is (you saw this coming, right?): it depends. Screening controls work differently depending on the combinations of hardware and software. However, there is a basic hierarchy we can set down that specifies which screening controls override which others—in other words, which controls predominate. If you want special screening to apply to one job, you might apply the settings using the controls for the printer driver or Print dialog box. But if you want an object to use special halftone settings in any document where that object is used, apply the settings to that object.

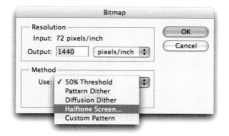

Figure 24-4
Converting
an image to a
bitmapped halftone
in Photoshop CS

Table 24-1 shows, in brief, the order in which screening controls override each other. Let's look at each item in order.

Vendor-specific methods. If you're printing to an imagesetter that uses a specialized screening technique like Agfa Balanced Screening or Heidelberg HQS, you may not get the screen settings you expect. These techniques use screening "filters" that catch all screening instructions and replace the frequency/angle combinations with the closest settings that are available in their optimized sets. These screening technologies can override all the screen-

ing you specify, whether it's in an object, an application, or a driver.

If custom screening instructions exist anywhere in your document, check with your service bureau to ensure that the custom screening won't be overridden. Sometimes specifying an odd screen can cause problems, too. Heidelberg uses 102 and 108 lpi to turn on different levels of stochastic screening in the imagesetter's RIP! It's unlikely you'd choose these frequencies, but beware, nonetheless.

Output device default. Every PostScript output device has a built-in default screen setting. That means that if you print a plain ol' job with no halftone screen settings in it, you get that device's defaults for the whole job. On imagesetters and other devices with hard disks, those defaults can be changed.

Printer driver. Printer drivers are the software modules that an operating system uses to "drive" printers; PostScript drivers actually write much or all of the PostScript code that gets sent to the printer. Halftone settings are minimal in print drivers, although the Windows XP PostScript driver allows you to choose between printer defaults and choosing your own screen frequency and angle.

Table 24-1
What overrides
what (Upper items
override lower
items)

Where applied	Affects screening of		
	Individual objects	**Entire document**	**All documents**
Vendor-specific methods			●
Output device default			●
Printer driver			●
Application (using Print dialog box)		●	
Objects within publications	●		
EPS files (embedded)	●		
Objects inside EPS files	●		

Application (using Print dialog box). Many applications provide control over halftone screens for your print jobs (as we cover in "Halftoning in Software," earlier in this chapter). Halftone screen control could be located in a variety of places depending on the application. In graphics applications, you often find two sets of halftone controls: one that allow the program to set halftone values that bypass the printer and driver settings; and another that directly controls the printer and driver settings themselves. In the former case, you might be sending custom halftones; in the latter, setting the printer's screen frequency.

Objects within publications. In some applications—FreeHand and CorelDraw, for example—you can select individual objects (text or graphics) and set a screen for those objects. In others, such as Page-Maker and QuarkXPress, you can apply screens to individual bitmapped images. These are called *object-level settings*, and they override the *application-level settings*, which apply to the rest of the job.

EPS files. Almost every program lets you save pages as EPS files (even if the pro-gram doesn't, PostScript printer drivers do). These files can be saved with halftone screening information included. When you place this file in another program, those internal screening instructions override any screening controls set by the program you're printing from. The custom screen-ing affects only the EPS that contains the instructions. The application, driver, or device defaults apply to the rest of the job.

Objects within EPS files. An EPS file that contains screening instructions can also include individual elements within the file that have *their own* screening instructions. For example, an EPS from Macromedia FreeHand might have a gray box that has an object-level halftone screen applied to it. The EPS file's settings apply to the whole graphic, but are overridden for individual objects that have their own settings within the EPS file.

Streamlining the Process

It's true, you might not need to know the detailed mechanics of who does the half-toning, when, and how. But the time will come (probably tomorrow) when you will. By understanding when and where half-toning happens, you can really control the process, and get the kind of results you want without overrunning your hard disks, clogging up your laser printers, and short-circuiting your imagesetter.

Halftoning Late in the Process

In Chapter 13, *Getting Good Color*, we point out that images retain maximum color flexibility when you convert them to an output-specific color space as late in your workflow as possible, because converting to an output-specific color space is usually a one-way street. It's the same with halftones. Once you convert an image from continuous tones to halftones, converting the image in the other direction will never recover the same level of quality. If there's any possibility that the job will be printed again under different conditions, avoid converting a scan to a halftone manually—leave that job to the output device or its printer driver (unless you are creating a special effect). Similarly, you haven't heard us talk about generating halftoned images directly from your scanning software, because doing so usually locks down the image too early in the process.

25

The Glorious Spot

SPOT SHAPES FOR QUALITY AND SPECIAL EFFECTS

Although it's at the very heart of the half-tone, we rarely hear designers talk about the spot, even in the most heated discussions on reproducing images.

We understand. In the majority of printing situations, spot shape is admittedly a minor quality factor. In the olden days before computer-to-plate (CTP) publishing, halftone dots were so abused on the way to print that even carefully created elliptical spots (or whatever) might just as well have been simple round blobs. CTP makes it easier to take a spot from conception straight onto the printed page with fewer intermediary steps.

In either the older paper–film–plate or newer CTP production workflows, it's still worth looking at spot control for specific purposes. If you're producing cosmetics catalogs, want to create special halftone effects, or need to solve tonal shift problems, controlling the halftone spot shape may be just the ticket.

On the Spot

As we mention in Chapter 20, *Frequency, Angle, and Spot Shape*, you can create halftone spots in a number of different shapes. Although you might want to create special-effect screens for design reasons—which we discuss at the end of the chapter—it's more likely that you will choose spot shapes to minimize spot variation in the reproduction process, and avoid a phenomenon called optical jump.

Optical Jump

Back in Chapter 22, *Reproducing Halftones*, we explain how halftone spots can fill empty areas that represent shadow

Figure 25-1
Optical jump

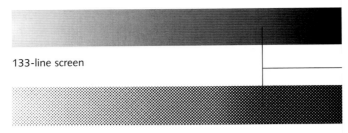

133-line screen

15-line screen

Note the optical jump at around 75-percent gray, where the halftone spots start to touch.

detail if you don't adjust your tonal values accordingly. That merging can result in an apparent jump in gray level. **Figure 25-1**, for instance, shows a smooth blend from black to white. At about the 75-percent point, however, where the halftone spots meet and begin to merge, there's an apparent jump in the smoothness of the blend.

You can reduce optical jump by choosing your spot shape—especially important when you're working with blends (or graduated fills, or fountains, or whatever you want to call them) and with photographs that include smooth transitions in the midtones (as in Caucasian faces).

Spot Variation

You might also want to consider spot shape because different spots fare differently in the tortuous path through the reproduction process. As we've noted before, spots tend to vary in size as they move through the process. Most spots get bigger (spot gain), though some very small spots (5 or 10 percent and below) tend to disappear entirely. The shape of the spot can affect the variation because some spots retain their shapes well in highlight areas, some in the midtones, and some in shadow areas.

Spot Shapes

PostScript offers several kinds of spots, each of which has distinct characteristics. Let's look at the six most common kinds of spots you might use or encounter.

Round Spots

The simplest halftone spot is round (**Figure 25-2**). The spot starts small, and increases in area until it fills the halftone cell. The round spot fares well in light tints and highlight areas; 5- and 10-percent tints with round spots are less likely to wash out and vanish. The round spot is especially prone to optical jump, however, and to serious spot gain in dark tints and shadow areas.

The first problem with the round spot is that all four sides of a round spot touch its neighboring spots all at once—at a given tint level. So at about 75 percent, where all four sides meet, there's a marked optical jump.

The second problem occurs in the dark tint areas (over 80 percent or so). The round spot that held the ink in place so well in highlight areas is now touching other spots. The technical term for the white shape between the spots (the area not covered by ink) is "that strange square pointy thing that looks like a diamond in a deck of cards." The fine, pointy areas in this shape have a tendency to fill in with ink, obliterating the subtle differences in dark tones and clogging up everything to black.

Other than the original PostScript version 23 Apple LaserWriters sold in the late 1980s, there are almost no printers that use this simple round spot. However, if you don't use a PostScript output device and are relying on your scanning, image-processing, or page-layout software to make

Figure 25-2
Spot shapes

Gradient

Round Spot

Diamond Spot

Elliptical Spot

Square Spot

Cross Spot

your halftones (see Chapter 24, *Who Does the Halftone?*), there's a reasonable chance that these simple spots are the only option. You can check by printing a graduated tint from black to white with a coarse screen frequency, and examining it carefully.

The Transforming PostScript Spot

Starting long ago, with PostScript version 38, PostScript devices started using a variation on the round spot as their default. It actually changes shape as it gets bigger, so we call it a transforming spot (we discuss another transforming spot—the transforming elliptical spot—later in this chapter). In *PostScript Screening: Adobe Accurate Screens*, author Peter Fink calls this spot a Euclidean spot.

This PostScript spot starts out round, then at around 50-percent gray it chang-

es shape, first becoming square, and then inverting so that instead of a big black round spot, it appears as a small white spot on a black background. This is similar to the effect you'd get if you were creating halftones traditionally (photographically).

This spot is less prone to spot gain than a normal round spot, because the round white spot in dark areas doesn't fill in with ink as easily as the strange square pointy thing. However, in many cases, it makes the optical jump problem even worse because there's a definite visual effect made by the checkerboard at around the 50-percent mark. This effect is especially noticeable in small graduated blends because the gray levels are densely packed in a small space.

Oval Spots

In another attempt to solve the problems of round spots, some programs produce an oval spot. This shape reduces the optical jump somewhat, because there are two meeting points—first where the ends meet and next where the sides meet. So instead of a single, large optical jump at 70 percent, you get two lesser optical jumps, at about 50 and 80 percent (the percentages where the ends and sides touch vary depending on how elongated the oval is).

While the oval spot has some advantages (like the round spot, it holds up well in highlight areas), it's really just a poor imitation of the true elliptical spot, which we discuss next. An oval spot is the shape you get when you choose the Elliptical Spot in QuarkXPress. Other programs may also use an oval spot when what you really want is elliptical. Again, you can tell what you're getting by printing out a sample at a low screen frequency (coarse enough to see the spots easily).

Elliptical Spots

Lithographers and screen printers have used an elliptical or "chain" spot (**Figure 25-2**) for years because it effectively battles both optical jump and spot variation. First of all, note that the elliptical spot is not really an ellipse. It's more of a rounded-corner diamond—slightly squashed, or elongated, so it's a bit bigger in one direction than in the other. The shape addresses the problem of optical jump very nicely because—like the oval dot—there are two meeting points: at the ends, and on the sides. So you end up with two smaller optical shifts—at about 50 and 80 percent—instead of one big one at 70 percent. Also, since the pointy ends of the diamonds merge slowly, the optical jump is less marked.

The elliptical spot holds up pretty well in dark areas, because the area that remains white is shaped like a diamond, as well. That shape doesn't fill in as easily as the strange square pointy thing that results with round and oval dots. It still doesn't hold up quite as well as a round or oval white area, however.

Note that this elliptical spot is not very elongated—it's actually close to a rounded-corner diamond—because if it was very elongated, you'd end up with something that looked like a line screen (or a chain-link screen, or what some lithographers call a corduroy screen) in tints between about 35 and 65 percent (read: really ugly).

Transforming Elliptical Spots

The best halftone spots we've seen are the transforming elliptical spots that Photoshop creates when you select the Ellipse option. The transforming elliptical spot starts out as an oval, changes into an elliptical spot at around 45 percent, then inverts, appearing as an oval white spot on a black background.

Transforming elliptical spots have all the advantages of elliptical spots in that they avoid optical jumps in the midtones, but they have the advantages of oval spots in highlight and shadow areas. Light areas don't wash out, and dark areas don't clog up. The only tiny improvement we'd hope for is that there be one more transformation—from oval to round at about 15 and 85 percent, since round spots are even better than oval for holding the ink in light areas, and holding out the ink in dark areas. Well, maybe someday.

Square Spots

Square spots (**Figure 25-2**) are sometimes used in high-quality color catalog work, because they give the impression of sharpness—especially in the midtones that are so important to cosmetic photography and the like—without having to use a whole lot of sharpening on an image (see Chapter 15, *A Sharper Image*, for more on sharpening and its problems). They give this impression partially because the corners of the dots suggest sharpness to our visual system, but also because they result in an optical jump in the midtones. That optical jump gives the midtones contrast—notably in human faces—and makes them look "sharp."

Figure 25-3
Line screen

Square spots have also been used traditionally in photoengraving for letterpress printing. Many programs offer the option of using a square spot. Though it's mainly useful for the somewhat specialized worlds of catalog and letterpress printing, it's also useful for creating special-effect screens, which is what we cover next.

Special-Effect Spots

Up to this point, this chapter has concentrated on spots for run-of-the-mill halftoning situations—for reproducing photographs and tints using relatively high screen frequencies (50 lpi and higher). However, when you get into low screen frequencies where you can actually see the spot shape, it's another world. In this world, spots can be fun, fun, fun. You can use them to produce trendy and hip designs, and to give photographs an eye-catching, stylized look.

You can use any of the spot shapes discussed above at low screen frequencies, of course, but there are some spot shapes that are useful only in really coarse screens (like under 20 lpi). Let's look at a few of these popular special-effect spot shapes.

Line screens. A line screen, in which the halftone appears to be made of straight lines, is a commonly used special halftone effect. There's really nothing special about it: it's also just a pattern of spots. It's just that each spot is shaped like a little line. The little line spots blend with each other to form long lines through the image (**Figure 25-3**).

Other special-effect screens. You're not confined to Photoshop's dot shapes if you want to create special-effect screens. You can buy plug-ins like Cutline or EtchTone (**www.andromeda.com**) that can apply line screens which simulate engraving effects (**Figure 25-4**). However, there's a difference between the look you get from running a plug-in filter and the screen effects you see in portraits published in *The Wall Street Journal*—the artists at the Journal draw the lines by hand to follow the contours of the face.

There are also a number of other special-effect spots you can create in PostScript—triangles, donuts, diamonds, pinwheels, and so on. The problem is that to create them, you have to be proficient in writing spot functions in PostScript-language code, and that's a lot harder than running a filter. Also, note that some PostScript imagesetters, especially those that are called "Post-Script compatible" (that is, they aren't licensed from Adobe, but carry out most

Figure 25-4
Andromeda Cutline and EtchTone

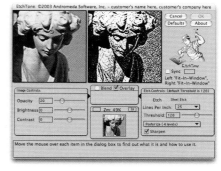

of the same functions as Adobe PostScript) can choke on PostScript patterns or produce bizarre results you didn't expect.

If you use any type of screen for a special effect, remember that it's only useful at a low line screen where the pattern is apparent to the unaided eye. There's no reason to use these at high screen frequencies.

Photoshop patterned screens. Here's another way to make a custom halftone screen using Adobe Photoshop:

1 Make a new grayscale image in Photoshop with the height and width you want the pattern to appear. For example, if you want a 10 lpi custom screen, make a file .1 inches tall and .1 inches wide. The resolution should be at least 800 spi—we usually use 1200 spi—though it should not be higher than your final printer resolution.

2 Create a pattern in this file that has a wide spectrum of tones, from black to gray to white. For instance, you could draw a crescent moon and run a Gaussian blur on it.

3 Select all the pixels and choose Define Pattern from Photoshop's Edit menu; give the pattern a name.

4 Now open a grayscale image that you want to halftone, choose the Image menu's Mode submenu, and then choose the Bitmap item. In the Bitmap dialog box, choose Custom Pattern

and pick your pattern from the popup menu. Make sure the Output Resolution you've set in the Bitmap dialog box is the same as the resolution you picked in Step 1.

When you click OK, the image becomes halftoned using the pattern as a custom spot shape. The darker pixels in the pattern are "turned on" first (in lighter areas), and the lighter pixels are "turned on" later (in darker areas).

You can do this for a color image, too, but you must first split the channels up into multiple files (use the Split Channels command in Photoshop's Channels palette), convert each to a bitmap, convert them back to grayscale, and finally use the Merge Channels feature (again, in the Channels palette) to put them back into a color file. This is one of those tips that takes longer to explain than it does to actually perform!

That Hits the Spot

Altering a halftone spot shape won't help much to get rid of a moiré problem (see Chapter 28, *When Grids Collide*) or improving the appearance of a lousy scan. In fact, the spot shape probably isn't even something that most people will see. Like good typography, the spots should rarely stand out and announce their presence. But if you're interested in high-quality work or in creating special effects in your halftone images, modifying spot shape can help.

26

Stochastic Screening

HALFTONING ALTERNATIVES

Figure 26-1
Round halftones (top) and stochastic screening (bottom)

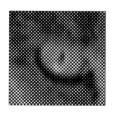

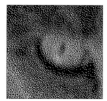

You probably noticed that our traditional recipe for halftoning was spiced up a notch by veiled promises of an exotic flavor called *stochastic screening*. If this has whetted your appetite, watch out: the plate is hot. A halftone is a black-and-white simulation of gray using different-sized spots. But who says you have to make grays that way?

Stochastic screening is also called *FM* (Frequency Modulated) screening. It's a method of creating halftones that better reproduces detail and can print with more than four colored inks while avoiding ugly patterns and moirés. Instead of regularly spaced halftone spots, stochastic screens appear like a random diffusion dither of spots, with more spots in darker areas and fewer spots in light areas (**Figure 26-1**).

While stochastic screening has made inroads into the prepress market, its big-gest impact has been on desktop inkjet printers, where methods based on stochastic screening are nearly universal and halftone spots are rarely used.

Why Go Stochastic

Traditional halftones are a pretty clunky way to reproduce images: Image detail is lost, especially at halftone screens below 150 lpi, and patterning may occur in color images if the halftone grid doesn't print at exactly the correct angle or if you try to print with more than four colors. Stochastic screening solves these issues while raising other concerns.

Stochastic Advantages

The limitations and disadvantages of traditional halftones are the corresponding benefits of stochastic screens. The stochastic screen has no angle, frequency, or shape. There are no tonal jumps or places where straight lines get fuzzy. And because you're working at the effective resolution of the output device—1200 dpi or higher—you can actually work with lower sample resolutions in your images without loss of quality.

Hey, Hey, No Moiré

We're getting a little ahead of ourselves in talking about moirés, or patterns that appear when halftone screens are overlaid at certain angles—we illustrate that concept in Chapter 28, *When Grids Collide*. But because there aren't any grid angles (or grids) with stochastic screening, there aren't any patterns that can results from clashes among colors printed at different angles. That means you can print with more than the four CMYK colors without fear of patterning. For example, postage stamps in Canada are printed with stochastic screening because they combine as many as 11 different inks and require very fine detail to be reproduced.

Stochastic screening also eliminates a kind of patterning called *content moirés*, which may occur when a grid appears in an image—like the knit in a sweater. These content moirés are insidious because they sometimes don't show up in proofs. Printing traditional halftones at very high line screens solves this problem, but stochastic screening retains the detail of the original pattern without causing a moiré, so you don't have to pay as much attention on press

 Unfortunately, there is no industry-wide term to describe the small element used in stochastic screening. We often use "speck" to differentiate it from a traditional halftone "spot." However, because these specks are typically clusters of device dots—just like traditional spots—we just as often say "spot." In some cases, the stochastic speck is actually a device dot (the smallest mark a device can make), but we still prefer speck or spot.

nor do you need to track down a fine-art printing house. One large-circulation knitting magazine we know of uses stochastic screening for this reason.

Plus, because there aren't overlapping spots, you lose rosette patterns as well. Press registration has a wider latitude with stochastic screening because it's harder to see when it's off.

Detail Definition

Is it God or the Devil in the details? Neither—it's spots that make or break detail. Images with fine detail—like a person's hair, grass, texture of clothing, or other natural objects—require high-frequency halftone screens to even approach a photographic feel. The reason is that detail in traditional halftones is limited to the line screen (it's like having 150 pieces of detail per inch in a 150 lpi halftone). Stochastic screening retains detail better because the detail can be resolved down to the spot or printer resolution. For example, you can easily have 300 or more pieces of detail per inch.

Tonal Shift and Color Fidelity

Halftone spots reach a point in their tonal scale when they become large enough to start touching their neighbors. You can monkey with spot shape—elliptical instead of round, supercells instead of a regular grid—but you're still left with a point at which tonal values jump as the ink fills in and the interstices are suddenly white holes in a black grid. Stochastic screening doesn't suffer from this problem, because there is no discrete tonal point at which specks start to touch. The distribution of specks allows better color fidelity and a smoother tonal range because of this.

The quarter-tone and three-quarter-tone values tend to have the most spot gain, but the gain is diffuse, avoiding real jumps. The gamma curves that are device-, paper-, and even press-dependent for creating stochastic-screened images can take the pain out of this as well.

Lower Resolutions

Stochastic screening lets you get equivalent results with lower-resolution images (fewer samples per inch) and lower-resolution output (fewer printer dots per inch). In theory, a 150-spi image output with stochastic screening at a high resolution should appear equal to a 225-spi (or even 300-spi) image output at 150 lpi using halftone spots. The reason: both are reproducing 150 differences in tonal value per inch. This is why those crummy 72-spi images from Web sites print significantly better using stochastic screening than with traditional halftones.

Figure 26-2 shows a side-by-side comparison of a conventional halftone and a stochastic version of the same image.

You know you can use a 1.5:1 spi:lpi ratio for traditional halftones, but what resolution do you really need for stochastic screens? Just because you can use a lower resolution doesn't mean you should. If you're trying to achieve maximum quality, you should probably shoot for a resolution between 300 spi and 450 spi (the human eye doesn't really resolve detail smaller than that anyway).

Steps Forward

Stochastic screening is possible and desirable today because of several simultaneous developments in printing and graphics arts preparation.

Computer-to-Plate (CTP)

Computer-to-plate (CTP) output removes all the intermediate photographic and contact steps that can introduce errors, spot gain, and density problems (see Chapter 22, *Reproducing Halftones*). Without these steps, it's easier to reliably image stochastic patterns.

CMYK+ Color

To get better, more saturated, more accurate printing of color images, several systems came out that use CMYK plus two or more other inks, including High-Fidelity (Hi-Fi), Pantone Hexachrome, and six-color inkjet printers with lighter-colored cyan and magenta inks. The problems with printing four inks using halftones are difficult enough (see Chapter 28, *When Grids Collide*), but with five or more colors it's almost impossible to avoid moiré patterns. Stochastic screening removes the moiré hurdle by not having a grid or angles that interfere and cause patterning.

Better Graphic Arts Materials

The plate material or lithographic film that's exposed, output, or contacted has a resolution of its own, which is a chemical limitation. In the '90s, these materials improved, allowing reproduction of higher halftone screens and tiny stochastic spots with more reliability and consistency.

Processing Power

It can take a lot of horsepower to process images into stochastic patterns—much more than halftoning. The ever-doubling performance of computer chips lets even entry-level imagesetters and personal computers run software that can create high-resolution (1200 dpi or higher) stochastic output without real delays versus conventional halftoning.

High End or Low End?

Some folks see stochastic screening as a technique for high-end output, like coffee table books. However, if you can already afford to use a waterless press running plates with traditional halftones at 200–300 lpi, there's little reason to bother with stochastic screening. Instead, stochastic screening makes more sense for catalogs, magazines, direct mail pieces, and brochures. The fine detail and rich color that stochastic screening makes possible also increases the "touch" value of the pictures in the catalog—turning more browsers into buyers.

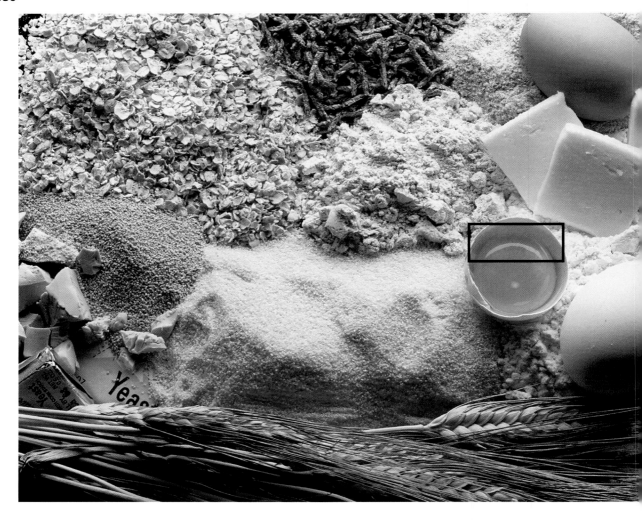

A conventionally screened image above, with a detail from the magenta plate called out. Halftone spots create the tonal values.

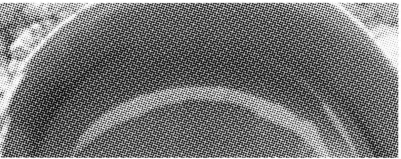

Figure 26-2 Conventionally screened halftone vs. stochastically screen image

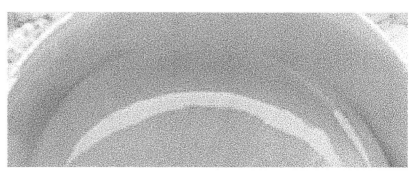

The same image printed in four colors as a stochastic pattern using Isis Imaging's Icefields software without linearization. (No comparison of color accuracy is intended.) The detail at right shows the same magenta plate detail made up of tiny concentrations of dots.

What's in This Spot?

As we mentioned earlier, stochastic screening works because there's no grid of spots. When you see many spots together, they look like a darker value than when you see just a few. But what are those stochastic spots made of? It turns out that these spots aren't actually that different after all.

Whether you're talking about traditional halftones or stochastic halftones, the spots have to be tiny to represent tonal values without being recognizable by the human eye. Printing in "draft" mode on a color inkjet printer usually produces spots that are big enough to see from a foot away or more. Try printing at "high quality" on glossy paper, and the spots are so small that the image appears to be continuous tone, like a photograph.

When it comes to stochastic screening on an imagesetter or platesetter, the spots may be even smaller—as small as 15–40 microns. That's 15–40 millionths of a meter (15–40 µm), or around .00125 of an inch. This is the size of a 2- or 3-percent traditional halftone spot at 150 lpi.

These stochastic specks are generally made up of "clusters" of device dots. For example, just like traditional halftone spots, a platesetter makes clusters of two or three device dots per side to create a single reproducible stochastic spot. However, while traditional halftone spots get larger and smaller, stochastic spots typically remain the same size. Of course, there is always a caveat: Some "hybrid" systems (which use "second-order" stochastic screening) now vary the size of these stochastic spots. They may even vary how "stochastic" the screen is, causing a single image to contain areas of stochastic dither and areas of a more regular grid.

Random Difficulties

We don't want you to think that printing stochastic screens is all wine and roses; there still are problems in knowing what results you will obtain in some areas of the printing process.

Proofing

For many years prepress professionals have complained that both film-based and digital proofing devices have a hard time showing what a stochastic image will look like when printed. The argument is that the stochastic spots are so small that the proofer can't hold them. True, the quick-and-dirty proofers down at Harry's Printing and Burger Hut probably can't. Stochastic screens are so fine that too much dust and smoke can cause problems.

But a high-resolution stochastic print (let's say, an FM screen from a 3360 dpi imagesetter, made of a cluster of 3 device dots per side, or 1120 dpi) is about the equivalent of a 200 lpi screen. Anyone comfortable with proofing a high-frequency traditional halftone should feel at home proofing a stochastic screen.

Radio, Radio

Here's a tidbit for those of you who liked physics in high school. Halftone screens are amplitude modulated (AM) while stochastic screens are frequency modulated (FM). It's just like AM and FM radio. With AM radio, the signal is a waveform that has cycles of identical duration that are equal distances apart; but the height of the waves changes, and that encodes the sound. FM radio varies the space between cycles to achieve the same effect.

AM and FM radio and screening have another thing in common. AM radio can use relatively low frequencies, in the 500- to 1200-kilohertz (thousands of cycles per second) range, because the amplitude is what's conveying the information. AM halftones can be created at relatively low frequencies as well, like 133 lpi in a grid using just 1270-dpi printers.

FM radio requires a much higher frequency, from about 88 to 108 megahertz (*millions* of cycles per second), because the information is being conveyed down near the resolution of the radio signal itself—the shifts from frequency to frequency requires a finer resolution to express sound. Stochastic screening likewise requires much higher resolutions to express itself—at least 800 to 1200 dpi versus just 133 or 150 lpi.

Spot or Speck Gain

Those tiny stochastic spots also result in somewhat more spot gain on press than traditional halftones. For example, where a traditional halftone might cause a 17-percent spot gain on press, the equivalent stochastic image might result in as high as 25- or 30-percent speck gain. However, that's not a problem as long as you compensate for the gain when preparing your images, just as you need to compensate for gain in traditional halftones. This is one area where requesting a test from your printer (on your particular paper stock) helps in the long run.

Speckling in Flat Colors & Highlights

The easiest way to identify a printed image that's been screened using stochastic algorithms is that the spot distribution, although close to random, looks like speckling (noise) in regions of flat colors and in highlights where the specks are more widely dispersed. For instance, in an image of a busy garden under a clear blue sky, the leaves and flowers in the garden may look incredible in a stochastic image, but the blue sky might look…well, oddly speckled. The larger the speck size, the more

obvious the speckling. Our eyes are used to seeing flat areas using traditional flat halftones, and the noise in the FM screen looks "wrong."

That's why some "second order" stochastic screens actually mix diffusion and grid systems together.

Dust

Remember that dust can be in the 15- to 30-micron range and appear in final printed pieces when you print on a press that can hold out the speck. This argues for reduced-dust, controlled environments for film- and platemaking. This might force you to use a printer for CTP or film output, or to find a service bureau that can produce output in those clean conditions—and pack and ship the film in an almost hermetic container.

Regular Patterns and Dithering

As we noted earlier in the chapter, there are other AM and FM screening terms besides the ones we've discussed so far, so let's take a slight detour to discuss two of these terms before finishing this chapter up.

Regular-Pattern Halftones

Regular-pattern halftones are similar to the halftones you know so much about now. However, instead of the "cluster" spots (where tonal values are represented by spots that grow from the middle out), the printer dots get turned on in the halftone cell in any order the software or you define. If you look at **Figure 26-3**, you can see how tonal values increase.

In PostScript output, this definition comes in the form of a halftone spot-function, which must be specially programmed in the PostScript. You can also create custom regular-pattern halftones in a program like Photoshop by converting grayscale images to Bitmap mode using a predefined Custom Pattern (see Chapter 25, *The Glorious Spot*). Ultimately, however,

Figure 26-3
Regular-pattern halftones

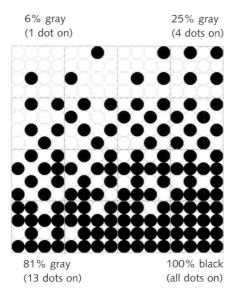

6% gray
(1 dot on)

25% gray
(4 dots on)

81% gray
(13 dots on)

100% black
(all dots on)

the only reason you'd want to use something like this is for a special effect. Note that custom PostScript spot functions are not supported by a number of non-Adobe PostScript printers (PostScript "clones" or "emulators").

Dithering

Dithering has been talked about in various chapters in this book already, and you may wonder what makes it different from stochastic screening. Stochastic screening relies on a pregenerated lookup table of 255 different cells while error diffusion is a random pattern of spots.

The distinction is critical only for high-resolution offset film and plates. At lower resolution, stochastic screening has too few printer dots and random dithers look better. And some dithers are better than others; using a Diffusion Dither in Photoshop will provide nowhere near the quality as a professional stochastic screen.

Collisions Ahead

We now leave the safe world of stochastic specks, where angle, frequency, and moiré simply don't exist, to go back into our workaday land of color shift, registration problems, and the collisions of grids. In the next chapter, *Band Aid*, we address how a journey of a thousand miles is stopped at the 255th step.

27

Band Aid

SMOOTHING THE STAIR STEPS

"Why can't I get a smooth graduated blend? Why are all these bands in my fountain? How can I get rid of this shade-stepping?" These questions get asked every day by desktop publishers. The problem is easy to see, especially in blends that extend over a large area (**Figure 27-1**). And it's usually almost as easy to fix.

We start this chapter by discussing how banding occurs, and then talk about how blends are made and how you can create them to avoid banding.

Shade-Stepping

Banding typically appears in blends because of the inherent limit in reproducing gray levels with digital halftones. As we discuss in Chapter 21, *Frequency vs. Gray Levels,* there are only so many levels of gray that you can achieve at a given screen fre-

 Before we go any further, for the sake of everyone's sanity, let's agree that the terms fountain, blend, degradé, vignette, *and* gradient *(or* graduated*) fill all refer to the same thing. Whatever you want to call it, this kind of fill is very popular among desktop publishers, especially among those working with illustrations. We'll use the term "blend" because it is most common and saves ink.*

quency and output resolution. For example, if you're printing at 133 lpi on a 1270-dpi imagesetter, you cannot achieve more than 92 levels of gray. So, when you're printing a nice, smooth blend that contains all 256

Figure 27-1
Banding in gradient fills

levels of gray, you're still only getting 92 of those grays. If the blend extends over a large enough area, each step is large enough that you actually see all 92 bands of gray.

What can you do about this? You can either fix the output side by lowering the screen frequency of your halftones or by printing on an imagesetter with a higher resolution (or both); or you can make changes in the input to avoid crossing these boundaries (described in "Making a Blend"). In many cases, you have to fix the output side to obtain a result anywhere close to what you want.

Let's look at the preceding example again. If we change the screen frequency from 133 to 80, we can achieve 252 levels of gray at 1270 dpi—which reduces banding considerably, but produces coarse, highly visible dots.

A better solution is to print the higher screen frequency on a 2540-dpi imagesetter, where we'd theoretically be able to print 366 levels of gray. But PostScript imposes a limit. If we went up to, say, 3360 dpi, we could have 640 levels of gray—a smooth blend, indeed. (See Chapter 21, *Frequency vs. Gray Levels*, for more details.)

When printing to a non-PostScript printer, the number of levels available depends on the screening method the printer uses. On a desktop inkjet printer, you typically get more levels by raising the printer driver's quality or resolution setting. On other types of output devices, you'll need to find out how many levels of gray or color the device can produce.

The Size of the Steps

There are two factors to consider when figuring out whether your blend will contain shade-stepping. If your blend doesn't contain about 256 levels of gray, there is an increased likelihood that banding will appear. Note that this banding is much less visible at coarser screen frequencies. However, often a bigger problem is how big each step is. Imagine 256 steps of gray from black to white over a 1-inch space. Each step is going to be really tiny, because each step is only ½₅₆ inch.

Okay, now stretch your imaginary blend out to 20 inches. Now each step has to be much bigger to fill the gap. You can figure out how big one step is by dividing the total length of the blend by the number of gray levels possible for that blend (which we just figured out in the previous section). For example, if you know that you only have 204 levels of gray possible for a blend over 10 inches, then you know that each step will be .05 inch (10 inches ÷ 204 steps).

If the step is big enough, it becomes obvious next to its neighboring steps. Typically, values between .01 inch and .03 inch (.25 to .75 millimeters, or 1 to 2 points) are small enough to blend together well. In the preceding example, the .05-inch step may be too large for a smooth blend, especially since you are not achieving a full 256 levels of gray.

Making a Blend

How you create a blend and the blend's inherent characteristics can have a big impact on whether you get banding, and how much. There are four cases to consider in which blends are involved. Each of these cases has unique parameters that can make the difference between a stairstepped affair and seamless gradation.

Blending Using Blend or Gradient Features

Some programs, such as Macromedia Free-Hand, do all the work for you; you just say, "Fill this box with a graduated blend from black to white" and it does it. **Figure 27-2** shows FreeHand's Graduated Fill option. Other programs, such as QuarkXPress, Adobe InDesign, Adobe Illustrator, and

Figure 27-2
The Graduated Fill option in FreeHand's Fill Inspector

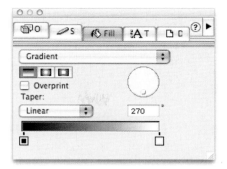

 Blends don't have to be confined to fills. You can use the Gradient palette in Adobe InDesign to apply a gradient to a stroke (line), if you ever find yourself needing such an effect.

CorelDraw, use similar techniques. These programs send PostScript instructions to the printer on creating the fill—the on-screen display is just a preview.

If you apply a graduated fill using a program's fill feature, the program should calculate the proper number of steps needed to print the blend without banding (see the next section). Some programs, such as Macromedia FreeHand, let you choose between a linear and a logarithmic fill. Because of the way the eye perceives light— see our density discussions in Chapter 2, *Scanners*—logarithmic fills often appear to have a smoother transition from black to white.

Blending by Creating Additional Objects

Some programs also give you tools for creating gradients a different way: by blending two objects. You select the two objects containing the beginning and ending tints, choose the number of steps you want in between, and the program creates that many new gradually shaded or colored objects between the two end points (**Figure 27-3**).

But how many steps should you use between the objects? The following formula makes it easy.

Number of steps = (output resolution ÷ screen frequency)^2 × percent change in color

We know this might be a daunting equation at first, but let's look at why it's really pretty easy. The first part of the equation is the same as the one we look at in Chapter 21, *Frequency vs. Gray Levels*. By dividing the output resolution by the screen frequency and then squaring that number, you find the number of gray levels that you can possibly print, limiting the total to no more than 256. Next, by multiplying that value by the percent change in your blend, you find the number of gray levels that are possible in your particular blend.

For example, you have a blend that transitions from 10-percent to 90-percent gray, or an 80 percent change in color. You're printing it on a PostScript Level 2 imagesetter at 2540 dpi with a 150 lpi screen. That calculates as 2540 divided by 150, or roughly 17, which when squared is about 287. Multiply that by 80 percent and you get 230 levels of gray. Contrast that with the number of possible tones to represent the range of 10 to 90 percent, or 80 percent

Figure 27-3
Creating a blend between two objects

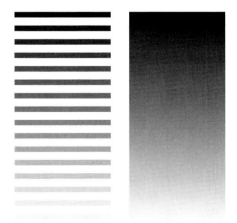

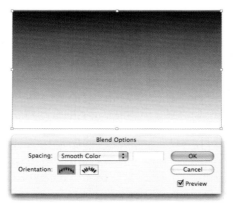

Figure 27-4 Blend Options dialog box in Illustrator

Figure 27-5
Photoshop's Gradient features

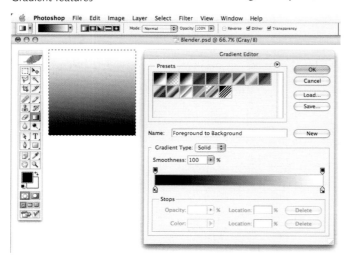

of 256, and you get 204. Because this is the maximum number of grays you could possibly achieve in this situation, there's really no need to use more steps than that in the blend (each step has its own gray level).

If the resulting number of steps causes gaps between objects, add more steps or make the objects wider. Otherwise, your blend will look like garbage. This formula simply ensures that you have *at least* enough steps to take advantage of 256 possible gray levels.

The Blend Options dialog box in Adobe Illustrator (**Figure 27-4**) calculates the number of steps needed for you. You often end up with 254 levels (the other two levels are those of the two original objects).

Color Blends

Remember that when you separate process colors, each plate becomes in essence a black-and-white image. That means that shade-stepping can and does occur on each plate separately. Therefore, when you're figuring out how likely it is that you'll get banding, you need to look at each color plate. Typically, banding is worst in the color with the smallest percent change. For example, if you're blending a color made of 70-percent cyan and 40-percent magenta to white, the magenta plate is more likely to band than the cyan because it's only using 40 percent of the available grays (see the equation earlier in this chapter).

On the other hand, if banding occurs on the yellow plate, chances are that it won't appear as prominently as it would on the cyan plate. Also, color blends are sometimes less likely to band because each color can mask the aberrations of the other. That is, the sum of the colors is smoother than each of the parts.

Blends in Bitmapped Images

Programs that work with bitmapped images, such as Adobe Photoshop and Corel Photo-Paint, create blends in a different way—on your computer, not in the PostScript processor. The interface is similar: you select options in the program that indicate a blend from this color to that color, and the program does it for you (**Figure 27-5**). However, because the program works with bitmapped images rather than objects (see Chapter 10, *What is a Bitmap?*), the blend is produced as a giant grid of dots, each of which can have a different gray level.

With bitmapped blends, the smoothness of the gradation is mostly dependent on the resolution and number of gray (or color) levels in the bitmap. If you're working with an 8-bit (256-gray) file or a 24-

Figure 27-6 Adding noise to a blend

Banding and Reproduction

Believe it or not, banding is one area where your final printed output may look better than what you see on screen or in a proof. We've seen many situations in which banding is obvious and annoying in Chromalins or MatchPrints, but completely invisible in the final printed output. The vagaries of printing mechanics—notably the spot variation we discuss in Chapter 22, *Reproducing Halftones*—actually tend to mask the banding, blurring the bands together so they're much less noticeable.

So, when there's a lot of spot variation—on uncoated stock and newsprint, with colored papers, and on web presses—this "band-blurring" is more pronounced. It's not a sure thing, however; sometimes you'll still get the banding effect even in these circumstances.

Getting Great Blends

When it comes right down to it, you probably shouldn't try to create blends larger than about 6 inches using an object-oriented illustration program like Illustrator, FreeHand, or CorelDraw—at least not in high-quality printing situations. If you expect more band-blurring in the print job, you can go up to nine or 10 inches. On the other hand, smaller blends work fine with these programs. If you need blends longer than that, create them in a bitmap-editing program, adding a little noise to smooth out the banding.

bit (16-million-color) file, and your image resolution is at least equal to halftone frequency, you should be fine.

There is a real advantage to creating blends in a bitmapped program as opposed to an object-oriented program: the ability to add "noise" that disguises banding. If you include in each gray level some pixels that are of a slightly different gray level, your eye merges all those pixels together, resulting in an apparently smoother blend (**Figure 27-6**).

Some output devices (such as those using PostScript 3) can add noise to vector gradient blends at printing time. If you're not using a device like this, you should create your blend in Photoshop and apply the Add Noise filter. In typical images, where the image resolution is about 1.5 or 2 times the halftone frequency, we suggest using a noise level of about 4 or 5. If the ratio is less, you might have to reduce the amount of noise.

28

When Grids Collide

AVOIDING PATTERNS AND MOIRÉS

Chain-link fences. Porch screens. Bad television anchor jackets. All around us are examples of big grids made of little, repeating squares. There's a fascinating optical illusion that happens with screens like these: it's called a moiré ("mwah-RAY") pattern (**Figure 28-1**).

Moiré patterns are caused by our eyes' perception of straight lines and repeating patterns. One grid, all by its lonesome, never has a problem with these patterns. It's when you have two or more grids overlay each other that the wires in your perceptual system may get crossed, and these little gremlins may start to appear.

One way to think about moiré patterns is by thinking of a pool of water. If you drop one stone in the water, you get a radiating circle of concentric waves. If you drop *two* stones in the water, however, you get a complex pattern of high points where

two waves meet and low points where two troughs meet. Moiré patterns are based on the same kind of *standing-wave* or *interference* pattern.

With scanning and halftoning, we're often faced with the kind of multiple overlaid grids that tend to result in moiré patterns. What are the halftones, after all? They are big grids of spots. What is scanning? It's turning a real-world picture into a grid of sample points. What is laser printing and imagesetting? It's laying down a grid of black dots. Everywhere we turn in the scanning and halftoning world, we find ourselves looking at grids. And, therefore, we all too often find ourselves looking at moiré patterns.

There are four main situations in which you might run into problems of conflicting patterns:

Figure 28-1
Moiré patterns

- ▶ Printing color separations, which in most cases involves overlaying two or more halftone screens

- ▶ Scanning and printing previously halftoned images

- ▶ Printing halftones of grayscale and color images that include regular patterns

- ▶ Printing black-and-white images that include repeating patterns

Color Separations

By far the most common cause of moiré patterns is improper screening in color separations. If the angles and frequencies of the overlaid screens aren't just right, moiré patterns result (**Figure 28-2**).

We discuss moirés in color separations later in this chapter and in Chapter 29, *Angle Strategies*.

Figure 28-2
Moiré patterning in process separation

Halftoning Halftones

When you see a photograph in print, it's most likely been halftoned. That's not the only way to print it, but it's the most common (see Chapter 26, *Stochastic Screening*). But scanners can't tell if an image is already halftoned; they just scan it in, sample by sample, as though it were a normal photograph. The halftone spots on the printed page aren't turned back into gray levels—they're scanned as collections of black samples.

For this reason, there are two opportunities for interference patterns: between the original screen and the scanner sample grid, and between the original screen (which is picked up by the scan) and the output screen. Fortunately, there are a few techniques you can use to reduce the patterns in the scanned image.

Fixing the Patterning

You can sometimes reduce the patterning in scanned images by adjusting the image scaling and output screen frequency, using trial-and-error until you get it to work. The idea is to create an integral relationship between the original's screen frequency and the output frequency (1:1, 2:1, etc.). However, if the screen angles don't match, that's another potential source of patterning. And unfortunately, it's a pretty darn hard thing to adjust for. A better solution (though still not perfect) is to eradicate the original halftone pattern before you print, using Photoshop, Corel Photo-Paint, or another program.

Photoshop. When our friend Jeff McCord agreed to produce a program for the Seattle International Film Festival a few years ago, he didn't realize that the artwork he needed to scan included many images that were pulled from previously printed material, even clippings on newsprint. If he learned anything from the job, it was how to scan, clean up, and print previously halftoned photographs using Photoshop.

His favorite method for grayscale images is to apply the Despeckle filter in Photoshop first. Then you can adjust levels and apply unsharp masking (see Chapter 12, *Tonal Correction*, Chapter 13, *Getting Good Color*, and Chapter 15, *A Sharper*

Image). The Despeckle filter is excellent for removing the weird traces of patterns in the scanned images. On the other hand, you have to be very careful with the Unsharp Mask filter (and other sharpening techniques) because they can re-accentuate the halftone pattern in the scan.

For scans of color halftones, Jeff likes to use Photoshop's Median filter with a specification of no more than 2 or 3 pixels. This filter has much the same effect in evening out the moiré patterning, but he finds it works better on color images.

Other people prefer other methods. Using blurring filters, followed by sharpening, often works well to remove some patterning. However, you lose detail, which you can't get back by sharpening. Similarly, downsampling the image (reducing its resolution) to as low as 25 percent of its original size and then upsampling it (interpolating samples) back up to its original size has much the same effect, and similar problems.

Note that people are often concerned with patterning they see on the screen with scans of previously halftoned images. However, you need to remember that the patterns you see at a 2:1 screen ratio may disappear when you look at the image at a 1:1 screen ratio. This is simply a conflict between the original screen and the monitor's pixel grid. The 1:1 screen ratio is the one you should pay attention to most.

Scanning software. Most scanning packages now include a *descreening* option; we mention it in Chapter 5, *How to Read Your Scanning Software*. In some scanning software, this feature uses an algorithm that tries to detect and fix the screening pattern. Other programs let you enter the line screen frequency of the original, which can make it easier for the software to detect the pattern; that is, if you're right about the original's screen frequency.

Content Moirés

A less common problem, but one that we think you should at least be aware of, arises when you're scanning images that themselves include repeating patterns—the tight weave in a close-up of a silk tie or the mesh screen on the front of an electric heater, for instance. These patterns can interfere with the grid of the printed halftone screen, resulting in *content moirés*. Fortunately, content moirés don't happen often, and they're rarely important if the object only has a small role in the picture.

You can correct for content moirés by adjusting the image size or the output screen frequency, once again seeking to establish an integral relationship between the image pattern and the output screen frequency. Unfortunately, with content moirés it's a trial-and-error process. Stochastic screening is another way to reduce content moirés by eliminating halftone grids altogether (see Chapter 26, *Stochastic Screening*).

Content moirés can also be a problem when printing screen shots containing patterns or dithered-color files like GIF images. In both cases, the source of the image (the monitor pixel grid) uses such a low resolution that the screen pixels display a visible pattern just by their nature. The effect is especially pronounced on monitors set to display 256 colors or less. Fortunately, today's high-bit displays allow Mac OS and Windows to use tones instead of patterns in their user interfaces, making monitor image moirés less common than they used to be. To minimize the chance of seeing this problem, before you take screen shots make sure the monitor is set to display more than 256 colors, and replace any patterns in the user interface with solid colors.

Black-and-White Bitmap with Repeating Patterns

Any black-and-white (or bilevel) bitmap that includes a repeating set of dots can cause patterning, because the pattern conflicts with the grid of laser printer or imagesetter dots. The worst offenders are images that are halftoned at scan time (see Chapter 24, *Who Does the Halftone?*). These scans—which are just big grids of black-and-white dots grouped into a regular pattern of halftone cells—result in a special kind of patterning. We call this—for want of a better name—*plaid patterning* (**Figure 28**-3).

Whether it's screen shots or scanned halftones, the solution for patterning in bilevel bitmaps is to scale the image so image resolution has an integral relationship to output resolution. That is, if you're printing on a 300-dpi printer, your images (at their final size, *after* they're placed on a page and scaled) should have a resolution of 100 dpi, 150 dpi, or whatever. There should be a 1:1, 2:1, or similarly integral relationship between image samples and printer dots.

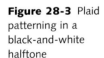

Figure 28-3 Plaid patterning in a black-and-white halftone

This requirement imposes limitations on the scaling percentages you can use for these types of images. The best advice is to decide in advance exactly what size you need an image to be on a page, then scale and crop images as you scan them,

We used to run into plaid patterning in screen shots of bilevel computer displays, but since displays have become high-bit we are probably more likely to encounter bilevel screen shots on handheld consumer devices like MP3 players or cheap PDAs.

rather than scaling them in your page-layout software. However, if you already have the scans and need to make them fit your spread, you can calculate the acceptable scaling percentages using the following formula:

```
Scaling percentage = original image
resolution ÷ output resolution × any
integer
```

Output resolution in this formula is for your *final output device*, not for your proofing device (if they're different, that is). You may still get plaid patterns on your proof output, but you won't when you imageset the file.

By substituting different integers in this formula, you can build a little table of acceptable scaling percentages for a job. Since different programs have different levels of percentage scaling accuracy, it's a good idea to test some images at different scaling percentages on your final output device.

Minimal Moirés

For the rest of this chapter, we talk about how halftone screens interact when you make color separations and overlay them on press. These overlaid screens provide the flexibility of color printing, but they can also pose real moiré problems. Moirés are mainly a problem with process color work, in which four (or even more) screens might be overlaid, but they are also a con-

Figure 28-4
Moiré patterns
with different
angle offsets

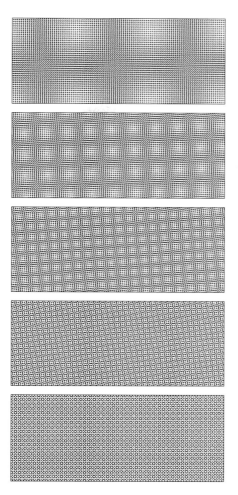

(though with asymmetrical spot shapes, the orientation of the spots varies around the full 360-degree arc, making it less likely for them to cause moirés). So the largest angle difference possible between two overlaid screens is 45 degrees. If you're creating duotones for a two-color job, the angles of the two color screens should be offset by 45 degrees. Put the dominant color—often black—at 75; the secondary color—typically lighter—should be at 30.

Continuing with this logic, the largest angle offset we could hope for between three screens is 30 degrees (90÷3). Angle offsets smaller than this produce moirés that are too large, hence too apparent.

But, hey: There are four process colors, not three. If you want the angle offsets to be at least 30 degrees, what do you do? Through years of trial and tribulation, the printing industry has standardized on a combination of four halftone angles: three at 30-degree offsets and one 15 degrees off. Cyan is at 15 degrees, black at 45, magenta at 75, and yellow at 0.

Because yellow is the lightest and least noticeable color, it can safely be set to 0 degrees, even though 0 degrees is a highly noticeable angle, and it's only 15 degrees from its nearest neighbor. Note that cyan is sometimes set at 105 degrees; however, with symmetrical spots it's really the same thing as 15 degrees (and even with asymmetrical spots, it doesn't make much difference).

When you overlay the four process colors using these angles, the resulting moiré patterns are as small as they can be. If these angles are off even slightly, however, you can run into big-time patterning problems. We discuss the problem of getting accurate frequencies and angles in the next chapter, *Angle Strategies*.

The Rosette

It's a popular misconception that when you overlay four halftone screens at the angles

sideration with spot-color work (especially with duotones and tritones), where two or three screens might collide. However, there are some angle combinations that minimize the optical illusion.

The larger the difference in angle between two overlaid grids, the smaller the resulting pattern, and the less apparent it is (**Figure 28-4**). So if one grid is at 0 degrees and another is at 5 degrees, there is a very apparent pattern. If you rotate the second grid to 45 degrees, the pattern shrinks to the point that—at a sufficient viewing distance—it seems to disappear.

Note that a 90-degree grid is essentially the same as one at 0 degrees, just as a 135-degree grid is the same as one at 45-degrees

Figure 28-5 An open-centered rosette

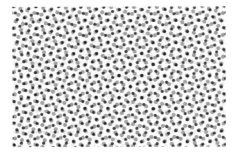

we just described, you don't get any patterning. You do, in fact, produce a pattern. It's just that the pattern is small and relatively innocuous, to the point where people don't call it a moiré; it's called a *rosette* (**Figure 28-5**).

Whenever you're printing halftones, you have a pattern of cells—the squares in the grid in which a halftone spot is formed. Since halftone spots are formed from the center of the cell and grow to the outsides, when you overlay a number of cells at different angles, the rosette forms a shape. Because of the rotation, it looks roughly circular. (You can only see rosettes clearly when the spots haven't grown too large.)

At low screen frequencies, the rosette pattern is quite evident, as any pattern would be. But at higher screen frequencies, the thousands of rosettes blend together to create a smooth "surface" for the image. At a sufficient viewing distance, the patterns blend together to give an impression of photographic detail.

There are two sorts of rosettes you can make in a four-color image: open-centered and close-centered (**Figure 28-5** shows an open-centered rosette).

Open-centered. Open-centered rosettes don't have a spot in the center of the rosette; this center is created by sliding the overlaid rotated screens to one direction or another to control where the rosette is formed. The open-centered pattern is sometimes called *robust* because it resists

color shifts in the image even when slight misregistration occurs. On the other hand, images with open-centered rosettes display a more visible pattern, and at lower screen frequencies tend to be somewhat lighter than similar images produced with closed-center rosettes. This makes sense because so much white paper shows through, and there's less spot gain due to ink overlap.

Because of the more pronounced pattern in open-centered rosettes, they are most appropriate for use at higher screen frequencies where the patterns are small and hard to see—150 lpi and higher. Agfa imagesetters use its Balanced Screening, which produces open-centered rosettes (but it can be coerced into producing closed-center rosettes by setting the imagesetter to positive and the imaging application to negative).

Closed-centered. A closed-center rosette pattern lets much less paper show through, so you have a better chance of color brilliance. Also, the rosette pattern is less apparent, so it's more usable at lower screen frequencies. However, registration is more critical; minor misregistration can cause significant color shifts. It also grows spot sizes by spreading ink more. Heidelberg's imagesetters use High-Quality Screening (HQS), which produces closed-centered rosettes. Note that a closed-centered rosette becomes an open-centered rosette in the highlights of an image.

Moiré Reducers

Moiré patterns can easily appear in your four-color images due to even minor flaws in either halftone angle or frequency. We talk about how to reduce those patterns in the next chapter, *Angle Strategies*, but we'd first like to discuss a couple of moiré reduction approaches that don't relate directly to accurate frequencies and angles.

Imagesetter software. Every imagesetter company has a different approach to how they generate halftone spots, but they all have built-in solutions to moirés. Heidelberg has High-Quality Screening (HQS) and Agfa uses Balanced Screens; even Adobe built a system called Accurate Screens that's part of several other imagesetters. All of these systems use either one or more of the solutions we describe in the next chapter, such as irrational screening or supercell screening, or their own proprietary combination.

Usually, you shouldn't even have to ask about moiré solutions; any major imagesetter manufactured in the last five or so years will have a perfectly reasonable solution built right in.

If you are using any special effects halftones, you need to ask your service bureau to disable the default screening.

Stochastic screening. In Chapter 26, *Stochastic Screening*, we mention that stochastic, or frequency-modulated, screening is a viable alternative to traditional halftone screening. One of the great benefits of stochastic screening is the impossibility of moiré patterning: There are no angles or frequencies to speak of, so no patterning can occur other than mechanical problems such as misregistration on press.

Go Forth and Moiré No More

Today, there's really no reason you should ever see a moiré pattern in process color work when you're creating output from a modern imagesetter. But you may have to watch with whom you work. Glenn once wasted a considerable amount of time working with a service bureau that produced moirés from its imagesetter. Eventually, he took the job to another shop with identical equipment, but the right configuration. The moirés disappeared.

29

Angle Strategies

GETTING IRRATIONAL

The curious paradox with digital imaging is that although it allows a precision well beyond what the eye can see this precision results in significant limitations in the real world. We look at one limitation in Chapter 21, *Frequency vs. Gray Levels*: The higher your halftone screen frequency, the fewer gray levels you can achieve at a given resolution.

In this chapter, we look at some other limitations at the boundaries of imaging and printing: attainable angles and screen frequencies. The fact is, not only do you often *not* get the precise output you asked for, but you sometimes can't even force a printer or imagesetter to bend to your will because the math doesn't work: the printer can't build a halftone cell given the settings you've chosen.

For example, if you select a 60-lpi, 45-degree screen on most 300-dpi laser printers, you actually receive output that's at 53 lpi. If you select the same screen but with a 44-degree angle, you receive output at 60 lpi, but the angle has snapped to 37 degrees—the printer rotates your request to its mathematically closest angle and frequency combination to produce its results.

This chapter addresses how PostScript and imagesetter software overcome the limitations of building halftone spots to produce output and simultaneously eliminate the color moirés we discuss in the previous chapter, *When Grids Collide*. We work this magic by implementing an interesting combination of angle, frequency, and halftone cell creation.

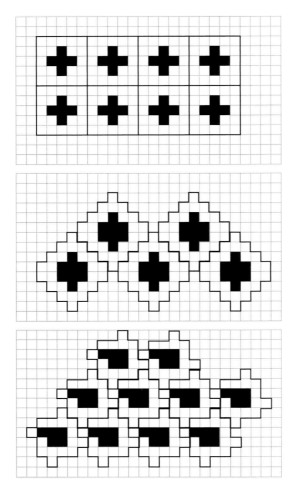

Figure 29-1
Digital halftone cells

Figure 29-2 Cells
and dot boundaries

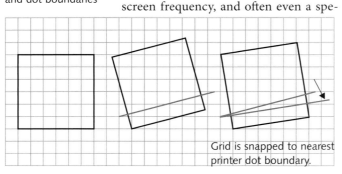

Grid is snapped to nearest
printer dot boundary.

Requesting Angles and Frequencies

In earlier chapters, we explain how to specify a halftone screen in a variety of ways: you choose a certain angle, a particular screen frequency, and often even a spe-cial spot shape. However, due to the limitations of the digital world, you don't always get as output what you precisely specified because the values you ask for can't always be created in a grid of dots.

Halftone spots are built inside halftone cells, which are made up of device dots. In typical digital screening, each of these cells looks exactly the same. They're like complex patterned tiles, and they have to fit together seamlessly. But there are only certain frequency/angle combinations at a given resolution for which this seamless tiling is possible.

Changing the Angle and Frequency

In order to rotate a halftone screen, you have to rotate the cell. Similarly, if you want to lower or raise the screen frequency, you have to make the halftone cells larger or smaller (**Figure 29-1**). The limitations occur because the halftone cell must fall on exact printer dot boundaries (**Figure 29-2**), and the cells have to tile.

Because cells have to tile, there are only so many combinations of frequencies and angles available at a given resolution. If the frequency and angle combination that you request isn't available, the default action is for PostScript to use its best guess at the nearest approximation (**Table 29-1**).

Increasing Printer Resolution

Although $\frac{1}{300}$ inch seems pretty small, a dot at that size is enormous compared to the eye's ability to perceive patterns. It's like building an oak dining room table using only two-by-fours. The smaller the size of each printer dot, the better your halftone spots because smaller dots increase the number of available frequency and angle combinations. When working at a finer resolution, you can rotate or adjust the size of the halftone cell, and have more pos-sibilities of whole dots to which a rotated grid can snap (**Figure 29-3**).

Table 29-1
Requested versus
actual frequency
and angle at
300 dpi

| Requested Angle | Requested Frequency | | | |
| | 50 lpi | | 60 lpi | |
	Actual Angle	Actual Frequency	Actual Angle	Actual Frequency
0	0	50.0	0	60.0
1	0	50.0	0	60.0
2	0	50.0	0	60.0
3	0	50.0	0	60.0
4	0	50.0	0	60.0
5	9	49.3	0	60.0
6	9	49.3	11	58.8
7	9	49.3	11	58.8
8	9	49.3	11	58.8
9	9	49.3	11	58.8
10	9	49.3	11	58.8
11	9	49.3	11	58.8
12	9	49.3	11	58.8
13	9	49.3	11	58.8
14	9	49.3	11	58.8
15	18	47.4	11	58.8
16	18	47.4	11	58.8
17	18	47.4	11	58.8
18	18	47.4	22	55.7
19	18	47.4	22	55.7
20	18	47.4	22	55.7
21	18	47.4	22	55.7
22	18	47.4	22	55.7
23	18	47.4	22	55.7
24	22	55.7	22	55.7
25	31	51.4	22	55.7
26	31	51.4	27	67.1
27	31	51.4	27	67.1
28	31	51.4	27	67.1
29	31	51.4	27	67.1
30	31	51.4	37	60.0
31	31	51.4	37	60.0
32	31	51.4	37	60.0
33	31	51.4	37	60.0
34	31	51.4	37	60.0
35	31	51.4	37	60.0
36	37	60.0	37	60.0
37	37	60.0	37	60.0
38	37	60.0	37	60.0
39	37	60.0	37	60.0
40	37	60.0	37	60.0
41	37	60.0	37	60.0
42	45	53.0	37	60.0
43	45	53.0	37	60.0
44	45	53.0	37	60.0
45	45	53.0	45	53.0

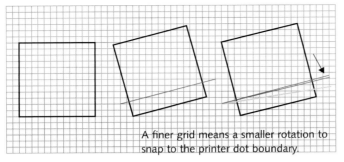

A finer grid means a smaller rotation to snap to the printer dot boundary.

Figure 29-3 Finer-resolution dots

If you had an infinite number of dots, you could have any combination of frequency and angle you wanted. However, despite David's experience with the transcendental in his book *The Joy of Pi,* none of us has had much experience with the infinite.

Rational Versus Irrational Screening

All the halftone screening that we've talked about in this book so far is called *rational tangent screening*. We also want to talk about *irrational* tangent screening. Both of these terms have been thrown around in the creative publishing press a lot, so we'd better clarify them.

These names derive from the sort of "snapping to the nearest dot" that we've been talking about here. When you can describe an angle as the hypotenuse of a triangle formed by whole dots, such as eight dots across and three dots up, you're describing a rational tangent angle. In fact, any angle

Figure 29-4
Irrational tangent screening

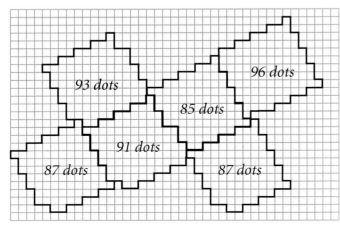

93 dots

96 dots

85 dots

91 dots

87 dots

87 dots

that you can create by using whole dots (whole integer numbers) is rational. The digital halftoning that we've been describing up to now works this way.

However, as we've seen in this and other chapters, many angles aren't generated this way, at least not at a particular screen frequency and output resolution. For example, with rational screening there is no way to get a true 15-degree halftone screen from an imagesetter. You can get close, but you can't achieve exactly 15 degrees because there are no integer values of dots that result in that angle.

Irrational tangent screening was developed and implemented on various RIP and imagesetter combinations to deal with this problem. In irrational screening, each halftone cell is not exactly the same size; some have more printer dots in them, some have fewer (**Figure 29-4**). By fudging the process like this, you can achieve a halftone grid that is extremely close to the requested frequency and angle.

The problem with irrational screening was that it was at one time incredibly processor-intensive (read: slow to print). Unlike rational screening, in which each of the 256 possible spots is built and cached for fast access, with irrational screening, each and every spot must be calculated on the fly as the image is being generated. Fortunately, the amazing advances in processor speeds over the past decade have made irrational screening quite practical.

The irregular nature of irrational screening reduces the likelihood of moirés by reducing the possibility of repeating halftone patterns.

Supercell Screening

If you take rational and irrational screening technologies and combine them at two entirely different levels of detail, you get an interesting hybrid called *supercell screening*. A *supercell* is a collection of smaller halftone cells, each of which may be made up of a different number of printer dots.

Figure 29-5
Supercell screening

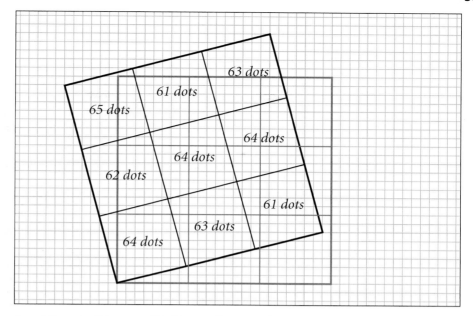

So, while each of these small halftone cells may contain a different number of printer dots (much like irrational screening), the whole supercell collection is repeated and tiled throughout the halftone, exactly like typical, rational screening (**Figure 29-5**). The micro level is irrational; the macro level, rational.

A supercell can produce a more accurate screen/angle combination because it's much bigger than its constituent halftone cells, so there are more potential corner points for rotated grids to snap to. This sort of screening can greatly help in reducing or eradicating patterning; however, there's often a performance hit. It's faster than irrational screening, but not as fast as standard rational screening.

The advantage of this form of screening is that moirés are much less likely when you lack the repeating, rational patterns at the micro level.

When You Need an Angle

Just as Einstein viscerally rejected quantum thermodynamics because of its lack of rationality with our perceived nature of the universe, so, too, did presses and lithographers once reject irrational screening and strange angles because it seemed impossible. No longer. These techniques are widespread and are one of the many tools in a designer's arsenal for avoiding moirés and other patterning problems.

Glossary
& Index

Glossary

Aliasing	Jagged edges seen in diagonals and curves more often in lower-resolution images or displays, such as computer screens. A sailing ship's rigging in front of a bright sky may look zig-zaggy at lower resolutions. See anti-aliasing.
Analog	A continuously variable value or reading—for example, a sine wave—as opposed to a pulse or discrete value, like data stored on a CD. Often used to describe electromechanical waves, such as radio signals, which can be modulated by amplitude (AM) or frequency (FM). See digital.
Anti-aliasing	Reducing the effects of aliasing by shading areas immediately adjacent to a jagged aliased edge. Although the anti-aliased image appears less distinct up close, from a normal viewing distance the brain perceives it as sharper and smoother.
Area array	A two-dimensional matrix. For example, the grid of image sensors used in many digital cameras in which all the sensors are exposed simultaneously to light. In this case, an area array works like a film frame.
Artifacts	Errors, such as grainy sample points, introduced by conditions and software in the scanning and image-editing processes. Artifacts also appear around high-contrast edges in JPEG files.
Bicubic sharpening	A method of resampling an image more intelligently and with better results than nearest neighbor or bilinear resampling. In Adobe Photoshop, when upsampling an image (such as for a photo enlargement), generally use Bicubic Smoother. When downsampling an image, generally use Bicubic Sharper.
Bilevel image	A 1-bit, black-and-white image. Also called a flat bitmap. See bitmap.
Bit depth	A measure of how many colors or tonal gradations can be represented in each sample of a digital image. The more bits, the greater number of shades of gray or different colors that can be represented. A sample of an 8-bit grayscale image can have one of 256 shades. A sample of a 24-bit image can store one of more than 16 million different colors. See bitmap, deep bitmap, flat bitmap.

Bitmap	A bit is the tiniest unit of computer storage, representing either a one or a zero. A map is jargon for a table, like a spreadsheet—the information is organized two-dimensionally, into rows and columns. A bitmap is a table that describes where bits are located—as in an image. See bit depth, deep bitmap, flat bitmap.
Blend	A smooth transition from one color or tone to another. Also known as: degradé, fountain, gradient (or graduated) fill, and vignette.
Blow out	A loss of highlight detail in the lightest areas due to spot variation, too small a dynamic range on the scanner or digital camera, improper exposure, or exaggerated linear or non-linear tonal correction. Blow out also can occur as an element of spot variation with rules or lines that approach the width of the smallest halftone spots, as in line art, boxes, and callouts.
Bluelines	Blueprint-paper contact prints or proofs of lithographic film (negative or positive), which let you see tiny imperfections and fix errors before the film is turned into an offset printing plate.
CCITT	The abbreviation for the International Telegraph and Telephone Consultative Committee that developed encoding for facsimile transmission and reception. There are several different standards; Group 3 and Group 4 are the most common.
CMYK	A color model that describes colors as a combination of Cyan, Magenta, Yellow, and blacK pigments. Commonly used in offset printing. Theoretically, black is not necessary as it could be created by mixing the three other colors. However, that not only creates an excess of ink, but would also result in an ugly brown instead of a proper black due to imperfections in the ink.
Collimated	A focused or point light source. In a film enlarger or scanner, a collimated light source is generally thought to produce sharper images, but can also over-emphasize silver film grain and other unwanted details like dust and scratches.
Color model	A system for describing color, usually by defining a few basic (primary) colors and then describing the range of colors that can be produced by combining them. There are three major classes of color models: a subtractive model that defines a combination of pigments, inks, or paints, and is described as CMY (cyan/magenta/yellow); an additive model that describes combinations of projected colors (like those on a computer monitor), or RGB (red/green/blue); and a device-independent model that objectively describes a color without reference to primary physical components.
Color resolution	The number of different shades of color that can potentially be resolved, stored or utilized by a device. For example, in a 24-bit image, each sample has three 8-bit values—one each for red, green, and blue which results in over 16 million possible colors.
Color space	The set or range of colors represented by a device or ICC profile. Multiple color spaces can exist for a color model; Adobe RGB and sRGB are two different color spaces within the RGB color model. See working space.
Content moirés	Interference patterns that occur when a grid appears in an image—like the knit in a sweater—that matches the frequency of a halftone screen. These content moirés may not be apparent in proofs. See moiré pattern.
Contone	A continuous-tone image as opposed to an image made up of spots or created by dithered dots. Images on photographic film or paper are contone.

Contrast curve	An image filter which is controlled by a chart that maps input gray levels to output gray values. Typically, the horizontal axis of the chart describes the levels of gray—from white to black—of the input image (the image that you start out with). The vertical axis describes the levels of gray of the output image (what you'll end up with). Same as gray-map curve.
CTP	Computer-to-Plate technology, in which there are no intermediate analog steps between the data and the plate that's used on the offset printing press. CTP platesetters directly expose plate material from the digital data.
Deep bitmap	Any image that has more than one bit describing each sample. See bit depth, bitmap.
Density	A measure of the opacity of photographic film, or how much light can shine through it (or reflect off it, in the case of prints). The more opaque or dense the film is, the greater tonal range the photographic emulsion can capture. The lightest and darkest tones a particular film can capture—the minimum and maximum tonal values—are called the "DMIN" and the "DMAX." A film's entire tonal range is measured by subtracting the minimum from the maximum, as with a DMAX of 3.3 minus a DMIN of 0.3 producing an overall density of 3.0D.
Descreening	The process of canceling (or attempting to cancel) a halftone screen by converting the half-tones back to continuous tones and colors. Many image-editing applications have descreening features, although they vary in their performance.
Device resolution	The resolution of an output device. For example, a monitor might be 72 ppi, and an imagesetter might be 2400 dpi. Device resolution can be confusing because its relationship to an image's resolution depends on what kind of device it is. For example, when creating Web graphics or other images for display on a computer monitor, you want each image pixel to correspond to a monitor pixel. But for very high-resolution devices like imagesetters and photo printers, the image resolution shouldn't be anywhere near the output resolution because the human eye can't resolve image detail that small.
Device-independent (CIE) color	A class of color model that works with the color-management systems that improve color correspondence between the monitor, color printouts, and final printed output. These models don't describe a color by the components that make them up (RGB or CMYK, for instance). They describe what a color looks like. All of them are based, more or less, on the standards defined by the Commission Internationale de l'Eclairage (CIE) in 1931. Also known as Perceptually Based Color.
Diffuse	Soft. In photography usually used to describe the quality of a light source.
Dithering	Using a non-regular non-grid pattern of dots to simulate colors or tones. Dithering is sometimes visible to the naked eye as a kind of speckling; it can create problems in flat colors, where it is often noticeable. It's better hidden (and put to better use) in photographs, giving the impression of a real tonal range. See stochastic screening.
Dots	The smallest marks that laser printers and imagesetters make. Printer resolution is measured in dots per inch (dpi). Do not confuse with spots (the elements of a halftone), pixels (the picture elements on a computer screen), or samples (the smallest details a scanner can resolve).
Dot gain	Growth of halftone spots on an offset press, which we call Spot Gain. This use of "dot" instead of "spot" is a holdover from conventional halftoning terminology.
Downsampling	The process of algorithmically reducing the number of samples in an image without distorting its visible content. See resampling and interpolation.
dpi	Dots per inch. The resolution of a printer. See ppi and spi.

Drum scanner	High-resolution scanner in which the media to be scanned (usually a photograph) is taped or otherwise affixed to a drum. The drum is rotated at a high speed as the media is scanned. Usually expensive and slow but still produces the best scanned results.
Dynamic range	The lightest and darkest levels that a scanner can potentially recognize. A wider dynamic range can result in better shadow and highlight detail.
Effective resolution	The resolution of an image at its final output dimensions. Effective resolution is only different than image resolution when an image is scaled using a program that doesn't resample image data—like scaling an image in a page-layout application—because that changes the density of samples over a different area without changing the resolution encoded in the image file.
Encapsulated Postscript (EPS)	A file format that contains PostScript, and typically other information, such as metadata and a preview image.
FireWire	The marketing name for the IEEE 1394a and 1394b standards, a high-speed serial interface pioneered by Apple Computer and adopted by Sony as i.Link. Apple offers FireWire 400 (1394a) and FireWire 800 (1394b).
Flat bitmap	A 1-bit image. Also called a bilevel image. See bitmap.
Flicker	A side effect of interlacing that occurs when adjacent horizontal lines on a CRT exist on different fields. If an image contains a horizontal line that's less than two video lines tall, alternating parts of it will repeatedly disappear and reappear as the fields it sits on redraw, and so the line appears to flicker.
Fountain	See blend.
FPO	For Position Only; an image that is placed for positioning, but which will later be replaced with a final, probably higher-resolution, image.
Gamma	How tonal values are distributed in an image or a video display, controlled by the midtone value. Gamma is usually displayed as a curve on a graph, showing where values are compressed, expanded, or shifted.
Gamut	The range of colors or grays as mapped against all possible colors in a color space. A gamut is usually shown as a three-dimensional shape carved out of a larger idealized palette.
GIF	Graphics Interchange Format. A graphics file format originally developed in 1987. GIF files can contain a maximum of 256 different colors, which are stored in a palette that is part of the GIF file itself. Supports transparency. Commonly used on the Web for low-resolution photos or images with areas of flat color.
Gray Component Replacement	Often referred to as GCR. See Undercolor Removal.
Gray-map curve	See contrast curve.
High-bit files	A term sometimes used for files that contain more than 8 bits per channel.
Histogram	A chart of the number of samples set to each gray or color level in a bitmapped image. The number of pixels (or the percentage of those pixels in the image) is typically the vertical axis, and the level of gray or color is a horizontal range. For example, a histogram can tell us that there are 10 sample points that are totally black, 34 sample points that have a gray level of 1 (out of 255 levels of gray), 40 sample points that have a gray level of 2, and so on.

Hot-pluggable   Devices that can be connected and disconnected without turning them off. For example, USB is a hot-pluggable standard.

Huffman encoding   An encoding scheme invented in 1952 which is used as part of a number of other compression schemes, like LZW and deflate.

ICC and ICM profiles   International Color Consortium and Image Color Management. These files store color descriptions of scanners, printers, presses, monitors, or even theoretical color spaces. A profile makes the difference between saying "red" and "red on this particular device."

Image resolution   The resolution of the grid of pixels that comprises a scanned image file. Image resolution simply defines the size of each pixel in the image. Image resolution can differ from scanner resolution if you scale or resample the image at any point in the process of taking an image from a scan to a print (or display).

Indexed color   A method for producing color that uses a specific color look-up table. Indexed-color bitmaps can use a table containing up to 256 colors, chosen from out of the full 24-bit RGB palette. A given sample's color is defined by reference (an index) to the abbreviated table: "this sample is color number 123, this sample is color number 81," and so on. GIF is an indexed color format.

Interlaced images   Images whose data are stored in an alternating form in the file so that the image gradually loads in lines or a blur as the file itself is retrieved. Initially introduced when the World Wide Web was typically accessed with slow modems; an interlaced image would show the viewer something while waiting for the entire image to load.

Interlacing   A display technique used by most televisions. Instead of drawing each video frame from the top down, interlaced displays draw each frame in two passes, similar to an interlaced GIF. One pass contains the odd-numbered lines, and the other pass contains the even-numbered lines. This technique was developed so that motion would be smoother on early televisions, which could not produce the frame rates of today's monitors. The opposite of interlacing is progressive scan, used in most high-definition televisions and computer monitors.

Interpolation   The process of increasing the number of samples in an image. Different interpolation methods produce different results, but they mostly introduce softness or blurriness. Also called upsampling.

Irrational tangent screening   A processor-intensive screening procedure in which each halftone cell is not exactly the same size; some have more printer dots in them, some have fewer. This can achieve a halftone grid that is extremely close to a specified frequency and angle, which is not always possible in more traditional (rational) screening schemes, while helping to avoids moirés.

Jaggies   See anti-aliasing.

JPEG   An image file format developed by the Joint Photographic Experts Group. JPEGs lose quality each time they're saved, due to the format's lossy compression scheme. JPEG allows bitmaps 8, 24, and 32 bits deep to be stored with variable compression (from high compression and lousy quality, to low compression and high quality).

JPEG 2000   A file format that makes use of wavelet compression, which lets the format provide improved quality at the same compressed file sizes as compared to conventional JPEG. There's no cross-compatibility between JPEG and JPEG 2000. Supports metadata.

Layer masks	An alpha channel attached to a specific layer of an image that uses grayscale values to control transparency. Black areas of the mask create transparent areas on the mask's layer, so that you can see through to the layer under it. White areas are completely opaque. ("Black conceals, white reveals.") Gray areas have partial opacity. Called Clip Masks in Photo-Paint.
LED	Light emitting diode. A semiconductor that emits light (usually at a discrete wavelength) when voltage is applied to it. Although generally not very bright, LEDs have the advantages of requiring little voltage and lasting a long time.
Line art	An image made up of lines or areas of black (no gray or color). A printed halftone is actually line art that simulates a grayscale or color image.
Linear array	In scanning, denotes a single row of image sensors that comprises the scanning element. To fill a frame with an image, the sensor row moves down the image, scanning each line of the image plane.
Linear correction	The most basic method of tonal correction that can be made using brightness and contrast controls in most image-editing programs. See nonlinear correction.
Lithographic	A process that can only create solid areas—without tone or tint. Offset presses are lithographic because they can only print a given ink color in a given location. Unlike photographic film and paper, tints must be simulated by halftones. Imagesetter output is usually called lithographic film or lithographic paper because it shares the same properties as offset lithography—dots are either on or off.
Lossless	A compression scheme in which no data is lost. This scheme is used in file formats such as LZW-compressed TIFF.
Lossy	A compression scheme in which data is lost, such as JPEG.
lpi	Lines per inch. The measure of fine detail in a halftoned image.
LZW	Lempel-Ziv-Welch, named for the inventors. A compression scheme that compresses data by looking for patterns throughout a file. These patterns, called phrases, are identified and stored in a table. Formerly covered by patent, which has expired.
Magic number	The first several bytes of data that Unix looks at to identify what type of file it is.
Metadata	Data about the data, commonly used to describe additional information about an image, such as camera model, aperture, time photo was taken, and so on. Newer image file formats, like JPEG 2000 and TIFF, support metadata.
Moiré patterns	Wavy lines that appear in an image when two or more grids or sets of parallel lines overlap each other. Can occur after images are screened, or when the TV weatherman wears a horizontally striped shirt.
Mottling	Blotchiness sometimes seen in areas of smooth gradation usually in lower-resolution scans. In people's faces, it looks like a poor complexion. Mottling may be due to a noisy scan, irregularities in the original image, or simply the content of the image. At the outer limits, it can even be caused by the scanner picking up the grain of the film. Sharpening can accentuate those irregularities.
Newton rings	Interference patterns that result from the contact of film stock and glass. These are most commonly seen on drum scanners, where the film is taped up against a cylinder, but high-resolution flatbeds can demonstrate the same problem. The solution is to use a special mounting oil between the film and the glass, which floats the film and removes the appearance of rings.

Noise
The introduction of random fluctuation into information, almost always due to imperfections in analog equipment, such as image sensors. Noise appears in scanned or digitally captured images as values that are too high or low compared with the original image data that was sampled.

Nonlinear correction
Modifying the tones of an image by changing the relationship of the input gray levels to output gray values in a nonlinear way. For example, you may change the highlights more than the midtones or shadows. When you use nonlinear correction to bring out shadow detail, you lose some detail in the highlights, but because the biggest problem with desktop scans is bringing out shadow detail, the trade-off is well worth it. Sometimes called gamma correction.

Object-level settings
Some graphics applications allow individual objects on a page to have specific settings; for example, in QuarkXPress, screens can be applied at different values to individual bitmapped objects. Object-level settings override the application-level settings, which apply to the rest of the job, but may be stripped out (overridden) by the output device.

Object-oriented graphics
Images that are described mathematically as a series of lines or curves, rather than by a bitmap. The distinction between bitmaps and objects is slightly fuzzy, because object-oriented files can include bitmaps as objects in their own right; they just usually don't allow you to make any changes to them. Also called draw graphics or vector graphics.

OCR
Optical Character Recognition. The process of turning a scanned image of text into ASCII through pattern-recognition, analysis, and heuristics.

Optical resolution
In a scanner, the actual number of sensors per inch (or centimeter). Optical resolution is typically across a scanner's shortest direction, while a figure (usually higher) across the length of the scanner is based on the stepper motor's capabilities.

Orange mask
An orange-colored layer in color negative photographic film that exists to compensate for inadequacies in color rendition of the dyes used in the film. Also called color mask.

Page-description language
A sequence of instructions that describe the exact appearance and location of objects on a virtual page, which is then translated into some form of output. PostScript is a page-description language.

Parallel port
A class of connector used by computers. Somewhat outdated. Before USB was widely accepted, most scanners were connected to IBM PC-compatible computers via the parallel port.

Path
An outline or vector. A closed path around an image may be used as a clipping path—a mathematically pure line that defines an edge.

Perceptually based color
See device-independent (CIE) color.

PDF
Adobe Acrobat file format that is both child of and big brother to EPS. Devised as a paperless document file that could be created from PostScript output and closely reproduce the original document. PDF has become ubiquitous as a simple way to distribute, display, and print virtual copies of material intended for print, as well as a method of delivering final prepress files to a printer for offset press reproduction.

Photo CD
A Kodak standard for storing images on CD.

Pixels	Picture Element. A single x,y coordinate on a monitor that can represent a different tone or color value. Display resolution is measured in pixels per inch (ppi), or as pixel dimensions (for example, 1024 by 768). Photoshop uses ppi for image resolution, but we use samples per inch (spi) in this book, as it refers specifically to the actual image data, not its representation at varying degrees of magnification onscreen.
Pixel aspect ratio	The proportions of a pixel. Most often used in video, where pixels can be rectangular rather than square. If you draw a square on a rectangular-pixel system like a television graphics workstation, then move that file to a square-pixel system like a Mac OS or Windows computer without any compensation, the square will look unnaturally thin because the square computer pixels aren't the same proportions as the rectangular TV pixels.
Platesetter	A high-resolution output device that produces output on printing plate material.
PNG	Portable Network Graphics. An image file format that uses lossless compression, can interlace images, is displayable in browser windows, and can use an indexed color palette of up to 256 colors. PNG can store either deep bitmaps (from 1 to 16 bits for grayscale and 24 or 48 for RGB) or an indexed color map. The format was designed for the Web, so there's no support in the specification for CMYK. The biggest problem with PNG files today is that the majority of surfers are using browsers that can't display the advanced features available in the PNG format.
Posterization	An obvious stair-stepping from one gray level or color tone to another, quite different, gray level or color tone—rather than a smooth transition. It is primarily a problem in graduated blends or halftones of photographs with smooth transitions from white to black.
PostScript	A programming language optimized for translating type and graphics from a graphics or other software program onto plain paper and lithographic paper, film, and plate material. PostScript is generated by graphics applications and sent to a printer, which interprets that page-description program by building a high-resolution bitmap in its memory. That bitmap is in turn placed via laser onto an output medium. See *also* EPS.
ppi	Pixels per inch. The resolution of a monitor. See dpi and spi.
Prepress	The preparatory stage before actual printing, when your service bureau receives and prepares your layout, image, and font files to run on press.
Rational tangent screening	The traditional method of creating halftones in which all halftone cells have the same number of dots. See irrational tangent screening.
Res	The term used by some service bureaus to refer to the resolution of a scanned image. Res is another word for samples per millimeter. Scanner operators often scan at "res 12," meaning 12 samples per millimeter or 304 spi. Pronounced "rez."
Resampling	Increasing or decreasing the number of samples throughout an image without cropping, usually accomplished using an image-editing or scanning program. See downsampling and interpolation.
Resolution	The number of samples in each unit of measurement of an image, such as the number of printer dots in a linear inch. Resolution is always measured across a line in a base measurement unit such as inches or centimeters, not as the area of a square. See image resolution and scanning resolution.
RGB	An additive color model based on the primary colors of red, green and blue. Monitors, film recorders, and televisions use this model.

Rosette	A pattern formed by the overlap of a set of halftone screens, each of which is rotated at a slightly different angle. An open-centered rosette reduces the number of places where larger halftone spots overlap by placing halftone spots in a ring.
Run Length Encoding (RLE)	A simple form of lossless compression for images that is an option when saving into formats like TIFF and BMP. RLE works by looking for the same value multiple times in a row.
Sampling resolution	See scanning resolution
Scanning mode	An option set in scanning software to optimize the scan for different types of originals. Modes often available are line-art, dithered, halftoned, grayscale, and color.
Scanning resolution	The resolution at which the scanner samples the original art or photograph. It's defined and limited by the scanner hardware, and controlled through scanning software.
Screen	The measure by which sampled image data or areas of tint or gradations are translated into halftone spots, in lines per inch (lpi).
SCSI	Small Computer Serial Interface. A data transfer method that was the de facto standard for the Mac since the earliest days. All consumer Macs and PCs have migrated to USB and/or FireWire, but SCSI has its legacy and its adherents. (Pronounced "skuzzy.")
Sharpening	The process of emphasizing slight differences by increasing contrast on adjacent tonal areas, which helps our eyes pick out detail. Most scanning and image-editing applications offer sharpening filters.
Spatial resolution	The number of bitmap units you can potentially resolve in physical space (as in 96 pixels per inch).
spi	Samples per inch. Used to measure the resolution of scans and bitmapped image data.
Spots	The elements of a halftone. In digital halftoning, the little shapes comprised of printer dots that create the illusion of a continuous-tone image.
Spot gain	Growth of halftone spots on press through ink spreading on paper, known more commonly as dot gain.
Spot variation	The changes that take place between the spots generated with a screen and the results off the press. Small spots might get smaller, midtone spots might grow by 15 percent, and spots in shadow areas might grow by 20 percent. Thus a graphical representation of spot variation across the tonal scale is typically a curve, not a line.
Stochastic screening	A halftoning screening process that uses a randomly distributed speck in varying concentrations to create tonal values. There's no grid and the speck size usually doesn't change. Many specks together look like a darker value than just a few. Collections of larger spots seem like darker tones than collections of smaller spots. Often used in cases where a content moiré would result.
Suspects	Errors that occur when optical character recognition software attempts to turn an image of letters into ASCII code. You usually perform an initial test run of a page and check for suspects, or words that the OCR software is uncertain about its match for or which a dictionary doesn't include.

TIFF	Tagged Image File Format. A widely used, industry-standard bitmapped file format for prepress and high-quality image storage. It can have theoretically unlimited bit depth, but most software reads or writes some standard sizes: 1 to 8, 24, 32 (for CMYK), or 48 (for high-bit RGB) bits per sample. TIFF can encode grayscale, RGB, indexed-color, or CMYK color models. It can be saved in compressed and uncompressed formats. Almost every program that works with bitmaps can handle TIFF files, whether for placing, printing, correcting, or editing the bitmap.
Tints	A solid area of gray or color. Usually referred to in percentages. A light gray tint, where the halftone spots are a tenth of their full size, is a 10-percent tint.
Tonal resolution	Another term for bit depth. The number of tonal or color steps you can potentially resolve within each unit of the bitmap (as in 8 bits per pixel). Also known as color resolution.
Tonal sensitivity	The ability of a scanner to accurately represent similar, adjacent tonal values as distinct from each other. Some scanners are great in the lighter and darker areas of a scan, but muddy in the midtones, where most of the Caucasian flesh tones are found. Others are less sensitive in the shadow areas.
Tone	How the colors or gray levels throughout a picture relate to one another.
Undercolor Removal (UCR)	A technique to reduce the total amount of ink printed by a press in a particular area by reducing unnecessary combinations of inks that don't add to the printed color's appearance. Some printers prefer gray component replacement (GCR), which only reduces ink coverage in neutral gray areas of the image.
Unsharp masking	A sharpening process that works by combining a slightly blurry (unsharp) version of an image with the original. This combination results in sharp details in high-contrast areas (the edges, where adjacent light and dark samples are markedly different), without creating tonal shifts in low-contrast areas (areas of smooth gradation, where rapid tonal shifts would destroy the subtle transitions).
Wavelet	Mathematical representation of the difference between two sets of data: an original set (like an image) and a set that's half the original's size (like a downsampled image). Important in some compression methods such as JPEG 2000.
Web safe palette	A set of 216 colors that both the Mac OS and Windows operating systems can display without using a patchwork of other colors to simulate ones it can't display. (This patchwork is called dithering.)
Working space	In Photoshop, the default color space profile for an image. Each color model has its own working space. For instance, Photoshop's default working space for new RGB images is sRGB, though we recommend changing it to Adobe RGB. See color space.

Index

#

8-bit color display, 91
8-bit images, 127, 153
8 bits per channel, 89, 107, 108, 110, 127–128
16-bit images, 128, 153
16 bits per channel, 89, 107, 108
24-bit color display, 90, 92
24-bit images, 127

A

A/D converters. *See* analog-to-digital converters
Absolute Colorimetric rendering intent, 164
ACDSee, 45
Acrobat, creating PDF files, 217
Acrobat Distiller, 217
Acrobat PDF files. *See* PDF files
adaptive analog-to-digital converters, 18
adjustment layers, Photoshop, 152–153, 182–183
Adobe Acrobat, creating PDF files, 217
Adobe Acrobat Distiller, 217
Adobe Gamma, 167–168
Adobe InDesign CS, 80, 258
Adobe PDF files. *See* PDF files
Adobe Photoshop Album, 45
Adobe Photoshop CS
   adjustment layers, 152–153, 182–183
   Auto Color command, 176–177
   Bitmap mode, converting to, 268
   Burn tool, 182
   Color Halftone filter, 267
   Color Settings dialog box, 175
   Crop tool, 184
   Custom CMYK dialog box, 175, 176
   custom halftone screens, 276
   Despeckle filter, 186, 292–293
   direct access to scanner, 20–21
   Dodge tool, 182
   Dust and Scratches filter, 186
   Fade Unsharp Mask command, 196

File Browser, 45–46
Free Transform command, 183–184
Gamut Warning view, 165
halftoning images, 267–268
Healing Brush tool, 187–188
Histogram palette, 152
History Brush, 182, 187
History feature, 153
Hue/Saturation command, 179
Image Size dialog box, 136, 138
interpolation methods, 138
Levels dialog box, 150–152, 176, 259
Measure tool, 183
Median filter, 186, 293
Missing Profile dialog box, 172–173
multiple windows for same image, 165
Patch tool, 188
Print with Preview dialog box, 267
Profile Mismatch dialog box, 172, 173–174
Proof Colors option, 165
Proof Setup options, 127, 130, 165, 176, 183
Rubber Stamp tool, 187–188
Separation Setup options, 176
Shadow/Highlight command, 181–182
Unsharp Mask filter, 193–195, 197–199, 293
Adobe RGB color, 67, 108, 232, 234
aliasing
   associated with unsharp masking, 192–193
   interpolation and, 138
   scan resolution and, 80
alpha channels. *See also* layer masks
   JPEG 2000 file format, 209
   TIFF file format, 207
   in Web-bound images, 95–96
AM (Amplitude Modulated) screening, 282
amber tint. *See* orange mask
ambient lighting, 168
Amount setting, Unsharp Mask filter, 194, 198–199
analog-to-digital converters, 4, 16–17, 18
analog video capture, 100
Andromeda Software, 184

angles, halftone screens. *See* screen angles
archiving files, 48–49
   backups vs. archives, 49
   CD archives, 49
   compression and compressed files, 226
   DVD archives, 49
   hard drive archives, 49–50
   media rotation, 51
   migrating from obsolete media, 51–52
   offsite archives, 51
   redundancy, 50
   tape archives, 50–51
   ZIP compression standard, 226
area arrays, 27
Argo, 334. *See also* recurring dogs
arrays, digital cameras, 27
art digital printmakers, 107
artwork appearing in images, 37
ASCII encoding
   ASCII-encoded bitmaps, 130–131
   EPS file format, 214
aspect ratio
   cropping scan area, 57
   film recorders and, 110
   pixel aspect ratio, 97–98
   scaling percentage settings, 59
asset management. *See* image management
assigning profiles, 170, 171, 172, 173
Auto Color command, Photoshop, 176–177
auto-exposure control, 61, 64

B

backing up files, 48–49
   backups vs. archives, 49
   CD backups, 49
   DVD backups, 49
   hard drive backups, 49–50
   media rotation, 51
   migrating from obsolete media, 51–52
   offsite backups, 51
   redundancy, 50
   tape backups, 50–51
banding. *See* blends, banding in

C

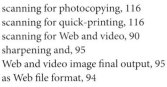

Credits & Permissions

All photography and illustration not otherwise credited provided by the authors.

Figure 7-4, page 92. Images on pages 280 and 281 courtesy of PhotoDisc, Inc., from *The Signature Series*: 4, *The Painted Table* and 8, *Study of Form and Color*; and their regular series, volume 6, *Nature, Wildlife and the Environment*.

Figure 10-4, page 128, illustration © Simon Tuckett.

Figure 12-2, page 145, Udaipur in figure © Carol Thuman.

Figure 19-2, 20-1, 20-3, pages 192, 243, 244, illustration © 1993 Steve Stankiewicz.

The following images are reprinted with permission from the Special Collections Division, University of Washington Libraries.

Figure 12-4, 12-5, 12-6, 21-1, pages 147, 148, 149, 248; photo #80.A.W&S
Figure 20-2, 20-4, 28-3, pages 244, 245, 294, photo #659
Figure 15-1, page 190, photo by Goetzman Photo
Figure 15-6, page 192, photo by Clifford Photo, negative #UW9685
Figure 15-7, page 193, photo by Todd, negative #UW 10511
Figure 15-12, page 198, 199, photo by Lee, negative #20056
Figure 22-1, page 253, photo by A. Curtis, negative #30744

Phoenix Books
Lambertville, NJ
Sat 21 July 2012
$6.50

Colophon

This book has a rich history dating back to 1993 and 1998, when we produced the first and second editions. Each version of the book has tracked the developments in output and offset printing technology.

Output and printing. The first edition was output to film via a service bureau in Seattle. We produced the film and shipped it to Peachpit Press's printer, which produced blueline proofs. There were no color pages.

The second edition was produced CTP for the black and white pages, while the dozen color plates were separated to film in Vancouver, B.C., and then sent off to the printer.

This edition is four-color throughout and was entirely produced through CTP and onscreen proofing. It was processed on a Creo Prinergy and output at 2400 dpi onto Kodak Thermal Gold plates. Kodak Approval proofs were used to check color.

Typefaces. The book is set in Minion Pro, the OpenType version of Roger Slimbach's classic Adobe face. The sans serif type used throughout for headings, captions, and other matter is Syntax, designed by Hans Eduard Meyer.

Software. We used the entire Adobe Creative Suite on Windows XP and Mac OS X 10.2 and 10.3 to create this book, which was written and edited in Microsoft Word. It was designed and laid out in InDesign CS. Illustrations were created and edited in Illustrator CS and Photoshop CS. GoLive CS was used to manage a production Web site for the book and to design the book's permanent Web site, **www.rwsh.com**. Acrobat 6 was used for soft proofing and correction. iView Media Pro managed images.

Computing power. This book was written, edited, and produced with two Apple PowerBook G4s (two different 15-inch FireWire 800s), a PowerBook G3 (FireWire/500 MHz), a Power Computing PowerCenter Pro with Sonnet G4/800 upgrade card, and a dual-1.25 GHz G4 Power Mac. Four PCs—running Windows XP—also contributed to the editing and production.

Production management. The team that wrote this book was based in the Seattle area, but we rarely saw each other face to face. With cable modem and DSL service readily available, files were exchanged through a Mac OS X fileserver using AppleShare and Samba, and a Linux fileserver running Apache and an FTP server. Most communication happened through email.

Corrections and revisions were marked in Acrobat 6 and exported as comment files (FDFs). Because of the advances in on-screen editing and color, the book was printed in its entirety on a laser printer only once in the entire production process.

Coffee and Wi-Fi. Diva Espresso and Herkimer Coffee contributed mightily to the production of this book through regular infusions. Wi-Fi networking was also a major part of our writing and production process, allowing us to roam across the country, the city, and the rooms of our houses.